LAW AND MORALITY

LAW AND MORALITY

Edited by

Louis Blom-Cooper QC
and Gavin Drewry

With a Preface by

Bernard Crick

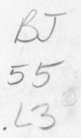

Duckworth

First published in 1976 by
Gerald Duckworth & Co. Ltd
The Old Piano Factory
43 Gloucester Crescent, London NW1
Editorial introductions and arrangement © 1976 Louis Blom-Cooper and
Gavin Drewry

ISBN Cloth 7156 0805 3
ISBN Paper 7156 0804 5

Filmset in 9/10 Baskerville by
Specialised Offset Services Limited, Liverpool,
and printed in Great Britain by
REDWOOD BURN LIMITED
Trowbridge & Esher

Contents

Preface

I am glad to have been in part responsible for seeing the need for this book and still more glad to have been able to persuade Louis Blom-Cooper Q.C. and Gavin Drewry to compile and introduce it. The subject-matter of the relation of law and morality is topical, and yet it is often neglected in education. Legal education is growing wider in scope. The problems discussed in this book – of attitudes to punishment (including the death penalty), to family law, to sexuality, to obscenity and pornography, to religion and blasphemy – inevitably demand a broader consideration than the apparently simple accumulation of case law and the apparently simple question 'What is the law?' The time has long since passed when it was believed that the lawyer could somehow stand apart from the ordinary concerns of mankind and achieve objectivity by means of a studied neutrality or unconcern, or could by professional training and etiquette render himself immune to those broad social conditions and tendencies which influence others. Much of law is technical – and we neglect techniques at our peril – but we still have to ask what the technique is being used for, what it *should* be used for. The old indifference, tempered with hostility, of common lawyers towards jurisprudence is now, though not entirely a thing of the past, yet waning rapidly. The student of law may not need to be also, in a full technical sense, a student of philosophy or the social sciences, but he is not likely to be much good as a lawyer if he does not appreciate the importance and relevance of these fields and know where to go to inform himself further. The questions raised in this book make this view of law seem inescapable.

The student of politics or of sociology, particularly of political and social philosophy, has been taught in recent years in a way that has reacted too far and too much against the old, arid, purely institutional or constitutional approach that was prevalent in the first quarter of this century. A student of politics may now pursue a course of studies from which any element of constitutional law is absent. A political philosopher may only discuss historical cases or purely invented cases, whereas under his nose, as it were, there are in the courts the most intellectually fascinating and often socially important cases raising all the old tensions between law and justice, with which – as the authors of this book remind us – political philosophy has been concerned since Plato.

Political philosophy has, however, lately begun to pull away both from purely positivist approaches and from a purely linguistic analysis. Ethical philosophy has come back into politics. The general debate between Lord Devlin and Professor H.L.A. Hart on the relation of law to morality is now one of the central pre-occupations of political philosophy. What is usually lacking is the kind of concrete example so well set out in this book. What is true for the student of political or social philosophy is also true, in this case, for the general philosopher. Anyone concerned with actual processes of reasoning on matters of morality will find much to stretch him here.

The structure of valid ethical arguments is hardly something to be determined *a priori*. Arguments about punishment, for instance, simply have to be followed through cases and then subjected to philosophical criticism; they cannot be judged by standards or definitions set up in advance. If there is a case in court to be argued at all, it shows that the law is ambiguous and that values and interests differ. Both the fascination and the acuteness of the general problem today of the relation of law to morality – Does law rest upon morality? Should law concern itself with private morals? – arise because we no longer live in a society in which there is a single clear moral code (whatever its basis) or in which there is consensus in the Ciceronian sense of common agreement as to right and interest. Only a fanatic would contend that in a lawcourt he is defending right against wrong or making an assault upon evil, or deny that he is far more likely to be grappling with a rival view of what is right, what is good.

That does not, of course, imply a moral relativism: that all values are equal and that there is no possibility of rational argument or judgment. One examination, one case may be better than another by some easily agreed standard; one case may involve implications which, after a while, the advocate himself is not willing to follow; one case may involve flagrant self-contradiction when extended into a neighbouring, but significantly different, concern. We argue, in fact, more about the validity of analogies than about the validity of principles. Perhaps at the end of the day, for instance, we find that nothing can bridge the moral gap between the Catholic and the humanist over the question of abortion. But it still does not follow that the two will be at each other's throats. Each may well accept the mere convenience of legal restraints even on behaviour they consider right, or of lessening restraints on behaviour they consider wrong.

For it is extremely important, though extremely hard for some, to grasp that law and morality may sometimes be quite separate things. To give a simple example, I hold a moral objection to the sale and consumption of addictive substances which are damaging both to health and sociability. But I am highly selective, on all kinds of grounds, in advocating which should be banned as a matter of public policy, or which should no longer be banned. The point is that strong moral disapproval does not necessarily imply that there should be a law. Indeed sometimes the attempt to enforce morality is self-defeating. Conversely, that there is a law, and that people should be punished for breaking it, does not always imply moral disapproval. Sometimes it is necessary for there to be some rule, such as driving on the left side of the road (or the right); breaking it is clearly 'wrong', but equally it would clearly be odd to call right-hand drivers 'immoral'.

In many of the questions of addiction, sexual morality, anti-social behaviour, it is necessary to distinguish between permissiveness and tolerance, and between disapproval and legal proscription. 'Permissiveness' describes the attitude of people who do not care what goes on. Some people are permissive about things that concern others deeply. Often people do care, do disapprove, as I do concerning drugs and pornography; but there are ways of expressing disapproval which do not involve legal sanctions. And because I am not in favour of tightening the laws on obscenity and bringing back censorship for the stage, I will not have anyone blackguard me by saying that I am permissive about these things.

Perhaps we need both less formal restraint and less permissiveness, but also more open rebuke and critical tolerance – up to a point, of course; and the ultimate point, all the old authorities seem to agree, was when society was in danger. This is a possibility. One can easily be too tolerant. Any society will defend itself against internal corruption by law and power. But it will not be a tolerant, decent, liberal society if it listens too much to those unhappy folk who cry 'social collapse is imminent' every time they read in a newspaper about the immoral behaviour of others. It is simply unlikely that increased sexual permissiveness is endangering the safety of the state, the stability of society. If moralists use an empirical argument, they have to show their evidence. But equally I am not much impressed by those who cry 'Democracy in danger' every time a magistrate confiscates some dirty books. Don't exaggerate; proportion is all.

These are but provocative digressions by way of preface, to insinuate, indeed assert, that this is a thought-provoking and thoughtful book, and one equally important to lawyers, philosophers and social scientists.

Bernard Crick
Professor of Politics
Birkbeck College
University of London

Introduction

From the time of Plato it has been clear to all thinking men that laws are not necessarily just, and from the time of the Romans, that all that is thought to be moral need not necessarily be embodied in law. From the period when a faintly recognisable legal system emerged as an adjunct of monarchical government, lawyers, theologians and philosophers – the dividing line implicit in the use of such labels is often jagged or blurred – have tried to make deductions about both the rationale underlying the promulgation (and subsequent modification) of legal rules and the duty to obey such rules.

Thus discussion of law and morality has numerous historical ramifications which reflect changing political circumstances, changing social values, and changing fashions of thought. Appropriate to one set of social conditions was a 'natural law' school which attempted to justify legal rules as being based on the divine revelation to the lawgiver. The 'positivist' school, associated in Britain with John Austin, was a direct reaction to such an approach. This school of thought eschewed value-judgments about the moral content of legal rules, and presented them as end-products of an established constitutional process, as *grundnorms*, or as the commands of the sovereign.

Both viewpoints are academically unfashionable in contemporary British jurisprudence; they have been superseded by schools of thought with their roots in the social sciences. Natural lawyers tend to be sneered at as old-fashioned mystics whose ideas cannot measure up to the yardsticks of the rigorous discipline of modern social science. Positivists are attacked for their dubious claims to have found an approach free of value-judgments. They are accused of perpetuating an unquestioning attitude to the substantive content of legal rules and are condemned for being obsessed with the constitutional sources of law. We ourselves do not propose to add to this debate, save to remark that in contemporary discussions on law and morality there can still be heard distinct echoes of this old and vapid conflict. In the introduction to Chapter 1, we indicate more fully our approach to the jurisprudential arguments.

It is quite impossible to present a realistic picture of the issues of law and morality by considering them from only one standpoint. This book, by deploying a varied range of documents, falls into two parts: first, a selection of items germane to the general debate; and second, items illustrating specific areas of that debate. Chapter 1 traces the endless but fascinating philosophical-cum-sociological debate about the theoretical relationships between law and morals. Later chapters illustrate how moral arguments permeate particular areas of substantive law.

The first chapter, therefore, is a scene-setter: in it are extracts from the writings of eminent academics and lawyers, ranging from John Stuart Mill and Sir James Fitzjames Stephen in the nineteenth century, to Lord Devlin and H.L.A. Hart in the twentieth. Our main problem has been to do even rough justice to the work of such distinguished and prolific authors. While we have tried to extract the pith and marrow of diverse and sophisticated arguments in necessarily truncated form, this chapter is not by any stretch of the imagination a definitive account. It is a fairly substantial *hors d'oeuvre* intended to whet, rather than to satiate, the appetite.

The compilation of the later chapters has raised difficulties of an equally formidable but somewhat different character. The philosophical debate about law and morality has produced a wealth of elegant argument directed principally at an academic audience: the personal ideologies of these authors can be deduced by reading between the lines of their writing. When we come to the field covered in our later chapters – the moral content of the debate about 'the law in action' – the arguments employed tend, by definition, to have a high, though largely unconcealed, ideological content. When proposals for law reform are discussed in public it often happens that dogma faces dogma. The final outcome is dictated as much by political fashion and administrative expediency as by force of unassailable logic and moral rectitude. Many of the documents in this second part can be understood only in the wider context of the *politics* of law reform.

It is, however, a gross oversimplification to depict this as an unending fight between pressure groups over some 'great issue', ending in victory for one side or the other. Pressure groups are amoeboid structures which change radically over a period of time, as do the causes for which they campaign. We have, therefore, selected documents which we consider in many cases to be typical of the various species of argument deployed. Our own introductory essays and headnotes, coupled with extracts from other commentators placed at strategic points among the documents (but concentrated mainly in Chapter 1) place them in the context of the wider debate on law and morality.

'Morality', colloquially, is a code of social behaviour; it is something which is both within the individual and which also encapsulates him by virtue of his membership of society. A common feature of debates on law reform is that individuals and groups seek to persuade others that their own morality is, or should become, part of the shared morality embodied in a legal rule. Persuasion may take the form of invoking a value system (like Christianity or Marxist-Leninism) already widely accepted as demonstration of the rectitude of a moral stand, and adopting a particular interpretation of a part of that system. When this happens it is sometimes difficult for outsiders to identify the crucial variables, since both opponents and proponents of reform may invoke the same basic values as part of their case: 'the will of God' can be used equally as a *casus belli* or as a plea for peace. The same is true of debates with a high individual-moral content which involve 'facts' open to a variety of interpretations: the deployment of criminal statistics relating to murder by both sides in the debate on abolishing capital punishment is a case in point. The difficulty here is that statements about morality must be interpreted in the light of a mass of circumstantial factors and complementary arguments. The ethically desirable cannot be derived from social facts or social needs, but the ethically desirable must surely be the sociologically possible.

As social values change, so the law itself undergoes change; in some instances, the law does not merely reflect contemporary change in social mores but lags lamentably behind. The retention of archaic laws relating to Sunday observance (see chapter 8) is an instance where political factors have discouraged mobilisation of institutional facilities for change. On the other hand, much law marches in the vanguard of public sentiment. The abolition of capital punishment, as with most penal reform, would never have come about (at least when it did) if the 'man on the Clapham omnibus' (see 1.10) had been the final arbiter on the matter. (Here, perhaps, is one powerful argument against referenda.) Clearly, as J.S. Mill so clearly recognised, collective morality is something which cannot be identified just by counting heads any more than by canvassing the opinion of the mythical 'average' man.

It is wholly unrealistic to treat 'morality' in isolation from other determinants of political or judicial behaviour. A statement that law is *related* to social morality is a resounding truism. It is the precise character of the relationship that has so far defied analysis. Equally, to assert that law is a *product* of morality is a half-truth. Apart from fruitless conjecture about the chicken and the egg, it would be necessary, in order to effect a synthesis of legal rules from moral principles, to find a satisfactory way of identifying the latter. We are still more than a Clapham omnibus ride away from being able to do that. To adopt the 'realist' line of argument, 'the law' at any given time is no more than what judges will say it is; what the private citizen believes the law to be (and *a fortiori* what he thinks it *ought* to be) is something quite different, and relates closely to highly individualistic ideas about morality.

A particular legal rule may be coterminous with the moral beliefs of many individuals and groups, or it may be in conflict with those beliefs. Whether such conflict leads to pressure for change depends upon a variety of factors: for example, the occurrence of a much publicised instance of injustice may lead either to the formation of a pressure group to remedy the social ill thereby revealed, or to the strengthening of support for a pressure group already in existence. Moral beliefs may affect attitudes and behaviour in areas where, for one reason or another, the law does not intervene (female homosexuality, for example). Where this happens, the fact of non-intervention may be seized upon by reformers as a lever with which to secure changes in other, analogous areas where legal rules do intervene (in this case male homosexuality). Partial reforms may be the thin end of the wedge for more comprehensive changes at a later date – a fact of which opponents of change are all too well aware – for example, the English Divorce Reform Act 1969 quickly led to pressure (so far unsuccessful) for similar changes to be effected in the case of Scotland. And the opposition to abortion law reform was in part based on the allegation that voluntary euthanasia would be next on the shopping list of zealous social reformers. Conversely, many legal rules operate in technical areas about which the private citizen usually knows very little and cares even less. The moral connotations of legal rules thus vary greatly from case to case.

'Morality' vis-à-vis the law constitutes an external environment which interacts with the law-making process, not because law-makers are blessed with divine insight into the 'general will', but rather because laws tend to be based upon value-loaded information which percolates to the law-makers (whose own individual values have a disproportionate influence upon the process). Their frames of reference are derived from various socialising mechanisms and fed by channels of political communication which may distort this information. In the vocabulary of political functionalism, demands are first articulated and aggregated, then converted by the political system (Parliament, the courts, etc.) into authoritative decisions in the form of changes in the body of legal rules. In practical terms, laws are synthesised by reference to, *inter alia*, ideological commitment, political expediency, and the constraints imposed by the inflexibility of institutionalised procedures.

We have selected various subject-areas where argument about moral issues seems to have played a particularly prominent part in shaping the law, or where social tensions have been generated by the failure of law-making institutions to take account of changing *mores*. Some of the areas selected – for example, human sexuality and the morality of punishment – involve arguments about morality in a particularly acute and overt form. But even in these areas, and to an even greater extent in others (such as divorce, legal status, and international law) the moral aspects of the argument must be examined alongside a whole range of other sociological and philosophical considerations.

Viewing the march of legal history from the particular standpoint of the latter half of the twentieth century, one is constrained not to stand aloof from our own cultural experiences. It is all too easy, for example, to lapse into the complacency of those who, having been vouchsafed the 'truth', can smugly proclaim how silly and unenlightened our predecessors have been by comparison with ourselves. All generations look back in horror or disgust at the apparent barbarities of their ancestors. But while this may have a substratum of truth, it cannot be held *a priori* that all that has gone before is worse than what we have now.

The war between advocates of absolute freedom of expression at almost any cost, on the one hand, and the battalions of anti-pornographers on the other, has in no sense been one of contemporary light against atavistic darkness. Nor is the current vision all light and no dark. Sincerity of belief in one's own brand of morality is no more the monopoly of the 'liberal-minded' than it is of the forces of reaction; the sincerity of the Christian is inherently no better or worse than that of the atheist; the Marxist's belief in his creed is no more or less 'valid' in any absolute sense than that of the fascist. Self-righteousness is one thing, rightness is very much another. Silliness or disingenuousness are not the prerogative of any one group – both sides in the debate on capital punishment, for example, have at one time or another been guilty of various kinds of specious reasoning.

Ours is a pluralistic society, and pluralism, by definition, implies a diversity of moralities, each entitled to (but not necessarily getting) a fair hearing. So this book is not about *the* morality of a society but rather about the ebb and flow of a plurality of beliefs in conflict.

This has been the nub of our problem. Space has not permitted us to be equally fair to every point of view or to adopt a time-span long enough to follow the swing of the moral pendulum through more than a small segment of its full arc. We have not avoided taking sides: we have probably adopted the posture of a rather smudged brand-label of twentieth-century liberalism. We hope that this confession will forewarn the reader of what to expect and go some way towards appeasing those whose standpoint may differ substantially.

We have allocated different subjects to different chapters. This in itself has raised a number of further difficulties, and we must warn the reader that our chapter divisions do not constitute impenetrable bulkheads sealing off the various subjects discussed. The issue of birth control, for example, raises problems relevant to human sexuality as well to the law relating to the family; the same subject has sometimes arisen (for example, see 5.17, the trial of Bradlaugh and Besant) in the context of prosecutions for publishing obscene material. Capital punishment can be discussed either under the rubric of 'punishment' or of 'sanctity of life'. Nothing in this area can be compartmentalised for, when law and the agents of law enforcement are mobilised to stamp out public immorality, they cast their net over a jurisprudential area that defies definitional boundaries.

Similarly, it is misleading to erect artificial barriers between civil and criminal law, since in many contexts the distinction concerns only the form and not the substance of legal proceedings. Nineteenth-century debates about adultery are chiefly concerned with its status as a matrimonial offence in the civil contract of marriage. An important factor here is that lawmakers are often more reluctant to brand behaviour of this kind as 'criminal' than they are to discourage it through the medium of the civil law, where ostensibly the State's role is neither to punish nor (directly) to stigmatise, but to provide a remedy to resolve the disputes between private citizens. The inherently implausible and patently unreal postures of judges in civil or criminal proceedings, acting as referees in private encounters, underlines the artificiality of the distinction between civil and criminal law. In form they act as arbitrators, but in substance they are the embodiment of the established code of social behaviour.

Our list of subjects is in no sense exhaustive – inevitably some important issues have been omitted, and not every mine has been quarried. Some of the subjects we have chosen are dealt with more comprehensively than others. Some sense of the momentum of the processes of interaction between law and morality is conveyed by including material which ranges over a fairly long time-span, although our principle objective has been to place some topical and perennial issues in historical perspective.

On the whole, 'official' or 'semi-official' material, such as judgments, parliamentary debates, pressure groups' literature, and the utterances of opinion leaders, has been included in preference to items from more obscure sources, such as diaries, memoirs and letters. This inevitably involves distortion in favour of the well-known. Such an approach is largely dictated by the character of the law-making process, for the law is changed by concerted and publicly authoritative pressures, and not by lone voices crying in the wilderness. On the other hand, one cannot afford to ignore altogether the remonstrations of the individual person prominent in the less influential strata of society. Today's rebel may be tomorrow's opinion leader: we have, therefore, included some more recondite material where this seems appropriate. Social morality (if it exists at all) is encapsulated in the very sinews of society. As such it is a symbiosis, rather than a summation of private moralities.

Note on style

In editing the extracts from documents we have stuck faithfully to the original texts, except to correct obvious errors of spelling or punctuation or to eliminate stylistic archaisms which jar upon the modern ear. Where several sentences are omitted we generally indicate the break by leaving a blank line in the text; brief omissions are indicated by dots. Numbered footnotes are editorial.

1

The General Debate

It was Dean Roscoe Pound, in his *Social Control Through Law*, who quoted William James as saying that the worst enemies of any subject are the academic teachers thereof. The subjects he had particularly in mind were medicine and law. In these activities the practitioner is in constant contact with the realities of human existence. He doubtless comes to his profession well versed in the ideas inculcated by academic teachers, but quickly either revises those ideas or casts them aside. The professor, on the other hand, is accused of taking the facts of life largely from the relations of others (including practitioners) and assuming them as received data. He generalises from them, it is alleged, and formulates conceptions and theories from which he deductively evolves other theories. On all this he builds a body of teaching which is often obstinate and resistant to reality. He is faithful to his theoretical model and obtusely resists the non-translatability of theoretical views into practical life.

Academics will quickly retort that this accusation of ivory tower obscurantism is a grievous caricature; that all scholarship worthy of the name is firmly founded upon empirical experience. Yet there is a moral in all this for those who through the years have debated the true relationship of law and morality. It is a characteristic of the literature that the battleground has been exclusively the philosophical plane. Natural lawyers and legal positivists, like all good intellectual antagonists, have rejected each other's arguments while agreeing at least on the terrain over which they should fight – and it has not been the professors alone who have formed the cohorts of troops. They have successfully dragged the legal practitioner away (on the rare occasion when he can be caught indulging his rare appetite for jurisprudence) from his traditional pragmatism into the philosophical arena.

Law is too vital an ingredient in the conduct of human society to be extrapolated from its essentially social environment. The theoreticians must, of necessity, be constantly aware of the changing law that pervades any dynamic society. As Dean Pound acutely observed, there is no place for a philosophy of law that seeks to force law into a Procrustean bed of its system; nor do we want an arid sociology of law that hides behind the skirts of a recondite methodology and which does not acknowledge in empirical terms the relationship between law and social *mores*. Given this understanding of the background to the debate, how does the law-and-morality issue stand today?

We are constantly reminded how the current debate is a carbon copy of that earlier dialogue, a century ago, between John Stuart Mill and Mr Justice Fitzjames Stephen. One new dimension has been added to the debate in the century of lull between Stephen's *Liberty, Equality, Fraternity,* published in 1873 (1.5) and Devlin's Maccabaean lecture *Morals and the Criminal Law* published in 1958 (1.10). It is the awareness – promoted initially by German writers like Jhering – that the law is a living entity responding (or failing to respond) to social stimuli.[1]

The relationship between law and morals is in effect quadripartite, but it is only the fourth part that engages our current interest. The first part is an historical and causal question. Has the law been influenced by moral principles? No one doubts the answer is affirmative; conversely law has influenced moral principles. The Suicide Act 1961 no doubt accurately reflected the long-standing moral view that to take one's own life was not a crime against the law, a view which had not always been shared by the judiciary (originally for reasons having to do as much with property as with theological morality). The statutory abolition of the crime of suicide in its turn buttressed and affirmed the moral attitude (6.8 to 6.12).

The second part questions whether law necessarily refers to morality at all; do morals and law overlap in practice, simply because both share the common vocabulary of rights and duties? It is here that the natural lawyers and legal positivists have engaged most fiercely in controversy. The antagonists have found temporary refuge in the sterile argument about whether law is open to moral criticism.

Can a rule of law, 'properly' derived (in constitutional terms) be held to conflict with some moral principle? Those who witnessed Parliament, through the vehicle of the War Damage Act 1965, reversing retrospectively the House of Lords' decision in *Burmah Oil Co. Ltd* v. *Lord Advocate*,[2] and thus depriving a large corporation of its fruits of litigation, would acknowledge readily the dissociation of law and political, if not social, morality. In any event, does it matter that the law is immorally enacted, if we are all bound by it? Its enforceability (if not its actual enforcement) is unlikely to be affected by such theoretical objections. Perhaps political morality can be defined only in terms of the franchise, and the efficacy of representative government – though again the argument rests on a philosophical and psychological, rather than on an empirical plane.

Argument about the enforceability of 'immoral' law – so topical in view of reactions to the Industrial Relations Act 1971 and to the Housing Finance Act 1972 – is closely bound up with questions about political obligation and the basis of State authority that have exercised the minds of every major political philosopher since Aristotle and Plato. There have been those, for example, who have preached disobedience to laws curbing traditional rights of trade unionists on the grounds that such law is distinguishable from 'ordinary' law by virtue of its supposedly pernicious ideological content. Civil disobedience has a long and chequered history and events have often vindicated, even canonised, the dissentients and misfits of a bygone age who have had the foresight to anticipate a subsequent moral trend. Those branded as criminals by political systems of which we disapprove (e.g., opposition groups in Rhodesia, South Africa, the Soviet Union and Nazi

1. The point is neatly put by Professor Hart in his *Law, Liberty and Morality* (London, 1963).

2. [1965] A.C. 75.

Germany) are depicted as heroic fighters for freedom. But law is law: advocacy of selective disobedience of legal rules is a two-edged sword and one which chips away at the foundations of the rule of law itself.

It is to a fourth issue, closely bound up with the third, that the modern controversialists have devoted much of their energies. It concerns the legal enforcement of morality. It is no accident that Lord Devlin's essay into this field (1.10) was prompted by the thesis propounded by the Wolfenden Committee on Prostitution and Homosexuality (1.7) – namely that there are areas of private morality which are none of the law's business. The modern debate has focused on the answer given by John Stuart Mill to the question: ought immorality, as such, to be subject to legal sanctions? Mill's classic response was 'The only purpose for which power can rightfully be exercised over any member of a civilised community, against his will, is to prevent harm to others' (1.3). The modern variant of this is that society is entitled to legislate only against those forms of behaviour which are calculated to cause social damage. Otherwise, society should discontinue external control, leaving behaviour in such areas to the control of individual consciences and built-in social controls unsupported by legal rules[3]. The main response of those who decry this 'hands off' philosophy is that abandonment of formal controls will mean that many will abandon all control, and the sufferer will be society as a whole.

This argument is altogether too absolutist. The disinclination of the law to be involved in sustaining a generalised morality does not mean that control should be abandoned – only that the desire and need for control will be the more successfully maintained by other agencies at work in society than by the heavy-handed instrument of the law.

The more sophisticated argument in favour of legal enforcement of morality, for which Lord Devlin is the most renowned proponent, is that law rests on a stable and identifiable community sentiment of what is moral and right. Both courts and legislators, so the argument runs, may and should rely upon morality rather than upon their own consciences and intelligence. This argument leads to the pseudo-democracy of a consensus among the riders on the Clapham omnibus (supposedly personifying the overwhelming majority of citizens). It is one of the arguments advanced by proponents of the referendum as an instrument not just of populism but even of democratic government.

Lord Devlin proclaims that the morals of society are those standards of conduct of which the reasonable man approves. Common morality depends upon the collective wisdom or unwisdom of reasonable men. But who is the reasonable man? Half a century of Freud, and the work of social and clinical psychologists over the latter half of that time, has cast serious doubt on the reality of the man who travels daily on the Clapham omnibus, unaware of the exalted status accorded to him by the legal fraternity. Under the skin of the real man lurks a whole range of repressed feelings and concealed prejudices in which rationality often faces an unequal struggle. In this respect the lawyers have signally failed to emulate the economists who abandoned, as of dubious utility, the concept of economic man.

3. See E. Vallance (ed.), *The State, Society and Self-Destruction* (London, 1975).

Given that such a creature exists, presumably the reasonable man is the man whom legislators and judges recognise as instantly acknowledging the moral rectitude of the laws prescribed at any point of time. He cannot be a person who thinks the law is wrong, because as Lord Devlin states: 'If the rational man disapproves of laws governing homosexuality and abortion [neither of which, at the time of his writing, had been legalised by Act of Parliament] he will not share in the common morality'. Thus, the reasonable man is the person who at a fixed point of time approves (or would so, if apprised of the law in question) of everything that is on the Statute Book and what is declared to be the common law. (Supposedly, the reasonable man might also disapprove of the law which is in desuetude.) Therefore, his reasonableness must change at the moment that the Statute Book is revised by new Acts of Parliament – although, as Lord Devlin himself declared in a different context, reasonableness does not change at the stroke of midnight when a new law comes into force.[4] Insistence upon so high a degree of punctuality would bring the point near to absurdity.

Lord Devlin's elegant argument prompted a vigorous response from the distinguished legal philosopher, H.L.A. Hart (1.11) who, among other things, attributes to Devlin the extreme view that social morality is a seamless web requiring obedience *in toto*. The following year (1964) saw the appearance of Lord Devlin's rejoinder in a book expanding upon the theme of his Maccabaean lecture and, in particular, devoting an entire chapter to a riposte to Hart.

The controversy lingers on and occasionally comes to the surface in judicial contexts. It is interesting to note that the leading judgment in the case, *Shaw* v. *D.P.P.* (1.9), in which the House of Lords resurrected the long forgotten crime of 'conspiracy to corrupt public morals' and asserted the role of the courts as *custos bonos mores*, was that of the arch formalist and eschewer of law-making, Viscount Simonds.[5]

Professor Judith Shklar, a distinguished Professor of Government at Harvard University, has made a refreshing contribution to the subject in a long essay, entitled *Legalism*, published in 1964 (1.13). She pertinently observes that the argument between natural lawyers and legal positivists is essentially a family quarrel among legalists, and 'that is perhaps, why outsiders find it tiresome'.[6] The natural lawyer and the legal positivists agree about the necessity of following rules; they disagree about what to do when a conflict between rules occurs.

But the question of choice is crucial to the practitioner, irrespective of morality. The judge who regards his decision as morally repugnant, but consoles himself with the remark that his court is not a court of morals, is in fact living up to the moral precept that the judicial role is to give effect to the

4. *Hughes* v. *Architects' Registration Council of the United Kingdom* [1957] 2 Q.B. 550, 559.

5. It was endorsed, with one whole-hearted (Lord Diplock) and one half-hearted (Lord Reid) dissent, in *Knuller* v. *D.P.P.* [1973] A.C. 435. But see Law Commission Working Paper No. 57 (1974) where it is proposed that conspiracy to corrupt public morals and to outrage public decency should cease to be criminal where the object of the conspiracy falls short of being a crime (para. 113).

6. *Legalism* (Cambridge, Massachusetts, 1964) p.106.

law. What the judge is doing, in the last analysis, is giving effect to a choice of values – a choice in favour of legal certainty rather than of uncertainty. And that certainty, in turn, depends upon supposedly ascertainable moral principles. In some circumstances, 'uncertainty' may actually promote a desirable flexibility – but this is not 'law' in terms of the morality of legalism. Whether the judge's decision is socially acceptable or not will depend upon the observer's standpoint; the decision will appear 'unjust' if it does not conform to his system of moral rules. Even judges sometimes express distaste for the results of their application of the strict letter of the law (1.14). If the observer is a natural lawyer he will declare that it is not only morally obnoxious but will also condemn it to 'grammatical death through definitional execution'. It will be said that it is not *to be* a legal decision at all, implying that it is undeserving of existence and hence need not be obeyed. The positivist lawyer will approve the judge's stance without advising the citizenry of its duty to obey or defy the decision.

Professor Shklar thus concludes:

> Whatever their disagreements, both sides agree that justice is a matter of the equal application of rules. The pursuit of rules – pre-established, known and accepted – is the end moreover, not only of law but all legalistic morals. It is this common aim that makes law and legalistic morality not separate entities but a single continuum. And the name of that continuum is justice. Rigorously applied in courts, more compromisingly in daily life, the virtues of acting according to rules may be practised in varying degrees of intensity, but the cast of mind, the moral attitude, remains constant. As such it is but one morality among others. It is this circumstance that legalism in its exclusiveness finds so difficult to accept and so impossible to adjust to – in theory, no less than in practice.[7]

The argument of the legalist makes the relationship of law and morality a non-issue. Mill, Stephen and their respective contemporary disciples may be forgiven, in an age when jurisprudential thinking was permeated by arid Austinian positivism, for straying into the wilderness of non-issues. It is hardly forgivable for modern jurists to have followed the same fruitless trail still further into the desert and to have become impaled on dialectical cacti. Many modern sociologists have both applauded the Hartites and been appalled at the Devlinites. The positivists, it must be said, have at least demonstrated the aridity of the argument, even though they have chosen to indulge in their gladiatorial combat on the abstract plane of legalism. Professor Shklar, viewing the debate from the platform of government and politics, has pronounced a plague on the houses of both natural lawyers and legal positivists.

Do we then need to concern ourselves with the moral content of law? In seeking an answer to the philosophical conundra implicit in that question, one could usefully recall what Joseph Butler (1692-1752), Bishop of Durham in the early eighteenth century, said to an illiterate congregation in

7. *ibid.*, p.109.

part of one of his fifteen famous sermons [8] – 'Things and actions are what they are, and the consequences of them will be what they will be; why then should we desire to be deceived?'

Professor Shklar, in her concluding remarks, invites lawyers in pursuit of justice to consider the notion of justice and to see what the single-minded devotion to that virtue entails. She means much what Bishop Butler had in mind. Look at human conduct, see how it acts and re-acts to human rules and do not bedevil the study with philosophical discussions that are devoid of practical considerations. If you can discover how legal rules are in fact translated into social action then the justice of those rules will be the more readily observable and can be underpinned, if so desired, by theoretical concepts of law and morality. To indulge in the search for a theoretical underpinning for legal rules without reference to the actual enforceability of those rules is, to say the least, unhelpful to the administrators of a legal system. It is to some of these activities that we turn.

1.1   The basis of crime : Blackstone's view

Sir William Blackstone (*1723-80) became first Vinerian Professor of English Law at Oxford. He was later a Justice of Common Pleas and, for a short period, of the King's Bench. His famous* Commentaries on the Laws of England *were first published in the period 1765-9 in order to forestall clandestine sales of his lectures. Although Blackstone was seriously criticised by, among others, Austin and Bentham for his intellectual rigidity, his* Commentaries *achieved a lasting success and had a profound influence upon the development of legal thought in Britain and, more particularly, in the United States of America. His views represented in large measure those of the judiciary at that time, and the* Commentaries *are still sometimes cited as authority in legal proceedings.*

The extracts used in this book are from the eighth edition of the Commentaries, *published in 1778, which was the last edition to be published in the author's lifetime.*

All crimes ought ... to be estimated merely according to the mischiefs which they produce in civil society: and, of consequence, private vices, or the breach of mere absolute duties, which man is bound to perform considered only as an individual, are not, cannot be, the object of any municipal law; any farther than as by their evil example, or other pernicious effects, they may prejudice the community, and thereby become a species of public crimes. Thus the vice of drunkenness, if committed privately and alone, is beyond the knowledge and of course beyond the reach of human tribunals: but if committed publicly, in the face of the world, its evil example makes it liable to temporal censures. The vice of lying, which consists (abstractedly taken) in a criminal violation of truth, and therefore in any shape is derogatory from sound morality, is not however taken notice of by our law, unless it carries with it some public inconvenience, as spreading false news; or some social injury, as slander and malicious prosecution, for which a private recompence is given. And yet drunkenness and malevolent lying are in *foro conscientiae* as thoroughly criminal when they are not, as when they

8. *Fifteen Sermons*, No. 7, Sermon 16.

are, attended with public inconvenience. The only difference is, that both public and private vices are subject to the vengeance of eternal justice; and public vices are besides liable to the temporal punishments of human tribunals.

1.2 Legislation as a means of promoting morality

William Wilberforce (*1759-1833) is most commonly associated with the abolition of slavery (1807) and with penal reform. A man of strong missionary zeal and Christian idealism, he was renowned for his rigorous advocacy of the enforcement of morals by means of the law. In 1787 he founded the influential Proclamation Society (see 8.1) for the suppression of vice. The extract that follows is taken from his notes on 'The Importance of Legislative Measures for Promoting Public Morals'.*

A community is made up of individuals, and generally it cannot be denied that to be virtuous is to be happy; but if this be true of all mankind, how peculiarly so in the lower orders which constitute the bulk of every community! Among them the question is not merely between the soul's calm sunshine, the peace within, the moderated desires and unruffled comforts, the calm survey of the past and anticipation of the future, compared with short deliriums of pleasure too dearly purchased by the misery of ungoverned passions, by a self-accusing conscience, and the consciousness of abused advantages ... while in every face the man reads a condemnation of his conduct ... which when he looks within is confirmed by the reproaches of his mind ... but ...

Immorality in the lower and even middling classes leads directly to temporal ruin; and while as in the higher classes all the comforts of virtue are forfeited, and all the disquietudes of vice incurred, there is superadded the suffering arising from the loss of hope, the declining condition of life, family jars and discord, bodily health ruined – too naturally leading to the violation of the laws of the land.

Consider in the case of every class, what is given up of pleasure, and what is incurred of pain.

Let it be remembered that the bulk of mankind must maintain themselves by their own efforts; consequently, that industry, sobriety, punctuality, temperance, health, regularity, are virtues necessary to their living in any tolerable enjoyment of the comforts of life.

Take a man whose irregularities and excesses render his home a scene of self-reproach and discord, and he is in a fine state of preparation for becoming an ale-house politician – a tool of faction. Our natural proneness to acquit ourselves and lay blame on others, disposes men to charge on the conduct of their rulers or the institutions of their country, those sufferings which flow from their own imprudence, folly, or vices. He complains perhaps of the tax-gatherer, when it is from his indolence that the means of paying his taxes are wanting. In the resorts of dissipation and vice he finds also comrades of a similar stamp. He loses by degrees a sense of those domestic pleasures, with the actual enjoyment of which his vicious habits are incompatible. He has no fire-side comforts, no little ones or faithful partner to look up to him with gratitude and affection.

These best pleasures of our nature the Almighty has put within the reach of the poor no less than the rich, as in the natural world the best things are the most common.

How little then is it true humanity to strew temptation in the way; to multiply inducements to idleness, dissipation, and vice; to draw into and encourage those smaller deviations and transgressions which infallibly lead to fatal consequences, and bring on a train of vicious habits and sufferings, while all the virtues with their attendant comforts fly away to seek an asylum in the cottages of the sober and industrious!

How much more criminal this in the legislature, which should watch over the welfare of the state, and guard with peculiar care the rights and comforts of the poor!

Are not these truths indisputable? And if so, what cruel mockery is it for enlightened men to pretend to be pleading the cause and promoting the interests of the lower orders, when contending against the checks to idleness, dissipation, and vice, and for multiplying the means and increasing the facilities of giving into illicit gratifications! Does it not argue an utter contempt for the comforts of those very people for whose interests they affect to feel?

How criminal then must be the legislature, whose duty it is to watch over the happiness of the people, when it not only neglects its office, but even assumes the directly opposite course, and tempts those very persons it should restrain! There is a selfishness also in this, since we should not tempt to vices which were immediately injurious to ourselves; yet like all selfishness it is short-sighted, for it soon reaches us after destroying the family comforts of the sufferer. ...

For the dissipated, vicious man is almost sure to be disaffected. Think then of the difference between having a hardy, contented, domestic people, eager to defend their wives and families, in the place of a set of discontented, factious men, to whom any change would be gain, and whose natural habits prompt them to take the side of licence and misrule against law and order.

The legislators of antiquity were so deeply impressed with all these truths, that it was their deepest study, and primary aim, to preserve from deterioration the public morals.

All this observe is true of morals independently of religion, but religion is also indispensably necessary, and religion is destroyed on the one hand by loose morals, just as, on the other, where religion declines the morals will be infallibly corrupted.

Sanction of oaths, property, person, life, honour, depend on them; the very cement that compacts society together. ...

But the truth is, cases will often arise in which the present temptation will be so strong, (importunate), the immediate interest or gain so powerful, the chance of detection so small, that the virtue of most men would give way, unless sustained by the consciousness of an invisible Spectator. What check remains, if the man is not aware that though removed from every human eye he is still in the presence of a Being who witnesses his most secret conduct, and who both can and will call him to account for actions which may escape and elude all human observation? It is the habitual effect of this restraint which strengthens the moral principle, and the force of this restraint in each particular instance is greater or less according to the power of habit. Release a man then from this habitual restraint, and you prepare him at once for every degree of perfidy and crime, without fear or remorse, without pity or compunction.

Morals necessary above all for a free country. The slaves of a despot may be kept in subjection by fear; but a free country can only be safe from without – as it can alone be at peace within – while it is sustained by the zealous attachment, and affectionate and patriotic loyalty of its people.

The degree of liberty every man possesses will make him the master of his own actions, and factions will spring up, and liberty will be corrupted into licentiousness.

The necessity of religion among the bulk of the people, i.e. the lower orders, is the greater, because that great principle of honour which it would scarcely be too strong to term the religion of the higher orders does not exist among them. Consider then what the former would be without the restraint of honour, and estimate what the latter without religion.

The immoral man cannot be a good citizen, because not a happy man. The unhappy wish for change, and impute to their government the distresses which flow from their own vices or imprudence.

Though the doctrine is unpopular, I am always disposed to call in private character and conduct to elucidate the motives of public.

1.3   Mill – *a nineteenth-century view of liberty under the law*

John Stuart Mill *(1806-73) was the renowned philosopher of the Utilitarian school. His essay 'On Liberty' (1859) from which this extract is taken is still regarded as one of the most profound and elegant contributions to the debate on law and morality.*

The object of this Essay is to assert one very simple principle, as entitled to govern absolutely the dealings of society with the individual in the way of compulsion and control, whether the means used be physical force in the form of legal penalties, or the moral coercion of public opinion. That principle is, that the sole end for which mankind are warranted, individually or collectively, in interfering with the liberty of action of any of their number, is self-protection. That the only purpose for which power can be rightfully exercised over any member of a civilised community, against his will, is to prevent harm to others. His own good, either physical or moral, is not a sufficient warrant. He cannot rightfully be compelled to do or forbear because it will be better for him to do so, because it will make him happier, because, in the opinions of others, to do so would be wise, or even right. These are good reasons for remonstrating with him, or reasoning with him, or persuading him, or entreating him, but not for compelling him, or visiting him with any evil in case he do otherwise. To justify that, the conduct from which it is desired to deter him must be calculated to produce evil to some one else. The only part of the conduct of any one, for which he is amenable to society, is that which concerns others. In the part which merely concerns himself, his independence is, of right, absolute. Over himself, over his own body and mind, the individual is sovereign.

It is proper to state that I forego any advantage which could be derived to my argument from the idea of abstract right, as a thing independent of utility. I regard utility as the ultimate appeal on all ethical questions; but it must be utility in the largest sense, grounded on the permanent interests of a man as a progressive being. Those interests, I contend, authorise the subjection of individual spontaneity to external control, only in respect to those actions of each, which concern the interest of other people. If any one does an act hurtful to others, there is a *prima facie* case for punishing him, by law, or, where legal penalties are not safely applicable, by general disapprobation. There are also many positive acts for the benefit of others, which he may rightfully be compelled to perform; such as to give evidence in a court of justice; to bear his fair share in the common defence, or in any other joint work necessary to the interest of the society of which he enjoys the protection; and to perform certain acts of individual beneficence, such as saving a fellow-creature's life, or interposing to protect the defenceless against ill-usage, things which whenever it is obviously a man's duty to do, he may rightfully be made responsible to society for not doing. A person may cause evil to others not only by his actions but by his inaction, and in either case he is justly accountable to them for the injury. The latter case, it is true, requires a much more cautious exercise of compulsion than the former. To make any one answerable for doing evil to others is the rule; to make him answerable for not preventing evil is, comparatively speaking, the exception. Yet there are many cases clear enough and grave enough to justify that exception. In all things which regard the external relations of the individual, he is *de jure* amenable to those whose interests are concerned, and, if need be, to society as their protector. There are often good reasons for not holding him to the responsibility; but these reasons must arise from the special expediencies of the case: either because it is a kind of case in which society have it in their power to control him; or because the attempt to exercise control would produce other evils, greater than those which it would prevent. When such reasons as these preclude the enforcement of responsibility, the conscience of the agent himself should step into the vacant judgment seat, and protect those interests of others which have no external protection; judging himself all the more rigidly, because the case does not admit of his being made accountable to the judgment of his fellow-creatures.

But there is a sphere of action in which society, as distinguished from the individual, has, if any, only an indirect interest; comprehending all that portion of a person's life and conduct which affects only himself, or if it also affects others, only with their free, voluntary, and undeceived consent and participation. When I say only himself, I mean directly, and in the first instance; for whatever affects himself, may affect others through himself; and the objection which may be grounded on this contingency, will receive consideration in the sequel. This, then, is the appropriate region of human liberty. It compromises, first, the inward domain of consciousness; demanding liberty of conscience in the most comprehensive sense; liberty of thought and feeling; absolute freedom of opinion and sentiment on all subjects, practical or speculative, scientific, moral, or theological. The liberty of expressing and publishing opinions may seem to fall under a different principle, since it belongs to that part of the conduct of an individual which concerns other people; but, being almost of as much importance as the liberty of thought itself, and resting in great part on the same reasons, is practically inseparable from it. Secondly, the principle requires liberty of tastes and pursuits; of framing the plan of our life to suit our own character; of doing as we like, subject to such consequences as may follow: without impediment from our fellow-creatures, so long as what we do does not harm them, even though they should think our conduct foolish, perverse, or wrong. Thirdly, from this liberty of each individual, follows the liberty, within the same limits, of combination among individuals; freedom to unite, for any purpose not involving harm to others: the persons combining being supposed to be of full age, and not forced or deceived.

No society in which these liberties are not, on the whole, respected, is free, whatever may be its form of government; and none is completely free in which they do not exist absolute and unqualified. The only freedom which deserves the name, is that of pursuing our own good in our own way, so long as we do not attempt to deprive others of theirs, or impede their efforts to obtain it. Each is the proper guardian of his own health, whether bodily, *or* mental and spiritual. Mankind are greater gainers by suffering each other to live as seems good to themselves, than by compelling each to live as seems good to the rest.

* * *

What, then, is the rightful limit to the sovereignty of the individual over himself? Where does the authority of society begin? How much of human life should be assigned to individuality, and how much to society?

Each will receive its proper share, if each has that which more particularly concerns it. To individuality should belong the part of life in which it is chiefly the individual that is interested; to society, the part which chiefly interests society.

Though society is not founded on a contract, and though no good purpose is answered by inventing a contract in order to deduce social obligations from it, every one who receives the protection of society owes a return for the benefit, and the fact of living in society renders it indispensable that each should be bound to observe a certain line of conduct towards the rest. This conduct consists, first, in not injuring the interests of one another; or rather certain interests, which, either by express legal provision or by tactic understanding, ought to be considered as rights; and secondly, in each person's bearing his share (to be fixed on some equitable principle) of the labours and sacrifices incurred for defending the society or its members from injury and molestation. These conditions society is justified in enforcing, at all costs to those who endeavour to withhold fulfilment. Nor is this all that society may do. The acts of an individual may be hurtful to others, or wanting in due consideration for their welfare, without going to the length of violating any of their constituted rights. The offender may then be justly punished by opinion, though not by law. As soon as any part of a person's conduct affects prejudicially the interests of others, society has jurisdiction over it, and the question whether the general welfare will or will not be promoted by interfering with it, becomes open to discussion. But there is no room for entertaining any such question when a person's conduct affects the interests of no person besides himself, or needs not affect them unless they like (all the persons concerned being of full age, and the ordinary amount of understanding). In all such cases, there should be perfect freedom, legal and social, to do the action and stand the consequences.

1.4   *Utilitarianism and moral duty*

The following letter was written by Mill in November 1867 in reply to an inquiry by E.W. Young concerning a passage in Mill's essay 'Utilitarianism'.

AVIGNON, 10*th November* 1867.

Dear Sir, – I beg to acknowledge your letter of the 23rd ultimo.

I do not claim any greater latitude of making exceptions to general rules of morality on the utilitarian theory than is accorded by moralists on all theories. Every ethical system admits the possibility, and even frequency, of a conflict of duties. In most cases the conflict occasions no great difficulty, because one of the duties is in general obviously paramount to the other. The difficulty arises when the choice is between a very great violation of a duty usually subordinate and a very small infringement of one ordinarily of more peremptory obligation. In such a case the former, I cannot but think, may be the greater moral offence. When I mentioned, as a case of this kind, the case of stealing or taking by force the food or medicine necessary for saving a life, I was thinking rather of saving another person's life than one's own. A much stricter rule is required in the latter than in the former, for the obvious reason that there is more probability of self-deception or of dishonesty. But I am far from saying that the rule should never be relaxed, even when the case is one's own. A runaway slave by the laws of slave countries commits a theft: he steals his own person from his lawful owner. If you say this is not morally theft, because property in a human being ought not to exist, take the case of a child or an apprentice who runs away on account of intolerable ill usage. There is in the doctrine I maintain nothing inconsistent with the loftiest estimation of the heroism of martyrs. There are times when the grandest results for the human race depend on the public assertion of one's convictions at the risk of death by torture. When this is the case martyrdom may be a duty; and in cases when it does not become the duty of all, it may be an admirable act of virtue in whoever does it, and a duty in those who as leaders or teachers are bound to set an example of virtue to others, and to do more for the common faith or cause than a simple believer. I do not know whether what I have written will do anything towards removing your difficulty, but I have not leisure to enter further into the subject.

1.5   A Victorian jurist's riposte to Mill

Sir James Fitzjames Stephen (*1829-94*), *the noted criminal lawyer, judge and author, crossed swords with J.S. Mill in a manner replicated in this century by Lord Devilin and Professor Hart (see 1.10 and 1.11). A prolific writer from his early days, one of his best known essays, 'Liberty, Equality, Fraternity' (1873) was a direct riposte to Mill. It was published before Stephen became a High Court Judge in 1879 and during a period when he was contributing regularly to the* Cornhill Magazine.

No better statement of the popular view – I might, perhaps say of the religious dogma of liberty – is to be found than that which is contained in Mr Mill's essay on the subject. His works on Utilitarianism and the Subjection of Women afford excellent illustrations of the forms of the doctrines of equality and fraternity to which I object.

There is hardly anything in the whole essay [On Liberty] which can properly be called proof as distinguished from enunciation or assertion of the general principles quoted. I think, however, that it will not be difficult to show that the principle stands in much need of proof. In order to make this clear it will be desirable in the first place to point out the meaning of the word liberty according to principles which I think are common to Mr Mill and to myself. I do not think Mr Mill would have disputed the following statement of the theory of human actions. All voluntary acts are caused by motives. All motives may be placed in one of two categories = hope and fear, pleasure and pain. Voluntary acts of which fear is the motive are said to be done under compulsion, or omitted under retraint. A woman marries. This in every case is a voluntary action. If she regards the marriage with the ordinary feelings and acts from the ordinary motives, she is said to act freely. If she regards it as a necessity, to which she submits in order to avoid greater evil, she is said to act under compulsion and not freely.

If this is the true theory of liberty – and, though many persons would deny this, I think they would have been accepted by Mr Mill – the propositions already stated will in a condensed form amount to this: 'No one is ever justified in trying to affect any one's conduct by exciting his fears, except for the sake of self-protection;' or, making another substitution which he would also approve – 'It can never promote the general happiness of mankind that the conduct of any persons should be affected by an appeal to their fears, except in the cases excepted.'

Surely these are not assertions which can be regarded as self-evident, or even as otherwise than paradoxical. What is all morality, and what are all existing religions in so far as they aim at affecting human conduct, except an appeal either to hope or fear, and to fear far more commonly and far more emphatically than to hope? Criminal legislation proper may be regarded as an engine of prohibition unimportant in comparison with morals and the forms of morality sanctioned by theology. For one act from which one person is restrained by the fear of the law of the land, many persons are

restrained from innumerable acts by the fear of the disapprobation of their
neighbours, which is the moral sanction; or by the fear of punishment in a
future state of existence, which is the religious sanction; or by the fear of
their own disapprobation, which may be called the conscientious sanction,
and may be regarded as a compound case of the other two. Now, in the
innumerable majority of cases, disapprobation, or the moral sanction, has
nothing whatever to do with self-protection. The religious sanction is by its
nature independent of it. Whatever special forms it may assume, the
fundamental condition of it is a being intolerant of evil in the highest degree,
and inexorably determined to punish it wherever it exists, except upon
certain terms. I do not say that this doctrine is true, but I do say that no one
is entitled to assume it without proof to be essentially immoral and
mischievous. Mr Mill does not draw this inference, but I think his theory
involves it, for I know not what can be a greater infringement of his theory of
liberty, a more complete and formal contradiction to it, than the doctrine
that there are a court and a judge in which, and before whom, every man
must give an account of every work done in the body, whether self-regarding
or not. According to Mr Mill's theory, it ought to be a good plea in the day
of judgment to say 'I pleased myself and hurt nobody else'. Whether or not
there will ever be a day of judgment is not the question, but upon his
principles the conception of a day of judgment is fundamentally immoral. A
God who punished any one at all, except for the purpose of protecting
others, would, upon his principles, be a tyrant trampling on liberty.

The application of the principle in question to the moral sanction would
be just as subversive of all that people commonly regard as morality. The
only moral system which would comply with the principle stated by Mr
Mill would be one capable of being summed up as follows: 'Let every man
please himself without hurting his neighbour;' and every moral system
which aimed at more than this, either to obtain benefits for society at large
other than protection against injury or to do good to the persons affected,
would be wrong in principle. This would condemn every existing system of
morals. Positive morality is nothing but a body of principles and rules more
or less vaguely expressed, and more or less left to be understood, by which
certain lines of conduct are forbidden under the penalty of general
disapprobation, and that quite irrespectively of self-protection. Mr Mill
himself admits this to a certain extent. In the early part of his fourth chapter
he says that a man grossly deficient in the qualities which conduce to his
own good is 'necessarily and properly a subject of distaste, or in extreme
cases even of contempt', and he enumerates various inconveniences to which
this would expose such a person. He adds, however: 'The inconveniences
which are strictly inseparable from the unfavourable judgment of others are
the only ones to which a person whould ever be subjected for that portion of
his conduct and character which concerns his own good, but which does not
affect the interests of others in their relation with him.' This no doubt
weakens the effect of the admission; but be this how it may, the fact still
remains that morality is and must be a prohibitive system, one of the main
objects of which is to impose upon every one a standard of conduct and of
sentiment to which few persons would conform if it were not for the
constraint thus put upon them. In nearly every instance the effects of such a

system reach far beyond anything that can be described as the purposes of self-protection.

Mr Mill's system is violated not only by every system of theology which concerns itself with morals, and by every known system of positive morality, but by the constitution of human nature itself. There is hardly a habit which men in general regard as good which is not acquired by a series of more or less painful and laborious acts. The condition of human life is such that we must of necessity be restrained and compelled by circumstances in nearly every action of our lives. Why, then, is liberty, defined as Mr Mill defines it, to be regarded as so precious? What, after all, is done by the legislator or by the person who sets public opinion in motion to control conduct of which he disapproves – or, if the expression is preferred, which he dislikes – which is not done for us all at every instant of our lives by circumstances? The laws which punish murder or theft are substitutes for private vengeance, which, in the absence of law, would punish those crimes more severely, though in a less regular manner. If there were laws which punished incontinence, gluttony, or drunkenness, the same might be said of them. Mr Mills admits in so many words that there are 'inconveniences which are strictly inseparable from the unfavourable judgment of others'. What is the distinction in principle between such inconveniences and similar ones organized, defined, and inflicted upon proof that the circumstances which call for their infliction exist? This organization, definition, and procedure make all the difference between the restraints which Mr Mill would permit and the restraints to which he objects. I cannot see on what the distinction rests. I cannot understand why it must always be wrong to punish habitual drunkeness by fine, imprisonment, or deprivation of civil rights, and always be right to punish it by the infliction of those consequences which are 'strictly inseparable from the unfavourable judgment of others.' It may be said that these consequences follow, not because we think them desirable, but in the common order of nature. This answer only suggests the further question, whether nature is in this instance to be regarded as a friend or as an enemy? Every reasonable man would answer that the restraint which the fear of the disapprobation of others imposes on our conduct is the part of the constitution of nature which we could least afford to dispense with. But if this is so, why draw the line where Mr Mills draws it? Why treat the penal consequences of disaprobation as things to be minimized and restrained within the narrowest limits? What 'inconvenience', after all, is 'strictly inseparable from the unfavourable judgment of others'? If society at large adopted fully Mr Mill's theory of liberty, it would be easy to diminish very greatly the inconveniences in question. Strenuously preach and rigorously practise the doctrine that our neighbour's private character is nothing to us, and the number of unfavourable judgments formed, and therfore the number of inconveniences inflicted by them can be reduced as much as we please, and the province of liberty can be enlarged in a corresponding ratio. Does any reasonable man wish for this? Could any one desire gross licentiousness, monstrous extravagance, ridiculous vanity, or the like, to be unnoticed, or, being known, to inflict no inconveniences which can possibly be avoided?

If, however, the restraints on immorality are the main safeguards of society against influences which might be fatal to it, why treat them as if they were bad? Why draw so strongly marked a line between social and legal penalties? Mr Mill asserts the existence of the distinction in every form of speech. He makes his meaning perfectly clear. Yet from one end of his essay to the other I find no proof and no attempt to give the proper and appropriate proof of it. His doctrine could have been proved if it had been true. It was not proved because it was not true.

The doctrine of liberty in its application to morals

So far I have considered the theoretical grounds of Mr Mill's principle and its practical application to liberty of thought and discussion. I now proceed to consider its application to morals.

... Mr Mill's whole case ... appears to me so weak that I fear that I may have misunderstood or understated it. If so, I have done so unconsciously. As it stands it seems to involve the following errors.

First, there is no principle on which the cases in which Mr Mill admits the justice of legal punishment can be distinguished from those in which he denies it. The principle is that private vices which are injurious to others may justly be punished, if the injury be specific and the persons injured distinctly assignable, but not otherwise. If the question were as to the possibility in most cases of drawing an indictment against such persons I should agree with him. Criminal law is an extremely rough engine, and must be worked with great caution; but it is one thing to point out a practical difficulty which limits the application of a principle and quite another to refute the principle itself. Mr Mill's proviso deserves attention in considering the question whether a given act should be punished by law, but he applies it to 'the moral coercion of public opinion', as well as to legal coercion, and to this the practical difficulty which he points out does not apply.

Secondly, the arguments against legal interference in the cases not admitted to be properly subject to it are all open to obvious answers.

Mr Mill says that if grown-up people are grossly vicious it is the fault of society, which therefore ought not to punish them.

This argument proves too much, for the same may be said with even greater force of gross crimes, and it is admitted that they may be punished.

It is illogical, for it does not follow that because society caused a fault it is not to punish it. A man who breaks his arm when he is drunk may have to have it cut off when he is sober.

It admits the whole principle of interference, for it assumes that the power of society over people in their minority is and ought to be absolute, and minority and majority are questions of degree, and the line which separates them is arbitrary.

Lastly, it proceeds upon an exaggerated estimate of the power of education. Society cannot make silk purses out of sows' ears, and there are plenty of ears in the world which no tanning can turn even into serviceable pigskin.

Mr Mill's other arguments are, that compulsion in such cases will make people rebel, and, above all, that the moral persecutor himself may very probably be mistaken.

This is true and important, but it goes to show not that compulsion should not be used at all, but that its employment is a delicate operation.

The Brahmins, it is said, being impressed with the importance of cattle to agriculture, taught people to regard the bull as a holy beast. He must never be thwarted, even if he put his nose into a shop and ate the shopkeeper's grain. He must never be killed, even in mercy to himself. If he slips over a cliff and breaks his bones and the vultures are picking out his eyes and boring holes between his ribs, he must be left to die. In several Indian towns the British Government has sent half the holy bulls to Mohammedan butchers, and the other half to draw commissariat wagons. Many matters go better in consequence of this arrangement, and agriculture in particular goes no worse. Liberty is Mr Mill's Brahminee bull.

1.6 Public opinion and legal change

Best v. **Samuel Fox and Co. Ltd** *concerned a claim for damages by a wife for the loss of her husband's consortium resulting from injury at work. The House of Lords held unanimously that a wife has no right of action for the loss of her husband's consortium, even though the common law does give such a right to the husband.*

On behalf of the appellant it is urged that a husband can bring an action for the loss of the consortium of his wife by means of any tort which deprives him of that consortium and that in the circumstances prevailing today a wife must have a similar right. Even, however, if it be assumed that in enticement cases the husband and wife have equal rights it does not follow that today they have equal rights and liabilities one towards the other in all respects. I do not think it possible to say that a change in the outlook of the public, however great, must inevitably be followed by a change in the law of this country. The common law is a historical development rather than a logical whole, and the fact that a particular doctrine does not logically accord with another or others is no ground for its rejection.

1.7 Private morality and the criminal law : the Wolfenden Report

The Report of the Departmental Committee on Homosexual Offences and Prostitution, under the chairmanship of Sir John (now Lord) Wolfenden, restates the classical Mill thesis that the law should not intrude into the sphere of private morality. The words contained in this extract (paras 60 and 61) were a catalyst for the ensuing debate between Devlin and Hart.

On its recommendation that homosexual acts by consenting male adults in private should cease to be punished by law, Mr James Adair dissented.

60.   We recognise that a proposal to change a law which has operated for many years so as to make legally permissible acts which were formerly unlawful, is open to criticisms which might not be made in relation to a

proposal to omit, from a code of laws being formulated *de novo*, any provision making these acts illegal. To reverse a long-standing tradition is a serious matter and not to be suggested lightly. But the task entrusted to us, as we conceive it, is to state what we regard as a just and equitable law. We therefore do not think it appropriate that consideration of this question should be unduly influenced by a regard for the present law, much of which derives from traditions whose origins are obscure.

61. Further, we feel bound to say this. We have outlined the arguments against a change in the law, and we recognise their weight. We believe, however, that they have been met by the counter-arguments we have already advanced. There remains one additional counter-argument which we believe to be decisive, namely, the importance which society and the law ought to give to individual freedom of choice and action in matters of private morality. Unless a deliberate attempt is to be made by society, acting through the agency of the law, to equate the sphere of crime with that of sin, there must remain a realm of private morality and immorality which is, in brief and crude terms, not the law's business. To say this is not to condone or encourage private immorality. On the contrary, to emphasise the personal and private nature of moral or immoral conduct is to emphasise the personal and private responsibility of the individual for his own actions, and that is a responsibility which a mature agent can properly be expected to carry for himself without the threat of punishment from the law.

[Mr Adair:] It is with regret that I find it necessary to dissociate myself from the other members of the Committee on what is undoubtedly the most important recommendation in Part Two of the report – to take homosexual acts committed in private by consenting male adults out of the realm of the criminal law ...

As I look at the matter, we are investigating in this part of our inquiry a course of conduct which is contrary to the best interests of the community, and one which can have very serious effects on the whole moral fabric of social life. It is one of those forms of conduct falling within the group to which the words of the Street Offences Committee ... apply as being 'conduct it has always been thought right to bring within the scope of the criminal law on account of the injury which they occasion to the public in general'. The influence of example in forming the views and developing the characters of young people can scarcely be overestimated. ... If the recommendation be adopted, the moral force of the law will be weakened. I am convinced that the main body of the community recognizes clearly the moral force of the criminal law of the land. Many citizens, it must be admitted, regard the prohibitions expressly imposed by the law as the utmost limits set to their activities and are prepared to take full advantage of any omission or relaxation. It would be surprising if there are not considerable numbers with this philosophy among those with whom we are concerned in this inquiry, and the removal of the present prohibition from the criminal code will be regarded as condoning or licensing licentiousness, and will open up for such people a new field of permitted conduct with unwholesome and distasteful implications.

1.8   Lord Denning on crime, sin and morality

Lord Denning (*b. 1899) has been Master of the Rolls since 1962. He is renowned for his robust and idiosyncratic approach to legal problems; his views on the relationship between law and morals are much more predictable, as shown by the following report in* The Times *of his address to the 1957 Conference of the Law Society, at which time he was a Lord of Appeal in Ordinary. His Lordship began with a reference to the Wolfenden report and then continued:*

... As far as morals in the sense of right standards of behaviour are concerned, I would say most emphatically that standards and morals are the concern of the law, and that whether done in private or in public.

A great part of our legal system is concerned with laying down right standards of behaviour, what people should or should not do. And for a great many people and those who have no religion and no conscience the law is the only standard. The law influences public opinion and, conversely, public opinion influences the law. They act and react on one another. So it is of the highest importance that the law should lay down right standards which commend themselves to right thinking people as being correct.

But, of course, it is not the process of the criminal law which is to be invoked in every case. The criminal law has its proper sphere, but the law in the wider sense covers all spheres of human activities. It is impossible to draw a hard and fast line between crime and sin.

Criminal law is concerned with laying down in its own sphere proper standards of behaviour. And where do we get our proper standards from? From our own moral standards. And are these born with us? Surely they have been inherited through the centuries and are determined by the precepts of religion and of good itself. I would say that without religion there can be no morality and without morality there can be no law.

1.9   'Ladies' Directory' case

Shaw v. **D.P.P.,** *when Viscount Simonds and Lord Reid reflected opposing legal attitudes to the courts' powers in enforcing moral standards.*

The majority's decision in Shaw, *that disinterred an offence of conspiracy to corrupt public morals, was the subject of fierce criticism throughout the 1960s. Despite the reversal of the rule that the House of Lords was bound by its own decisions, the House, presided over by Lord Reid, declined in 1972 to reverse its earlier ruling (* Knuller *v.* D.P.P., *see 7.8).*

[Viscount Simonds:] My Lords, as I have already said, the first count in the indictment is 'Conspiracy to corrupt public morals', and the particulars of offence will have sufficiently appeared. I am concerned only to assert what was vigorously denied by counsel for the appellant, that such an offence is known to the common law, and that it was open to the jury to find on the facts of this case that the appellant was guilty of such an offence. I must say categorically that, if it were not so, Her Majesty's courts would strangely

have failed in their duty as servants and guardians of the common law. Need
I say, my Lords, that I am no advocate of the right of the judges to create
new criminal offences? I will repeat well-known words: 'Amongst many
other points of happiness and freedom which your Majesty's subjects have
enjoyed there is none which they have accounted more dear and precious
than this, to be guided and governed by certain rules of law which giveth
both to the head and members that which of right belongeth to them and
not by any arbitrary or uncertain form of government.' These words are as
true today as they were in the seventeenth century and command the
allegiance of us all. But I am at a loss to understand how it can be said
either that the law does not recognise a conspiracy to corrupt public morals
or that, though there may not be an exact precedent for such a conspiracy as
this case reveals, it does not fall fairly within the general words by which it is
described. I do not propose to examine all the relevant authorities. That will
be done by my noble and learned friend. The fallacy in the argument that
was addressed to us lay in the attempt to exclude from the scope of general
words acts well calculated to corrupt public morals just because they had
not been committed or had not been brought to the notice of the court
before. It is not thus that the common law has developed. We are perhaps
more accustomed to hear this matter discussed upon the question whether
such and such a transaction is contrary to public policy. At once the
controversy arises. On the one hand it is said that it is not possible in the
twentieth century for the court to create a new head of public policy, on the
other it is said that this is but a new example of a well-established head. In
the sphere of criminal law I entertain no doubt that there remains in the
courts of law a residual power to enforce the supreme and fundamental
purpose of the law, to conserve not only the safety and order but also the
moral welfare of the State, and that it is their duty to guard it against
attacks which may be the more insidious because they are novel and
unprepared for. That is the broad head (call it public policy if you wish)
within which the present indictment falls. It matters little what label is
given to the offending act. To one of your Lordships it may appear an
affront to public decency, to another considering that it may succeed in its
obvious intention of provoking libidinous desires it will seem a corruption of
public morals. Yet others may deem it aptly described as the creation of a
public mischief or the undermining of moral conduct. The same act will not
in all ages be regarded in the same way. The law must be related to the
changing standards of life, not yielding to every shifting impulse of the
popular will but having regard to fundamental assessment of human values
and the purposes of society. Today a denial of the fundamental Christian
doctrine, which in past centuries would have been regarded by the
ecclesiastical courts as heresy and by the common law as blasphemy, will no
longer be an offence if the decencies of controversy are observed. When Lord
Mansfield, speaking long after the Star Chamber had been abolished, said[9]
that the Court of King's Bench was the custos morum of the people and had
the superintendency of offences contra bonos mores, he was asserting, as I
now assert, that there is in that court a residual power, where no statute has

9. *Rex* v. *Delaval* (1763) 3 Burr. 1434, 1438, 1439.

yet intervened to supersede the common law, to superintend those offences which are prejudicial to the public welfare. Such occasions will be rare, for Parliament has not been slow to legislate when attention has been sufficiently aroused. But gaps remain and will always remain since no one can foresee every way in which the wickedness of man may disrupt the order of society. Let me take a single instance to which my noble and learned friend Lord Tucker refers. Let it be supposed that at some future, perhaps early, date homosexual practices between adult consenting males are no longer a crime. Would it not be an offence if even without obscenity, such practices were publicly advocated and encouraged by pamphlet and advertisement? Or must we wait until Parliament finds time to deal with such conduct? I say, my Lords, that if the common law is powerless in such an event, then we should no longer do her reverence. But I say that her hand is still powerful and that it is for Her Majesty's judges to play the part which Lord Mansfield pointed out to them.

[Lord Reid:] My Lords, I turn to the first count.

In my opinion there is no such general offence known to the law as conspiracy to corrupt public morals. Undoubtedly there is an offence of criminal conspiracy and undoubtedly it is of fairly wide scope. In my view its scope cannot be determined without having regard first to the history of the matter and then to the broad general principles which have generally been thought to underlie our system of law and government and in particular our system of criminal law.

It appears to be generally accepted that the offence of criminal conspiracy was the creature of the Star Chamber. ... The Star Chamber perhaps had more merits than its detractors will admit but its methods and principles were superseded and what it did is of no authority today. The question is how far the common law courts in fact went in borrowing from it.

I think that Lord Goddard C.J. was repeating the generally accepted view when he said: 'A conspiracy consists of agreeing or acting in concert to achieve an unlawful act or to do a lawful act by unlawful means'. ... But what is an 'unlawful act'? To commit a crime – yes, but what about offences which can only be dealt with summarily and punished lightly: they are certainly unlawful acts but (I quote from the Law of Criminal Conspiracies, by R.S. Wright J., p.83) they 'are not in themselves of grave enough consequence to be matters for indictment. ... ' To commit a tort – yes in certain cases, but for somewhat similar reasons it seems to be at least doubtful whether it is an offence to conspire to commit a tort which is neither malicious nor fraudulent nor accompanied by violence.

Then there is undoubtedly a third class of act which an individual can do with impunity but a combination cannot. Perhaps the best known example is conspiring to injure a man in his trade if done without justification.

There are two competing views. One is that conspiring to corrupt public morals is only one facet of a still more general offence, conspiracy to effect public mischief; and that, like the categories of negligence, the categories of public mischief are never closed. The other is that, whatever may have been done two or three centuries ago, we ought not now to extend the doctrine further than it has already been carried by the common law courts. Of course I do not mean that it should only be applied in circumstances precisely similar to those in some decided case. Decisions are always authority for other cases which are reasonably analogous and are not properly distinguishable. But we ought not to extend the doctrine to new fields.

Even if there is still a vestigial power of this kind it ought not, in my view, to be used unless there appears to be general agreement that the offence to which it is applied ought to be criminal if committed by an individual. Notoriously, there are wide differences of opinion today as to how far the law ought to punish immoral acts which are not done in the face of the public. Some think that the law already goes too far, some that it does not go far enough. Parliament is the proper place, and I am firmly of opinion the only proper place, to settle that. When there is sufficient support from public opinion, Parliament does not hesitate to intervene. Where Parliament fears to tread it is not for the courts to rush in.

1.10   Lord Devlin on morals and the criminal law

Lord Devlin *(b. 1905) was a leading judicial figure in Britain during the years 1948-64 and a proponent of the legalistic view of enforcement of morals in the tradition of Stephen. His famous Maccabaean lecture on 'Morals and the Criminal Law' in 1957, from which this extract is taken, set in train the continuing and seemingly endless philosophical debate. The lecture has been published as one of a collection of essays in a volume entitled* The Enforcement of Morals *(London, 1965) pp.12-20.*

I think ... that it is not possible to set theoretical limits to the power of the State to legislate against immorality. It is not possible to settle in advance exceptions to the general rule or to define inflexibly areas of morality into which the law is in no circumstances to be allowed to enter. Society is entitled by means of its laws to protect itself from dangers, whether from within or without. Here again I think that the political parallel is legitimate. The law of treason is directed against aiding the King's enemies and against sedition from within. The justification for this is that established government is necessary for the existence of society and therefore its safety against violent overthrow must be secured. But an established morality is as necessary as good government to the welfare of society. Societies disintegrate from within more frequently than they are broken up by external pressures. There is disintegration when no common morality is observed and history shows that the loosening of moral bonds is often the first stage of disintegration, so that society is justified in taking the same steps to preserve its moral code as it does to preserve its government and other essential institutions. The suppression of vice is as much the law's business as the suppression of subversive activities; it is no more possible to define a sphere of private morality than it is to define one of private subversive activity. It is wrong to talk of private morality or of the law not being concerned with immorality as such or to try to set rigid bounds to the part which the law may play in the suppression of vice. There are no theoretical limits to the power of the State to legislate against treason and sedition, and likewise I think there can be no theoretical limits to legislation against immorality. You may argue that if a man's sins affect only himself it cannot be the concern of society. If he chooses to get drunk every night in the privacy of his own home, is any one except himself the worse for it? But suppose a quarter or a half of the population got drunk every night, what sort of society would it be? You cannot set a theoretical limit to the number of people who can get drunk before society is entitled to legislate against drunkenness.

... How are the moral judgments of society to be ascertained? By leaving it until now, I can ask it in the more limited form that is now sufficient for my purpose. How is the law-maker to ascertain the moral judgments of society? It is surely not enough that they should be reached by the opinion of the majority; it would be too much to require 'the individual assent of every citizen. English law has evolved and regularly uses a standard which does not depend on the counting of heads. It is that of the reasonable man. He is not to be confused with the rational man. He is not expected to reason about anything and his judgment may be largely a matter of feeling. It is the viewpoint of the man in the street – or to use an archaism familiar to all lawyers – the man in the Clapham omnibus. He might also be called the right-minded man. For my purpose I should like to call him the man in the jury box, for the moral judgment of society must be something about which any twelve men or women drawn at random might after discussion be expected to be unanimous. This was the standard the judges applied in the days before Parliament was as active as it is now and when they laid down rules of public policy. They did not think of themselves as making law but simply as stating principles which every right-minded person would accept as valid. It is what Pollock called 'practical morality', which is based not on theological or philosophical foundations but 'in the mass of continuous experience half-consciously or unconsciously accumulated and embodied in the morality of common sense'. He called it also 'a certain way of thinking on questions of morality which we expect to find in a reasonable civilized man or a reasonable Englishman, taken at random'.[10]

Immorality then, for the purpose of the law, is what every right-minded person is presumed to consider to be immoral. Any immorality is capable of affecting society injuriously and in effect to a greater or lesser extent it usually does; this is what gives the law its *locus standi*. It cannot be shut out. But – and this brings me to the third question – the individual has a *locus standi* too; he cannot be expected to surrender to the judgment of society the whole conduct of his life. It is the old and familiar question of striking a balance between the rights and interests of society and those of the individual. This is something which the law is constantly doing in matters large and small. To take a very down-to-earth example, let me consider the right of the individual whose house adjoins the highway to have access to it; that means in these days the right to have vehicles stationary in the highway, sometimes for a considerable time if there is a lot of loading or

10. *Essays in Jurisprudence and Ethics* (London, 1882) pp. 278 and 353.

unloading. There are many cases in which the courts have had to balance the private right of access against the public right to use the highway without obstruction. It cannot be done by carving up the highway into public and private areas. It is done by recognizing that each have rights over the whole; that if each were to exercise their rights to the full, they would come into conflict, and therefore that the rights of each must be curtailed so as to ensure as far as possible that the essential needs of each are safeguarded.

I do not think that one can talk sensibly of a public and private morality any more than one can of a public or private highway. Morality is a sphere in which there is a public interest and a private interest, often in conflict, and the problem is to reconcile the two. This does not mean that it is impossible to put forward any general statements about how in our society the balance ought to be struck. Such statements cannot of their nature be rigid or precise; they would not be designed to circumscribe the operation of the law-making power but to guide those who have to apply it. While every decision which a court of law makes when it balances the public against the private interest is an *ad hoc* decision, the cases contain statements of principle to which the court should have regard when it reaches its decision. In the same way it is possible to make general statements of principle which it may be thought the legislature should bear in mind when it is considering the enactment of laws enforcing morals.

I believe that most people would agree upon the chief of these elastic principles. There must be toleration of the maximum individual freedom that is consistent with the integrity of society. It cannot be said that this is a principle that runs all through the criminal law. Much of the criminal law that is regulatory in character – the part of it that deals with *malum prohibitum* rather than *malum in se* – is based upon the opposite principle, that is, that the choice of the individual must give way to the convenience of the many. But in all matters of conscience the principle I have stated is generally held to prevail. It is not confined to thought and speech; it extends to action, as is shown by the recognition of the right to conscientious objection in war-time; this example shows also that conscience will be respected even in times of national danger. The principle appears to me to be peculiarly appropriate to all questions of morals. Nothing should be punished by the law that does not lie beyond the limits of tolerance. It is not nearly enough to say that a majority dislike a practice; there must be a real feeling of reprobation. Those who are dissatisfied with the present law on homosexuality often say that the opponents of reform are swayed simply by disgust. If that were so it would be wrong, but I do not think one can ignore disgust if it is deeply felt and not manufactured. Its presence is a good indication that the bounds of toleration are being reached. Not everything is to be tolerated. No society can do without intolerance, indignation, and disgust; they are the forces behind the moral law, and indeed it can be argued that if they or something like them are not present, the feeling of society cannot be weighty enough to deprive the individual of freedom of choice. I suppose that there is hardly anyone nowadays who would not be disgusted by the thought of deliberate cruelty to animals. No one proposes to relegate that or any other form of sadism to the realm of private morality or to allow it to be practised in public or in private. It would be possible no doubt to point out that until a comparatively short while ago nobody thought very much of cruelty to animals and also that pity and kindliness and the unwillingness to inflict pain are virtues more generally esteemed now than they have ever been in the past. But matters of this sort are not determined by rational argument. Every moral judgment, unless it claims a divine source, is simply a feeling that no right-minded man could behave in any other way without admitting that he was doing wrong. It is the power of a common sense and not the power of reason that is behind the judgments of society. But before a society can put a practice beyond the limits of tolerance there must be a deliberate judgment that the practice is injurious to society. There is, for example, a general abhorrence of homosexuality. We should ask ourselves in the first instance whether, looking at it calmly and dispassionately, we regard it as a vice so abominable that its mere presence is an offence. If that is the genuine feeling of the society in which we live, I do not see how society can be denied the right to eradicate it. Our feeling may not be so intense as that. We may feel about it that, if confined, it is tolerable, but that if it spread it might be gravely injurious; it is in this way that most societies look upon fornication, seeing it as a natural weakness which must be kept within bounds but which cannot be rooted out. It becomes then a question of balance, the danger to society in one scale and the extent of the restriction in the other. On this sort of point the value of an investigation by such a body as the Wolfenden Committee and of its conclusions is manifest.

The limits of tolerance shift. This is supplementary to what I have been saying but of sufficient importance in itself to deserve statement as a separate principle which law-makers have to bear in mind. I suppose that moral standards do not shift; so far as they come from divine revelation they do not, and I am willing to assume that the moral judgments made by a society always remain good for that society. But the extent to which society will tolerate – I mean tolerate, not approve – departures from moral standards varies from generation to generation. It may be that over-all tolerance is always increasing. The pressure of the human mind, always seeking greater freedom of thought, is outwards against the bonds of society forcing their gradual relaxation. It may be that history is a tale of contraction and expansion and that all developed societies are on their way to dissolution. I must not speak of things I do not know; and anyway as a practical matter no society is willing to make provision for its own decay. I return therefore to the simple and observable fact that in matters of morals the limits of tolerance shift. Laws, especially those which are based on morals, are less easily moved. It follows as another good working principle that in any new matter of morals the law should be slow to act. By the next generation the swell of indignation may have abated and the law be left without the strong backing which it needs. But it is then difficult to alter the law without giving the impression that moral judgment is being weakened. This is now one of the factors that is strongly militating against any alteration to the law on homosexuality.

A third elastic principle must be advanced more tentatively. It is that as far as possible privacy should be respected. This is not an idea that has ever been made explicit in the criminal law. Acts or words done or said in public or in private are all brought within its scope without distinction in principle. But there goes with this a strong reluctance on the part of judges and legislators to sanction invasions of privacy in the detection of crime. The police have no more right to trespass than the ordinary citizen has; there is no general right of search; to this extent an Englishman's home is still his castle.

This indicates a general sentiment that the right to privacy is something to be put in the balance against the enforcement of the law. Ought the same sort of consideration to play any part in the formation of the law? Clearly only in a very limited number of cases. When the help of the law is invoked by an injured citizen, privacy must be irrelevant; the individual cannot ask that his right to privacy should be measured against injury criminally done to another. But when all who are involved in the deed are consenting parties and the injury is done to morals, the public interest in the moral order can be balanced against the claims of privacy. The restriction on police powers of investigation goes further than the affording of a parallel; it means that the detection of crime committed in private and when there is no complaint is bound to be rather haphazard and this is an additional reason for moderation. These considerations do not justify the exclusion of all private immorality from the scope of the law. I think that, as I have already suggested, the test of 'private behaviour' should be substituted for 'private morality' and the influence of the factor should be reduced from that of a definite limitation to that of a matter to be taken into account. Since the gravity of the crime is also a proper consideration, a distinction might well be made in the case of homosexuality between the lesser acts of indecency and the full offence, which on the principles of the Wolfenden Report it would be illogical to do.

The last and the biggest thing to be remembered is that the law is concerned with the minimum and not with the maximum; there is much in the Sermon on the Mount that would be out of place in the Ten Commandments. We all recognize the gap between the moral law and the law of the land. No man is worth much who regulates his conduct with the sole object of escaping punishment, and every worthy society sets for its members standards which are above those of the law. We recognize the existence of such higher standards when we use expressions such as 'moral obligation' and 'morally bound'. The distinction was well put in the judgment of African elders in a family dispute: 'We have power to make you divide the crops, for this is our law, and we will see this is done. But we have not power to make you behave like an upright man.'

It can only be because this point is so obvious that it is so frequently ignored. Discussion among law-makers, both professional and amateur, is too often limited to what is right or wrong and good or bad for society. There is a failure to keep separate ... the question of society's right to pass a moral judgment and the question of whether the arm of the law should be used to enforce the judgment. The criminal law is not a statement of how people ought to behave; it is a statement of what will happen to them if they do not behave; good citizens are not expected to come within reach of it or to set their sights by it, and every enactment should be framed accordingly.

1.11 Utilitarianism redivivus? The views of Professor Hart

H.L.A. Hart, *philosopher, sometime legal practitioner and academic lawyer, became Professor of Jurisprudence in the University of Oxford in 1952. He is a leading exponent of the Mill doctrine in modern guise and effective proponent of that doctrine in his writings, of which the best example is the collection of essays,* Law, Liberty and Morality *(parodying Stephen's own title) from which the following extract is taken.*

When we turn to the positive grounds held to justify the legal enforcement of morality it is important to distinguish a moderate and an extreme thesis, though critics of Mill have sometimes moved from one to the other without marking the transition. Lord Devlin seems to me to maintain, for most of his essay, the moderate thesis and Stephen the extreme one.

According to the moderate thesis, a shared morality is the cement of society; without it there would be aggregates of individuals but no society. 'A recognized morality' is, in Lord Devlin's words, 'as necessary to society's existence as a recognized government', and though a particular act of immorality may not harm or endanger or corrupt others nor, when done in private, either shock or give offence to others, this does not conclude the matter. For we must not view conduct in isolation from its effect on the moral code: if we remember this, we can see that one who is 'no menace to others' nonetheless may by his immoral conduct 'threaten one of the great principles on which society is based'. In this sense the breach of moral principle is an offence 'against society as a whole', and society may use the law to preserve its morality as it uses it to safeguard anything else essential to its existence. This is why 'the suppression of vice is as much the law's business as the suppression of subversive activities'.

By contrast, the extreme thesis does not look upon a shared morality as of merely instrumental value analogous to ordered government, and it does not justify the punishment of immorality as a step taken, like the punishment of treason, to preserve society from dissolution or collapse. Instead, the enforcement of morality is regarded as a thing of value, even if immoral acts harm no one directly, or indirectly by weakening the moral cement of society. I do not say that it is possible to allot to one or other of these two theses every argument used, but they do, I think, characterise the main critical positions at the root of most arguments, and they incidentally exhibit an ambiguity in the expression 'enforcing morality as such'. Perhaps the clearest way of distinguishing the two theses is to see that there are always two levels at which we may ask whether some breach of positive morality is harmful. We may ask first, Does this act harm anyone independently of its repercussion on the shared morality of society? And secondly we may ask, Does this act affect the shared morality and thereby weaken society? The moderate thesis requires, if the punishment of the act is to be justified, an affirmative answer at least at the second level. The extreme thesis does not require an affirmative answer at either level.

Lord Devlin appears to defend the moderate thesis. I say 'appears' because, though he says that society has the right to enforce a morality as such on the ground that a shared morality is essential to society's existence, it is not at all clear that for him the statement that immorality jeopardizes or weakens society is a statement of empirical fact. It seems sometimes to be an *a priori* assumption, and sometimes a necessary truth and a very odd one. The most important indication that this is so is that, apart from one vague reference to 'history' showing that 'the loosening of moral bonds is often the first stage of disintegration', no evidence is produced to show that deviation from accepted sexual morality, even by adults in private, is something which, like treason, threatens the existence of society. No reputable historian has maintained this thesis, and there is indeed much evidence against it. As a proposition of fact it is entitled to no more respect than the Emperor Justinian's statement that homosexuality was the cause of earthquakes. Lord Devlin's belief in it, and his apparent indifference to the question of evidence, are at points traceable to an undiscussed assumption. This is that all morality – sexual morality together with the morality that forbids acts injurious to others such as killing, stealing, and dishonesty – forms a single seamless web, so that those who deviate from any part are likely or perhaps bound to deviate from the whole. It is of course clear (and one of the oldest insights of political theory) that society could not exist without a morality which mirrored and supplemented the law's proscription of conduct injurious to others. But there is again no evidence to support, and much to refute, the theory that those who deviate from conventional sexual morality are in other ways hostile to society.

There seems, however, to be central to Lord Devlin's thought something more interesting, though no more convincing, than the conception of social morality as a seamless web. For he appears to move from the acceptable proposition that *some* shared morality is essential to the existence of any society to the unacceptable proposition that a society is identical with its morality as that is at any given moment of its history, so that a change in its morality is tantamount to the destruction of a society. The former proposition might be even accepted as a necessary rather than an empirical truth depending on a quite plausible definition of society as a body of men who hold certain moral views in common. But the latter proposition is absurd. Taken strictly, it would prevent us saying that the morality of a given society had changed, and would compel us instead to say that one society had disappeared and another one taken its place. But it is only on this absurd criterion of what it is for the same society to continue to exist that it could be asserted without evidence that any deviation from a society's shared morality threatens its existence.

It is clear that only this tacit identification of a society with its shared morality supports Lord Devlin's denial that there could be such a thing a private immorality and his comparison of sexual immorality, even when it takes place 'in private', with treason. No doubt it is true that if deviations from conventional sexual morality are tolerated by the law and come to be known, the conventional morality might change in a permissive direction, though this does not seem to be the case with homosexuality in those European countries where it is not punishable by law. But even if the conventional morality did so change, the society in question would not have been destroyed or 'subverted'. We should compare such a development not to the violent overthrow of government but to a peaceful constitutional change in its form, consistent not only with the preservation of a society but with its advance.

1.12 Crash-helmets: legislation against self-destruction

The following is part of a debate on a motion in the House of Commons to take note of the Motor Cycle (Wearing of Helmets) Regulations 1973. The motion was carried by 54 votes to 15. (Subsequent parliamentary skirmishes have taken place over proposals to legislate for the compulsory wearing of seat belts in cars.)

[Mr J. Enoch Powell (Wolverhampton South-West)]: All hon. Members have had considerable correspondence on this subject in recent weeks. Whatever conclusion they have reached, they will have been impressed with the responsible attitude which virtually all their correspondence showed, and by the fact that most of the people from whom it came were people who have had long experience of motor cycling and who place the strongest emphasis on example as well as personal practice in taking all reasonable precautions when motor cycling.

The correspondence showed a greater grasp than many of my hon. Friends of the real principle that is at issue in these regulations. The writers of the letters realise that the law is making it a criminal offence for a person to behave in a way which endangers solely the person concerned and in no way places any other person at risk. At no stage, either in this discussion or on the previous occasion to which my hon. and learned Friend the Member for Buckinghamshire, South (Mr Ronald Bell) referred, has it ever been suggested that a motor cyclist by wearing or not wearing a helmet increases or diminishes the risk to other road users.

Mr Alan Haselhurst (Middleton and Prestwich): Does not my right hon. Friend agree that if another party is involved in an accident with a motor cyclist who is not wearing a helmet and that motor cyclist perishes, the other party might suffer considerable mental anguish for the rest of his life?

Mr Powell: I am not sure whether my hon. Friend is not trying to strengthen my argument. Certainly, his intervention must direct hon. Members' minds to what precisely is at issue and what this criminal offence is concerned with. It is not concerned with the effect upon other people's minds, upon their emotions, upon their feelings. The issue is whether any increase of risk whatsoever to any other road user is involved, and no one has claimed that it is.

In creating this criminal offence we are doing something for which at present there is no parallel. There is no criminal offence to be found on the Statute Book the nature of which endangers the safety of the person concerned and no one else.

Mr William Shelton (Clapham): Suicide.

Mr Powell: Suicide is not a criminal offence.

Mr Norman Fowler (Nottingham, South): Drugs.

Mr Powell: I am aware of the point about drugs. My hon. Friend the Member for Cannock [Mr Patrick Cormack] can quote innumerable instances where an employer or a person who sells an article or offers a facility is required to behave in a particular way with a view to the potential safety of the employee or the purchaser or whatever second or third party it may be; but we shall look in vain for a parallel to this criminal offence where the individual himself is solely concerned and inflicts no risk upon any other.

My hon. Friend the Member for Nottingham, South (Mr. Fowler) mentioned drugs, and I admit that this is the nearest we have come to establishing a criminal offence such as I have defined. Nevertheless, even there the nature of drug-taking in many cases is such that it cannot but inflict harm upon others. I am not saying that can be absolutely stated, and I concede that we have an approach to this nature of criminal offence in the context of drugs; but certainly in no other area has a criminal offence of this nature been created. We are debating something which is new and which is a major departure of principle; and it is at any rate right that we should recognise that we are doing it and consider why.

We are told that every one has people who are dependent on him – most of us do – or linked with him humanly in one way or another, and that therefore we ought to create a criminal offence in order to punish a person for endangering the support or affectionate feelings of those with whom he is linked, or prevent him from doing so.

The House must perceive how far we shall be taken if we embark upon that course. There is hardly a single decision which a man can take, certainly no important decision, no decision even about what sport to engage in, without affecting potentially the welfare of his family, the interests of his friends and the affections of those with whom he is linked. If we do this thing on such grounds, we shall be laying the basis for a series of new laws which will reach right into every act, every form of behaviour, every choice of the average citizen.

The last and the most beguiling argument – and I imagine it is the argument which operates upon those hon. Members who will reject my argument and that of my hon. and learned Friend the Member for Buckinghamshire, South [Mr Ronald Bell, who initiated the debate] – is that if this crime is created there will be fewer road casualties from this cause. That is the most alarming argument of all that could be used in this House of Commons: that because by doing so we could reduce the number of deaths from a particular cause – not deaths inflicted by other people's carelessness, not deaths resulting from the omission of precautions which those who manufacture articles or sell them could have been caused to take, but deaths resulting from private and uniquely personal decisions – therefore we can make it a crime to take that sort of risk.

That argument is the most dangerous because it is the most beguiling. When one bastion after another of individual freedom, of independence, is breached, it does not happen in an unpopular context. It does not happen when the reasons for doing so are unattractive. It does so when sentiment and emotion and the feelings of all of us are engaged. None of us likes to contemplate the notion of a young man whose life could have been saved being lost because he was not wearing a crash helmet. Our first natural instinct and reaction, having legislative power in our hands, is to use that legislative power.

But that is where the danger lies. The abuse of legislative power by this House is far more serious and more far-reaching in its effects than the loss of individual lives through foolish decisions. [*Interruption.*] I say just that and I repeat that as a Member of the House of Commons speaking to the House of Commons. The maintenance of the principles of individual freedom and responsibility is more important than the avoidance of the loss of lives through the personal decision of individuals, whether those lives are lost swimming or mountaineering or boating, or riding horseback, or on a motor-cycle.

We are sent here to make laws and to preserve liberties. If we allow this regulation to stand, we shall have failed in the duties we were sent here to perform.

1.13   The 'law and morality' debate debunked

Judith N. Shklar *is Professor of Politics at Harvard University. In the extract that follows, taken from her elegant and stimulating book,* Legalism (*1964), she exposes the aridity of much of the conventional argumentation about law and morality.*

'If the core of natural law theory is the proposition that law and morals intersect, positivism lives to deny that proposition. This does not mean that natural lawyers are not interested in distinguishing law from morals. On the contrary, both positivists and natural lawyers agree not only that the aim of legal theory is the definition of law, but that the way to define law is to discover those specific characteristics which set it apart from other social rules, especially those of morality. If this common preoccupation has provided the chief bones of contention, it has also come to make the two contestants seem increasingly similar. Long-standing enmity is, after all, an intimate human relationship, and old enemies often resemble each other more closely than they suppose. In the present case, as a result of concentrating on each other, the subject of debate between natural lawyers and positivists has been limited to those issues, and those alone, which bear on their dispute.

To an outsider – an historian of ideas, for instance – both natural lawyers and legal positivists seem at first to be primarily interested in definitions. Indeed, most legal theory looks like a heap of definitions piled one upon another.

... Ideology is not conscious distortion. It is, rather, a series of personal responses to social experiences which come to colour, quite insensibly often, all our categories of thought. The liberalism of Kelsen or Hart, for example, is perfectly open and avowed, as is that of many of their admirers. It is that very liberalism and the standards of intellectual objectivity that it demands, however, which make it apparently difficult for those thinkers to recognize the extent to which their preferences mold their conceptions about law and morals.

... The task of law in practice is to preserve order against ideology; that of theory, to structure a notion of law free from all that is subjective, contingent, or ideological. The price of historical irrelevance does not seem too high in that case. As for Professor Hart, what liberal denies that his attacks upon those who want to improve the moral conduct of their fellow citizens by applying governmental pressures are as necessary and valid as were those of John Stuart Mill? There is nothing one can object to in these efforts to protect the private life of every individual against the absolutism of those moralists who would employ the force of government to impose their preferences upon others. It does not, however, follow that, because this is desirable, it is also logically necessary or conceptually possible to separate law and morals. No one argues that this separation has ever been maintained in practice, either in the past or in the present. Indeed, the age of totalitarianism is one in which this separation is rejected more than ever by a greater number of governments. The simple point is that the separation of law and morals is not self-evidently necessary, even on that most empty, formal, and 'pure' plane where history is purposely forgotten. The entire formulation is not a matter of logical classification, of conceptual clarity, of 'science', or of analytical coherence. It is an expression of the liberal desire to preserve individual autonomy, and to preserve the diversity of morals which is in constant danger of ideological and governmental interference.

Even those positivists who are most anxious to avoid committing themselves to a too specific notion of morality concede that there is at least a difference in the kind of pressure that is brought to bear upon people. Moral pressure takes the form of an appeal to a person's own standards. It is a call to what is commonly spoken of as conscience. Moreover, morality is voluntary, and so 'I could not help it' is an excuse in morals but not necessarily in law. The pressure exerted by law is ultimately coercive, and in any case refers to a rule outside the individual's private system of values. In addition, it has been suggested, again by a convinced positivist, that morality is more important to the individual ultimately than law. What 'important' means is not very clear, but the implication is that it refers to behaviour and ideas that should not be controlled by law. Lastly, it is suggested that morality and especially mores, unlike law, are not subject to deliberate and rapid change. This notion has been traditionally stressed by conservatives anxious to limit the legislative urges of radicals. It has come to appeal to liberals, again, one suspects, in order to limit governmental action – not necessarily radical action, of course. One cannot forebear to mention that this notion is plainly false. In an age of concentrated propaganda, morality and mores *are* subject to quick and deliberate change. The morality of large numbers of Germans surely underwent extensive and rapid changes during Hitler's regime. In fact, every one of the suggestions that treats law and morality as two separate blocks of rules that are just 'there' to be identified can be shown to be too narrow – to have excluded some moral possibility or historical manifestation.

The most interesting thing about natural law theory and its replacements is their indestructibility. Their endurance cannot, moreover, be ascribed simply to the well-known survival power of the Roman Catholic Church. Natural law has also been built into the judicial systems of most Western countries. It is, finally, as a guide to legislation, whether monarchical, parliamentary, judicial, or administrative, that it has fulfilled its greatest function. The belief in an objective common good has remained very powerful, and this is not surprising; it certainly makes the responsibility of deciding less onerous if one can believe that there are prefabricated rules waiting to be recognized and followed in legislation. There is, indeed, every reason to believe that the several revivals of natural law thinking in the twentieth century have all been part of more general ideological movements in favour of unity, and of wider searches for political values transcending those of the competing groups. The first revival in Europe before the First World War was at least partially a defensive reaction to the socialist doctrine of inevitable class war, as well as to parliamentary party fragmentation. The present revival in Europe seems to represent a search for *some* set of values in a situation of more or less complete political apathy, where people are haunted, nevertheless, by memories of fascism and prospects of Soviet penetration. In America the recent successes of natural law theory are surely part of the general cry for 'national purpose', for a 'united moral front'. To this must be added the native passion for ever more 'consensus', and an implicit belief in 'a common good' or 'the public interest' towards which the nation is perpetually moving. In all these cases, whether it be a simple appeal to 'political truth', to the common good, or to 'social solidarity', natural law has played its ideological part, as it would wherever unity has, for some reason, come to appear a vital political need and agreement has been treated as an end in itself. In response to the continuing appeal and even intellectual respectability of such attitudes, the liberal heirs of Austin are bound to renew their determination to keep law and morality apart. Professor Hart is at his best when he is brilliantly demolishing the views of those who, like Justice Devlin, defend legislated morality. That, after all, is the *raison d'être* of analytical positivism.

The various ideologies of agreement now current are by no means all genuinely higher law doctrines. On the contrary, some display an extraordinary pseudo-pragmatism. It is, for instance, Justice Devlin's contention that society will fall apart unless an accepted morality is enforced by the public authorities. Even without the threats of the Cold War, which have stimulated the 'need for values' and the call for a national purpose in the United States, it is here argued that, not only does *a* notion of morality prevail in England, but that social disaster must follow any failure to give it the backing of coercive legislation. The tricky question of who really knows what is moral is answered by referring the doubter to 'the man on the Clapham bus' whose moral attitudes can be taken as representative of all England, or at least of all of England that matters. Here one is in the presence of the mythical 'average man', whose uses have at last been discovered by conservatives. The unquestioning mind is taken as the best index of public opinion, morality is then identified with this opinion, and the survival of society is made to depend upon its being the sole guide for public policy, with no further need to check the facts of the case. That tolerance and freedom might also be values, that the moral successes of public enforcement remain dubious, are matters which do not even seem to occur to this type of mentality.

What is taken as axiomatic by Justice Devlin and his American counterparts is that freedom cannot be the basis of legal justice. The distinction that is never made here is not the one between law and morals, but the one between educative and legalistic moral and political values. The argument is always presented in the form of a rather self-evident proposition: that no policy is totally value-free, that the enforcement of *some* morality is inevitable, and that those who deny this fact in order to defend moral freedom are either foolish or wicked, or both. The point is well taken but it hardly meets the issues, for freedom and diversity are values, too, and individualism and impersonal justice are types of morality as well. To defend them is not to deny the obvious – that, whatever 'society' does, it promotes some set of values. However, the defenders of the 'man on the Clapham bus' not only are urging upon us a very specific and narrow set of norms; they are doing it in order to bring conformity into a pluralistic society, and under the false pretence of defending moral values against the amoral.

1.14　The case of the un-Christian rector

Law, justice and morality are, or can be, very different commodities as Lord Justice Davies' judgment in Hayward v. Chaloner *clearly shows. The facts of the case were that, in 1939, a small piece of land was let to the rector of the parish of Bilsthorpe, Nottinghamshire, for a nominal rent. The owners ceased to ask for rent after 1942, and successive rectors used the land as part of their gardens. In about 1960 the then rector began negotiations to sell his land – adding to it the parcel of his neighbours' land which he claimed as his by the rule of 'adverse possession'.*

The plaintiffs sued for possession in the county court – and won. But the rector appealed to the Court of Appeal. The appeal judges made it abundantly clear that they had no sympathy with the merits of the appeal, but the appellant persisted. Lord Denning M.R., dissenting from his brethren, would have dismissed the appeal. His judgment was followed by these observations of Lord Justice Arthian Davies:

Davies, L.J.: I bitterly regret that, despite the reasoning of my Lord's judgment, I am unable to agree to the dismissal of this appeal. Most unfortunately, the law, as I conceive it to be, as applied to the facts of this case, is clear and has resulted in the extinction of the plaintiffs' title to this little piece of land and its acquisition by the incumbent of Bilsthorpe. I have had the advantage of reading beforehand the judgment which Russell L.J. is about to deliver as to the legal position. I agree with it in its entirety; and no purpose would be served if I were to go over the same ground.

But to my mind it is quite impossible to leave the case at that and to abstain from making any observations as to the merits. I shall endeavour to make those observations in as moderate language as possible.

I should say at the outset that there can be no possible criticism of Mr Garland, counsel who appeared for the appellant in this court. He conducted the case, which one could not help feeling that he found distasteful, with dignity, fairness and firmness throughout.

But as for his client, that is another matter. It may well be that at first the rector genuinely believed that this little piece of land belonged to the Church. He had only been there since 1962, and no rent had been paid since 1942. But when the dispute arose, things altered. I say nothing about the rector's effort to obtain some sort of documentary admission from the female plaintiff on April 1, 1965, of which the county court judge plainly disapproved, and pass straight to the hearing of the action in the county court.

At the end of that hearing the facts were established beyond any doubt. The plaintiffs had an indisputable paper title to this piece of land. The plaintiffs and their aunt before them – all people, it would appear, of small means – had for many years – well over the statutory twelve years – forborne to demand the rent of 10s. a year; and the reason for their forbearance was their loyalty and generosity to their church. As Mr Hayward said in evidence, if the rector had given him ten shillings he would have put it in the offertory box. Judgment was given against the rector.

One might have thought that at this stage the rector would think that honour was satisfied, if honour has any part in this case, and that the only Christian and decent thing to do would have been to accept the decision, particularly as we have been told by Mr Garland that not even now has there been a binding contract by the rector to sell this land.

But no. An appeal was brought to this court. At the end of the hearing the court indicated its strong views on the merits of the case and reserved its judgment in order that the matter should be further considered by the Church authorities, in the hope that wiser, more generous, and more Christian counsels should prevail and that the defendant should withdraw from the position hitherto taken up.

But Mr Garland, after the elapse of about a month, appeared again before the court and informed us that he was instructed to ask the court to give judgment. Who it was who was responsible for this attitude we do not know. It may be that it was the rector himself: or it may be, from what Mr Garland told us, that it was the diocesan patronage board. Whoever it was, he wanted his 'pound of flesh'. In the absence of a Portia to help us, he must in my judgment have it.

2

Capital Punishment

The abolition of capital punishment in Great Britain, effected provisionally in 1965[1] and finally in December 1969,[2] was brought about as much as a result of a moral revulsion to the practice of hanging as of the inefficacy of the sanction as a means of keeping down the murder rate. Throughout the protracted debates – few social issues can have been so volubly worked over – there has been a strong undercurrent of emotional argument. An extensive raking over of the theory of general deterrence became, in fact, the thin disguise for basic emotional attitudes.

From the beginnings of the campaign to limit the death penalty, the supposed uniqueness of the crime of murder and its alleged threat to civilised social order has frequently been said to justify the imposition of the unique penalty: that it is necessary for social equilibrium to retain a differential inequality between the penalty for murder and for 'lesser' crimes (see 2.3). Allied to this resistance to penal innovation has come the oft-repeated argument, epitomised in the writings of William Paley, that the death penalty is a powerful, if not unique deterrent (see 2.1). This was an argument used by the parliamentarians, ecclesiastics and judges to resist the nineteenth-century reforms limiting the death penalty virtually to the crime of murder. Meanwhile, the hard-headed commercial community was urging that experience told the merchants that the death penalty for property offenders at least was wholly ineffectual to stem the tide of their depredations (see 2.4 and also 2.5).

The twin threads of the inefficacy and inhumanity of hanging were best exemplified in the campaign which led to the abolition of public executions in 1868 following the report of a Royal Commission (a minority of which recommended outright abolition of the death penalty). Revulsion at the sight of a hanging, even when it was not botched by an inept hangman strangling the condemned man by misplacing the rope on the neck, was matched by the growing awareness that Tyburn was the scene of a proliferation of pickpockets – presumably undeterred by the sight of the consequences of their indulged criminality (see 2.6).

The nineteenth-century fight against the death penalty for petty crime began around 1810 with the foundation of a Society for the Diffusion of Knowledge upon the Punishment of Death.[3] The battle inside Parliament

1. The Murder (Abolition of Death Penalty) Act 1965 came into force on 9 November 1965; capital punishment remains statutorily in force for high treason and for piracy with violence.
2. In December 1969, Parliament determined, by affirmative resolution of both Houses, that the 1965 Act should remain in force without a time-limit.
3. James B. Christoph, *Capital Punishment and British Politics*, London, 1962, pp.15

was led by Sir Samuel Romilly (2.3) and Sir James Mackintosh, but a succession of Bills passed by the Commons were defeated in the Lords and it was not until the 1830s that advances were made. By 1837, the number of capital crimes had fallen from over two hundred at the beginning of the century to a mere fifteen; and it took another two decades for the number to diminish further to four.

Until the twentieth century, the failure of penal policy to differentiate between murderers persisted. The first breach in the stronghold of the death penalty for murder came with the establishment of a new crime of infanticide in 1922. Here again the moral revulsion felt, not only by the public but also by members of the judiciary, that mothers mentally disturbed during post-parturition should be executed, led to the modest reform to reduce child-killing by the victim's mother during its first year of life to manslaughter.[4] This feeling was matched a half century later by the desire to impose only non-custodial penalties on mercy killers[5] (see, however, 6.7).

The remainder of the century witnessed a nucleus of influential citizens agitating to remove the ultimate sanction. Two groups above all contributed finally to the demise of the public hangman. Ever since William Temple, when Archbishop of York, publicly declared his opposition to the death penalty (2.9) the bishops became a potent force at the instance of the abolitionists. And the judges, under the Lord Chief Justiceship of Lord Parker (1958-71) finally came round, perhaps rather grudgingly, to the view that the Homicide Act 1957 which distinguished between capital and non-capital murder was both unworkable and illogically discriminatory, and that it was better to go forward to abolition than back to the capital penalty for all murders.

In part, the judicial move towards reform was a reaction to the broad hint thrown out by the Royal Commission on Capital Punishment 1949-53 (2.10) and to the fulsome belief in the virtues of capital punishment propounded by Lord Parker's predecessor (2.11). Lord Goddard's espousal of the death penalty during the 1948 Criminal Justice Bill's parliamentary passage was unashamedly retributive in approach and his followers never adopted the more subtle technique, fashionable in the debates in the 1960s, of deploying the inconclusive statistical evidence to support the deterrent argument. One of the most telling (because of its lack of dogmatism) refutations of Lord Goddard came from another Law Lord, Lord Morris of Borth-y-Gest (2.12) who, in the abolition debate of December 1969, married neatly the emotional and the intellectual arguments.

The undercurrent of support for the restoration of hanging receives a new boost with every child-murder or police-shooting and was given a new lease

---

ff. This excellent study, by a political scientist, traces the debate about capital punishment from its early origins up to about 1960; for a brief account of subsequent events see G. Drewry, 'Parliament and hanging: Further episodes in an undying saga', *Parliamentary Affairs*, vol. 27, pp.251 ff. (1974).

4. D. Seaborne Davies, 'Child-killing in English law', in *The Modern Approach to Criminal Law* (Macmillan, 1945), pp. 301 ff.

5. Twelfth Report (Penalty for Murder) of the Criminal Law Revision Committee, Cmnd. 5184 (January 1973) paras 12 and 42.

of life late in 1974 in the wake of terrorist bomb outrages in English cities. The deterrent argument lingers on after the death penalty has been consigned to an historical limbo (2.13). However, the public controversy over capital punishment is revealed more and more for what it is, and always essentially was – a conflict of values over human life (2.14).

2.1 Archdeacon Paley on the proper ends of punishment

William Paley *(1743-1805) was appointed Archdeacon of Carlisle in 1782 and, three years later, published his influential work* Principles of Morals and Political Philosophy, *from which the following extract is taken. His view that 'the proper end of punishment is not the satisfaction of justice but the prevention of crimes', and that 'punishment is an evil to which the magistrate resorts only from its being necessary for the prevention of a greater', had a marked influence upon the development of ideas about crime and punishment at the turn of the eighteenth century. In particular, Paley had a profound belief in the deterrent effect of capital punishment.*

Of crimes and punishment

The proper end of human punishment is not the satisfaction of justice, but the prevention of crimes. By the satisfaction of justice, I mean the retribution of so much pain for so much guilt; which is the dispensation we expect at the hand of God, and which we are accustomed to consider as the order of things that perfect justice dictates and requires. In what sense, or whether with truth in any sense, justice may be said to demand the punishment of offenders, I do not now inquire; but I assert, that this demand is not the motive or occasion of human punishment. What would it be to the magistrate, that offenders went altogether unpunished, if the impunity of the offenders were followed by no danger or prejudice to the commonwealth? The fear lest the escape of the criminal should encourage him, or others by his example, to repeat the same crime, or to commit different crimes, is the sole consideration which authorises the infliction of punishment by human laws. Now that, whatever it be, which is the cause and end of the punishment ought undoubtedly to regulate the measure of its severity. But this cause appears to be founded, not in the guilt of the offender, but in the necessity of preventing the repetition of the offence: and hence results the reason, that crimes are not by any government punished in proportion to their guilt, nor in all cases ought to be so, but in proportion to the difficulty and the necessity of preventing them. Thus the stealing of goods privately out of a shop may not, in its moral quality, be more criminal than the stealing of them out of a house; yet being equally necessary, and more difficult, to be prevented, the law in certain circumstances denounces against it a severer punishment. The crime must be prevented by some means or other; and consequently, whatever means appear necessary to this end, whether they be proportionable to the guilt of the criminal or not, are adopted rightly, because they are adopted upon the principle which alone justifies the infliction of punishment at all. From the same consideration it also follows, that punishment ought not to be employed, much less rendered severe, when the crime can be prevented by any other means. Punishment is an evil to which the magistrate resorts only from its being necessary to the prevention of a greater. This necessity does not exist, when the end may be attained, that is, when the public may be defended from the effects of the crime, by any other expedient. The sanguinary laws which have been made against counterfeiting or diminishing the gold coin of the kingdom might be just until the method of detecting the fraud, by weighing the money, was introduced into general usage. Since that precaution was practised, these laws have slept; and an execution under them at this day would be deemed a measure of unjustifiable severity. The same principle accounts for a circumstance which has been often censured as an absurdity in the penal laws of this, and of most modern nations, namely, that the breaches of trust are either not punished at all, or punished with less rigour than other frauds. Wherefore is it, some have asked, that a violation of confidence, which increases the guilt, should mitigate the penalty? – This lenity, or rather forbearance of the laws, is founded in the most reasonable distinction. A due circumspection in the choice of the persons whom they trust; caution in limiting the extent of that trust; or the requiring of sufficient security for the faithful discharge of it; will commonly guard men from injuries of this description; and the law will not interpose its sanctions to protect negligence and credulity, or to supply the place of domestic care and prudence. To be convinced that the law proceeds entirely upon this consideration, we have only to observe, that where the confidence is unavoidable, – where no practical vigilance could watch the offender, as in the case of theft committed by a servant in the shop or dwelling-house of his master, or upon property to which he must necessarily have access, – the sentence of the law is not less severe, and its execution commonly more certain and rigorous than if no trust at all had intervened.

It is in pursuance of the same principle, which pervades indeed the whole system of penal jurisprudence, that the facility with which any species of crimes is perpetrated, has been generally deemed a reason for aggravating the punishment. Thus, sheep-stealing, horse-stealing, stealing of cloth from tenters or bleaching-grounds, by our laws, subject the offenders to sentence of death: not that these crimes are in their nature more heinous than many simple felonies which are punished by imprisonment or transportation, but because the property, being more exposed, requires the terror of capital punishment to protect it. This severity would be absurd and unjust, if the guilt of the offender were the immediate cause and measure of the punishment; but is a consistent and regular consequence of the supposition, that the right of punishment results from the necessity of preventing the crime; for if this be the end proposed, the severity of the punishment must be increased in proportion to the expediency and the difficulty of attaining this end; that is, in a proportion compounded of the mischief of the crime, and of the ease with which it is executed. The difficulty of discovery is a circumstance to be included in the same consideration. It constitutes indeed, with respect to the crime, the facility of which we speak. By how much therefore detection of an offender is more rare and uncertain, by so much the more severe must be the punishment when he is detected. Thus, the writing of incendiary letters, though in itself a pernicious and alarming injury, calls for a more condign and exemplary punishment, by the very obscurity with which the crime is committed.

2.2   *Johnson on hanging as a penalty*

Samuel Johnson *(1709-84) the famous lexicographer, author and traveller, wrote the influential journal* The Rambler *(with occasional contributions from others) during the period 1750-2. It is from* The Rambler *that this extract on capital punishment is taken.*

Death is, as one of the Ancients observes ... *of dreadful Things the most dreadful*, an Evil, beyond which, nothing can be threatened by sublunary Power, or feared from human Enmity or Vengeance. This Terror should, therefore, be reserved as the last Resort of Authority, as the strongest and most operative of prohibitory Sanctions, and placed only before the Treasure of Life, to guard from Invasion what cannot be restored. To equal Robbery with Murder is to reduce Murder to Robbery, to confound in common Minds the Gradations of Injury, and incite the Commission of a greater Crime, to prevent the Detection of a less. If only Murder were punished with Death, very few Robbers would stain their Hands in Blood; but when, by the last Act of Cruelty no new Danger is incurred, and Security may probably be obtained, upon what Principle shall we bid them forbear?

It may be urged, that the Sentence is often mitigated to simple Robbery; but surely this is to confess that our Laws are unreasonable in our own Opinion; and, indeed, it may be observed, that all but Murderers have, at their last Hour, the common Sensations of Mankind pleading in their Favour.

From this Conviction of the Inequality of the Punishments to the Offence proceeds the frequent Solicitations of Pardons. They who would rejoice at the Correction of a Thief, are yet shocked at the Thought of destroying him. His Crime is extenuated by comparing it with his Misery, and Severity defeats itself by exciting Pity.

The Gibbet, indeed, certainly disables those who die upon it from infesting the Community, but their Death seems not to contribute more to the Reformation of their Associates than any other Method of Separation. A Thief seldom passes much of his Time in Recollection or Anticipation, but from Robbery hastens to Riot, and from Riot to Robbery; nor when the Grave has closed upon his Companion has any other Care than to find another.

The Frequency of capital Punishments rarely hinders the Commission of a Crime, but generally prevents its Detection, and is, if we reason only upon prudential Principles, chiefly for that Reason, to be avoided. Whatever may be urged by Casuists or Politicians, the greater Part of Mankind, as they can never think that to pick the Pocket and to pierce the Heart are equal, will scarcely believe, that two Malefactors so different in Guilt can be justly doomed to the same Punishment; nor is the Necessity of submitting the Conscience to human Laws so plainly evinced, or so clearly stated, but that the Pious, the Tender, and the Just, will always scruple to concur with the Community in an Act which their private Judgment cannot approve.

2.3   An attempt to abolish hanging for theft

Sir Samuel Romilly *(1757-1818) became Solicitor-General in 1806 and after the fall of the Ministry in 1807 devoted himself to abolishing capital punishment for offences other than murder. This extract is taken from his journal, dated 30 May 1810, and followed the rejection by the House of Lords of his Bill to abolish hanging for the crime of stealing property to the value of five shillings from a shop.*

30th, *Wed*. The second reading of the Bill to abolish capital punishment for the crime of stealing privately to the amount of five shillings in a shop, came on to-day in the House of Lords, on the motion of Lord Holland, who had taken charge of the Bill. It was rejected by a majority of 31 to 11; the Ministers having procured a pretty full attendance of peers, considering the advanced season of the year, to throw it out. Amongst these were no less than seven prelates; the Archbishop of Canterbury, the Bishops of London and Salisbury, Dampier Bishop of Ely, Luxmore Bishop of Hereford, Sparke the new Bishop of Chester, and Porter an Irish Bishop. I rank these prelates amongst the members who were solicited to vote against the Bill; because I would rather be convinced of their servility towards government, than that, recollecting the mild doctrines of their religion, they could have come down to the House spontaneously, to vote that transportation for life is not a sufficiently severe punishment for the offence of pilfering what is of five shillings' value, and that nothing but the blood of the offender can afford an adequate atonement for such a transgression. Lord Ellenborough, the Lord Chancellor, and Lord Liverpool, were the only peers who spoke against the Bill; and Lord Holland, Lord Erskine, Lord Lauderdale, Lord Lansdowne, and Lord Suffolk for it. Lord Grey voted for the Bill but did not speak; Lord Melville and Lord Redesdale were among the silent voters against it. The argument principally relied on by those who spoke against the Bill was, that innovations in Criminal Law were dangerous, and that the present measure was part of a system to innovate on the whole criminal code. It was said that the House should consider, not merely the Bill itself, but the speculations in criminal jurisprudence of the author of the Bill: that he had been the author of the Act, passed two years ago, to abolish the punishment of death for the crime of picking pockets; and that the consequence of abolishing that punishment had been a very great increase of the crime. So Lord Ellenborough and the Lord Chancellor took upon themselves to affirm the fact to be from information which they said they had received. But how, it may well be asked, and was indeed asked by Lord Lansdowne in the course of the debate, do they know that the crime has increased? All they can know is, that prosecutions are much more frequent than they were before the Act passed; and this, instead of affording any argument against the Bill, proves its efficacy. It was stated, when the Bill was proposed, that the inordinate severity of the punishment appointed by law prevented those who had been robbed from prosecuting, and by that means procured complete impunity to the offenders. Take away, it was said, this most severe punishment, and you will have many more prosecutors.

The punishment is taken away; many more prosecutions are preferred; and this is the very fact which these men, blinded by their gross prejudices, put forward as proof that the measure has been unsuccessful. It is, on the contrary, the strongest proof of its success; and would afford us a triumph, if we were capable of enjoying it, on the justness of our speculations. Lord Ellenborough said that there was no knowing where this was to stop; that he supposed the next thing proposed would be, to repeal the law which punishes with death the stealing to the amount of five shillings in a dwelling-house, no person being therein: and then he declared that that act it was which afforded security to the poor cottager that he should enjoy the fruits of his labour; and he pathetically described the situation of the poor, relying with confidence on the security the law afforded them for the scanty comforts which they were allowed. No person, however, has yet proposed to abolish this law; and it is not very easy to see what there is in common between the two laws, except the words 'five shillings'. However, whether similar or not, the law he spoke of was not brought under the consideration of the House by the Bill under debate. He spoke of transportation, the severest punishment which the Bill allowed to be inflicted on the offender, as one which had few terrors for those who violate the law, and described it as being considered by them, and, as I understood him, as being justly considered, as only 'a summer airing by an easy migration to a milder climate'. The part, however, of his speech which appeared to me to be the most objectionable was that in which he said that he doubted whether the judges had not erred by too much lenity; and that it was probably that fault on their part which he encouraged these attempts to alter the law. I am not here stating his words, for I cannot recollect them, but what he said was pretty much to this effect. The inference to be drawn from this is pretty obvious, that in order to discourage such attempts in future, and to deprive these lovers of innovation of one of their arguments, namely, that the practice of the law is on this subject at total variance with its theory, it may be right to enforce the law more rigorously.

2.4 Nineteenth-century petitions against hanging for property offences

Two petitions follow, one from the Corporation of London in 1819 and the other from the Jurors of London in 1831, both opposing the death penalty for minor crimes against property.

THE PETITION OF THE CORPORATION OF LONDON
(January 25, 1819)

The petition,
As presented by the Sheriffs of London and Middlesex,
January 25, 1819

To the Honourable the Commons of the United Kingdom of Great Britain and Ireland in Parliament assembled. The humble Petition of the Lord

Mayor, Aldermen, and Commons of the City of London, in Common Council assembled,

Showeth, THAT your Petitioners are greatly interested in the Police both for the City of London, and for the County of Middlesex, where His Majesty's commissions for the trial of offenders issue yearly, and eight sessions at the least are held every year; and they are impressed with the conviction, that their representations upon the present state of the Criminal Law, and its effects on public morals, will be deemed worthy the consideration of your Honourable House.

That upwards of 200 crimes, very different in their degrees of enormity, are equally subject to the punishment of Death, which is enacted not only for the most atrocious offences, – for burglary, for rape, for murder, and for treason, – but for many offences unattended with any cruelty or violence, for various minor crimes, and even for stealing privately to the amount of five shillings in a shop.

That from the returns upon the table of your Honourable House, it appears that crimes have for some years been rapidly increasing, both in number and malignity, to the injury of the rising generation, and the debasement of the national character.

That there were committed for trial in Middlesex in the years

1812	...	1,663
1813	...	1,707
1814	...	1,646
1815	...	2,005
1816	...	2,226
1817	...	2,686

The capital convictions in Middlesex were, in the years

1812	...	132
1813	...	138
1814	...	158
1815	...	139
1816	...	227
1817	...	208

There were executed in Middlesex in the years

1812	...	19
1813	...	17
1814	...	21
1815	...	11
1816	...	29
1817	...	16

There were committed for trial in the different Jails in England and Wales, in the years

1805	...	4,605	1815	...	7,818
1812	...	6,576	1816	...	9,091
1813	...	7,164	1817	...	13,392
1814	...	6,390			

There were confined in Newgate, of boys only, of 17 years and under, in the years

1813	...	123
1816	...	247
1817	...	359

That without the interference of your Honourable House, in adapting the state of the Criminal Law to the state of the moral and religious sentiments of the nation, the increase of crimes must be progressive, because, strong as are the obligations upon all good subjects to assist the administration of justice, they are overpowered by tenderness for life – a tenderness which, originating in the mild precepts of our religion, is advancing, and will continue to advance, as these doctrines become more deeply inculcated into the minds of the community.

That many injured persons have refused to prosecute, because they cannot perform a duty which is repugnant to their natures, by being instrumental in the infliction of severity contrary to their ideas of adequate retribution; and by such impunity young offenders, instead of being checked in their first departure from virtue, are suffered to advance from small offences to crimes of great atrocity.

That some Jurymen submit to fines rather than act as arbiters of life and death in cases where they think the punishment of death ought not to be inflicted.

That some Jurymen are deterred from a strict discharge of their duty, and acquit guilt or mitigate the offence so as not to subject the offender to the punishment of death, and thus assume a discretion never intended to be vested in juries, and relax the sanctity of a judicial oath, upon which the integrity of the trial by jury much depends.

That, amongst other instances, a jury, rather than be instrumental in inflicting the punishment of death for larceny to the amount of 40s. from a dwelling, found a 10*l.* note to be worth only 39s.

That another jury, influenced by the same motives, found two bills of exchange, value of 10*l.* each, and eight Bank notes, value of 10*l.* each, worth the same sum of 39s.

That your Petitioners cannot omit to urge upon your Honourable House, that even this disinclination to enforce the law is not confined to the injured parties, and to juries, but extends to the learned judges, who, impressed with a similar feeling, have exercised their ingenuity in discovering means by which the real value of the property stolen should not be found by the jury; and where convictions have taken place, constantly recommend a great part of the convicts to the royal mercy; and His Majesty's advisers, influenced by the same anxiety to preserve human life, readily apply and easily obtain from the throne a remission of the sentence.

That your Petitioners do not apply to your Honourable House with any feeling but of gratitude and respect, for the administration of the law by the learned judges, or for this exercise of the royal prerogative, by causing law and justice in mercy to be executed in every judgment; but they are impelled to submit to your consideration the state of the law itself, which produces evasions dangerous to the community, and which must continue to produce them, as they depend not upon the sentiments of any individuals, but upon certain and general principles of our nature, upon the advanced state of civilisation in the country, and upon the diffusion of Christianity, by which we are daily taught to 'love each other as brethren, and to desire not the death of a sinner, but rather that he should turn from his wickedness and live'.

Your Petitioners, therefore, humbly pray, that your Honourable House will take the premises into your most serious consideration, and adopt such measures as the importance of the subject requires, and as to the wisdom of your Honourable House may seem meet.

THE LONDON JURORS' PETITION (September 6, 1831)

To the Right Honorable The Lords Spiritual and Temporal of the United Kingdom of Great Britain and Ireland in Parliament assembled.
The Petition of the undersigned Inhabitant Householders of the City of London, liable to serve as Jurors,

Humbly Sheweth,

That your Petitioners view with deep regret, the excessive and indiscriminate severity of the Criminal Laws, which annex to Offences of different degrees of moral guilt the punishment of *Death*, and confound the simple invasion of the rights of property, with the most malignant and atrocious crimes against the person and the life of man.

That the recent Acts passed with the professed intention to amend and improve the Criminal Laws, have not remedied the evil of which an enlightened community have the greatest reason to complain, but have still left those laws a disgrace to our civilisation, by retaining the opprobrious distinction of being the most sanguinary of any in Europe.

That Christianity, common reason, and sound policy, demand that the laws which affect the liberties and the lives of men, should proportion the punishment to the offence, and not teach cruelty to the people by examples of vindictive legislation.

That where public opinion does not go along with the laws, the persons who suffer under them are regarded as the victims of legislative tyranny, or judicial caprice, and not as criminals whose doom has been pronounced by the voice of dispassionate justice.

That the criminals executed in this country are selected out of a far greater number sentenced to death, and where *the practice* condemns *the law*, the law ought to be altered, that criminals might suffer the punishment of their guilt by the authority of *defined statutes*, and not by the uncertain and capricious rule of *judicial discretion*.

That in the present state of the law, juries feel extremely reluctant to convict where the penal consequences of the offence excite a conscientious horror on their minds, lest the rigorous performance of their duty as jurors should make them accessory to judicial murder. Hence in Courts of Justice, a most unnecessary and painful struggle is occasioned, by the conflict of the feelings of a *just* humanity with the sense of the obligation of an oath.

That witnesses also are very frequently reluctant to give evidence, as well as juries to convict, lest they might bring upon their consciences the stain of blood, and thus criminals who, under a more rational and considerate code of laws, would meet the punishment due to their crimes, escape with *complete impunity.*

That for these reasons, your Petitioners humbly pray your Right Honorable House to take the Criminal Laws into your consideration, for the purpose of the *revision* and *amendment* of the same, by drawing a distinction between the simple invasion of the rights of property, and crimes of violence and blood, and by abolishing the penalty of *death* in all cases in which the Legislative power cannot justify in the eyes of GOD and man, that last and dreadful alternative – *the extermination of the offender.*

And your Petitioners will pray, etc.

(Signed by the different foremen, respectively, of seven Old-Bailey Grand Juries of 1830, and by upwards of 1,100 merchants, traders, etc., who either have served, or are liable to serve as jurors.)

2.5   Public executions : a dubious deterrent

This editorial note in The Spectator *(1831) comments upon distasteful scenes at public executions and notes the apparent absence of any deterrent effect.*

At one of the recent executions of an incendiary, it is reported in the newspapers, that 'great numbers of people attended the execution; and because the execution was delayed a few minutes over nine o'clock, they began whistling and clapping, something in the style of the gallery at the theatre when there is any delay'. Such is the beneficial effect of the punishment of death upon the feelings of the people. It is notorious that pickpockets are never so active as at an execution. On a similar occasion in the North, some time ago, when the peasantry had come from far and near to see a man hanged, and he was reprieved a short time before the hour fixed for his death, discontent of the loudest kind was manifested. The people exclaimed in true Yorkshire, 'What a *sheem* to bring us all this way for *naught!*' They are mistaken who value highly the effect of public executions on morals: executions are considered in the light of very serious melodramas, where sympathy may sometimes be excited for the sufferer, and no horror for the crime, and by which, in fact, the fear of capital punishment is weakened.

2.6   A Dickensian tirade against public executions

Charles Dickens *(1812-70) opposed capital punishment through the mouths of his fictional characters. He also waged a war against the horrors of public executions through the correspondence columns of newspapers. The following letter was written to* The Daily News *(1846).*

Gentlemen, In the very remarkable Report made to the State Assembly of New York, in 1841, by a select committee of that body, who arrived at the conclusion, 'that the punishment of death, by law, ought to be forthwith and for ever abolished' in that part of America, there is the following suggestion:

' ... Whether there sleep within the breast of man, certain dark and mysterious sympathies with the thought of that death, and that futurity which await his nature, tending to invest any act expressly forbidden by that penalty, with an unconscious and inexplicable fascination, that attracts his thoughts to it, in spite of their very shuddering dread; and bids his imagination brood over its idea, 'till out of those dark depths in his own nature, comes gradually forth a monstrous birth of Temptation. ...'

Strongly impressed by this passage when I first read the report; and believing that it shadowed out a metaphysical truth, which, however wild and appalling in its aspect, was a truth still; I was led to consider the cases of several murderers, both in deed, and in intent, with a reference to it; and certainly it gathered very strong and special confirmation in the course of that inquiry. But, as the bearing, here, is on capital punishment in its influences on the commission of crime; and as my present object is to make it the subject of one or two considerations in its other influences on society in general; I, for the present, defer any immediate pursuit of the idea, and merely quote it now, as introducing this lesser and yet great objection to the punishment of death:

That there is, about it, a horrible fascination, which, in the minds – not of evil-disposed persons, but of good and virtuous and well-conducted people, supersedes the horror legitimately attaching to crime itself, and causes every word and action of a criminal under sentence of death to be the subject of a morbid interest and curiosity, which is odious and painful, even to many of those who eagerly gratify it by every means they can compass; but which is, generally speaking, irresistible. The attraction of repulsion being as much a law of our moral nature, as gravitation is in the structure of the visible world, operates in no case (I believe) so powerfully, as in this case of the punishment of death; though it may occasionally diminish in its force, through strong reaction.

When the murderers Hocker and Tawell had awakened a vast amount of this depraved excitement, and it had attained to an unusually indecent and frenzied height, one of your contemporaries, deploring the necessity of ministering to such an appetite, laid the blame upon the caterers of such dainties for the Press, while some other newspapers, disputing which of them should bear the greater share of it, divided it variously. Can there be any doubt, on cool reflection, that the whole blame rested on, and was immediately and naturally referable to, the punishment of death?

Round what other punishment does the like interest gather? We read of the trials of persons who have rendered themselves liable to transportation for life, and we read of their sentences, and, in some few notorious instances, of their departure from this country, and arrival beyond sea; but *they* are never followed into their cells, and tracked from day to day, and night to night; *they* are never reproduced in their false letters, flippant conversations, theological disquisitions with visitors, lay and clerical: or served up in their whole biography and adventures – so many live romances with a bloody ending. Their portraits are not rife in the print-shops, nor are their autographs stuck up in shop-windows, nor are their snuff-boxes handed affably to gentlemen in court, nor do they inquire of other spectators with eye-glasses why they look at them so steadfastly, nor are their breakfasts, dinners, and luncheons, elaborately described, nor are their waxen images in Baker-street (*unless they were in immediate danger, at one time, of the gallows*), nor are high prices offered for their clothes at Newgate, nor do turnpike trusts grow rich upon the tolls that people going to see their houses, or the scenes of their offences, pay. They are tried, found guilty, punished; and there an end.

But a criminal under sentence of death, or in great peril of death upon the scaffold, becomes, immediately, the town talk; the great subject; the hero of the time. The demeanour in his latter moments, of Sir Thomas More – one of the wisest and most virtuous of men – was never the theme of more engrossing interest, than that of Hocker, Tawell, Greenacre, or Courvoisier. The smallest circumstance in the behaviour of these, or any similar wretches, is noted down and published as a precious fact. And read, too – extensively and generally read – even by hundreds and thousands of people who object to the publication of such details, and are disgusted by them. The horrible fascination surrounding the punishment, and everything connected with it, is too strong for resistance; and when an attempt is made in this or that goal (as it has been sometimes made of late), to keep such circumstances from transpiring, by excluding every class of strangers, it is only a formal admission of the existence of this fascination, and of the impossibility of otherwise withstanding it.

Is it contended that the fascination may surround the crime, and not the punishment? Let us consider whether other crimes, which have now no sort of fascination for the general public, had or had not precisely the gross kind of interest which now attaches to Murder alone, when they were visited with the same penalty. Was Forgery interesting, when Forgers were hanged? and is it less interesting now when they are transported for life? Compare the case of Dr Dodd, or Fauntleroy, or the Reverend Peter Fenn, or Montgomery, or Hunton, or any other generally known, with that of the Exchequer-Bill forgery in later times, which, with every attendant circumstance but death, or danger of death, to give it a false attraction, soon dwindled down into a mere item in a Sessions' Calendar. Coining, when the coiner was dragged (as I have seen one) on a hurdle to the place of execution; or Burglary, or Highway Robbery – did these crimes ever wear an aspect of adventure and mystery, and did the perpetrators of them every become the town talk, when their offences were visited with death? Now, they are mean, degraded, miserable criminals; and nothing more.

That the publication of these Newgate court-circulars to which I have alluded, is injurious to society, there can be no doubt. Apart from their inevitable association with revolting details, revived again and again, of bloodshed and murder (most objectionable as familiarizing people's minds with the contemplation of such horrors), it is manifest that anything which tends to awaken a false interest in great villains, and to invest their greatest villainies and lightest actions with a terrible attraction, must be vicious and bad, and cannot be wholesome reading. But it is neither just nor reasonable to charge their publication on the newspapers, or the gleaners for the newspapers. They are published because they are read and sought for. They are read and sought for: not because society has causelessly entered into a monstrous and unnatural league on this theme (which is would be absurd to suppose), but because it is in the secret nature of those of whom society is made up, to have a dark and dreadful interest in the punishment at issue.

Whether public executions produce any good impression on their habitual witnesses, or whether they are calculated to produce any good impression on the class of persons most likely to be attracted to them, is a question, by this time, pretty well decided. I was present, myself, at the execution of Courvoisier. I was, purposely, on the spot, from midnight of the night before; and was a near witness of the whole process of the building of the scaffold, the gathering of the crowd, the gradual swelling of the concourse with the coming-on of day, the hanging of the man, the cutting of the body down, and the removal of it into the prison. From the moment of my arrival, when there were but a few score boys in the street, and those all young thieves, and all clustered together behind the barrier nearest to the drop – down to the time when I saw the body with its dangling head, being carried on a wooden bier into the goal – I did not see one token in all the immense crowd; at the windows, in the streets, on the house-tops, anywhere; of any one emotion suitable to the occasion. No sorrow, no salutary terror, no abhorrence, no seriousness; nothing but ribaldry, debauchery, levity, drunkenness, and flaunting vice in fifty other shapes. I should have deemed it impossible that I could have ever felt any large assemblage of my fellow-creatures to be so odious. I hoped, for an instant, that there was some sense of Death and Eternity in the cry of 'Hats off!' when the miserable wretch appeared; but I found, next moment, that they only raised it as they would at a Play – to see the stage the better, in the final scene.

Of the effect upon a perfectly different class, I can speak with no less confidence. There were, with me, some gentlemen of education and distinction in imaginative pursuits, who had, as I had, a particular detestation of that murderer; not only for the cruel deed he had done, but for his slow and subtle treachery, and for his wicked defence. And yet, if any one among us could have saved the man (we said so, afterwards, with one accord), he would have done it. It was so loathsome, pitiful, and vile a sight, that the law appeared to be as bad as he, or worse; being very much the stronger, and shedding around it a far more dismal contagion.

The last of the influences of this punishment on society, which I shall notice in the present letter, is, that through the prevalent and fast-increasing feeling of repugnance to it, great offenders escape with a very inadequate visitation. Only a few weeks have elapsed since the streets of London presented the obscene spectacle of a woman being brought out to be killed before such as crowd as I have described, and, while her young body was yet hanging in the brutal gaze, of portions of the concourse hurrying away, to be in time to see a man hanged elsewhere, by the same executioner. A barbarous murderer is tried soon afterwards, and acquitted on a fiction of his being insane – as any one, cognizant of these two recent executions, might have easily foreseen.

I will not enter upon the question whether juries be justified or not justified in evading their oaths, rather than add to the list of such deeply degrading and demoralizing exhibitions, and sanction the infliction of a punishment which they conscientiously believe, and have so many reasons for believing, to be wrong. It is enough for me that juries do so; and I presume to think that the able writer of a powerful article on Johnstone's trial in *The Daily News*, does not sufficiently consider that this is no new course in juries, but the natural result and working of a law to which the general feeling is opposed. Mr Abercrombie, five-and-thirty years ago, stated it in the House of Commons to have become a common practice of juries, in cases of Forgery, to find verdicts 'contrary to the clearest and most indisputable evidence of facts'; and cited the case of a woman who was proved to have stolen a ten-pound note, which the jury, with the approbation of the judge, found to be worth only thirty-nine shillings. Sir Samuel Romilly, in the same debate, mentioned other cases of the same nature; and they were of frequent and constant occurrence at that time.

Besides – that juries have, within our own time, in another class of cases, arrived at the general practice of returning a verdict tacitly agreed upon beforehand, and of making it applicable to very different sets of facts, we know by the notable instance of Suicide. Within a few years, juries frequently found that a man dying by his own hand, was guilty of self-murder. But this verdict subjecting the body to a barbarous mode of burial, from which the better feeling of society revolted (as it is now revolting from the punishment of death), it was abrogated by common consent, and precisely the same evasion established, as is now, unfortunately, so often resorted to in cases of murder. That it is an evasion, and not a proceeding on a soundly-proved and established principle, that he who destroys his own life must necessarily be made – the very exceptions from this usual course in themselves demonstrate.

So it is in case of Murder. Juries, like society, are not stricken foolish or motiveless. They have, for the most part, an objection to the punishment of death: and they will, for the most part, assert such verdicts. As jurymen, in the Forgery cases, would probably reconcile their verdict to their consciences, by calling to mind that the intrinsic value of a bank note was almost nothing, so jurymen in cases of Murder probably argue that grave doctors have said all men are more or less mad, and therefore they believe the prisoner mad. This is a great wrong to society; but it arises out of the punishment of death.

And the question will always suggest itself in jurors' minds – however earnestly the learned judge presiding, may discharge his duty – 'which is the greater wrong to society? To give this man the benefit of the possibility of his being mad, or to have another public execution, with all its depraving and hardening influences?' Imagining myself a juror, in a case of life or death: and supposing that the evidence had forced me from every other ground of opposition to this punishment in the particular case, as a possibility of irremediable mistake, or otherwise: I would go over it again on this ground; and if I could, by any reasonable special pleading with myself, find him mad rather than hang him – I think I would.

CHARLES DICKENS

2.7   Stephen advocates capital punishment for murder

Sir James Fitzjames Stephen, *who later wrote a rebuttal of J.S. Mill's essay* On Liberty *(see 1.5), published the following defence of capital punishment in* Fraser's Magazine, *June 1864.*

After an interval of several years public attention has once more been directed to the question of the abolition of capital punishments; and this time the advocates of that measure have so far succeeded as to procure the appointment of a Commission to inquire into the whole subject. It is to be hoped that their inquiries will not be confined to the single question whether men shall continue to be hung for murder, but that it will extend to some other subjects closely connected with the principal point at issue, and often allowed to exercise great influence over the opinions formed respecting it.

The subject will be found to fall under the following heads: First, Ought capital punishment to be inflicted under any circumstances whatever? Secondly, Ought any alteration to be made in the definition of the crime for which it is inflicted; namely, Wilful murder? These three questions are perfectly independent of each other; and the matter will be greatly simplified if they are separately considered.

First, then, Ought capital punishment to be inflicted for any crime whatever, and particularly ought it to be inflicted for murder? We think it ought. First, because no other punishment deters men so effectually from committing murder; secondly, because no other punishment gratifies and justifies in so emphatic a manner the vindictive sentiment, the existence of which is one of the great safeguards against crime; thirdly, because no other way of disposing of great criminals is equally effectual, appropriate, and cheap.

First, no other punishment deters men so effectually from committing crimes as the punishment of death. This is one of those propositions which it is difficult to prove, simply because they are in themselves more obvious than any proof can make them. It is possible to display ingenuity in arguing against it, but that is all. The whole experience of mankind is in the other direction. The threat of instant death is the one to which resort has always been made when there was an absolute necessity for producing some result. Those who argue that the punishment of death does not terrify, may be challenged to answer this single question. Suppose a pistol were levelled at the head of a man proposing to commit murder, and suppose he knew that the death of his victim would immediately be followed by his own, does any one suppose that the murder would be committed? Again, men, in a good cause, and under the influence of good sentiments and favourable circumstances, are capable of acts of the most heroic courage; yet even in the heat of battle it is hardly possible to get men to encounter certain death. They will run great risks, but, as Sir William Napier said of himself, there is always 'a secret springing kind of hope', which sustains them. No one goes to certain inevitable death, except on compulsion. Put the matter the other way. Was there ever yet a criminal who, when sentenced to death and brought out to die, would refuse the offer of a commutation of his sentence for the severest secondary punishment? Surely not. Why is this? It can only be because 'All that a man has will he give for his life.' In any secondary punishment, however terrible, there is hope; but death is death; its terrors cannot be described more forcibly. If we look at the facts, not at the narrow and inconclusive facts which are put forward as statistical arguments on this subject (as to which more will be said hereafter), but at broad facts, notorious to all mankind, it is plain that the punishment of death, when rigorously inflicted, has tremendous deterring force. Take two instances – the Reign of Terror and the suppression of the Indian mutiny. Can any one say that in these cases the punishment of death did not deter? In the Reign of Terror the crime punished with death was disaffection, even in the slightest degree, to the establishment in France of a democracy. This crime was not recognized as such by the adherents of the old order of things. They did not consider themselves morally bound to favour the Revolution. Not only had they no scruples of conscience about opposing it, but they considered opposition to it as a virtuous action. They were brave men, and showed in fields of battle all over Europe how little they feared death; but they were cowed by the guillotine. The Reign of Terror was a reign in the proper sense of the word. The Revolutionary Government held down their antagonists, and forced them for the time being into submission. The same thing happened at the Indian mutiny. Hindoos care less for their lives, we are told, than Europeans. The mutineers, no doubt, thought themselves in the right; yet the tremendous vigour with which they were punished effectually put them down. By executing every man taken in arms, a lesson was read to them which as long as India is India will never be forgotten. It is idle to say that the process of shooting and hanging men by scores caused no terror. It did strike terror, and that a terror deep enough to enable a handful of Europeans to set their feet on the necks of enemies many times more numerous than themselves. The same lesson has been read repeatedly in different parts of the world. Did the Inquisition, with its stakes and its tortures, strike no terror into heretics? Did Alva do nothing towards terrifying the Flemings and the Dutch? Did hanging, shooting, and flogging play no part in putting down the Irish rebellion in 1798? Did the storming of Drogheda have no effect on other Irish towns? Did not Yeh, even in China, where human life is held far cheaper than with us, maintain his power at Canton by the execution of 70,000 men? Be bloody enough and pitiless enough, and human nature will give way. Few things, indeed, hardly even great virtues, will bear up against the threat of death enforced without shrinking by irresistible power. If this is the case where the object is to overcome the strongest passions of the human mind, such for instance as patriotism and religion, is it to be supposed that mere vice will fail to be affected by it? If the fear of death will make men desert their country and deny their God, is it to be supposed that it will have no influence at all on the mind of a man who is plotting murder? It would require the strongest evidence to prove a proposition so improbable; but if it were proved, it would prove too much. It would prove that legal punishments do not deter at all, for it can hardly be contended that of the two, the fear of penal servitude or imprisonment is more terrible than the fear of death. Mr Bright said, in the late debate, that the punishment of death 'is a terrible one to a man on the verge of the grave; but months before when the crime is committed and the passions are aroused, the punishment is of no avail whatever.' If this is so, what is to be said of penal servitude? The words are unfamiliar, and the notion which they convey confused the indefinite. Is it to be supposed that months before the trial, and at the time when the passions are aroused, the contingency of penal servitude will influence the criminal's imagination more strongly than the contingency of death? The notion is obviously absurd. The truth is, that if it is denied that the punishment of death deters from crime, the deterrent theory of punishment ought to be altogether given up, and we ought to resort to the doctrine maintained (amongst others) by Theodore Parker, that crime ought to be treated exclusively as a disease, and that punishment ought to be considered only as a medicine.

2.8 *Capital punishment : the view of a twentieth-century archbishop*

William Temple *(1881-1944), Archbishop of York 1929-42 and of Canterbury 1942-4, was active in the field of education and a member of the Labour Party during the 1920s. This article, 'The Death Penalty', which appeared in* The Spectator *in 1935 was a significant and, in the context of the time, advanced contribution to the debate on capital punishment.*

The present discussion of the Death Penalty has an importance that extends far beyond the subject itself. The retention or alteration of our present practice, now that the question has been sharply raised, must depend upon the moral principles accepted by the community for the government of its penal code. It has commonly been agreed that in all punishment there are three elements, which may, of course, be active in very varying proportions. These have usually been called the Retributive, the Deterrent and the Reformative. Personally, I hold that the essential element in what has been called retribution is not the infliction of pain to balance evil done, but is the action of the community in repudiating a criminal act. If, when a crime has been committed, the community does nothing, it is condoning the act, and to that extent becomes a partner in the guilt of it. If it treats the criminal merely as a subject for remedial care it is ignoring his moral character.

What is first of all required for the moral welfare of the community, and of the criminal himself, is that action should be taken in the name of the community making clear its repudiation of the crime. Thus the community clears itself by re-assertion of the outraged principle, and assists the criminal by recalling to his attention the principle against which he had offended. Almost inevitably this element in punishment takes the form of the infliction of pain or inconvenience, and inasmuch as every criminal act is an abuse of liberty, the appropriate form of retribution or repudiation is curtailment of liberty, that is to say, imprisonment. But for smaller offences the inconvenience of a fine may serve, and in the case of those who neither are, nor can reasonably be expected to be, fully formed in character, and therefore fully responsible for their conduct, it is both proper and just that the remedial element should be given so much preponderance as is best expressed through a training in the use of liberty rather than the removal of it. This, no less than the avoidance of contaminating contacts, is the ground for substituting special schools or probation for imprisonment in the case of juvenile offenders.

The deterrent element stands on a quite different ground. It is not primarily a moral principle at all, except so far as the character of a potential criminal may be safeguarded by the check upon his indulgence of criminal impulses. Strictly speaking it is not the infliction of punishment, but the law which directs it, in which the deterrent element is to be found. Obviously in the case of the criminal who has been detected the deterrent quality of the punishment has already failed. He has not been deterred; and the object of inflicting the punishment upon him, so far as the aim is deterrent, is not to deter him but to deter other people. It is, strictly speaking, the law which is, or seeks to be, deterrent when it enacts that whoever shall in future do such and such thing shall suffer such and such consequences.

Now, so far as punishment is deterrent only, it is treating the criminal as a means to an end, and though the law which condemned him may aim at preserving him from the crime, the actual infliction of the punishment is mainly concerned with other people. So far as this is true, it is non-moral; and if there were no other element in any instance of punishment, it would be immoral, for it is always immoral to treat a person only as a means to some end other than his own well-being. No form of punishment is so purely deterrent as the Death Penalty. It has, indeed, been urged, by T.H. Green for example, that the sentence of death may be the one shock needed to call the criminal to a sense of his guilt and so to stimulate repentance. Perhaps sometimes it is so. But there does not seem to be much evidence that in practice sentence of death has this tendency. Of course it is only on the hypothesis of immortality that the death penalty can be regarded as reformative at all; and it is doubtful whether many of those who incure it have a sufficiently vivid faith in a future life to accept the sentence of death as a temporary discipline.

Recent experience has shown that in many cases public opinion revolts against the execution of condemned criminals, and indeed the proportion of reprieves tends steadily to increase. Moreover, observation seems to leave no doubt with regard to the chief quality of effectiveness in deterrent punishment. It is not the severity of the penalty inflicted, but the certainty both of detection and of the exaction of the penalty required by law, whatever this may be. If then, as seems unquestionable, we have reached a stage where the expectation of execution has been rendered definitely uncertain, so that there is always hope of reprieve, the death penalty will be less deterrent than a life sentence without the possibility of reprieve. No doubt it is logically absurd to be more deterred by certain imprisonment for life than by possible execution with life imprisonment as the alternative; but few men are governed by logic, and criminals less than most: and as a matter of psychology the introduction of uncertainty, even though it only be as between death and a life sentence, weakens the deterrent influence of the present law as compared with a life sentence certain to take effect.

The fact that a man sentenced for life may gain his discharge after a long period does not have this effect of uncertainty, because his doing so is conditional upon something else altogether – namely, future good conduct.

What is required for effective deterrence is that there shall be prescribed for the crime a penalty which will then and there be inflicted. Our modern sentiment has robbed the death penalty of its chief defence. This is of great importance when we remember that all punishment should contain the remedial or reformative element, for, as has been said, this element is at its minimum in the death penalty. Unless, therefore, it can be pleaded that that penalty is uniquely deterrent, which in modern conditions it is not, the case against it seems overwhelming. Moreover, the cause which makes the reformative element so small exposes the death penalty also to a special risk of injustice. This is the finality of it so far as this world is concerned. It may be very rare that an innocent man is found guilty of murder. But we cannot be sure that it has never happened, or never will happen. Certainly there are on record cases where a reprieve has arrived only just in time, and sometimes this has been granted as a result of discovery that the guilt really attached to another person and that the condemned man was innocent. If a person has been found guilty and imprisoned and his innocence is afterwards established, nothing can restore to him the years of freedom of which he has been deprived; none the less he may return to his family and friends with his good name vindicated. But if a man has been hanged, the subsequent discovery of his innocence cannot avail him in this life. There must be overwhelmingly strong reason before a civil community takes the risk that is involved in the infliction of a punishment final in that sense. But, on the contrary, even apart from this consideration, the case for the death penalty seems definitely weak.

If the contention of these paragraphs is sound it would follow that we should, as soon as possible, remove the death penalty for murder from the statute book; but it would also follow that we should not ask for reprieves in the meantime, except in circumstances so peculiar that everyone could recognize that the exception does not infringe the rule.

There is one other consideration telling the same way which we have kept to the end because it is of quite supreme importance. It is the principle laid down by Jeremy Bentham that the State affects the conduct and actions of its citizens more by the standards governing its own action than by the penalties which it visits upon others. It is often said that execution for murder is justified because murder, being an outrage upon the sanctity of life, calls for a quite unique retribution or repudiation. That in itself may be true: but the State will do most to promote regard for the sanctity of life by paying regard to that sanctity itself. Its action in taking life where murder is proved will do more to undermine regard for life, and therefore even to encourage murder, than the terrible nature of the punishment could do to check the murderous impulse. This is an argument which in any special application is incapable of being tested; but the principle of it rests both upon a very wide observation of instances and upon the understanding of human character possessed by those who have most deeply penetrated its secrets. To me, at least, it seems clear that few public actions would at the present time so much demonstrate and secure an advance in the ethics of civilization as the abolition of the Death Penalty.

2.9 Capital punishment and deterrence: the Gowers Report

The following is taken from the Report of the Royal Commission on Capital Punishment, 1949-1953 (Chairman, Sir Ernest Gowers).

59. Capital punishment has obviously failed as a deterrent when a murder is committed. We can number its failures. But we cannot number its successes. No one can ever know how many people have refrained from murder because of the fear of being hanged. For that we have to rely on indirect and inconclusive evidence. We have been told that the first thing a murderer says when he is arrested is often 'shall I be hanged?' or 'I did it and I am ready to swing for it', or something of that kind. What is the inference to be drawn from this? Clearly, not that the death penalty is an effective deterrent, for he has not been deterred; nor that he consciously considered the risk of the death penalty and accepted it; still less that the death penalty was not so effective a deterrent as some other punishment might have been. The true inference seems to us to be that there is a strong association between murder and the death penalty in the popular imagination. We think it is reasonable to suppose that the deterrent force of capital punishment operates not only by affecting the conscious thoughts of individuals tempted to commit murder, but also by building up in the community, over a long period of time, a deep feeling of peculiar abhorrence for the crime of murder. 'The fact that men are hung for murder is one great reason why murder is considered so dreadful a crime.' This widely diffused effect on the moral consciousness of society is impossible to assess, but it must be at least as important as any direct part which the death penalty may play as a deterrent in the calculations of potential murderers. It is likely to be specially potent in this country, where the punishment for lesser offences is much more lenient than in many other countries, and the death penalty stands out in the sharper contrast.

2.10 Lord Goddard's maiden speech

Lord Goddard *(1877-1971) was Lord Chief Justice (1946-58) and an enthusiastic advocate of punishment (including the death penalty and corporal punishment) for its own sake. The extract here is from his forceful maiden speech on the second reading in the Lords on 28 April 1948 of the Government's Criminal Justice Bill into which the Commons had, on a free vote, inserted a clause providing for the suspension of the death penalty for five years. In the result, the clause was thrown out by an overwhelming majority in the Lords.*

[Lord Goddard]: Much of the debate which has so far taken place on this Bill has related to the question of capital punishment. It is unnecessary for me to traverse the ground that has already been covered, but I should like to look at the matter from another angle. I cannot help feeling that this is really part of a much wider subject – the true functions of criminal law in regard to crime and punishment. Reading the debates in another place and leading articles that have appeared in responsible and weighty journals, and listening to the speech of the noble Viscount, Lord Templewood, and others, it has seemed to me that there is a great tendency nowadays to consider that punishment should never be punitive, only reformative. I agree with all my heart that when you are dealing with the sort of cases which come before magistrates daily, and perhaps to a lesser extent before Quarter Sessions – that is, when you are dealing with the young criminal, the boy who is drifting into crime, the man who has made a slip from which he can be rescued, or even the old lag in whom there is still some good that, given a fair chance, he will be able to develop – reformation is the main thing for a court to bear in mind.

But that class is not the only class of criminal with which the law deals; and when you get to the Court of Assize an entirely different picture is presented. There you get cases in which there is definitely no question of reformation as it is ordinarily understood. If we are to punish only with a view to reformation, what is one to do, for instance, with the ordinary motor manslaughter case? No kind of case is more distressing. You have a man before you, very often a man of education, of position, of some culture, perhaps a successful business man. For one reason or another – it may be that he has been at a party and taken more than he ought – he gets an overweening confidence in his skill as a driver and takes a risk, which has dreadful results. Sometimes not only is one person killed; in one case which came before me some years ago four persons were killed in the twinkling of an eye. Was it too much to say, at any rate in the days before the restrictions were placed upon motoring, that the roads of this country were strewn with dead and dying? The statistics of the people killed on the roads are such that they make one shudder. It is not a question of 'reforming' drivers of the type I have mentioned. Such a man probably bitterly repents, and will be haunted to his dying day by what he has done. But, as I say, he makes the roads dangerous, and he must be punished.

There is one other consideration which I believe should never be overlooked. If the criminal law of this country is to be respected, it must be in accordance with public opinion, and public opinion must support it. That goes very nearly to the root of this question of capital punishment. I cannot believe that the public opinion (or I would rather call it the public conscience) of this country will tolerate that persons who deliberately condemn others to painful and, it may be, lingering deaths should be allowed to live. I am not afraid to make a confession on this point. It is a common reproach against Judges (though I believe it is absolutely groundless) that they are – the word generally used – reactionary, and are always on the side of severity. It is not so. It is an idea that I think has been fostered by the historical fact that a great predecessor in my office, Lord Ellenborough, in the early days of the last century, was a bitter opponent of the reforms then suggested to make a great number of offences which were then capital non-capital. I suppose that, to a large extent, he reflected the opinion of his time, and perhaps sufficient credit is not given to him, because at least he erred in good company. If your Lordships refer to the *Parliamentary Debates* of those days, you will find that nearly the whole of the Bench of Bishops supported him.

I know that in uttering this sentiment I shall not have the sympathies of everyone but, in my humble opinion, I believe that there are many many cases where the murderer should be destroyed. The cases which come before one, where there is no question of insanity, are sometimes so horrible that I confess that I have suffered feelings of actual physical nausea in having to listen to them. I know full well the danger of arguing from the general to the particular, but let me give your Lordships two instances to justify my view that some of these bestial murderers should be destroyed. Last November, I tried a case at Bristol. The prisoner, thank God, was not a British subject. He was a Pole, but he had been here for quite a long time. On his own confession, having finished his supper, during which he had had only a moderate quantity to drink, he said that he had had an overwhelming desire for sexual intercourse. He went out and, finding no young girl near his camp, went to a little village alehouse on the outskirts of the village, kept by an old woman of seventy-six. He entered that woman's house at dead of night, he went into her room, he raped her, he committed another nameless offence on that poor creature's body, and he killed her.

At the end of last sittings, another case came before me in the Court of Criminal Appeal. I regret to say that this time the prisoner was a British subject. In a mining village in South Wales, a young man of about twenty-two years of age who had had a little to drink – not much, for no one suggested he was drunk – while pushing his way down an alley knocked against an old woman who reproached him – reviled him, if you like, for I expect she used strong language at him. He struck at her so that she fell on the sidewalk and fractured her skull. Then he kicked her to death and raped her as she was dying on the pavement. When one is faced with cases like that, can one doubt that those who have to listen to them, and those who have to try to keep an impartial and cool judgment, come to the conclusion that some cases are so awful that the prisoner should be destroyed? I wish those whose opinions I respect, and whose views I can understand, would sometimes come and listen to an Assize at some towns that I could mention. The depravity of human nature is dreadful. In many cases, it is capable of reform. In God's name, where it is capable of reform let us reform it; but in the sort of cases that I have instanced to your Lordships I feel that no question of reform can in any possible circumstance arise.

2.11   *Speech by an abolitionist judge*

Lord Morris of Borth-y-Gest (*b. 1896*), *Lord of Appeal in Ordinary 1960-74, made the following speech which sharply differed in tone from that of Lord Goddard. It was made during the debate in the House of Lords on the Orders making permanent (in December 1969) the abolition of capital punishment, previously suspended for five years in 1965.*

Lord Morris of Borth-y-Gest: My Lords, I wish only to say, with the utmost brevity, why I favour the Motion of the noble and learned Lord the Lord

Chancellor. I do not take the view that it is never right for the State to take life; I do not take the view that it could never be proper to have the death penalty. But I do take the view that the death penalty ought to be retained only if it is shown that it is absolutely necessary and essential for the purpose of saving the lives of potential future victims. My approach to the problem has been along those lines.

It is now some years since I had the responsibility, the unenviable responsibility, of presiding at murder trials. My experience dates back to the late 1940s, when I had such share of that responsibility as came in the ordinary course of a Judge of the King's Bench Division. In those days – the late 1940s – a verdict by the jury of 'Guilty' could be followed only by one sentence of the court. So those whom my colleagues and I in those days saw in the dock and who were found by the jury to be guilty were all people who had not been deterred by the death sentence.

The experience of the judges was of observing a succession of people, if found guilty, to whom that applied. In many cases – probably the majority – the reason was that at the time of a killing no thought whatsoever had been given to the consequences. In a small number of cases if there had been any thought at all, the only thought was that there would be neither detection nor apprehension. But I must remember that it may be there were some whom we did not see in the dock only for the reason that they had been deterred. It may be there were some whom we saw on lesser charges and who were not arraigned on more serious charges only for the reason that they had been deterred. So one cannot be positive and certain. I hope that in expressing my view against capital punishment I should never be assertive or dogmatic. We can only do the best we can on the available evidence to form a conclusion.

So, starting with judicial experience tending to show that capital punishment was no deterrent, one can only do one's best to study the material in this publication of the Home Office Research Unit,[6] and to study the other available evidence. I approach the matter by accepting, as I think all in your Lordships' House accept, that capital punishment is something abhorrent in itself, something that ought to be resorted to only if it is shown that it is such a unique deterrent that, regrettably, unfortunately and unavoidably, it must be retained. I take the point put by the noble Lord, Lord Salter, a few moments ago. I have never thought that capital punishment could not be regarded as any kind of deterrent. I think the case instanced by the noble Lord, Lord Salter, was an illustration of a possible situation where there may be a deterrent effect.

But, my Lords, all these questions that so torment us and exercise our minds and our consciences are questions in which the argument is not all one way. Life would be very simple if we could all see a clear answer to every question. But I consider that in this matter the best one can do is to weigh up all the available evidence and come to a conclusion. The conclusion that I have reached is the conclusion that it is not shown that capital punishment has such an exceptional potency as a deterrent that it is essential we should keep it.

6. *Murder, 1957 to 1968* (H.M.S.O., 1969).

Is not the test whether we feel that the objections to what we all regard as abhorrent are outweighed by something that is shown to be a supreme, unfortunate but inevitable necessity? I do not think that that has been shown. Can we be sure that the utter and irrevocable certainty of the death penalty can always be matched by positive certainty of guilt? In no country, with the fairest system of law, with the most humane and conscientious judiciary, do I feel that we can be satisfied of that.

... The conclusion that I have reached, my Lords, is that it is not shown that we must retain this abhorrent form of penalty.

2.12 *Hanging as a deterrent: two opposing views*

John Sparrow *Warden of All Souls College, Oxford, and* **Louis Blom-Cooper QC**, *two letter-writers to* The Times *(31 December 1969 and 5 January 1970 respectively) on the deterrent effects of punishment for murder in the absence of the death penalty*

From Mr John Sparrow

Sir, – Whether or not Parliament's decision to abolish the death-penalty was a wise one, it is important that the public should appreciate its full significance, which – so far as I am aware – has nowhere been pointed out.

What was it that really determined the votes of the majority in either House upon this issue? The decisive factor was not the statistical evidence (which they did not wait to see completed), or any other evidence, about the effectiveness of the death-penalty as a deterrent; it was a deep conviction, based not upon reason but upon emotion, that the gallows – or any other machinery for judicial execution – is an anachronism and a horror, and should have no place in a civilised society in the twentieth century even if it provides the most effective means of deterring the potential murderer. A society which dispenses with the death-penalty and has a murder-rate of x *per annum* is *pro tanto* a healthier and more civilised society than one which reduces its annual murder-rate below x by maintaining the machinery of capital punishment: better a few more murders in the year than the possibility of even a single judicial execution.

This humanitarian view invites two comments: (i) it is held by only a small minority of the public, and (ii) most of those who hold it belong to categories – e.g. peers, M.P.s, bishops, academics – from which the murderer does not usually draw his victims; the people who are murdered are 'ordinary' people – bank-clerks, post-mistresses, policemen, prostitutes. It is natural that the enlightened minority should pay more heed to the outrage inflicted on their own sensibilities by the existence of the gallows than they pay to the risk of murder run by the mass of ordinary people and the loss of a few 'unimportant' lives.

But is it right – one may ask – that they should make this preference a basis for legislation? Will it not increase the sense of alienation, not only from the Government, but from Parliament itself, that is even now becoming widespread among the electorate? This, after all, is not an issue with which the enlightened are more concerned, or one (like, say, the Common Market) on which they are any better able to judge, than is the man in the street.

This is only half the story. The humanitarian feeling thus dominant among the 'enlightened' minority extends beyond the death-penalty to alternative punishments for murder, and to punishments for other crimes. Already the *Observer* has declared that 'Since some murderers may have to be detained for much longer than the so-called "average" of nine years in custody, conditions in our prisons must be made tolerable for them'.

This far-reaching suggestion – for it could hardly be intended that conditions should be made more tolerable for murderers than for those convicted of less serious offences – reveals clearly where we are being led by the trend of feeling responsible for the abolition of the death penalty: the goal is the removal from judicial penalties of every harsh or painful or humiliating element. Is there not a danger that if you remove these elements from judicial penalties you will also remove their efficiency as deterrents? To the extent that you make the penalty imposed upon x for an offence a 'tolerable' one you diminish the likelihood that it will deter y from committing a similar offence. The *Observer* was aware of this dilemma, but could offer no solution of it.

Parliament, it seems, has taken its first step along the road to Erewhon and Utopia – a desirable road, no doubt, but one along which it is possible to move too fast. The time has not arrived, at any rate in this country, when crime can be prevented by treating criminals as mental patients, or single contract debtors to the state, and hoping that this will serve as a sufficient warning to the thug, the cheat and the crook.

It is, no doubt, the function of Parliament to give a lead to the country at large in matters such as this; but it is useless, surely, to talk of 'leading', along this or any other road, if Parliament is so far out of touch with the mass of its constituents that they are not prepared to follow. But at least it is desirable that they should be made aware of where it is that their representatives are set to take them.

Yours faithfully,
JOHN SPARROW

From Mr Louis Blom-Cooper

Sir, – The Warden of All Souls, Mr John Sparrow, in his letter of December 31 pointing out the significance of Parliament's decision to abolish capital punishment, repeats the fallacious argument that the lessening of the severity of punishment weakens the deterrent effect of that punishment. He asks whether the removal from judicial penalties of every harsh or painful or humiliating element will not remove their efficacy as deterrents. The answer is in the negative.

The penalty inflicted on an offender can only be one of many factors that determines whether potential offenders of like crimes will commit those crimes. The detection rate, subjectively estimated by the potential offender, is the first line of deterrence. If the detection rate is high – as it is for murder – then the risk of being caught will be the greater and will tend to operate as an effective deterrent. Even if caught, the question then is, will the offender be successfully prosecuted? If the acquittal rate is low, then again the potential offender will be halted in his tracks before embarking on his escapade.

It is only when he has been caught and prosecuted to conviction that the penalty even begins to operate as a deterrent. And if, as in all crimes save that of murder, the court has a complete discretion (with only a maximum penalty prescribed) the potential offender cannot know what mitigating factors might operate to lessen the punishment imposed by the court. For murder, the potential offender may know that the penalty is the fixed one of life imprisonment. But this indeterminate sentence will not tell him how long he will have actually to spend in prison.

Hence the degree of punishment, let alone the physical and psychological conditions under which the prison sentence will be served, can operate only marginally on the mind of the potential offender – and this argument proceeds on the assumption that (a) potential offenders even think about the consequences of committing crime before they embark on it; and (b) even if they do apply their minds to penal consequences, they are in possession of sufficient information upon which they can take a calculated risk as to detection, prosecution, conviction and sentence.

Yours faithfully,
LOUIS BLOM-COOPER

2.13 A modern humanitarian analysis

W.J.H. Sprott *(1897-1971) was a distinguished academic in several fields of the social sciences, and a sometime associate of the Bloomsbury Group. This extract is taken from an essay entitled 'Conflicts of values' in* The Hanging Question, *published in 1969 shortly before the final debate on the abolition of hanging in December of that year.*

One's attitude towards the death penalty is a matter of one's scheme of values, and as such it has to be weighed against other, possibly conflicting, values to see which has priority. For my part the basic value is that I believe it to be wrong to kill human beings. Of course I admit that there may be circumstances when higher values are threatened, as in the case of a 'just' war, then one may have to grant that killing other human beings might be the lesser of two evils, but it is evil all the same.

It is not that I think life is 'sacred', whatever that may mean. I think of human beings as something more than featherless bipeds. In considering them I think one should not merely be concerned with the fact that they are breathing; one must also consider what I would call the 'quality' of their lives. This is a notion which I find impossible to define, let alone measure, but there are conditions in which the kind of thing I call 'quality' is either reduced to almost nothing, or unattainable. On the one hand if a person is suffering from a disease agreed to be incurable and causing considerable pain, then I think it right and proper that they should be eased into peace. On the other hand if a child is born so grossly malformed that it will never achieve a normal human life at all, then I am inclined to think it should not be allowed to live. Furthermore, apart from such extreme cases, I, like everyone else, think that many people, murderers and non-murderers, would be much better dead, considering the misery they spread around them, but in these cases I think one ought to wait for a happy accident, rather than taking steps to eliminate them.

I think the controversy can be seen as an episode in the long and hazardous process of human civilisation. In this matter I confess myself to be old fashioned enough to be a follower of L.T. Hobhouse. In his *Morals in Evolution* he traces the gradual uneven expansion of human decency. At first one had to behave decently to members of one's tribe; other people were fair game. Then contact with other peoples brought to mind that they might be more useful as friends than as enemies, so one extended one's decency to them. As time goes on codes of decent behaviour are formulated, more commercial and cultural contacts are made, and human sympathy expands to cover wider areas. Today when cultural contact is at a maximum there are, I believe, more people concerned with the fate of more people than ever before. We are fussed up about the slaughter in Vietnam and in Biafra. Why on earth should we care? They have nothing to do with us, but the majority of people in the world would feel that such a remark is outrageous.

Of course I do not subscribe to the doctrine that there is some 'hidden hand' at work ensuring this advance in civilised behaviour, nor do I claim that it has been any kind of even process; there have been set-backs, and doubtless more will come. I think it is due to the cumulative effect of increased range of interaction and to increased rationality. On the whole, if one has contact with other people, however strange they may be, one cannot help extending one's regard to them. Reason steps in to question any discrimination. If you believe that you ought to behave decently to other human beings of your own colour, reason asks why not behave decently to human beings of a darker hue? The Americans in the old days tried to get round it, significantly enough, by saying that Negroes were not human at all, and therefore do not count. This nonsense was soon exploded and the Americans have felt uneasy ever since.

In the small area of our treatment of murderers the same process has been at work. In the eighteenth century it was presumably thought right and proper to hang offenders for crimes that we would now think of as petty, until enlightened juries started to give perverse verdicts. Gradually the death penalty was abolished for all but a limited number of offences, in spite of a certain amount of opposition from the bench of bishops.

It was also thought proper that executions should take place in public view, so as to strike terror into potential offenders. Then this became a public scandal; people enjoyed the spectacle, which was felt to be indecent, and so far from striking terror, the occasion provided a field-day for pickpockets. So the condemned were hanged in comparative privacy, and the public who wished could only satisfy their ghoulish curiosity by reading about it in the newspapers.

Now we ask whether the disgusting affair need go on at all. Those who wish to have the death penalty are on the defensive; they have to make a case which will satisfy our sympathies and our reasons. I believe the trend is against them.

All this may be thought of as an attempt to bolster up soppiness with high-falutin' ideas. This does not worry me. If there were more soppiness about, the world would be a better place.

3

Non-Capital Punishment

Punishment of criminals is almost as endemic in society as crime itself (see 2.1). Indeed, penal sanctions have been until very recently (and still are to a very limited extent) used to enforce civil obligations (3.6 and 3.7). There are currently few signs that the prevalent belief in the social utility both of publicising penalties and of actually imposing penal sanctions is on the wane. Rather, the reverse: there is a pronounced reaction against a progressive penal policy that tends to concentrate attention wholly on actual offenders and their needs for treatment. Only a minority is persuaded of the disutility of punishing offenders (3.9). Even if the 'progressives' were to achieve their ultimate goal of expunging punishment from the penal system, there are grounds for thinking that society would still occasionally use the individual offender for general purposes of declaiming its aversion to grosser anti-social behaviour.

A prime objective of penal sanctions may well be to afford the opportunity for social catharsis, a healthy safety valve for the venting of community spleen against individual social disrupters. Social catharsis involves both recognition of some relief to the wrongdoer's immediate victim (if he survives) and the satisfaction to the general body of moral and God-fearing men of punishment of the wrongdoer. Unless and until catharsis is achieved, a sense of moral outrage remains unassuaged (compare 2.10). Moral contentment is the corollary of this catharsis. To what extent and in what form it is to be reflected in punishment of the offender must depend upon the particular criminal offence and the offender's degree of responsibility for the crime. Here, moral judgments, or at least social value judgments, are inevitable tools for determining penal policy. The crucial question in this area is: to what extent do pronounced penal sanctions need to be executed in practice? Must society's moral indignation be assuaged by knowledge of the offender's actual suffering? This problem is best exemplified by the debate on corporal punishment (3.1 to 3.4).

Quite apart from the pervasive and habitual need for social catharsis, we still cling to the fondly-held belief that social utility is achieved not merely by pronouncing from the Bench the appropriate penal sanction but also by the *example* of its infliction for a purpose other than accommodating a generalised desire for punishment. We believe (or pretend to believe) that only by such judicial action are we (or, at least, others) influenced to keep within the law. There is also embedded in this philosophy a strain of retribution, which depicts punishment as an offender's just deserts for disobeying society's code.

As long as we persist in the unproved (and unprovable?) theory of deterrence, we face the dilemma which we can resolve only by an uneasy compromise. As Professor Hart has observed,[1] penalties which we believe are required as a threat to maintain conformity to the law at its maximum may be too harsh a sanction and tend to convert the offender into a committed professional criminal. The use of measures less severe than are believed necessary for law observance may lower the efficacy and example of punishment on others. This dilemma proceeds upon the assumption that there is some way of measuring, with a degree of accuracy that is sadly lacking in such highly tentative social issues, the amount of punishment that will maximise the extent of conformity from the rest of us. At best, any punishment so motivated is a sop to public opprobrium; at worst, we deceive ourselves as to the efficacy of penal sanctions. If every offender standing convicted in the docks of our criminal courts were on one day to be given uniformly an absolute discharge, would this cause of itself even a trembling of the social equilibrium?

Those who acknowledge the inherent absurdity of the socially-erected dilemma tend to rationalise the resultant compromise by believing that the social influence of the threat and example of imprisonment is often independent of the severity of the punishment. But there is little indication that this attitude is reflected in the judiciary. There are currently two schools of thought: the majority, largely encouraged and controlled by the appellate courts, adopts the uneasy compromise of applying a tariff which supposedly embodies a need to effect maximum conformity (see 3.5) mitigated by the supposed responsibility and social needs of the particular offender. A minority of judges, either overtly or by implication, adopts a posture of social indignation and regards moral guilt as a proper ground for judicial punishment. Mr Justice Fitzjames Stephen's famous dictum, that it is morally right to hate criminals and a proper attitude of mind to treat criminals not with long-suffering charity but open enmity, is not without its modern exponents – Lord Goddard for one. It had a resounding rebuff from Sir Winston Churchill as long ago as 1910 (see 3.8).

The trouble about such an approach is that it is a caricature of the progressive viewpoint. The question is not: does the offender deserve to be punished in proportion to the gravity of his moral blameworthiness, even supposing we can measure the degree of wickedness displayed (though a consensus of commentators about an offender's just desserts might be achieved in most cases)? The dividing point is whether or not the punishment to be exacted will do any good (apart from the neutralising effect of temporary incarceration) both to the offender and to the society of which he is, willy-nilly, a member.

As long, therefore, as we have not dispensed with the belief that punishment is a necessary concomitant of a criminal conviction we are stuck with a choice of penal aims that are often antipathetic. In selecting the penal sanction we will inevitably have to acknowledge social and moral limitations. But moral considerations should never precede the ascertainment of social factors. Moral judgments about social action or inaction, when made without the basis of such information, proceed upon social assumptions that may turn out to be invalid. We need to examine the

---

1. *Punishment and Responsibility*, London, 1968, p.27.

efficacy of the sanction before we can judge the morality of legal enforcement.

3.1 The call for wider corporal punishment (1874)

Return of Names of Public Bodies and Functionaries who have, since the 1st day of January 1885, addressed to the Home Secretary Memorials, Presentments, or other Communications in favour of Legislation for the infliction of Corporal Punishment in cases of Offences under the Criminal Law Amendment Act, 1885,' against Children of less than Thirteen Years of Age, giving Dates and Substance of Recommendations.

Date	Names of Public Bodies or Functionaries, and Nature of their Address to the Home Secretary.	Substance of Recommendations.
8th April 1885	Presentment of Grand Jury of the Court of Quarter Sessions for the North Riding of Yorkshire.	In cases of indecent assaults on children of tender years, flogging to be inflicted at the option of the Court.
30th Oct. 1885	Presentment of Grand Jury of Northumberland at Assizes held at Newcastle-on-Tyne.	Future legislation to provide for the infliction of corporal punishment in cases of carnal knowledge of children under 12, unnatural offences, and indecent assaults on women.
10th Nov. 1885	Presentment of Grand Jury at Yorkshire Assizes (forwarded by Mr Justice Hawkins, who cordially concurred).	In view of the increasing number of outrages and indecent assaults on children of tender years, power should be given to Judge to sentence offenders to some 'additional and more deterrent punishment.' Flogging not expressly named.
18th Oct. 1886	Order of Court of Quarter Sessions for Durham.	Punishment of the lash to be authorised in cases of criminal assaults on girls under 13 years of age.
5th Nov. 1886	Memorial of Justices of the Peace for the Borough of Stockton-on-Tees.	Judges should be authorised to order flogging in addition to any other punishment in cases of criminal assaults on women and children.

11th Nov. 1886	Memorial of the Guardians of the Sunderland Poor Law Union.	Calls for legislation empowering Judges to order the lash in cases of indecent assaults on girls under 13 years of age.
17th Nov. 1886	Resolution passed at a special meeting of Justices of the Peace of the Borough of Gateshead-on-Tyne.	Further powers should be given to inflict flogging for criminal and aggravated assaults upon women and children.
18th Nov. 1886	Resolution of Town Council of Appleby.	Calling for legislation authorizing punishment of the lash in cases of criminal assaults on female children of and under the age of 13 years.
18th Nov. 1886	Resolution passed at a special meeting of the Magistrates of the city of Newcastle-on-Tyne.	Calls for power to be given by the Legislature to Courts of Assize and Quarter Sessions to order, in addition to any other punishment, corporal punishment with the 'cat' on prisoners convicted of rape, having carnal knowledge, and committing indecent assaults on females of or under 13 years of age, and of attempts to commit any of such offences.
13th Dec. 1886	Resolution passed at a special meeting of the Magistrates of the Borough of Berwick-on-Tweed.	Power should be given by the Legislature to Courts of Assize and Quarter Sessions to order (in addition to other punishment), the infliction of corporal punishment with the 'cat' upon prisoners convicted of rape, and committing indecent assaults on females of or under 13 years of age, and of attempts to commit such offences.
25th Jan. 1887	Memorial signed by ten of the Magistrates for the Borough of Jarrow.	Power to be given to the Supreme Court of Justice presided over by one of Her Majesty's Judges to order whipping, in addition to any other penalty in cases of assaults on females.

24th May 1887	Presentment of the Grand Jury, Central Criminal Court.	'The Grand Jury, in view of so many cases coming before them of criminal assaults by fathers upon their own children, feel called upon to express their strong opinion that, if the law permits, the liberal use of the lash ought to be added to any other punishment adjudged.'
1st July 1887	Memorial of the Mayor, on behalf of the Magistrates of the Borough of Tvnemouth.	Her Majesty's Judges to have power to order flogging in addition to any other sentence in cases of offences upon and against women and children under that part of the Criminal Law Amendment Act, 1885, which relates to the protection of women and girls, and their unlawful detention with intent to have carnal knowledge.
11th Mar. 1887	Presentment of Grand Jury of adjourned General Quarter Sessions for Surrey (the Court concurring).	Recommend in cases of outrages on children and unnatural crimes, flogging in addition to imprisonment.
15th Mar. 1888	Presentment of Grand Jury of Northumberland.	Power to be given to Judges at their discretion to order corporal punishment in cases of criminal assaults on children of tender years.

3.2   *Corporal punishment in the 1880s : call by the Judges for its extended use*

Amount of Flogging

By 26 & 27 Vict. c. 44., 50 strokes are allowed as the maximum, but the maximum is never inflicted. Several judges propose to lower it; Brett, J., to 30, Lush, J., to 25, Cockburn, C.J., to 24.

Mellor, J., considers that there ought to be power to order two floggings.

Offences for which it is proposed that Flogging should be authorised

Mellor, J.
(*a*)   Brutal assaults.
(*b*)   Rapes and attempt to commit rape.
(*c*)   Bad cases of indecent assaults on women and female children.

Bramwell, B.
(*a*)   All cases of cruelty, except those to which the sufferer consented.
(*b*)   Assaults to commit rape.
(*c*)   Stack firing.

Amphlett, B.
(*a*)   Assaults involving unlawful and malicious infliction of grievous bodily harm, whether felonies or misdemeanors, and whether causing death or not, and whether on men, women, or children.

Pigott, B.
(*a*)   All cases of felony, or attempts to commit felony, accompanied by brutal violence, and intending to cause and causing actual bodily harm.

Pollock, B.
(*a*)   Assaults with intent to do grievous bodily harm.
(*b*)   Assaults occasioning actual bodily harm, if the person assaulted is a woman or child.
(*c*)   Not indecent assaults.

Cleasby, B.
(*a*)   Assaults causing grievous bodily harm with intent to cause it.
(*b*)   Assaults causing grievous bodily harm.
(*c*)   Assaults causing actual bodily harm, except such assaults are on women.
(*d*)   Indecent assaults on children and rapes on children.

Quain, J.
(*a*)   Assaults of violence, especially those on women and children.

Lush, J.
(*a*)   Assaults occasioning actual bodily harm.
(*b*)   Rapes on children under 10.
(*c*)   Rapes where two or more persons are jointly concerned.
(*d*)   Attempt to throw a train off the rails. 24 & 25 Vict. c. 100. s. 32., 24 & 25 Vict. c. 97. s. 35.
(*e*)   Arson of stacks and farm buildings.

Blackburn, J.
(*a*)   Aggravated or repeated assaults.
(*b*)   Acts of malicious mischief, *e.g.*, stack firing, attempt to throw trains off the rails.

Archibald, J.
(a) Assault causing grievous bodily harm, when committed under circumstances of great brutality.
(b) Rape, or attempt to rape, by two or more persons.

Brett, J.
(a) Brutal assaults, if also cowardly, not, however, if punishment is penal servitude exceeding five years.
(b) Indecent assaults. 24 & 25 Vict. c. 100. ss. 50, 51.

Grove, J.
(a) Assaults which are at once brutal and cowardly, *e.g.*,–
  (1) Assaults on children.
  (2) Indecent assaults.
  (3) Unnatural crimes.
  (4) Unprovoked assaults of men on women.
  (5) Assaults inflicting bodily injury.

Kelly, C.B.
(a) Brutal assaults.

Cockburn, C.J.
(a) Brutal assaults where bodily injury was intended and resulted, not confined to women and children.
(b) Not indecent assaults, unless personal violence attended by bodily injury.

It thus appears that with respect to offences other than those of brutal violence, flogging is considered an appropriate punishment –
*(a) For rapes and attempts to commit rape: by Mellor, J.; Bramwell, B.; Grove, J.
*(b) For rapes, only if on children, or where two or more are concerned: by Lush, J.; Brett, J.
*(c) For rapes only where two or more are concerned: by Archibald, J.
*(d) For rapes and indecent assaults, if on children: by Cleasby, B.
*(e) For bad cases of indecent assaults on women and children: by Mellor, J.; Brett, J.
 (f) For acts of malicious mischief, as stack firing, attempting to upset a train: by Bramwell, B.; Blackburn, J.; Lush, J.

 * Pollock, B., is especially opposed to making these indecent offences punishable by flogging; so is Cockburn, C.J., unless bodily injury is inflicted.
 With respect to brutal assault, corporal punishment is considered by most of the judges an appropriate penalty, especially where the sufferer is a woman or child. Cleasby, B., on the other hand, would exclude flogging where the assault has been on a woman.

3.3   The Cadogan Report

Report of the Departmental Committee on Corporal Punishment, chairman Lord.
Cadogan: it was proposed to enact its recommendations in the Criminal Justice Bill
1938, but owing to the imminence of war the Bill never reached the Statute Book, and
corporal punishment was not abolished until the Criminal Justice Act 1948. It survives, as
an object of considerable recent controversy, on the Isle of Man.

Conclusions

59. After examining all the available evidence, we have been unable to
find any body of facts or figures showing that the introduction of a power of
flogging has produced a decrease in the number of the offences for which it
may be imposed, or that offences for which flogging may be ordered have
tended to increase when little use was made of the power to order flogging
or to decrease when the power was exercised more frequently. We are not
satisfied that corporal punishment has that exceptionally effective influence
as a deterrent which is usually claimed for it by those who advocate its use
as a penalty for adult offenders. We do not, of course, deny that it has some
deterrent effect. All forms of punishment have some deterrent influence, and
it is arguable that the more severe the punishment the greater the deterrent
effect. This alone, however, would not be a sufficient ground for retaining
the existing powers of corporal punishment. If it were, it would also be a
sufficient ground for making corporal punishment a possible penalty for
many other offences. The final test is, not whether corporal punishment has
any deterrent effect, but whether there are offences or classes of offences for
which long sentences of imprisonment or penal servitude are so ineffective
as deterrents that it is necessary, for the protection of society, to provide
whatever additional element of deterrence may be afforded by the further
penalty of corporal punishment.

60. Various suggestions have been made to us regarding the type of
offence for which corporal punishment might be an appropriate penalty.
The Lord Chief Justice was good enough to consult the Judges of the
King's Bench Division on the general question of the powers of superior
courts to order corporal punishment and to furnish, for our information, a
memorandum summarising their views. (The Lord Justice General was also
consulted, but he replied that no sentence of corporal punishment had been
imposed by any Judge of the High Court in Scotland for at least fifty years
and in these circumstances the Scottish Judges did not feel able to express
any views on the questions under consideration by the Committee.) The
memorandum furnished by the Lord Chief Justice showed that the Judges
of the King's Bench Division consider that corporal punishment operates as
a useful deterrent and are of opinion that it is desirable to retain the existing
powers to impose sentences of corporal punishment for garrotting, robbery
with violence, procuring, living on immoral earnings, and importuning by
male persons, and also for offences committed by boys under sixteen years
of age under section 4 of the Criminal Law Amendment Act, 1885. In
addition, the Judges were of opinion that, if it were thought desirable as a
matter of policy to extend the existing powers of whipping, the courts might

be empowered to sentence to corporal punishment male persons of any age convicted on indictment of unlawful carnal knowledge of a girl under thirteen years of age and also, perhaps, persons convicted on indictment of rape.

Other witnesses have made other suggestions for extending the existing powers of corporal punishment. The following is a full list of the additional offences for which it has been suggested that corporal punishment might be an appropriate penalty:— Rape: defilment of girls under thirteen years of age: incest committed by a father with a daughter under sixteen years of age: sodomy or gross indecency committed by older men on young boys: demanding money with menaces: sending or throwing explosive substances and throwing corrosive fluid: serious assaults with razors, bayonets, broken bottles, etc.: serious assaults on wives and children: gross cruelty to animals.

We find difficulty in discerning in this list of miscellaneous offences any common principle which could be accepted as a basis for differentiating between these offences for which corporal punishment is considered an appropriate penalty and those for which it is not. It appears to us that the nearest approach to a common factor in these additional offences for which corporal punishment has been suggested is that they are all, in varying degrees, offences which excite special indignation; and that, to this extent, the suggestion that corporal punishment should be applied to these offences is, in the last analysis, based on a purely retributive principle. The idea that corporal punishment should be used as a special retribution for specially detestable offences has a strong sentimental appeal: but we could not accept it as a safe guide in determining which offences should be made liable to this form of punishment. In our view corporal punishment must be justified by the deterrent, not the retributive, principle: and these suggestions for extending this penalty to fresh offences fail to satisfy the only test which we think it proper to apply — i.e., we have found no evidence to suggest that for these offences long sentences of imprisonment or penal servitude are so ineffective as deterrents that it is essential to add some further penalty for the protection of society.

61. There is the same difficulty in finding any common principle underlying the various offences for which corporal punishment may be imposed under the existing law. These offences have been selected, not by the application of any principle of logic, but merely by historical accident; and in consequence the existing law is full of anomalies. If, for example, in committing a violent rape a man has overcome his victim by seizing her by the throat, he is liable to corporal punishment under the Garrotters Act: but if his violence took the form of beating her on the head he is not liable to be flogged. If in snatching a woman's handbag a man pushes the woman away so that she falls, he is liable to corporal punishment for robbery with violence: but a man who commits a much more serious assault on a woman is not liable to a flogging if he does not rob her. The anomalies of the existing law are so obvious that it is unnecessary for us to dwell on them. It is clear that if corporal punishment were to be retained as a penalty for adult offenders, it would be necessary to sweep away the confused and miscellaneous provisions of the existing law and to build up a new system

based on some more logical principle. None of the witnesses who advocated the retention or extension of corporal punishment was able to put forward any principle which would form a practical basis for differentiating the type of offender for whom corporal punishment would be an appropriate penalty from those for whom it would not be appropriate. The only suggestion made to us on these lines was that corporal punishment should be reserved for cases in which gross and brutal violence had been used in the commission of the offence. In our view, however, even this suggestion is misconceived. We have no reason to believe that men who commit offences involving the use of violence are necessarily less amenable to reformative influences than those who commit other forms of crime. Many persons convicted of offences involving violence are dealt with effectively at the present time by reformative methods. Even in these cases, probation has sometimes been found an effective remedy – for example, we have been impressed by the evidence which we have heard regarding the measure of success achieved by the probation officers at the County of London Sessions in dealing with persons convicted of this type of offence. It is not to be assumed that, because a person has committed an offence involving the use of violence, he is necessarily more susceptible than others to the deterrent effects of corporal punishment and less likely to be deterred by other forms of punishment. In the last resort, the question whether a man is not likely to be deterred except by a sentence of corporal punishment cannot, in our view, be determined by the nature of the offence which he has committed: it turns entirely on the character and disposition of the man, irrespective of his offence. The suggestion that corporal punishment should be reserved for cases of gross and brutal violence is ultimately based, not on the view that persons who commit these offences cannot be effectively deterred by other methods, but rather on the argument that 'violence must be met by violence'. In a debate in the House of Commons in 1900, on a Bill proposing an extended use of corporal punishment, the late Lord Oxford met this argument in the following words: 'I regard the suggestions made in this debate as a revival of the theory, at once fallacious and barbarous, that a man who commits a peculiarly brutal offence should receive a proportionately brutal punishment. I can imagine nothing more repugnant to the most elementary principles of justice and common sense than to say that, because a man has committed a savage offence, those whose duty it is to enforce respect for the law should begin that man's punishment with correspondingly savage treatment.'

3.4 An endorsement of the Cadogan Report

The revival in Britain during the 1950s of the arguments in favour of corporal punishment led to the reference of the subject to the Home Office Advisory Council on the Treatment of Offenders, under the chairmanship of Mr Justice Barry. Its report in November 1960 endorsed the Cadogan Committee's conclusions.

Conclusions

83. In view of the great conflict of opinion on this subject, it would have been surprising if, at the outset of our enquiry, some of us had not thought

that the reintroduction of judicial corporal punishment might be justified as a means of checking the growing increase in crime generally and in offences of hooliganism in particular. That was, in fact, the case, but, having studied the views expressed to us and the available evidence, we consider that the findings of the Cadogan Committee are still valid, and have come unanimously to the conclusion that corporal punishment should not be reintroduced as a judicial penalty in respect of any categories of offences or of offenders.

84. Most of the arguments and considerations that have caused us to come to this conclusion are discussed in the earlier parts of this report. We think it may be convenient, however, if we summarise briefly here those that have carried most weight with us.

85. First, it is clear that there is a marked cleavage of opinion on the question whether or not judicial corporal punishment should be reintroduced, not only among ordinary members of the public but also among those who, because of their knowledge and experience, are better able to express informed opinions on this matter. There is also a marked divergence of view, both among those who are opposed to judicial corporal punishment and those who favour it, on particular aspects of the problem. There is, however, a measure of agreement that the reintroduction of this penalty would be a retrograde step, although we are not sure that it is generally realised quite how retrogressive it would be. Many people appear to think that before its abolition by the Criminal Justice Act, 1948, corporal punishment was available for a wide variety of offences, and that as only twelve years have elapsed since that Act was passed it would be quite reasonable now to regard the abolition of judicial corporal punishment as having been an experiment and to decide that, the experiment having been a failure, the provision should be revoked. In fact, between 1861 and 1948 judicial corporal punishment was available for a narrowly limited range of offences, and for adults was in practice used only for offences of robbery with violence. The advocates of reintroduction, however, do not wish to limit this penalty to the same offences as before, but to make it available either for offences of all kinds or at any rate for all offences involving violence against the person – in particular those committed by young hooligans. If that were to be done it would mean putting the clock back not twelve years but a hundred years.

86. Secondly, the present demand for the reintroduction of judicial corporal punishment seems to be limited to this country. Other countries which have dispensed with it show no desire to reintroduce it, though many of them are faced with problems similar to those that exist here. The demand for it in this country is often the subject of adverse comment abroad, and its reintroduction would be certain to damage our reputation as the country which has been a pioneer in the use of enlightened methods of penal treatment.

87. Thirdly, we consider that, in these circumstances, the reintroduction of judicial corporal punishment could be justified only if there was a reasonable assurance that it would substantially reduce crime and afford real protection to potential victims. We think that there cannot be any such assurance. There is no evidence that corporal punishment is an especially

effective deterrent either to those who have received it or to others. We recognise that in a limited number of cases a sentence of corporal punishment would deter both the offender who received it and other potential offenders; but the same could be said of many forms of drastic and severe punishment which have long since been abolished as affronting the conscience of a civilised community. We are not satisfied that the numbers likely to be deterred are sufficient to justify the reintroduction of a form of punishment that has the manifold disadvantages discussed elsewhere in this report.

88. Fourthly, judicial corporal punishment is out of line with modern penal methods and would militate against the success of reformative treatment, such as probation or borstal training.

89. Fifthly, many of the new methods contemplated by the Criminal Justice Act, 1948, have not yet been fully tried, and they are to be greatly developed in the immediate future. In particular, many more detention centres are to be made available. It is, therefore, too soon to conclude that these methods, and others that are to be introduced (such as those for dealing with young offenders that we recently recommended) are inadequate to deal with the problems which have led to the demand for the reintroduction of corporal punishment.

90. Finally, there are a number of practical objections and difficulties ... which strengthen the case against judicial corporal punishment. The most important of these objections is the delay that must occur between the commission of the offence and the infliction of the punishment. This would be particularly harmful to juvenile offenders.

91. We recognise that if our conclusion is accepted many people will feel that, unless alternative measures to check the continuing increase in crime are introduced, the present situation will become worse, and while, as we have explained ... we think that this may not be so grave as is generally supposed, we agree that there is cause for concern. It is no part of our task to suggest alternative measures, but we think it right to mention two that we brought to our attention by many of our witnesses and correspondents.

(a) We were impressed by the argument that the greatest deterrent to crime is not the fear of punishment but the certainty of detection. This can only be achieved by the provision of a fully staffed and efficient police force in all areas. We feel sure that this consideration will be borne in mind by the Royal Commission on the Police in the course of their deliberations.

(b) We have found a widespread feeling that the courts sometimes appear to deal surprisingly leniently with offenders convicted, often not for the first time, of offences of violence. We recognise that there are usually good reasons, not apparent to those who do not know the full circumstances of the case, for what may appear to be a lenient sentence. We have no doubt, however, that there are cases in which a severe and exemplary punishment is often salutary; and we consider that the existing powers of the courts are adequate to meet this need.

92. We hope that our own recommendations for the treatment of young offenders will be implemented before long, and that the various methods of treatment contemplated by the Criminal Justice Act, 1948, will be fully

developed. We are convinced that these methods are likely to prove more effective in the long run than negative methods such as corporal punishment.

3.5 Sentencing: the Judges' tariff

The sentencing policy of the courts is recognised as containing an element of a tariff of prescribed punishments. Only a notional tariff exists, but R.M. Jackson uncovered the following remarkable memorandum on 'Normal Punishments', prepared by the judges in 1901.

The extent of divergence in the assessment of punishment by Judges of the High Court, sitting in Courts of criminal jurisdiction, has been much exaggerated. In almost every class of crime, and pre-eminently in the case of manslaughter, the Judge, in fixing the punishment, has to discriminate between widely different degrees of moral culpability, and to weigh an infinite variety of circumstances and situations. The Legislature has wisely provided a large latitude in punishment. Justice demands, at times, that this latitude should be boldly used; and demands constantly the use of it in a slighter degree. Any attempt to mete out punishment to offenders in the same class of crime at a rigidly uniform rate could result only in the frequent perpetration of injustice. If due allowance is made for these essential considerations, there is nothing in the sentences of Judges of the High Court of Justice which are recorded in the criminal statistics (apart from the question of the advisability of flogging as a punishment) to indicate the existence of any established difference of principle or of general practice in the sentences of Judges of the High Court of Justice.

At the same time, the Judges of the King's Bench Division are agreed that it would be convenient and of public advantage in regard to certain classes of crime to come to an agreement, or, at least to an approximate agreement, as to what may be called a 'normal' standard of punishment: a standard of punishment, that is to say, which should be assumed to be properly applicable, unless the particular case under consideration presented some special features of aggravation or of extenuation.

They have, accordingly, considered carefully the Report of a Committee which was early in last year entrusted with the duty of investigating this subject, as well as the written comments upon that Report which have been made by Members of the Bench, and a scheme of punishment in certain cases drawn up by Mathew, J.; and the result of their deliberation is embodied in this Memorandum. It will be seen that in some cases it has not been found practicable to do more than recommend a range of punishment within certain limits.

I. Offences against property, without violence

The inclination of the Court towards leniency of punishment which has marked the last 20 years has, on the whole, been justified by results.

But, as the Reports published annually by the Home Office and the Statistics of Crime which they contain seem clearly to indicate, the leniency has gone too far in regard to those who are habitual criminals. In the case of such criminals, alike for the protection of property and as the best chance of reclaiming the offender the Judges are of opinion that, as is indicated below, a sentence of penal servitude should, as a general rule, be passed upon such persons as have already been convicted of similar offences and appear to be seeking regularly to make a livelihood out of crime.

It is, however, carefully to be borne in mind that there are offenders who have been previously convicted of dishonesty who are not professional criminals; and the mere repetition at intervals of acts of dishonesty ought not to be treated as in itself suffcient to stamp the convict as a member of the class to which reference has just been made. There are, for example, persons who from one cause or another have been temporarily disabled from earning wages and yield to the pressure of want; and again, persons who, although leading a generally honest life of work, do at times commit acts of dishonesty, owing to a special temptation, or, as often happens, under the influence of drink. For such occasional criminals imprisonment* seems to us to be, as a rule, sufficient punishment.

Juvenile offenders under 16 years of age should not be sentenced to any term of imprisonment unless there has been a previous conviction.

Larceny
  (*a*) *In the case of a first offence:*
      For juveniles under 16, no term of imprisonment.
      For adults, a discharge upon recognisances, or a short term of imprisonment.
  (*b*) *In the case of subsequent convictions:*
      If intervals of honest conduct, imprisonment for from 6 to 12 months.
      If the prisoner whilst at liberty has been making crime his source of livelihood, penal servitude from 3 to 5 years.

Embezzlement
  (*a*) *In the case of a first offence:*
      Same treatment as for convictions for larceny (*supra*).
  (*b*) *In the case of subsequent convictions:*
      In ordinary cases imprisonment, 4 to 12 months.
      If the offence is systematic, and/or the amount embezzled is large, penal servitude, 3 to 5 years.

False Pretences
  (*a*) *In the case of a first offence:*
      Same treatment as for convictions for larceny (*supra*).
  (*b*) *In the case of subsequent convictions:*
      Imprisonment, 4 to 12 months. If the prisoner has been getting his living by crime, penal servitude, 3 to 5 years.

Forgery
  (*a*) *For first offences, when the offence is akin to larceny, or obtaining by false*

* *Note.* – The term 'imprisonment' in this Memorandum is to be understood as covering both imprisonment with, and imprisonment without, hard labour.

pretence, as, e.g., forging an order for goods or an endorsement for a cheque:
Same treatment as for convictions for larceny (*supra*).
(*b*) *In the case of subsequent convictions:*
Where the offence is of the same sort and is not effected systematically, imprisonment, 6 to 12 months.
Where the offence is effected systematically, penal servitude, 3 to 5 years.

Forgery or uttering of Bank Notes, Bills or Deeds, or where there is a Conspiracy to Defraud and/or to a Large Amount by Forged Documents.
Penal servitude, 3 to 10 years.

Fraudulent Personation of Pensioners
In the case of adult convicts, imprisonment, 3 to 9 months.
In the case of convicts under 16, same treatment as in case of larceny (*supra*).

Post Office Cases (Stealing of or from Letters)
Imprisonment, 8 to 15 months.

Fraudulent Personation of Owners of Stocks or Public Funds, or of Personal Representatives of Deceased Persons
Penal servitude, 7 to 12 years.

II.   *Offences against property, with violence to property*
Burglary, Housebreaking, Shopbreaking, &c.

These offences, as is stated in the official Home Office Report, are mostly the work of professional criminals, and, where the offence is of a serious kind and is not a first offence, the normal sentence should be one of penal servitude, 3 to 5 years. But it is important to bear in mind that an offence which really differs little or nothing in point of gravity from thieving may technically constitute in law one or other of these offences, and may be set down as such in the Judge's private Calendar at the Assizes if the convict is charged with a subsequent offence. A burglary, a housebreaking, or a shopbreaking, may be really a petty offence against property, and should, in such a case, be treated, in the matter of punishment, as an ordinary larceny would be treated.

Arson
Stack burning, from 12 months' imprisonment to 3 years' penal servitude.
Setting fire to house, penal servitude, 5 years; and, where human life is endangered, 10 years.

III.   *Other offences relating to property*
Coining or Uttering Base Coin
On first conviction, imprisonment, 1 to 6 months.
On second conviction, imprisonment, 9 to 12 months.
On a third conviction, penal servitude, 5 to 7 years.

IV. *Offences against property, with violence to the person*
Robbery with Violence
After a previous conviction for a similar offence, penal servitude; and if serious bodily hurt has been inflicted, or the crime has been committed by several in concert, for a period not less than 5 years.

V. *Offences against the person*
Manslaughter
Where the death arises from an assault, and there is no intent to kill, the person should be punished as if he had been convicted for the infliction of such an injury as might reasonably be expected to result from the assault.

Attempts to Murder where Life is Endangered
Penal servitude, 7 to 12 years.

Felonious Wounding or Inflicting Grievous Bodily Harm with Intent, &c.
Imprisonment for 18 months, or penal servitude, not exceeding 5 years.

Shooting with Intent, &c.
Penal servitude, 5 to 10 years.

Administering Poison
The same.

Throwing Vitriol
Penal servitude, not less than 3 years.

Assaults, other than those above-mentioned, causing Bodily Harm, or Unlawful Wounding
Imprisonment, 6 to 18 months.

Rape on Females over 13 Years of Age
A period of from 5 to 7 years' penal servitude gives a reasonable range of punishment; to be increased if there are accompanying circumstances of aggravation, such, e.g., as rape by a gang or by a parent or a master, or with brutal violence, and to be reduced if there are extenuating circumstances.

[Mathew, J., has suggested a more detailed normal scale, as follows:

Where temptation and no great violence, imprisonment for 18 months, or penal servitude for 3 years. Where violent assault, penal servitude for 5 years. When done by several in concert, penal servitude for 10 years.]

It is agreed, however, that rape is an offence which covers varying degrees of wickedness, and the just punishment for which requires varying degrees of severity.

Rape on Children under 13 Years of Age, and Felonious Carnal Knowledge under the Criminal Law Amendment Act, 1885
If by a parent, in the absence of exceptional brutality or intimidation or cruelty, penal servitude 10 years.

If by an adult stranger, penal servitude for 7 years.

If by a youth under 18, and upon a child nearly 13 years of age, and with consent in fact, imprisonment for 3 to 12 months.

If by a youth over 18 years of age, under the same circumstances, imprisonment from 12 to 18 months.

If the convict is under 15 years of age, and there is no evidence of earlier wrongdoing of the like kind, and there has been no grave physical injury to the sufferer, no imprisonment, but a whipping, as authorised by the Criminal Law Amendment Act, 1885, s. 4.

[Wills, J., in cases of assaults of this nature, committed by fathers upon their children, approves of 12 to 16 years' penal servitude as a normal standard of punishment; and where helpless children have been forced by strangers, approves of 10 to 15 years' penal servitude as a normal standard of punishment.]

Indecent Assault
Imprisonment, 1 to 12 months.

Misdemeanour under the Criminal Law Amendment Act
Imprisonment, 1 to 12 months.

Procuring Abortion
5 years' penal servitude.

Sodomy
As to the punishment of this crime there is some difference of opinion amongst the Judges of the King's Bench Division. The recommendation of the Report, of which the majority approve, has suggested, in the case of an adult convict, that, where there is no violence and the other party is also adult, a sentence of penal servitude for 3 years, would, in the absence of special circumstances, be sufficent; that in the case of juvenile offenders under 16 years of age, the punishment should not exceed 6 months' imprisonment; and that, when the offence is committed by an adult upon a youthful and unwilling victim, a punishment of penal servitude up to a maximum of 10 years would be just. In the opinion of Wills, Wright, Bruce, and Phillimore, JJ., this scale of punishment is too low.

VI.   *Other offences*
Bestiality
The punishment for a first offence should not, except under very special circumstances, exceed 12 months' imprisonment, and if the offender is not over 16 years of age should not exceed 6 months' imprisonment.

[Wright, J., and Phillimore, J., are of opinion that this scale of punishment is unnecessarily high.]

Bigamy
If woman not deceived and/or prosecution vindictive, imprisonment not exceeding 6 months.

If woman deceived, imprisonment from 12 to 18 months, or penal servitude, in rather worse cases, from 3 to 5 years.

[Wright, J. suggests a normal sentence of 6 months' imprisonment when the woman is not deceived, and 3 years' penal servitude where the woman is deceived. Bruce, J., suggests 3 months as the minimum sentence.]

Perjury
Generally, imprisonment from 3 to 12 months.
Where a deliberate attempt to injure character, or to defraud, or to pervert justice, penal servitude from 5 to 7 years.

Concealment of Birth
Imprisonment for 2 months.
[Suggested by Bruce, J.]

Flogging as a punishment

As to the wisdom of inflicting in any case this form of punishment, there is a considerable divergence of opinion. But it is, at all events, the decided view of almost all, if not all, of the Judges of the King's Bench Division that, if flogging forms part of a sentence, (1) it should be only a single flogging, and (2) that it should be administered at the commencement of the term of punishment; and they are also of opinion that its infliction should be confined to cases where the criminal has either inflicted serious bodily hurt, or has made the assault in concert with others.

Grantham, Wright, Ridley, Bigham, Darling, Phillimore, and Bucknill JJ., are in favour of the extension of this form of punishment to cases of the grosser criminal assaults on women and children. Lawrance J., is of opinion that flogging is a punishment which might advantageously be adopted in some cases of assaults on children, but that, unless it were universally adopted it would be unwise to extend it to such cases. Ridley, J., has suggested that, wherever a person under the age of 17 years has been convicted of a criminal assault under Section 4 of the Criminal Law Amendment Act, 1885, the legislature should empower the Judge to order a whipping with the birch-rod in lieu of imprisonment, and Channell, J., is in favour of this suggestion.

(Signed) Alverstone, C.J.
(Signed) J.C. Mathew
(Signed) Alfred Wills
(Signed) Wm. Grantham
(Signed) J.C. Lawrance
(Signed) N.S. Wright
(Signed) Gainsford Bruce
(Signed) William R. Kennedy
(Signed) Edward Ridley
(Signed) John C. Bigham
(Signed) Charles Darling
(Signed) A.M. Channell
(Signed) Walter G.F. Phillimore
(Signed) T.T. Bucknill

Notes on the memorandum on normal punishments, by Bruce, J.

Larceny
   (a) In the case of a first offence, for juveniles under 16, no term of imprisonment.
I do not think that this should be laid down as a general rule. The Prison
Commissioners have lately made special arrangements for the training and
discipline of boys under 16, and I believe that there are many cases where it
would be distinctly mischievous to allow an act of theft to pass without
punishment. In many cases it is important to remove the boy from the
influence of vicious parents for a time, and it is not always a good thing to
send a boy to a reformatory for a long term. The Memorandum says
nothing about whipping as an alternative to imprisonment in the case of
boys under 16. In some cases, whipping is, I think, the proper punishment,
but I cannot regard it as a substitute for imprisonment in all cases.

Forgery
   For first offences of forging an order for goods or an endorsement to a cheque.
I do not agree that as a general rule a person who is for the first time
convicted of an offence of this kind should be discharged upon
recognisances. I think forgery is a much more serious crime than larceny,
and in the case of forgery I think only special circumstances can render a
discharge upon recognisances a right determination.

Manslaughter
I do not agree that an assault that causes death is to be punished just in
the same way as the assault would have been punished if death had not
ensued. The loss of life is, I think, always an element to be taken into
consideration in awarding punishment.

Felonious Wounding with Intent – Shooting with Intent, &c.
The intent is the essence of the offence, whether committed by means of
one instrument or another. I doubt whether it is right to make the
punishment for *wounding* with intent so much lighter than for *shooting* with
intent.

Perjury
I do not understand the force of the phrase *to pervert justice*; all perjury
tends to pervert justice. I suppose the phrase *to defraud* means to obtain gain
or advantage personal to the accused.

Concealment of Birth
What is the opinion of the Judges on this matter? I think we ought to be
able to agree upon a normal sentence.

3.6   An eighteenth-century attack on imprisonment for debt

Samuel Johnson *(see item 2.2) contributed the following article on imprisonment for
debt to* The Idler *in 1761. Imprisonment of debtors by their creditors was abolished in*

*1869, but it was another one hundred years before the Administration of Justice Act-1970
ended imprisonment for failure to pay a judgment debt.*

As I was passing lately under one of the gates of this city, I was struck with
horror by a rueful cry, which summoned me *to remember the poor Debtors.*

The wisdom and justice of the *English* laws are, by *Englishmen* at least,
loudly celebrated; but scarcely the most zealous admirers of our Institutions
can think that law wise, which when men are capable of work, obliges them
to beg; or just, which exposes the liberty of one to the passions of another.

The prosperity of a people is proportionate to the number of hands and
minds usefully employed. To the community sedition is a fever, corruption
is a gangrene, and idleness an atrophy. Whatever body, and whatever
society, wastes more than it acquires, must gradually decay; and every
being that continues to be fed, and ceases to labour, takes away something
from the public stock.

The confinement, therefore, of any man in the sloth and darkness of a
prison, is a loss to the nation, and no gain to the Creditor. For of the
multitudes who are pining in those cells of misery, a very small part is
suspected of any fraudulent act by which they retain what belongs to others.
The rest are imprisoned by the wantonness of pride, the malignity of
revenge, or the acrimony of disappointed expectation.

If those, who thus rigorously exercise the power which the law has put
into their hands, be asked, why they continue to imprison those whom they
know to be unable to pay them: One will answer, that his Debtor once lived
better than himself; another, that his wife looked above her neighbours, and
his children went in silk cloaths to the dancing school; and another, that he
pretended to be a joker and a wit. Some will reply, that if they were in debt
they should meet with the same treatment; some, that they owe no more
than they can pay, and need therefore give no account of their actions. Some
will confess their resolution, that their Debtors shall rot in jail; and some
will discover, that they hope, by cruelty, to wring the payment from their
friends.

The end of all civil regulations is to secure private happiness from private
malignity; to keep individuals from the power of one another; but this end is
apparently neglected, when a man, irritated with loss, is allowed to be the
judge of his own cause, and to assign the punishment of his own pain; when
the distinction between guilt and unhappiness, between casualty and
design, is intrusted to eyes blind with interest, to understandings depraved
by resentment.

Since Poverty is punished among us as a crime, it ought at least to be
treated with the same lenity as other crimes; the offender ought not to
languish, at the will of him whom he has offended, but to be allowed some
appeal to the justice of his country. There can be no reason, why any Debtor
should be imprisoned, but that he may be compelled to payment; and a
term should therefore be fixed, in which the Creditor should exhibit his
accusation of concealed property. If such property can be discovered, let it
be given to the Creditor; if the charge is not offered, or cannot be proved, let
the prisoner be dismissed.

Those who made the laws, have apparently supposed, that every deficiency of payment is the crime of the Debtor. But the truth is, that the Creditor always shares the act, and often more than shares the guilt of improper trust. It seldom happens that any man imprisons another but for debts which he suffered to be contracted, in hope of advantage to himself, and for bargains in which he proportioned his profit to his own opinion of the hazard; and there is no reason, why one should punish the other, for a contract in which both concurred.

Many of the inhabitants of prisons may justly complain of harder treatment. He that once owes more than he can pay, is often obliged to bribe his Creditor to patience, by increasing his debt. Worse and worse commodities, at a higher and higher price, are forced upon him; he is impoverished by compulsive traffick, and at last overwhelmed, in the common receptacles of misery, by debts, which, without his own consent, were accumulated on his head. To the relief of this distress, no other objection can be made, but that by an easy dissolution of debts, fraud will be left without punishment, and imprudence without awe, and that when insolvency shall be no longer punishable, credit will cease.

The motive to credit, is the hope of advantage. Commerce can never be at a stop, while one man wants what another can supply; and credit will never be denied, while it is likely to be repaid with profit. He that trusts one whom he designs to sue, is criminal by the act of trust; the cessation of such insidious traffick is to be desired, and no reason can be given why a change of the law should impair any other.

We see nation trade with nation, where no payment can be compelled. Mutual convenience produces mutual confidence, and the Merchants continue to satisfy the demands of each other, though they have nothing to dread but the loss of trade.

It is vain to continue an institution, which experience shews to be ineffectual. We have now imprisoned one generation of Debtors after another, but we do not find that their numbers lessen. We have now learned, that rashness and imprudence will not be deterred from taking credit; let us try whether fraud and avarice may be more easily restrained from giving it.

3.7 The Payne Report

The Report of the Departmental Committee on the Enforcement of Judgment Debts *(chairman Mr Justice Payne) recommended the abolition of imprisonment for debt and, by a majority, also recommended the abolition of imprisonment for the enforcement of maintenance obligations. The recommendations were substantially enacted in the Administration of Justice Act 1970.*

1098. (i) The theological, legal and economic sanctions which used to buttress marriage have in our own day dissolved into ties of habit or affection. Just as debtors pledge their property and not their persons to their creditors, so husbands and wives can only pledge their loyalty in marriage. We reject the suggestion that maintenance default be made a crime and we recommend the abolition of imprisonment for defaulters. We do not think that the policeman and the prison officer are appropriate agents for the regulation of family life because they bring penal sanctions into a social area where compensation and restitution are the only relevant and tolerable aims, and moral censure the only proper method of expressing disapproval. Citizens in 1969 do not think of failure to discharge matrimonial obligations as criminal behaviour and to treat it as such by imprisoning offenders in the absence of supporting public sentiment damages the law and degrades marriage.

1099. (ii) Some of our colleagues look forward to a time when the new system has been established and has shown that the payment of maintenance might be enforced without the sanction of committal; of course we should then recommend its abolition ... (section 2, paragraph 1068).

We have explained why we think the imprisonment of maintenance defaulters or of civil debtors is morally capricious, economically wasteful, socially harmful, administratively burdensome and juridically wrong. We wish it abolished forthwith. Legal history records many dire prognostications of abolishing this or that penalty or final sanction. The dangers of relying upon arguments which stress the present and practical importance of particular forms of deterrent threat may be underlined by recalling the 18th Century judge who remarked, in passing sentence of death: 'You are to be hanged not because you have stolen a sheep, but in order that others may not steal sheep'. The results of hesitancy in grasping the nettle of legal reform in this field may be illustrated by recalling the headings under which Bentham recorded his views on imprisonment for debt in 1778. They were: 'its inaptitude as an instrument of compulsion'; 'its inaptitude, applied as it is, as an instrument of punishment'; and 'its needlessness demonstrated by experience'.

3.8   National character and public attitudes to crime: the Churchillian view

Winston Churchill *(1874-1965): Churchill was speaking in the House of Commons in 1910 on Government policy towards the use of prisons.*

We must not forget that when every material improvement has been effected in prisons, when the temperature has been rightly adjusted, when the proper food to maintain health and strength has been given, when the doctors, chaplains, and prison visitors have come and gone, the convict stands deprived of everything that a free man calls life. We must not forget that all these improvements, which are sometimes salves to our consciences, do not change that position. The mood and temper of the public in regard to the treatment of crime and criminals is one of the most unfailing tests of the civilisation of any country. A calm and dispassionate recognition of the rights of the accused against the State, and even of convicted criminals against the State, a constant heart-searching by all charged with the duty of punishment, a desire and eagerness to rehabilitate in the world of industry all those who have paid their dues in the hard coinage of punishment, tireless efforts towards the discovery of curative and regenerating processes, and an unfaltering faith that there is a treasure, if you can only find it, in the heart of every man – these are the symbols which in the treatment of crime and criminals mark and measure the stored-up strength of a nation, and are the sign and proof of the living virtue in it.

3.9   The reformer's dilemma

Hugh J. Klare *was, for two decades until 1971, the distinguished secretary of the Howard League for Penal Reform, during which period that organisation moved from being an effective pressure group to being a sounding board for progressive penal policies at the Home Office. The article reproduced here, 'Striking a Balance in the Fight Against Crime', poses the dilemma for the penal reformer in the next two decades.*

The view of crime and punishment outlined by Mr John Sparrow (*The Times*, Feb. 24, 1970) is held by many people – probably by the majority. It was recently re-expressed when a committee of lawyers asked for 'demeaning' punishment. It was most starkly put by the eminent jurist Sir James Fitzjames Stephen in 1883 when he wrote that 'it is morally right to hate criminals' and went on to suggest that punishment should be informed by this feeling. What follows is not so much an attempt to counter the arguments which lead to such opinions, but to offer a reasoned account of another view.

This takes as its starting point the notion that society must be protected from all violent and dangerous offenders; not only from murderers but from all who ruthlessly pursue criminal activities. A second but equally important notion is respect for the human personality. A democratic and civilised society must constantly struggle to achieve the appropriate balance between what is right for society and what is right for the individual.

The fight against crime must reflect this balance and also take into account what is now known about the nature and origins of criminal behaviour. To take the last point first, there is a constant need to examine, develop, refine and evaluate social strategies capable of reducing criminogenic processes in society. Following the lives and careers of a large number of children in detail gives us clues. For we can then begin to see what, in terms of background and personality, distinguishes those who become delinquent from those who do not. The study of high delinquency areas also yields valuable information. This is a large subject which must be patiently pursued. We are a long way from being sure about the priorities of preventive policies though some seem obvious enough.

Such work is long-term. For short-term crime prevention, we must have an effective police force; the speedy administration of justice; and well-informed courts. This leads on to punishment and the need for a penal system which can, at one end, provide secure but humane facilities for those from whom society must be protected for a very long time; and, at the other, rehabilitative techniques designed to reduce the chances of a return to crime.

Police officers have recently had a pay award and recruitment is being stepped up. But efficiency had already increased. The proportion of offences cleared up by the police was 40.2 per cent in 1966. By 1968 it had risen to 41.9 per cent despite the fact that the number of indictable offences had gone up by nearly 10 per cent in the same period. Patently some progress has already been made. Much more remains to be done, particularly by methods such as the computerisation of fingerprints.

A word in parenthesis about violence. This is going up steeply and worries everyone. The problem must nevertheless be seen in proportion. Crimes against the person still constitute less than $1\frac{1}{2}$ per cent of all indictable offences. Included is anything from murder, manslaughter, wounding and assault to endangering railway passengers or abandoning children under two. (Woundings usually occur as a result of brawls. That is how members of a slum culture settle a conflict – they do not have recourse to lawyers.) The clear-up rate for crimes against the person is half as high again as for that of all other indictable offences taken together. That is no reason to be complacent. The strictest possible control of firearms, perhaps including stiff minimum sentences, should also be applied.

We must have speedy justice. It is not unusual now for accused persons to have to wait three, four or even five months in custody before their guilt or innocence is decided in a Court of Assize or Quarter Sessions. A royal commission under Lord Beeching has recommended the reorganisation of these courts.[2] The implementation of these recommendations will reduce waiting time.

We must have knowledgeable courts. They must decide which punishment fits the crime as well as the criminal. Too great a leniency is as wrong as too much severity. The courts have to express the disapprobation of society. It would be a mistake, both for the offender and for society, if magistrates attempted to be social workers. It might even be bad for the magistrates themselves – self-indulgence can easily masquerade as mercy. But they must have a knowledge of the penal system, they must understand local conditions and have sufficient information on the offender to see him and his crime in context. Finally, they have to bear in mind the sentences that other courts impose in similar circumstances.

Where the view here put forward differs sharply from Mr Sparrow's and others is in its concept of the penal system. 'Offenders', wrote the late Sir Lionel Fox, Chairman of the Prison Commission, 'are sent to prison *as* a punishment and not *for* punishment'. Those inside consist of a minority of professional criminals and a majority of people who are failures in life and failures in crime. Many of them come from a background of social and psychological deprivation. Deterrence, which works well for the haves, works most uncertainly for those who never have had a stake in society. The boy who fails after approved school may 'graduate' to borstal with some pride. His reference group is other young offenders. When men were still being flogged, some would show their scars at the drop of a hat: they were like medals.

Many prisoners are deeply convinced of their own worthlessness. They may have grown up among that rough lot at the end of the street, despised by the rest. They may have been carelessly conceived and uncaringly

2. Cmnd. 4153 of 1969; substantially implemented by the Courts Act 1971.

brought up. Perhaps they were illegitimate or more subtly rejected. Overprotection, too, can unfit a child and yet make him feel the world owes him a living. But social workers or psychiatrists, though they may discover such information, do not undervalue individual responsibility. On the contrary, some of the treatment methods they use, such as case-work and psychotherapy, are specifically designed to widen the area of choice, to increase inner freedom and to strengthen the sense of personal responsibility.

Prison deprives offenders of their liberty. It should not also take away from them what little dignity and self-respect they may possess. Work should not be demeaning but constructive and, where possible, socially useful. Prison officers must fulfil their custodial duties. But they, too, need the chance to be positive, to enter into relationships, to be helpful, to take pride in their job. There are, of course, some explosively violent or fiercely manipulative prisoners whose management is immensely difficult. For them we need small units, a high complement of hand-picked staff, great social skill.

But prisoners must not be humiliated and it is morally wrong to ask staff to impose such a regime. Just as it is wrong to pay someone to kill people, not in self defence but in cold blood, and on our behalf. But Mr Sparrow is right: this is a minority view. It has prevailed here and in other democracies. As crime and unrest increases, as it will for complex social reasons, such a view may come under ever greater pressure in the next decade or two. It cannot survive at all under repressive governments and in the dictatorships of left or right.

3.10   The morality of war crimes trials

Judith N. Shklar *(see 1.13) wrote on the difficult philosophical problems arising out of the attempts to deal judicially with war crimes.*

A national ideology as law: Tokyo
If the legal basis of the charge of waging aggressive war was not very solid, relying on such a general expression of sentiment as the Kellogg-Briand Pact, it was no more and no less ephemeral than that of all the other charges. It is only the future futility of this part of the 'codification' of international law and the fact that it was a charge that the defense was not allowed to discuss fully, that is objectionable. At Tokyo there were, however, problems which did not arise at Nuremberg. First of all, it is doubtful whether a trial as a legal drama could have had any great political effect in a non-European country so lacking in legalistic traditions. Secondly, the war in the East was one that could not be easily discussed in terms of proximate causality, which Nazism had made possible, indeed sensible, at Nuremberg. Lastly, the American prosecutor at Tokyo, Mr Keenan, unlike Justice Jackson, chose to put his case in natural law terms.

What could a trial teach the Japanese? What political traditions could it restore? None. The 'situational ethics' of the Japanese are inherently unlegalistic. An acceptance of each situation as demanding specific ethical responses and a near-fatalism in matters of personal behaviour have long acted against government by general rules and personal responsibility to such norms. Until the war personal conflicts were rarely resolved by a resort to courts; they were handled informally by local worthies, who made communal cohesion, rather than what is due to the individual claimant, the main object of conciliation. To see the deep roots that legalism and trials have in Western culture one need think only of the part which legal imagery plays in literature, in metaphor, and in religious discourse of every kind. The court of love, the court of conscience, the trial of wits, the court of honour, Judgment Day – how much these phrases tell us about ourselves! How many trial scenes appear in dramas and novels! How central to our everyday speech and to our imagination is the picture of a contest between diametrically opposed wills, judged according to some general rule! Even fate as we think of it behaves legalistically. The trial, the supreme legalistic act, has served us with an image around which we have structured a vast variety of experiences – ethical, religious, and aesthetic. Of all this there is no trace in Japan. The result is that a trial could not and did not dramatize anything for the Japanese. The general view was that it was a bit of a bore, but that the conquerors were behaving as one would expect conquerors to behave. They were responding to their situation, and so were the defeated leaders now on trial. There was no great sympathy for the latter, and no interest in the legalistic gymnastics of the former. The defendants themselves appear to have had much difficulty in understanding the trial, refusing to accept the extremely competent advice of their American counsel, preferring to follow their own legally irrelevant patterns of thought. Nevertheless, it would be quite erroneous to say that the Tokyo trial was an outrage – it was merely a complete dud.

4

Human Sexuality

Sex is a focal element in the debate on law and morality. Indeed, in popular parlance, the word 'morality' is often used synonymously with 'sexual morality'. We will encounter sexual elements in such issues as contraception (Chapter 5) abortion (Chapter 6) and obscenity (Chapter 7). The present chapter is concerned almost exclusively with the debate about the extent to which criminal penalties should be used to regulate sexual behaviour regarded as 'deviant' or 'perverted'.

Religious fundamentalists can find Biblical authority to condemn almost every kind of sexual activity which is not devoted exclusively to the procreation of children in wedlock. Societies with predominantly secular value systems tend to draw a firm distinction between crime and sin – to apply John Stuart Mill's principles, the State should regulate only that sexual activity which does measurable harm to third parties. But where is the line to be drawn; how is 'harm' to be defined and measured; and on whose shoulders should the responsibility rest for deciding these questions?

There is a general consensus that the concept of criminality based on 'harm' requires the State to protect those incapable of protecting themselves – certainly from forcible sexual advances, but also from 'corruption'. The prohibition of rape clearly falls into the former category. The prevention of corruption (particularly of the young) is clearly written into laws against obscenity (see Chapter 7). However, preserving the sexual innocence of young people extends to laws which hold that *all* sexual contacts between persons below a certain age are criminal *per se*. The arbitrariness of drawing a line at an 'age of consent' is illustrated by the varying points at which the line has been drawn in different societies and at different periods. But it is often mitigated in practice by more or less flexible attitudes adopted by prosecuting authorities and by the courts.

The 'corruption' element in sexual-criminal jurisprudence is founded, not merely upon a 'protective' argument, but also upon an implicitly Devlinite view that a challenge to the morality of the 'average man' is a threat to the entire social order. This argument is difficult to disentangle from the historically quite separate (though not unrelated) arguments about sin. The origins of criminal sanctions against sexual behaviour are frequently scriptural, while the implicit or explicit justification for retaining them is usually a fear of possible social disintegration. Social order is seen by some as being in a state of delicate equilibrium, needing only a slight nudge to precipitate society into an abyss of chaos and a hopelessly lost identity.

The divergence between social reality and traditional attitudes to sexual sins embodied in criminal law is nowhere more clearly illustrated than in the issue of homosexual behaviour. A long line of socio-sexual research (though much of it suspect on methodological grounds) leads clearly to the conclusion that not only is homosexuality widespread but also that few people can be classified as either exclusively heterosexual or exclusively homosexual in their orientation (4.1).

The sin of sodomy originates from the Biblical legend of Sodom and Gomorrah. In many ancient cultures, homosexual behaviour was condoned or even encouraged. However, buggery was made a capital offence in England in 1533. There are recorded instances of self-mutilation in order to avoid the urge to commit sexual acts which could lead to the extreme penalty. It was later written into the Offences Against the Person Act 1861 where it attracted a maximum penalty of penal servitude for life. The offence of gross indecency – the legal basis for modern social persecution of male homosexuals – came into being through a curious legislative aberration. The Criminal Law Amendment Bill, 1885, as originally drafted and passed by the Lords, was concerned with such matters as the keeping of brothels and abducting young women for immoral purposes. Henry Labouchere[1] tabled a new clause, taken *mutatis mutandis* from the French Criminal Code, imposing a seven year maximum sentence (later reduced to two years) for gross indecency between male persons. The clause passed, virtually without discussion – a reflection perhaps of the prudish attitude to the subject at that time.[2] Even today, male homosexuality is considered by some to be an unmentionable sin (4.4).

Legal sanctions against homosexual conduct were further extended by the Vagrancy Act (1898). However, by the early 1950s, informed public opinion began to agitate for reform. The cause was assisted by the Montagu case (4.3) and was taken up by MPs, including Desmond Donnelly and Kenneth Robinson. The Church of England Moral Welfare Council produced a liberal report on the subject; and the Wolfenden Committee (which deliberated in extreme secrecy) was set up in 1954.

Evidence to the Committee, both secular and ecclesiastical, was almost unanimous in condemning the *status quo*, and the outcome of the inquiry (see 1.7, *ante*), was nearly a foregone conclusion, though one member was moved to dissent. The Report was widely applauded and in 1958 the Homosexual Law Reform Society launched its campaign. After several unsuccessful attempts to secure the passage of private members' legislation, a Sexual Offences Bill was piloted through Parliament in 1967 by Mr Leo Abse (4.5).

The reform, de-criminalising homosexual acts between consenting male adults in private was a modest but welcome one, although the law is still unevenly enforced. More fundamentally, homosexuals are still treated like second-class citizens with nasty sexual habits. The campaign for radical changes in law and attitudes is still being waged with vigour by such pressure groups as the National Federation of Homophile Organisations and the Campaign for Homosexual Equality. Given the fuss required to secure the relatively minor advances of 1967, the immediate prospects for further reform seem remote.

Wolfenden's terms of reference also included prostitution – another

1. Liberal MP for Northampton, 1880-1906.
2. See Peter G. Richards, *Parliament and Conscience*, London, 1969, pp. 64-5.

sexual phenomenon of great antiquity, and another instance of the ambivalence of social attitudes towards sexual behaviour (see 4.10). English criminal law has, by and large, directed its sanctions against 'persons keeping bawdy houses' (*viz.* a Statute of 1755), against procuring, and/or abduction of minors (or anyone else, if unwilling) for sexual purposes; against 'vagrancy' (a pernicious catch-all concept); against poncing for profit; and, more recently, against soliciting in public places. Ambiguous attitudes (particularly marked in Victorian England) meant that the criminal law stopped short of banning prostitution as such, for (called by other names) it formed the basis of essentially bourgeois pleasures – an escape from the *ennui* of Victorian marriage. Instead, the law has been concerned generally to sweep the more outward manifestations under the carpet; to protect the young (until the Criminal Law Amendment Act 1885, passed in the wake of the Stead abduction case, the age of consent was as low as twelve years, and child prostitution was rife); and to protect the armed forces against the depredations of venereal disease.

To this last end, the notorious Contagious Diseases Acts (1864-9) were directed. These provided statutory inspiration for a 'special' police squad armed with draconian powers to detain suspected prostitutes who, after appearing before a magistrate, would be taken to hospital for examination and medical purification. The process could be infinitely repeated at the discretion of the police, and many of those detained were not prostitutes, although thereafter they were indelibly labelled as such. The crusade against the Acts was led by Josephine Butler, Harriet Martineau, and Florence Nightingale (4.6) and opposed by such formidable adversaries as Gladstone and Elizabeth Garrett Anderson – in fact (at first) by almost everyone. A Royal Commission reported on the subject in 1871[3] and its rather muddled conclusion (subject to numerous dissents on particular matters) was that the Acts should remain in force.

In a famous passage, the Commission considered an argument that might well be concealed between the lines of the debates on Lord Chorley's Bill to make solicitation of prostitutes by their male clients (usually by 'kerb-crawling') a criminal offence (see 4.12) nearly a century later:

> Many witnesses have urged that as well on grounds of justice as expediency, soldiers and sailors should be subjected to regular examinations. We may at once dispose of this recommendation, so far as it is founded on the principle of putting both parties to the sin of fornication on the same footing, by the obvious but not less conclusive reply that there is no comparison to be made between prostitutes and the men who consort with them. With the one sex the offence is committed as a matter of gain; with the other it is the irregular indulgence of a natural impulse.

The subject continued to be debated in various contexts for seventeen years (4.7 and 4.8) until the repeal of the Acts in 1886. Shadows of it still linger on in discussion of other aspects of women's rights. Josephine Butler's Association for Moral and Social Hygiene, originally formed to fight the

3. Cd. 408 of 1871.

Acts, survived into the twentieth century to crusade, *inter alia*, for equal standards of morality to be applied to men and women, and lives on today as the Josephine Butler Society.

Prostitution, since the Wolfenden Report (4.9) and the Street Offences Act 1959 which followed it, forms the subject only of sporadic debate. Of particular interest has been Lord Chorley's as yet unsuccessful campaign (4.12) to subject the male clients who seek the services of prostitutes to similar legal restrictions as apply to the prostitutes themselves under the Street Offences Act 1959 (4.11), a move subsequently endorsed in a Home Office working party's report on vagrancy and street offences.

One sin which has never been a secular crime in England is adultery (though it has been a capital offence elsewhere, for example in New England, and still remains notionally subject to criminal penalties in several States of the USA). This is the case in spite of the vigorous efforts of the self-appointed guardians of moral purity who thrived in the latter part of the eighteenth century and the beginning of the nineteenth century (4.13 and 4.15; also 1.2, 8.1, and 8.2). But the stigma that for so long attached to adultery as a matrimonial offence, and the penalties exacted from the adulterer in divorce proceedings, no doubt muted the cries of those who felt that explicitly criminal sanctions should be applied. The enactment of the Divorce Reform Act 1969 (see Chapter 5) undoubtedly reflects a less censorious social attitude to marital infidelity.

The offence of rape bridges the gap between violence to the person and the emotive and morally-laden concept of sex crime. In England, rape carries a maximum penalty of life imprisonment, though this is seldom imposed. The main problem raised by this offence is not a matter of morality *per se* but has to do with difficult forensic issues of proof and line-drawing (4.17 and 4.18). There is, for example, the perennial problem of the hysterical woman who tells lies and hopes that the mud will stick, as it often does; and the problem of where consent begins and ends – of the woman whose consent stops a fraction short of permitting sexual penetration. A modern feminist reminds us, however, of the dangerous (predominantly male) tendency to suspect secretly that, in the nature of things, the victim of a rape probably got what she asked for (4.19). This view was recently expressed by Mr Justice Melford Stevenson, who airily remarked during a trial for rape in 1974 that this was, as rapes go, an 'anaemic' kind of rape. Further controversy has surrounded a majority decision of the House of Lords in 1975 that a man cannot be guilty of rape if he honestly believes that the woman consented to have intercourse, even if that belief is unreasonable – *D.P.P.* v. *Morgan* [1975] 2 W.L.R. 913. The desire to protect rape victims from publicity has prompted an MP to introduce a Bill to provide for the anonymity of rape victims when giving prosecution evidence at a criminal trial.

Incest is not a commonly prosecuted offence – largely because, by its very nature, it takes places in a family context and often with complete mutual consent. The early history of incest is not very well documented (but see 4.20), though it was known as an ecclesiastical offence in feudal England and remained totally outside the ambit of the secular criminal code until the Punishment of Incest Bill was enacted in 1908 (after several unsuccessful attempts to procure the passage of legislation). One widespread attitude at this time seemed to be that incest was another totally unmentionable subject (4.22).

In recent years, the incidence of cases reported to the police has remained around three hundred a year, but the proportion of these going to trial is about one third. Not only is the offence difficult to detect, but it occurs in circumstances of familial intimacy where conclusive evidence is hard to come by. Traditionally, incest is considered to be based upon an atavistic taboo, much discussed by anthropologists, but the degree of public concern it has aroused in this country is negligible and idiosyncratic (4.21). Related to it – and giving rise to much greater controversy – are the debates on modifying the rules of consanguinity in marriage. These are discussed in Chapter 5.

4.1　*The search for evidence on human sexual behaviour: the Kinsey Report*

Alfred C. Kinsey *was one of the pioneer researchers in the field of human sexuality. The work of Kinsey and his associates in the Institute for Sex Research, Indiana University, has been the subject of fierce criticism on methodological grounds, but their first major work,* Sexual Behaviour in the Human Male *(1948), from which the following extract dealing with homosexuality is taken, has had a profound influence upon modern thinking about what constitutes 'normal' sexual behaviour.*

In view of the data which we now have on the incidence and frequency of the homosexual, and in particular on its co-existence with the heterosexual in the lives of a considerable portion of the male population, it is difficult to maintain the view that psychosexual reactions between individuals of the same sex are rare and therefore abnormal or unnatural, or that they constitute within themselves evidence of neuroses or even psychoses.

If homosexual activity persists on as large a scale as it does, in the face of the very considerable public sentiment against it and in spite of the severity of the penalties that our Anglo-American culture has placed upon it through the centuries, there seems some reason for believing that such activity would appear in the histories of a much larger portion of the population if there were no social restraints. The very general occurrence of the homosexual in ancient Greece ... and its wide occurrence today in some cultures in which such activity is not as taboo as it is in our own, suggests that the capacity of an individual to respond erotically to any sort of stimulus, whether it is provided by another person of the same or of the opposite sex, is basic in the species. That patterns of heterosexuality and patterns of homosexuality represent learned behaviour which depends, to a considerable degree, upon the mores of the particular culture in which the individual is raised, is a possibility that must be thoroughly considered before there can be any acceptance of the idea that homosexuality is inherited, and that the pattern for each individual is so innately fixed that no modification of it may be expected within his lifetime.

The opinion that homosexual activity in itself provides evidence of a psychopathic personality is materially challenged by these incidence and frequency data. Of the 40 or 50 per cent of the male population which has homosexual experience, certainly a high proportion would not be considered psychopathic personalities on the basis of anything else in their histories. It is argued that an individual who is so obtuse to social reactions as to continue his homosexual activity and make it any material portion of his life, therein evidences some social incapacity; but psychiatrists and clinicians in general might very well re-examine their justification for demanding that all persons conform to particular patterns of behaviour. As a matter of fact, there is an increasing proportion of the most skilled psychiatrists who make no attempt to re-direct behaviour, but who devote their attention to helping an individual accept himself, and to conduct himself in such a manner that he does not come into open conflict with society.

It is obvious that social interpretations of the homosexual behaviour of any individual may be materially affected by a consideration of what is now known about the behaviour of the population as a whole. Social reactions to the homosexual have obviously been based on the general belief that a deviant individual is unique and as such needs special consideration.

Administrators of penal and mental institutions are often much disturbed over the problem presented by a male who is committed for a homosexual offense. Such an individual is likely to receive especially severe treatment from the officials in the institution, and he may be segregated as a potential menace to the rest of the inmate body. If it is an institution in which trained psychologists or psychiatrists are employed, they are likely to give especial attention to the half dozen cases who are sent to the institution each year, on such charges. Our surveys in institutions, however, indicate that 25 or 30 per cent of all the inmates have had homosexual experience before admission. It is obvious that the male who happens to be sent in on a homosexual charge may present no more special problem to the institution in this regard than the other quarter or third of the inmate body, who might just as well have been sent in on such a charge. As far as the administration of a custodial institution is concerned, the problem of discipline does not depend upon the control of individuals who have some homosexual experience in their history, as much as it does upon the control of men who are particularly aggressive in forcing other individuals into homosexual relations.

The judge who is considering the case of the male who has been arrested for homosexual activity, should keep in mind that nearly 40 per cent of all the other males in the town could be arrested at some time in their lives for similar activity, and that 20 to 30 per cent of the unmarried males in that town could have been arrested for homosexual activity that had taken place within that same year. The court might also keep in mind that the penal or mental institution to which he may send the male has something between 30 and 85 per cent of its inmates engaging in the sort of homosexual activity which may be involved in the individual case before him.

On the other hand, the judge who dismisses the homosexual case that has come before him, or places the boy or adult on probation, may find himself the subject of attack from the local press which charges him with releasing dangerous 'perverts' upon the community. Law enforcement officers can utilize the findings of scientific studies of human behaviour only to the extent that the community will back them. Until the whole community understands the realities of human homosexual behaviour, there is not likely to be much change in the official handling of individual cases.

The difficulty of the situation becomes still more apparent when it is realized that these generalizations concerning the incidence and frequency of homosexual activity apply in varying degrees to every social level, to persons in every occupation, and of every age in the community. The police force and court officials who attempt to enforce the sex laws, the clergymen and business men and every other group in the city which periodically calls for enforcement of the laws – particularly the laws against sexual 'perversion' – have given a record of incidences and frequencies in the homosexual which are as high as those of the rest of the social level in which they belong. It is not a matter of individual hypocrisy which leads officials with homosexual histories to become prosecutors of the homosexual activity in the community. They themselves are the victims of the mores, and the public demand that they protect those mores. As long as there are gaps between the traditional custom and the actual behaviour of the population, such inconsistencies will continue to exist.

There are those who will contend that the immorality of homosexual behaviour calls for its suppression no matter what the facts are concerning the incidence and frequency of such activity in the population. Some have demanded that homosexuality be completely eliminated from society by a concentrated attack upon it at every point, and the 'treatment' or isolation of all individuals with any homosexual tendencies. Whether such a programme is morally desirable is a matter on which a scientist is not qualified to pass judgment; but whether such a programme is physically feasible is a matter for scientific determination.

The evidence that we now have on the incidence and frequency of homosexual activity indicates at least a third of the male population would have to be isolated from the rest of the community, if all those with any homosexual capacities were to be so treated. It means that at least 13 per cent of the male population (rating 4 to 6 on the heterosexual-homosexual scale), would have to be institutionalized and isolated, if all persons who were predominantly homosexual were to be handled in that way. Since about 34 per cent of the total population of the United States are adult males, this means that there are about six and a third million males in the country who would need such isolation.

4.2   Bishop John Robinson's view of the place of law in the field of sex

John Robinson *was Suffragan Bishop of Woolwich and is chairman of the Sexual Law Reform Society. The following is an extract from his Beckly Lecture delivered in conjunction with the Methodist Conference in July 1972.*

When we are confronted with something of which we deeply disapprove (especially if we have not thought deeply about it) there is an instinctive reaction to say 'There ought to be a law against it.' But this is to equate the place of criminal law with that of moral condemnation. Clearly, once we do think about it, this simple equation cannot be sustained. That way leads to the regimentation of morals and the police state. Let us then draw out the implications of the phrase, 'There ought to be a law against it.'

In the first place, the function of the law is primarily being seen as negative. We all know that you cannot (regretfully) make people good by Act of Parliament, but at least, it is argued, you can stop them straying too far. And the charge against the permissive society is that the controls have slipped: things are being permitted that ought not to be permitted.

The second implication is that society or its leading members have the right to control, to say what shall be permitted. And the function of law in such a paternalistic understanding of society is by its sanctions to promote the values, to enforce the morality, of those who know best, whether this is an oligarchy of self-appointed guardians or what John Stuart Mill called 'the tyranny of the majority'. Its function, as he said, in this way of thinking, is that of 'moral police,' to prescribe what it is good for us to read or think or do and to proscribe what it is not.

According to this concept the place of law in the field of sex is potentially unlimited – as indeed one can see from the fact that still under the Sexual Offences Act of 1967 anal sex between husband and wife in the privacy of their bedroom is in theory punishable with life-imprisonment. For this is the 'abominable crime' of buggery, and quite consistently if it is morally abominable it must be legally prohibited. But it is to America, the land of the free, that you must go for the full outworking of this theory.

There, with the sole exception of New Mexico, every possible sexual activity with the exception of 'normal' conjugal union and solitary masturbation (and even the latter in Indiana) has been declared criminal in one State or another and usually in most. This applies to prostitution (in all States) adultery and even fornication. No doubt much of this is dead wood, though in Boston as late as 1954 the sex laws were reported to receive 'normal enforcement,' and in 1948 there were 248 arrests for adultery in that city. Indeed, it has been estimated that, on the evidence of the Kinsey Report, 95 per cent of the American people should have been in gaol for sexual offences alone. But unenforced or unenforcible law is bad law, and if law is to be respected here or anywhere else it should be commendable on the ground that ' you *know* it makes sense.'

I quote these rather extreme instances because it is increasingly clear to me that if we are to have sexual laws that make sense it is not merely a question of trimming away dead wood, or the more absurd growths, but of looking again at the tree that was capable of producing such fruits. For they were entirely logical growths. If the function of law is the public enforcement of private morals, then, if you *can* prohibit what you think is morally wrong or offensive, you should.

I wish to argue that this whole theory is fallacious and that we shall not get out sexual laws right until we can detach ourselves from it and start again.

The function of criminal law is the positive one of preventing harm to others. This may, of course, involve prohibition or restriction – effective gun laws are an obvious case in point – but the *raison d'être* of the law is protection not prohibition. *And where there is no need for protection it should not intervene.* It is not there to express what Charles Davis has called 'the anger of morality,' however 'abominable' may be the object of its disapprobation. It is there as far as possible to enable people to be free, mature, adult human beings, or what the New Testament calls 'sons.' Of course, it cannot make people sons. But it has a rôle, a limited rôle, in hindering the hindrances. It is limited because the free processes of influence, education, example and persuasion are so much more productive. But as a last resort if a person refuses to respect the freedom of another there must be provision to compel him to do so.

Within the sexual area one could take as a starting point the statement of the report of the Wolfenden Committee on Homosexual Offences and Prostitution. The function of criminal law, it says, 'is to preserve public order and decency, to protect the citizen from what is offensive or injurious, and to provide sufficient safeguards, against exploitation or corruption of others, particularly those who are specially vulnerable because they are young, weak in body or mind, inexperienced, or in a state of special physical, official or economic dependence.'

On this basis the committee proceeded to ground its recommendations to obviate the offensive public manifestations of prostitution (though not to make it illegal) and to remove from the area of criminality homosexual acts between 'consenting adults in private.' This last, now famous, phrase provides in fact a convenient three-sided boundary to what the report described as that 'realm of private morality and immorality which is, in brief and crude terms, not the law's business.' *Per contra* we can use it as a guide to where the law has a right and a duty to protect the citizen – that is to say:

(1) Where there is not true consent;
(2) Where there is not adult responsibility;
(3) Where there is obtrusion on the public.

Let us consider each of these in turn, and we shall find that they get progressively more difficult to determine.

The first presents relatively little trouble, though consent is clearly a matter of degree, especially among those of diminished responsibility or in a state of 'physical, official or economic dependence.' Offences against consent would obviously include rape, enticement, deception, blackmail, and some (but not all) forms of prostitution – however much all forms of prostitution (and for that matter many marriages) may be judged morally, though not legally, exploitative. But if an adult freely and knowingly consents to sell himself or herself for sexual purposes, then the law has no right to intervene, though here as elsewhere it can properly protect against abuse the conditions of the market. But although this first condition is relatively simple, it is fundamental to the preservation of persons as persons. Each of the others must presuppose it is essential.

The second condition raises the question, 'What is the age of consent?' or, 'Who is a responsible adult?' Ideally one could argue that there should be no fixed age of consent. Wherever you draw the line, especially at the variable, and changing, age of puberty, it is bound to be arbitrary; therefore each case must be judged on its merits. But obviously an adult before having sexual relations with a boy or girl must know in advance whether he is breaking the law; it is no protection for a judge afterwards to opine that the young person was not old enough to give consent. A line must be drawn, however arbitrarily.

But a line for what? Under the law a person is deemed legally to be capable of different things at varying ages – for instance, of committing rape at 14, of getting married at 16, of voting at 18, of homosexual relations (if a man) at 21. In this connection, we are dealing not with the age at which we think young people *morally should* have sex relations, but with the age at which they *legally can* consent to what they are doing. And clearly this is potentially lower than for marriage, which involves heavier commitments and responsibilities.

Two things can, I think, be said straightaway: (a) The age for homosexual and heterosexual relations ought to be the same, since it is capacity for personal consent which is at issue not sexual proclivity – unless, of course, one applied the previous argument and said that since heterosexual relationships imply the possible procreation of children the age of responsibility for them should be higher; (b) The present age of consent for male homosexual relationships is absurdly high. It was fixed at a time when the age of majority in general was 21, though even then the evidence presented to the Wolfenden Committee by the Church of England Moral Welfare Council recommended that the age should be 17 for both sexes. Since female homosexual relationships have never been illegal, no age of consent for them has been defined, though presumably this is covered by the fact that any other sexual act with a girl under 16 is criminal.

I suggest that we start from the proposition that the legal age of consent for all sex relationships should be 16. Indeed, I believe that the only real argument is whether or not it should be lower. For two things follow from the age of consent: (a) Below it liability for criminal prosecution automatically arises; and few would want to see a teen-aged boy sent to gaol for fathering the child of a 15-year-old he intends to marry (as I gather can actually happen in permissive Denmark, where a girl under age is legally required to state the name of the father and thus expose him to prosecution); (b) It is, technically, aiding and abetting a criminal offence to prescribe contraceptives for those below the age of consent. But, alas, we know that it is precisely these who are at greatest risk. To be compelled to break the law in order to protect them and their potential unborn babies is a heavy responsibility and merely helps to bring the law into disrepute. And it also, of course, deters the young from seeking advice.

I do not find it easy to make up my mind on this issue. On the one hand, there is no doubt that the line drawn by the law does have a deterrent effect and protect children of school age who would otherwise be exposed to relationships for which they are not ready and to responsibilities which they are in no position to carry. Yet the criminal law is a very blunt instrument for this purpose and is in danger of being discredited if it is not implemented, or even respected, except in particularly blatant cases.

Those I have consulted who are actually dealing with the young people concerned would plead above all for the greatest scope for flexibility, taking into account not simply an arbitrary age but all the attendant circumstances. On this basis I think I am persuaded that probably the most creative, and as well as the most realistic, solution would be to lower the legal age of consent to 14, so that no one having intercourse with a person above that age should automatically be committing a criminal offence, but then to provide additional protections. There could properly be an extension of the period, say, from 14 to 17 when, under the Children and Young Persons Act, care and protection proceedings (with their dual criteria of admitted offence and need) would be available; and legislation could be designed to safeguard minors against adults exploiting or corrupting them through, as Wolfenden put it, their 'inexperience.'

Though a girl might 'consent' to prostitution at 16 or even 14, it could be a criminal offence for her to be employed in that relationship under 18. The same could apply to engagement for sexual displays and photography. Equally it might be possible (though it would be more difficult to frame or enforce the act) to provide additional protection for minors (through action initiated by a parent or guardian or others) against undesirable homosexual or heterosexual relations with older persons.

But here, as elsewhere, the place of criminal law is a limited one. Indeed, to introduce its scrutinies and its sanctions may often do more harm than good. Speaking of the effect of sexual experience on children, a former probation officer has said this in a letter from which he has allowed me to quote:

'Harm results much more from the tension between an individual's experience and that of his reference group than from the experience in itself. Some research on childhood "victims" of sexual offences would appear to bear this out in that it is the subsequent parental horror, police investigation, etc, which are significantly more disturbing than the offence. Consequently the best protection we can afford children is the extension of what experience or behaviour we can embrace, survive and ultimately be enriched by. Vis-à-vis *this* concept of protection I think law may well need to have a declaratory and educative function as well as merely a constraining one.'

Those are wise words, with broader application.

Finally, under this second condition – adult responsibility – it is clearly possible and desirable to include special protection of the young in any regulations made on the subject of censorship, film classifications, television timings, etc. – though one is bound to add that the evidence for youth actually being corrupted by, or even interested in, the kind of sex controlled or uncontrolled by such legislation is less than overwhelming. On the contrary, there is strong evidence, as I was being told in Denmark recently, that the vast majority of the patrons of pornography are married men between 45 and 55 and that most of the stuff is bought in remarkably large quantities by remarkably few people. But its issue of censorship and control brings us to the third and even more contentious line, that between private and public.

As the Wolfenden Report recognised, the point at which it becomes the law's business to intervene is when the legitimate privacy of the individual requires protection against intrusion. This cuts both ways. First, the individual can expect protection against the police, the press, informers, blackmailers, etc., bringing into the public realm what is essentially his private affair. But, equally, the individual member of the public can expect protection against having forced upon him through hoardings, advertisements, window displays, unsolicited mailings, through public entertainments and the mass-media, what invades his privacy by being, in the etymological sense of the words, 'indecent' or 'obscene', that is, inappropriate to the time or place or (if this is the ultimate derivation of obscenity) having presented on stage what should be off.

On the first aspect of privacy, there is still a good deal of tidying up of the law to be done, especially in bringing legislation (and still more its implementation) into line for heterosexual and homosexual relationships. The definition of privacy for homosexuals (if male) is still much more restricted than it is for heterosexuals. They cannot with security show the usual signs of affection in public, and even in a private house no other person may be present during homosexual relations. As the recent House of Lords judgment in the IT case[4] has confirmed, they may not use the press to make contact with one another for non-criminal purposes – a liberty not, as far as I know, denied to any other of Her Majesty's subjects.

As a positive principle one might say that any discrimination between the sexes should itself be made illegal. And this goes also for the inequality of penalties (e.g., for indecent assault on a man – 10 years, for indecent assault on a woman – 2 years). There is still no privacy at all guaranteed under the law for male homosexuals in Scotland and Northern Ireland, the armed services or the merchant navy. Moreover, the implementation of the Act remain disconcertingly uneven, with varying police policies and unpredictable interpretations of such vague concepts as a 'breach of the peace' or a 'public place'. It should surely be accepted that homosexuals should be harassed and prosecutions initiated only when public decency is palpably outraged or actual annoyance caused to specific persons.

Finally, under this heading of safeguarding civil liberties, careful attention needs to be paid to the law regarding 'incitement', under which a person can be prosecuted for encouraging others to do something which is not unlawful but 'which might be said to be immoral', and to growing resort by the judiciary to common-law charges especially the vague and oppressive charge, first involved in 1960 and still embodied in no legislation, of the 'conspiracy to corrupt public morals'.

In approaching the complex issues of censorship, let me first restate the general principle that it is not the job of the law to try to make people pure or to stop them being prurient. Specifically in regard to sexual obscenity one could say that the aim of the law should be not to prohibit those who want pornography (which is largely what it has bent its energies to doing) but to protect those who don't. In private, persons should be free and protected to read or see what they like – even if others dislike or disapprove of it intensely. In public, persons must be free and protected, within limits, from having forced upon them what they find indecent or objectionable. I say 'within limits'. For any restriction is a limitation of someone else's freedom

4. *Knuller* v. *D.P.P.* [1973] A.C. 435.

and is justifiable only if, in the words of a sub-committee of the Society of Conservative Lawyers, the material is 'grossly offensive to the public at large' – which can only be assessed by a publicly appointed committee answerable to the electors (rather than by a bench of magistrates) and, if challenged, by a jury.

This phrase, 'grossly offensive to the public at large', is taken from their recent report, 'The Pollution of the Mind', and constitutes the definition of what they believe should be a new offence of 'public indecency'. It would specifically provide control *only* over material displayed in a public place. But they also wish to recommend further restriction under a new definition of obscenity. 'We had no difficulty,' they say, 'in rejecting the present definition which includes the test of "tending to deprave and corrupt"', adding that experience had shown that 'the present definition and Acts are virtually unworkable'. They propose substituting the following:

Any material shall be obscene if: (1). It grossly affronts contemporary community standards of decency and, (2). The dominant theme of the material as a whole appeals to a lewd or filthy interest in sex or is repellent. They add the proviso that there shall be no conviction if the material can be proved nevertheless to be in the public good.

This is certainly a move in the right direction. A tendency to deprave or corrupt is virtually undemonstrable. Offensiveness, on the other hand, is an integral part of what it means for something to be obscene (and the obscene, unlike the erotic or the pornographic, has no necessary connection with sex, but covers ugliness, noise, stench, etc.). But equally by definition it must offend someone. Unless someone else's susceptibilities are violated by his having it forced on him there is no case for obscenity as such being criminal, however morally or aesthetically repugnant we may judge it to be. In other words, there has to be someone to object (and object in reasonable numbers and with reasonable seriousness) because his privacy is being invaded.

But then we are back at the charge of public indecency. And if this is properly applied, I see the need for no further criminal offence.

The real charge against pornography is that it is an anti-erotic – destructive of what God saw and, behold, it was very good. Fortunately, however, satiety sets in a good deal sooner than it does with either tobacco or alcohol. When you have seen the lot, you've seen the lot; and, ·as an American presidential report showed, there is a law of rapidly diminishing returns. I would prefer to speak of hard-bore rather than hard-core. The amount of actual damage it does is certainly a good deal less than that of either of the other two legalised commodities I have mentioned. This is not to say that its effect is negligible or that pornography does no harm – far from it – and, as with tobacco and alcohol, we must protect (especially the young) against the *abuse* of sex where we can. But the damage is paradoxically probably the opposite of what most people seem to fear. It is not the heightening or intensifying of the drive that is likely to result from a distorted sexual environment but its crippling and constricting.

This is even more true of damaging personal *relationships* – one bad encounter may permanently impair a person's sexual development. But you cannot ultimately protect against these by law. And distorted books and pictures about sex are likely to have attraction in the long term only for those whose sex *relations* have been a failure. In other words, pornography appeals *in an enslaving or addictive* way only to those who, for reasons that go much further back into childhood and adolescence, are sexually sick or lonely. They are depraved because they are deprived, and should be pitied rather than prosecuted – and above all helped. In so far as pornography, like excessive smoking or drinking, is a symptom of a sick society, let us apply all the cures and dissuasives we know. But censoring the symptoms is not only useless but counter-productive.

This is fully borne out in the field of sexual legislation by the experience of Denmark in abolishing censorship. After the first much-publicised flush the surviving sex-shops and live shows (the latter of which have never been public entertainments and require 24-hours club membership) are struggling to keep going on the tourist trade. With the lid of repression lifted, crimes of sexual violence (and not merely, as has been asserted, crimes that are no longer offences) have certainly dropped, as indeed – against the trend of all other crime – they may have begun to do in this country, where in 1971 they were 2 per cent down, in contrast with 14 per cent up for violence against the person.

Just as New Mexico, for all its absence of immorality laws, is apparently no more libidinous than any other American state, so abolition of censorship in Denmark does not promote lewdness (except among neighbouring nationals!) – rather, if anything the opposite. And the news that Scotland Yard intended to act merely on complaints from the public in place of a seek-and-destroy policy was not exactly received with elation by the bookshops managers of Soho. According to a *Sunday Times* report, 'one pessimist frankly admitted that he expected legalised porn to follow – with the catastrophic drop in prices that would mean'.

This sounds so paradoxical and to most people such rot that the logic behind it needs spelling out further. Indeed there is concealed here a perfectly intelligent objection, and intelligible fear, namely that to legalise is *ipso facto* to license. One of the main functions of the law it is said, is to 'set a good example'. What is lawful is what society approves: to make lawful what has hitherto been unlawful is equivalent to giving it the stamp of social approbation.

But just because something is legal it does not mean that it is approved. And to de-restrict it legally does not imply that it is morally to be encouraged. Such a step may merely be an acknowledgment that the law has been an ass or has ceased to correspond with social realities. Thus, to remove suicide from being a criminal offence is not to set society's approval upon it. And there is no reason to suppose that more people now attempt suicide *because* it is legal and therefore 'all right'. If they do, it is because modern life has greater strains.

In actual fact the force of law as a power for good in those areas is a good deal weaker than we tend to suppose. It is not the law that alters social attitudes so much as social attitudes the law. It is not because the law has changed – it hasn't – that more illegally conceived (and not merely illegitimate) babies are being born to girls under 16. It is because of a change of social mores and the half-arrival of contraceptives. To stiffen the law would not staunch the flow: it would merely make advice and protection more difficult.

The notion that 'anything goes' just because the law allows it reflects the paternalistic assumption that it is the function of law to tell people what is good for them and that what is not prohibited is thereby promoted. But it is precisely a sign of a civilised society that it progressively substitutes the free processes of social judgment for the sanctions of penal suppression.

The positive, and quite indispensable, function of law in the sexual field is to protect the young and feeble-minded and to guard the privacies of the individual, whether in private or in public. If we can reform it to do that effectively and constructively in a manner that commands consent and therefore respect, we shall have done a great thing. For the rest, the way is open, now more than ever, for the immense corporate task of helping to transform ourselves from a paternalistic society, through the adolescent pains and follies of a permissive society, *towards* a more genuinely mature society.

4.3 A first-hand view of penal policy towards homosexuality

Peter Wildeblood *was a reporter on the* Daily Mail. *He was involved in the Montagu case in 1953-4 and sentenced to eighteen months' imprisonment for homosexual offences. On his release, Wildeblood took every opportunity to fan the public sympathy aroused by the trial, and in 1955 published* Against the Law, *'a first hand account of what it means to be a homosexual'. This extract is from the Penguin edition.*

It has been said that the purposes of punishment are fourfold. The main objects are to deter the wrongdoer and others, and to reform him; the subsidiary objects are to compensate the injured party and to satisfy the indignation of the community. I doubt whether any of these ends are best achieved by prosecution.

I do not believe that a homosexual can be transformed into a heterosexual overnight by the shock of prosecution and imprisonment. The most that can be expected is that he will, while still experiencing an attraction towards his own sex, refrain from giving way to it again. On the other hand, I have never met a homosexual who has resolved to mend his ways as a result of being imprisoned. The laws under which these men are prosecuted appear to them so flagrantly unjust that there is no question of their feeling any remorse or shame for what they have done. This attitude, which may or may not be justified, is strengthened by the fact that no moral stigma attaches to adult homosexuality in the prison community. In this respect it differs from pederasty, or the seduction of boys; and under the combined pressure of disapproval from their fellow-prisoners and perhaps the realization that their actions are morally indefensible, pederasts do sometimes decide that they will never succumb to temptation again. Whether they carry out these resolutions, I do not know.

It must also be remembered that once a man has been taught to look upon himself as a criminal there is a tendency for him to abandon his standards of morality, not only in the respect in which he has been prosecuted, but in others as well. In the unmoral atmosphere of prison, it is easy to look upon all authority as an anonymous and baleful 'They', to be cheated and disobeyed.

I do not believe that the fact of my imprisonment, or that of Edward Montagu or Michael Pitt-Rivers, will deter a single person from committing acts such as those with which we were charged. Regrettably enough, I believe that the opposite may be true. I have already written about the influence of the Wilde case, and it has often been pointed out that a crime of a sensational nature which receives wide publicity is often followed by a wave of imitations, committed by people of weak intellect whose imaginations have been inflamed by the newspaper reports. After we were arrested and remanded on bail, Edward Montagu and I received many hundreds of letters from such people, including young boys. One boy of 15 used to try to telephone me almost every day during the week when I was waiting for the trial to begin. I find this horrifying and am sincerely grieved to think that I may, however unwillingly and indirectly, have been responsible for such a thing.

The homosexual world is, of necessity, compact and isolated. It is also extraordinarily out of touch with reality. I have already mentioned that a number of homosexuals, respected and discreet, were courageous enough to offer evidence to the Home Office Committee when it was set up. These, however, were exceptional. The great majority of the homosexual community shrugged its shoulders, expressed the opinion that the law would never be changed, and carried on with its dangerous and tragic way of life. Our case caused a momentary flutter, and a number of the better-known homosexuals left the country for a time, until they decided that it was safe to return. I am obliged to admit that most homosexuals are furtive and irresponsible, and that if a more tolerant and just attitude towards their condition is ever adopted by this country it will not be through their efforts. On the other hand, they are perhaps not entirely to blame. Their secretiveness and cynicism are imposed upon them by the law as it now stands.

I do not know how far my prosecution acted as a deterrent. Its purpose as an instrument of reform concerns me alone.

Long before I was prosecuted, I had considered the possibility of submitting myself to a 'cure', if any such existed. I had discussed the question with a number of doctors, without ever discovering one who professed to be able to effect any alteration in my sexual bias. Psychiatrists, psychotherapists, psychologists, and psychoanalysts, derive a large part of their incomes from men who fear that their homosexual instincts, if left unchecked, will involve them in prosecution and disgrace. It is not very surprising therefore, that there should be some resistance towards relaxation of the law among the official organizations of the medical profession. But individual doctors, if they are honest, will nearly always admit that there is nothing they can do. There is no magic cure. Extravagant claims were at one time made for treatment by means of sex-hormone injections. It has since been established that, although the injection of female hormones into a man produced a cessation of all desire, whether homosexual or heterosexual, the effect was only temporary and was sometimes accompanied by distressing physical changes. The man thus treated became a kind of hermaphrodite or eunuch, and suffered from the psychological upset natural to such a condition. A homosexual treated with male hormones, however, did not become more of a 'man'; his desires were merely intensified.

Psychotherapists claim that they are able to help in cases where the homosexual bias is weak, or when it is accompanied by self-condemnation or social maladjustment. The course of treatment is bound to take a very long time and cost a great deal of money, and its effects are always uncertain, depending on the willingness of the patient to be cured and the degree of trust which he feels towards his psychiatrist. Ironically enough, this kind of treatment is only likely to be successful with those who have failed to come to terms with their abnormality. With the man who has learned to accept his condition, it is almost certain to be useless.

In spite of this, it might have been possible for me to embark on such a course, if I had not been sent to prison. At Wormwood Scrubs, which is so often pointed out as a centre for the psychological treatment of offenders, the facilities for such treatment were not so much inadequate, as virtually absent. I met many men who had been told by judges that they were being sent for three, or five, or seven years to a place where they would be properly looked after and encouraged to mend their ways; but nothing whatever was being done for them. Out of 1,000 prisoners at the Scrubs, only 11 were receiving psychiatric treatment at the time I was there, and only a small proportion of these were homosexuals. Dr Landers, the Principal Medical Officer, was an intelligent and honest man who admitted the limitations of the system; but I could not help feeling that he would be doing more good if he had devoted his efforts to improving the revolting sanitary conditions of the place, instead of concentrating on the highly problematical redemption of such a small group.

Once I was in prison, as I have described, I was not only not encouraged to take psychological treatment, but actively discouraged. Men in prison, whatever their crime may have been, do not merely remain as bad as they were when they came in; by a visible process of moral erosion which goes on week after week and year after year, they become worse. This is particularly true of sex offenders, and I do not pretend to have been any exception.

4.4 *Homosexuality as violation of natural law*

The following letter was written in 1957 to The Times *by Sir Henry Slesser, a former Solicitor-General and Lord Justice of Appeal.*

Sir, – The advocates of the Wolfenden Report on homosexuality seek to compare the sins of fornication and adultery with perversion and argue that they should be similarly treated. They forget that homosexuality is contrary to natural law, which is not the case with normal sexual depravities.

It is, says Blackstone, 'a crime against Nature', known to the law in his time as '*peccatum illud horribile inter Christianos non nominandum*'. We find in a report in the time of Edward I that it was the sin 'not to be named'. Since the time of Henry VIII it has been a felony and it has been given in the

Offences Against the Person Act, 1861, the description, unique I believe, in the criminal law in its more serious aspects, of the 'abominable crime'.

This is the view entertained by lawyers, canonists and society at large since the time of Constantine, of something which we are now asked in this 'enlightened age' to exonerate from the criminal law when committed in private.

Yours obediently,
HENRY SLESSER

4.5 Legislative action to implement recommendations of the Wolfenden Report

Leo Abse *is Labour MP for Pontypool, an indefatigable social reformer in Parliament, and a solicitor in a prominent Cardiff firm. This speech opened the second reading debate on the Sexual Offences (No.2) Bill in 1966.*

Mr Leo Abse (Pontypool): I beg to move, That the Bill be now read a Second time.

It would be as well, perhaps, to remind the House of other occasions on which legislation which impinges upon human relationships has come before the House. There was a Bill, the Deceased Wife's Sister's Marriage Act, which finally became law in 1907, which it may be recalled, ended the prohibition on a man marrying the sister of his dead wife. Before that Bill became law it came to the House on scores of occasions. Indeed, on Second Reading it was passed by the House on at least 19 occasions and it was rejected in the House of Lords on at least 13 occasions.

No one reading the debates of that period can but wonder at the Jeremiahs and the moralists of those days of yesteryear in both Commons and Lords. That arose only because a slight change in the marriage laws was desired. If we read those debates, the passions that were aroused seem almost droll, and the threats to family stability and the institution of marriage which were then uttered now seem historical curiosities.

Yet I believe that there are lessons to be learned. We are prone in this country to extend our national debates on legislation touching on human relations to the point at which they sometimes verge almost on farce, and sometimes they are taken to the point of morbidity. We should remind ourselves that it is now well over twelve years since the Wolfenden Committee was appointed and it is almost a decade since it reported. From the time that the present Minister of Health first brought the issues before the House shortly after the Wolfenden Committee had reported, down to the occasion on which the House gave a Bill similar to this a Second Reading when it was introduced by Mr Humphrey Berkeley, the House has repeatedly and exhaustively tested the Wolfenden recommendations. This, alas, I almost apologise to the House, is certainly by no means the first occasion on which I have brought such a Bill to the House.

It is not surprising, therefore, in my view, that when Lord Attlee supported a Bill similar to this Bill in another place, one of the reasons that he gave for supporting the Bill and for trying to bring this debate to an end was that he feared that more was being said about homosexuality than need be said, a point of view with which I am certainly in full accord.

I am not suggesting that this Bill is as marginal as the Bill which I mentioned, the Deceased Wife's Sister's Marriage Bill, but it is well neither to exaggerate the effect which the law made here can have upon human conduct outside – a tendency almost to megalomania, a tendency to which we as legislators are prone – nor, when we are dealing with the problem, to exaggerate the size of the problem which we have to face.

It is true that no one knows the number of homosexuals that exist in this country. It was suggested in some evidence submitted to the Wolfenden Committee that there were some 750,000 in the land. The Home Office spokesman in another place indicated a figure of perhaps 500,000. These figures are sometimes blown up. They are blown up, on the one hand, by self-acclaimed moralists who always seem to be searching for immorality and, on the other hand, by homosexuals themselves, who in the case certainly of some of them are so oppressed with guilt reinforced, I believe by our laws, that when they wish to spread and to share their guilt, and to rid themselves of it, they sometimes have a tendency to exaggerate the numbers who are prone to this failure.

But whatever the precise numbers may be, all of us could agree that such is the unreality of our present laws that we can say as a descriptive fact that, apart from motorists, we are dealing with the largest number of those to be declared criminals in the land. To these men, what does the law say? It does not give them the choice of saying that they may live out their lives in discretion. It does not give them the choice that they may live out their lives away from public view provided that they do not flaunt their conduct. The law as it stands does not give them the choice to live out their lives provided that they never corrupt a young person.

In fact, the law gives them a brutal choice. It offers them either celibacy or criminality, and nothing in between. And since homosexual behaviour, it is to be assumed, is no less compulsive, though lamentably different in direction, than heterosexuality, we are demanding a code of behaviour from them which the heterosexualists among us know that we could not possibly sustain. I ask those of us who are blessed with the emotional security of a heterosexual life, those who are blessed with a good wife and with a family, those who have the blessing of children, have we the right to demand this code of behaviour from those whose terrible fate it is to be a homosexual? I do not think that we have, and in any event it is an unreal demand, and it is impossible for it to be met.

May I give the number of convictions of adults who commit homosexual acts in private? According to the survey of the Wolfenden Committee at that time, it was about 100 convictions a year, and, judging by the number of custodial offences revealed in the statistics, it is probably less now. Even to state these figures is to show how derisory is the conviction rate and how utterly unenforceable is the law. As Wolfenden said, there is an almost astronomical disparity between the number of illicit sexual acts which occur and those which are detected by the guardians of the law. If we assume that we have as many homosexuals as the Kinsey Report revealed were in existence in the United States – if we are in this unfortunate position – it means that in the 21 to 30 age group alone, judging by the rate of convictions that are taking place, there would be a 30,000-to-one chance of an illicit act leading to conviction in this country.

Therefore, we have an unenforceable Act, and it would require a massive recruitment of police and an invasion of privacy which all of us would find quite intolerable before the law could begin to be enforced. It is a bad law because it is unenforceable law, and it is bad law because it is utterly random in its application. It is totally lacking in certainty and perforce inequitable. The prurient curiosity of one chief constable may activate a whole spate of prosecutions in one county. On the other hand, the squeamishness, the diffidence, the robustness, the common sense, perhaps, of a chief constable in another county may mean that there are never any convictions at all in that country. Law of this nature applied in this way must be inequitable.

It is bad law, too, because the penalties that attach to it are utterly senseless. It is true that society knows no other way of dealing with the man who is a compulsive pederast, interfering with little boys, than to remove him from the community. Our knowledge is inadequate. But when we are talking of all these men whose relationships, in private, are with adults who give their consent, we know that to talk of sending these men to prison is, as has been said again and again, as therapeutically useless as incarcerating a sex maniac in a harem. This is the position, and we all know it. There is no rehabilitative element at all in the punishment that is meted out. It must be repugnant to us. It must be repugnant to the least bold penologist to realise that we have these penalties in which we can take no pride, that the penalties for adults committing homosexual offences in private are the most severe.

Although there are no rehabilitative effects flowing from the existing law, we know that there are other effects. One effect, so far as it is positive at all, is clearly to stigmatise thousands of our citizens as being outlaws and pariahs. We have to face the fact that we are dealing with large numbers of people – many of them, apart from this particular aberration, who are totally law-abiding. In many cases, it means that the homosexual feels that he is almost a selected minority specially chosen and persecuted, and he sees within the wider community, for good or evil, more permissive attitudes. He knows that fornication and adultery, although disapproved of, are not crimes. He sees that in almost the remainder of the Western world discreet homosexuals have been granted legal immunity, whereas in this country the homosexual lives in a land that persists in this eccentric doctrine that such behaviour should attract a maximum sentence of life imprisonment.

I do not regard it, therefore, as surprising that in such a climate of opinion there are not a few homosexuals who almost lapse into near paranoia. It is not surprising, when the law puts them outside the community, that they behave as many do, that they should react as some of them do in an anti-social manner, with all their original feelings of guilt reinforced by repressive laws. I do not think it is surprising that sometimes they protect their self-esteem by absurdly proclaiming their superiority intellectually and artistically to those of us who are mere heterosexuals. This is the reaction which we as a community almost provoke. Is it surprising that when we place them in this position they resort to one of the few means open to them by which they can still regard themselves as having an identity as human beings within society? Then when they make such statements we accuse them of being proselytisers.

Then there is another effect, a dastardly effect, of the present law which cannot be under-estimated. It is the fact that blackmail is the ambience which wraps itself around the existing law. On the last occasion when we had a debate, it was said that a former Attorney-General, Sir William Jowitt, had estimated that 90 per cent of the cases of blackmail which came to his attention contained an element of homosexual conduct. We know, too, that in the more recent review which the Wolfenden Committee conducted when it took a fixed period of time, it asserted that within that time there were 71 cases reported to the police of which 32 were connected with homosexual offences. We know that this can only be the tip of the iceberg, for any man who reports that he is being blackmailed as a consequence of a homosexual act knows that he is placing himself in jeopardy with the possibility of a prosecution. There are too many documented cases in recent years of hoodlums who, taking advantage of the existing position, have come to believe that they can rob a homosexual with impunity.

It is because of these sorts of reasons, rather than those which I was citing earlier, that the law is in disrepute with the general public. But whatever may have been the position 10 years ago, it cannot be gainsaid, in the light of the national opinion polls, the Gallup Poll and so on – however much we may discount them – that when we see the overwhelming majority of the public who, according to those polls, are in favour of changing the law in accordance with the Wolfenden recommendations, one cannot doubt that there is a severe public reaction to the law as it stands.

The paramount reason for the introduction of this Bill is that it may at last move our community away from being riveted to the question of punishment of homosexuals which has hitherto prompted us to avoid the real challenge of preventing little boys from growing up to be adult homosexuals. Surely, what we should be preoccupied with is the question of how we can, if it is possible, reduce the number of faulty males in the community. How can we diminish the number of those who grow up to have men's bodies but feminine souls?

It is clear from the number of homosexuals who are about that, unfortunately, little boys do not automatically grow up to be men. Manhood and fatherhood have to be taught. Manhood has to be learnt. The only way for it to be taught is by example. It is true that there are dangers to a boy – a sophisticated House knows it – if an over-possessive mother ties her son to her with a silver cord so that the boy is enveloped in a feminine aura out of which he is never able to break and assert his masculine independence. We know that this happens. But, equally, it is certain from all the research that has been done that there is particular vulnerability for those who have had jealous or loveless fathers, for those with inadequate fathers, and for those – these are in the greatest danger of all – who are fatherless either by death or desertion. These have no father substitute with whom they can learn to identify.

We hear often about mothercraft. We do not hear a great deal about fathercraft. The children of part-time parents, the children of the ambitious executive returning home after the boy is abed, perhaps, too, the children of over-busy Members of Parliament who work very hard from early in the morning till late at night and who sometimes say their children grow up without their knowing them – all these young people who, in effect, become *de facto* fatherless children, are hostages to fortune. In order to become men they need fathers with whom they can identify, not shadowy fathers, not hostile fathers, but fathers with whom they can learn, play and discuss things, fathers from whom they can have proper attention. Boys need more than pocket-money fathers who send them out to the cinema. They need real fathers.

If we pass this Bill, we can be more profitably engaged in discussing how to mobilise our social resources better so that, for example, we could have more male child care officers and far more male teachers. We could consider how we could have a legitimacy law such as the Church has been calling for recently to enable the putative father to give legal recognition to his son and so save the boy from the syndrome, of which we are learning so much, of the dangerously genealogically bewildered child. We could be considering how to do more to help widows with children and unmarried mothers. We could consider how to find ways and means of leading those fatherless children who, with no man about the house to lead them on their way through boyhood, become bewildered and, in the confusions of adolescence, lose their way to manhood.

I believe that continuance of the existing law fosters the illusion that solely by punishment we can prevent homosexuality. In my view, the passage of this Bill would free society from much of its morbid preoccupation with punishment. It could release its energies to the more constructive task of fostering stable family relations, family relations in which children can grow up certain of their identity and confident of their own rôle.

4.6   *How successful was the 1967 Act?*

Many homosexual organisations have argued strongly that the reforms embodied in the 1967 Act have left untouched the worst manifestations of legal discrimination against homosexuals. The view that the Act contains disturbing anomalies is strongly supported by Tom Harper, a distinguished legal journalist and sometime editor of the New Law Journal. His analysis also suggests possible shortcomings in the official Criminal Statistics.

The Campaign for Homosexual Equality and the National Union of Students have both called for changes in the law relating to sexual offences, and in particular for the removal of a number of anomalies in the Sexual Offences Act 1967 relating to homosexual conduct. So soon? Their representations may to some extent reflect the impatience of those with an axe or two to grind. Nevertheless, many of the issues involved are of the widest public concern, especially in view of their implications for law reform and criminology generally.

Insofar as it removed homosexual conduct, in private, between consenting adults aged 21 and over, from the ambit of criminal sanctions, the 1967 Act was hailed by some and denounced by others for bringing about a revolutionary change in the law. It represented, in fact, a major compromise between opposed and indeed incompatible attitudes to homosexual conduct, and like many other similarly motivated law reform measures (the Divorce Reform Act 1969, for example), its revolutionary character stemmed, not from the particular changes it effected, but from the fact that it had happened at all. In that respect, it recalls Dr Johnson's famous analogy between women preachers and dogs that walk on their hind legs. Compromise, however, rarely makes for good law, and it is not therefore very surprising that anomalies have so soon become apparent in the operation of the 1967 Act, even within the scope of what it purported to improve.

One of the most glaring anomalies in the present law relating to homosexuality has arisen, not directly from the 1967 Act, but from a later enactment – the Family Law Reform Act of 1970. This, among other things, lowered the age of legal majority from 21 to 18, but only for the purposes of the *civil* law. Where under the *criminal* law the critical age was 21, as it was under the 1967 Act, it remained unchanged. A criminal offence is therefore committed where homosexual acts take place, even in private and between consenting persons, if one of them is, say, 20 and the other is 21. In such circumstances, moreover, a criminal offence is committed *by both*. In consequence, whereas consent was the basis on which the 1967 Act excluded homosexual conduct in private from the sanctions of the criminal law, consent is totally irrelevant for that purpose if one participant in a homosexual relationship is under 21. Yet an individual of 18 is deemed to be capable of giving fully effective legal consent to marriage, and a girl of as little as 16 to a heterosexual extramarital relationship. Many similar disparities may be cited, moreover, in relation to legal consent for the purposes of contractual relationships of all kinds.

Quite apart from anomalies of the kinds already referred to, the actual operation of the Sexual Offences Act 1967 has had some puzzling results. From the annual volumes of *Criminal Statistics*, for both buggery and attempted buggery (two of the three categories of conduct to which that Act applies), the number of offences given as 'known to the police' and 'cleared up' declined during the years 1967-72. So did the number of those convicted of those offences. By contrast, offences of indecency between males – the third category – increased over the same period, from 840 to 1,069 'known to the police' (in the 1972 volume, just published, this formula was altered to 'recorded as known to the police'), and from 817 to 1,039 'cleared up', while the number of those convicted of this offence increased from 444 in 1967 to 1,137 in 1971, an increase of no less than 160 per cent. Even allowing for a slight reversal of this trend to 1,079 convictions in 1972, the overall rate of increase was very sharp indeed, compared with that for any other offence in the criminal calendar, and that during a period when the

1967 Act might have been expected to produce precisely the opposite result in the case of indecency between males. Sociologically and criminologically speaking, it is of obvious importance whether this increase involved indecency with young children or homosexual acts between adults which, on one technical legal ground or another, were caught by the criminal law. The published criminal statistics are, however, totally silent on the point, and the Home Office are able to provide no information on it. All they are able to say is that virtually the whole of the increase in convictions between 1967 and 1972 occurred in the Metropolitan Police district and Lancashire, which raises more questions than it answers.

Apart from the mere number of convictions for indecency between males, the official statistics tell us a little about the ages of the offenders. With remarkable consistency, the highest proportion of offenders throughout the period 1967-72 involved the 30-40 age group hardly varied from year to year: 29 per cent in 1967, 26 per cent in 1968, 30 per cent in 1969, 31 per cent in 1970, 30 per cent in 1971 and 31 per cent in 1972. Offenders in the under-21 age group may, of course, include both participators (or only one) in an ordinary homosexual relationship, as well as those who committed acts of indecency in the ordinary sense of the term. The proportion of offenders in this age group fell sharply from 12 per cent in 1967 to 6 per cent in 1968, and thereafter continued to fall steadily but much less steeply – to 5 per cent in 1969, 4.5 per cent in 1970 and 4 per cent in 1971, with a slight increase, to 4.7 per cent, in 1972. On the face of it, this might suggest that the exemption from prosecution which homosexuals aged between 18 and 21 were denied under the 1967 Act was being accorded to them by extra-statutory concession on the part of prosecuting authorities. The decline in convictions is, however, virtually entirely accounted for by offenders in the under-17 age group, for the numbers of those aged 17 to 21 remained almost constant throughout. At the opposite end of the scale, offenders aged 60 and over increased from 4.7 per cent in 1967 to 6.6 per cent in 1968, but subsequently declined to 6.5 per cent in 1969, 6.2 per cent in 1970 and 5.7 per cent in 1971, rising in 1972 again to 6.2 per cent.

It is easy enough to record the discoverable facts – such as they are. But because they are as incomplete as they are, the conclusions that can be drawn from the *Criminal Statistics* are of correspondingly limited value. There is a need, therefore, for two campaigns: one to get the law relating to sexual offences changed, so as to remove its evident and in many instances indefensible anomalies, and the other to promote the kind of statistical research which will throw light on how the law actually works. What is needed therefore – and it is needed in varying degrees for every kind of criminal conduct – is not more statistics but more meaningful statistics. For what, basically, I am writing about here is the inadequacy of technical legal classifications of crime. In response to a specific inquiry about the greatly increased incidence of the offence classified as 'indecency between males', the Home Office replied that 'it is difficult to think of any way of establishing with certainty the reasons for what appears to be an exceptional increase in offences of this kind.' This begs the crucial question: offences of *what* kind? Of course, every law student knows what 'indecency between males' signifies, but it signifies virtually nothing that matters to the student of anything else. According to *Criminal Statistics*, its 'sub-classifications' are 1. indecency 'by a man of the age of 21 or over with another male person under the age of 21', and 2. indecency 'by a man with another male person other than in 1.'. Curiously enough, even these categories are indistinguishable in *Criminal Statistics* because the figures given there are never related to the persons *with whom* indecency occurs, but only to those *by whom* it is committed. This is only one instance of the shortcomings of these annual stocktakings of the criminal scene. To discover others, all you have to do is to take any one of the tables they contain and work out what it does *not* tell you that the searcher after criminological truth ought to know.

4.7 *Opening shots in the campaign to repeal the Contagious Diseases Acts*

Daily News, 31 December 1869: protest signed by Harriet Martineau, Florence Nightingale, Josephine Butler, and more than one hundred other women. Although this statement provoked much abuse, it effectively launched the vigorous debate which led, seventeen years later, to the repeal of the Acts.

We, the undersigned, enter our solemn protest against these Acts.

1st – Because, involving as they do such a momentous change in the legal safeguards hitherto enjoyed by women in common with men, they have been passed, not only without the knowledge of the country, but unknown, in a great measure, to Parliament itself; and we hold that neither the Representatives of the People, nor the Press, fulfil the duties which are expected to them, when they allow such legislation to take place without the fullest discussion.

2nd –Because, so far as women are concerned, they remove every guarantee of personal security which the law has established and held sacred, and put their reputation, their freedom, and their persons absolutely in the power of the police.

3rd – Because the law is bound, in any country professing to give civil liberty to its subjects, to define clearly an offence which it punishes.

4th – Because it is unjust to punish the sex who are the victims of a vice, and leave unpunished the sex who are the main cause, both of the vice and its dreaded consequences; and we consider that liability to arrest, forced medical treatment, and (where this is resisted) imprisonment with hard labour, to which these Acts subject women, are punishments of the most degrading kind.

5th – Because, by such a system, the path of evil is made more easy to our sons, and to the whole of the youth of England; inasmuch as a moral restraint is withdrawn the moment the State recognises, and provides convenience for, the practice of a vice which it thereby declares to be necessary and venial.

6th – Because these measures are cruel to the women who come under their action – violating the feelings of those whose sense of shame is not wholly lost, and further brutalising even the most abandoned.

7th – Because the disease which these Acts seek to remove has never been removed by any such legislation. The advocates of the system have utterly failed to show, by statistics or otherwise, that these regulations have in any case, after several years' trial, and when applied to one sex only, diminished disease, reclaimed the fallen or improved the general morality of the country. We have, on the contrary, the strongest evidence to show that in Paris and other Continental cities where women have long been outraged by this system, the public health and morals are worse than at home.

8th – Because the conditions of this disease, in the first instance, are moral, not physical. The moral evil through which the disease makes its way separates the case entirely from that of the plague, or other scourges, which have been placed under police control or sanitary care. We hold that we are bound, before rushing into experiments of legalising a revolting vice, to try to deal with the *causes* of the evil, and we dare to believe that with wiser teaching and more capable legislation, those causes would not be beyond control.

4.8   *The fight against the Contagious Diseases Acts*

The National Association for the Promotion of Social Science was founded in 1841, largely by lawyers concerned with harnessing the social sciences to practical reform. Many of the articles published in the Association's Transactions *reveal an awareness of social problems well in advance of the period. This article written in 1871 by H.N. Mozley, a barrister, calls vigorously for repeal of the Contagious Diseases Acts.*

The first Contagious Diseases Act was passed in the year 1864. It was found that seamen and soldiers suffered greatly from venereal disease. Under these circumstances, the military and naval authorities not unnaturally looked to continental countries, and particularly to that country which is nearest to us, to see how the evil was dealt with there. Accordingly, they caused a law to be passed on the principle which has so long obtained in France, applicable however to naval and military stations only, and not nominally recognizing prostitution as an institution of Government.

It would be unjust to attach any very severe censure to the promoters of this legislation. They unquestionably acted to the best of their judgment for the promotion of the interests with which they were charged. They wished to render vice safe, not indeed for its own sake, but in so far as this safety might promote the efficiency of the army. True it is that they seem to have completely ignored the moral aspect of the question. But the moral aspect of the question was at that time very imperfectly understood. It had not then received the exhaustive discussion which it has since received, nor was it at that time doubted that the French army was in a fair state of efficiency, and owed that efficiency in a great measure to legislation founded on the same principle.

I have said thus much, because nothing is more common than to hear supporters of the Contagious Diseases Acts appeal to their own good motives as a reason (apparently) for the continuance of the system. In last month's *Blackwood*, for instance, we are told that there was no thought of legalizing vice; all that was desired was to check disease. We reply that the promoters of the system have in fact legalized vice, whether they intended it or not. If every law is to be judged according to the motives of its promoters, a good deal of the laborious inquiries which are from time to time instituted as to the operations of particular laws would become quite unnecessary.

What then is the objection to this kind of legislation as applicable to soldiers and sailors? First of all, it treats them not as moral and responsible beings, but as unreasoning brutes requiring the gratification of their lowest and most sensual appetites provided for. It develops to the utmost their animal propensities, and does its best to stifle all higher aspirations. A great deal has been said, and that justly, on the degrading effect this system must have upon the unfortunate women who are subjected to it. I submit, however, that the degradation inflicted upon our soldiers and sailors is quite as great. Assuming, then, that these Acts did increase the efficiency of the army and navy, we should submit that the means employed were not such as could be rightfully employed for the purpose; but, in fact, that which is immoral can never be really expedient; and especially might we infer that anything which tends to demoralize the soldier cannot promote his efficiency. Such an inference is fully confirmed by the history of the late continental war. And if it be said that the system is also in operation in Germany, I would reply that its introduction there is far more recent, and its operation more limited than in France. The demoralization produced by such legislation would necessarily take time to show itself. Again, did not the British army gain splendid victories at the beginning of the century before Contagious Diseases Acts were thought of for the country? Why then should they be supposed necessary at the present day?

We now proceed to consider the moral question, in the narrow sense of that term – How do the Acts tend to promote or discourage unchaste living? That they would, in any direct way, encourage chastity in men is a proposition which I have never heard contended for, even by the strongest supporters of the Acts. So far as the Contagious Diseases Acts are successful, to that extent they must encourage dissoluteness of living by removing the fear of its attendant dangers. If they do not do this, it can only be because they fail in their object. It is ridiculous to urge that the fear of evil will not operate to deter men from actions, whether of an innocent or guilty character. All penal legislation is based upon an opposite principle. Of course, it may well be that the sanction may be insufficient in many individual cases to counteract the temptation; but to say that the sanction would in no case be effectual is absurd. But then it is said that the Contagious Diseases Acts diminish the number of prostitutes in the stations to which they apply. This is a point on which there is a good deal of conflict of opinion, into which I do not propose to enter.

Now that I have touched slightly upon the particular branches of the question, I would now consider it with reference to the means employed. These are, to invade the personal liberty of certain women, on the ground that they are propagating disease. Now every law properly so called interferes, more or less, with the liberty of those affected by it. But the interference with liberty, as that phrase is understood in connection with the Contagious Diseases Acts, is a far more cruel thing than that interference with liberty which is implied by the existence of law. Again, viewing it merely as an interference with liberty, the question in every case must be, whether the restraint in the individual case is a necessary evil or not. And in attempting to answer this question, it is exceedingly pertinent to inquire whether there is any inequality in the application of the law which is not warranted by the circumstances or necessities of the case. If, for instance, a law having a certain object be applied only to class A, when there is no apparent reason why the object of the law would not be equally fulfilled by its extension to class B, its exclusive application to Class A is *primâ facie* vicious. If sound in its principles, it does not go far enough. There is nothing more common in British legislation than this kind of inequality, which proceeds generally from inadvertence. The Contagious Diseases Acts have been no exception to this rule. While, as I have said, acting with the utmost severity and cruelty towards unchaste women, they let unchaste men go scot-free. And the manner in which they act upon unchaste women is not such as to induce the world to suppose that the Legislature regards prostitution as in any way objectionable, but rather that it is a legitimate profession, and that the State has nothing to do but to see that those who exercise it are properly qualified to do so. If the medical evidence showed that the medical examination of profligate men could not serve the object of the promoters of the Acts, the present objection as regards inequality could not apply; but no such evidence has been given, so far as I am aware of. The argument is not at all grappled with by the Commissioners in their report. They attempt to justify the distinction made between the sexes, partly by a supposed difference in the moral delinquency of unchastity according to the sex of the wrongdoer, and partly by the question of the medical examination of soldiers and sailors, a question which seems to have been suggested by the remarks made by certain witnesses before the Commission, but which is utterly irrelevant to the question we are now discussing, which is, why, if unchaste women are subjected to periodical medical examinations, unchaste men, whether soldiers or sailors or civilians, should not be equally so subjected.

To revert to the other part of their argument, we may observe that this also is wholly beside the present question. Be it remembered that supporters of Contagious Diseases Acts are nothing if not 'sanitary reformers.' Sanitary reform, in fact, is the watchword of the party. In order to justify the different treatment of the sexes, it should have been shown that the examination of unchaste men would be useless as a measure of sanitary reform. Now a great deal of evidence has been given by supporters of the Acts as to the amount of disease imported by soldiers and sailors and foreign traders.

Of course, while we prefer to take the supporters of the Acts on their own ground, we must not be understood as admitting for a moment the supposed difference between male and female unchastity. Every individual case which it is necessary to consider must be considered upon its own facts: but what we are contending for is, that there is no *a priori* palpable difference between the sexes in the matter. If the Commissioners' statement of this question be the correct one (which we may assume for the sake of the argument), then we say the case of the unchaste man is certainly worse than that of the unchaste woman. What they say is that unchastity in man is an irregular indulgence. But what crime is there of which they may not be said? Man is naturally corrupt, and he is bound to fight against his evil inclinations; and nothing can be said worse of him than that he does not do this. While, however, we claim the distinction made between the sexes as an argument against the Contagious Diseases Acts, and all legislation based upon such a system, it must not be inferred that we should at all approve of a system of medical examination of men. Believing the whole system of the Contagious Diseases Acts to be founded on an erroneous principle, we are strongly opposed to its extension in any direction.

Now let us consider the inequality which this system creates between the rich and the poor.

Taking again as the basis of our argument the statement of the Commissioners, that female incontinence arises from love of gain, we ask, Do rich women sin from love of gain? If not, here is at once a difference made between the rich and the poor. Of course I do not contend that this inequality is in itself a conclusive objection to the system, else we should have to repeal our laws against theft and fraud in money matters, and other similar offences which, by the nature of the case, must be committed chiefly by the poor. But I do mention it as a reason for narrowly watching the operation of the system, and for urging upon the rich the question whether they would acquiesce so tamely in legislation of this kind if it were *their* wives and daughters, and not the wives and daughters of the poor, who are subjected to the police interference of the kind sanctioned by the Contagious Diseases Acts. And I cannot but think that these considerations acquire additional force from the appeals made from time to time to the selfish indifferentism of the upper classes by press writers in the interest of the Acts – appeals made in a very different spirit from that of the poet: 'Homo sum, humani nil a me alienum puto.' Wealthy ladies are told that they need never know of these things, and ought never to concern themselves about them. What can such writers mean except that the rich are specially protected by the circumstances of their position from the evils and abuses incident to the working of the Acts, and, that being so, they need not trouble themselves how the poor may be affected by them?

I would now advert to a popular fallacy by which it is often attempted to defend legislation of this kind. It is said that the Acts are not intended for the benefit of unchaste men, but for that of the innocent women and children whom they infect. The obvious answer to this is that any serious misconduct on the part of a father of a family will, more or less, affect his wife and children. Suppose, for instance, a clerk is tempted to embezzle his employers' money, will he escape punishment because if he were sent to prison his family would be ruined? We punish the guilty, though we know that the innocent will be involved, to a certain extent, in the punishment. Why should persons suffering from venereal disease be so specially under the protection of the law?

I would conclude with a few observations with regard to the principles of legislation involved. To check disease is not a *necessary* function of government; I mean, it is not the object, or even one of the objects, for which governments are constituted. It is outside of the *necessary* scope of governmental functions. I do not, of course, by this mean that it is not within the possible scope of legislation. Many things are done, and properly doen, by Government, because they cannot be so well done by any other agency. But, judging from legislative procedents, the suppression of vice has been not less the object of governmental action than the check of disease. And if this is as it should be, what is to be said for a law which encourages vice to the extent to which it checks disease? If the law succeeds, it encourages vice, in men at least; if it does not do so, it is because it fails in its effect. What would be thought of a law which, by way of checking pauperism, should provide for giving doles to beggars? You might thus in the individual cases relieve distress, but there can be no doubt that such a law would be followed by a great increase of pauperism. You would be attempting to get rid of a public mischief by hampering the very vice which feeds it. And so with the diseases resulting from incontinence. The law attempts to check these diseases by granting impunity to the vices which foster them.

4.9   Mill joins battle against the Acts

The following letter was written by John Stuart Mill and Helen Taylor (29 December 1879), to Professor J. Nichol of Glasgow, on the Contagious Diseases Acts.

Dear Sir, – The chairman of the late meeting on Women's Suffrage had already conveyed to me the invitation which I have been honoured with to attend and address a meeting; but though it would give me much pleasure to do so, I have been obliged to answer that my engagements do not permit of my visiting Glasgow this winter.

I do not care much to discuss the Contagious Diseases Acts with yourself because, being willing as you are to allow women their fair share in electoral representation, you hold a perfectly defensible position when you differ from them on a point of legislation which concerns them. The position of those men, however, who, while they refuse women any share in legislation, enact laws which apply to women only, admittedly unpopular among women, is totally different from yours, and appears to me as base as it is illogical, unless, indeed, they are prepared to maintain that women have no other rights than the cattle, respecting whom a kindred Act has been passed. I fully agree with you that the true fundamental point to be set right is the franchise. I will, however, without refering to all the points in your argument which I disagree with, note down one or two of my reasons for differing from you on the main question.

1. There is very strong evidence that in the country (France) where legislation similar to the Contagious Diseases Acts has been long in force and its full effects have been produced, it increases the number of the class of women to whom it applies. The comparative safety supposed to be given increases the demand, and the number of women temporarily removed from the market makes vacancies in the supply which has to be, and are, made up. This is not necessarily shown by statistical returns, inasmuch as those can take no account of the great mass of clandestine prostitution practised in evasion of the law, and which, if prevented, could only be so by a still

more tyrannical use of the powers given to the police, and by exposing respectable women to a still greater amount of injury and indignity than at present.

2. No reason can be given for subjecting women to medical inspection which does not apply in a greater degree to the men who consort with them. The process is painful even physically, and sometimes dangerous, to women – not at all so to men; and it is idle to say that its application to men is impracticable – the same kind and degree of espionage which detects a prostitute could equally detect the men who go with her. The law being one-sided, inflicted on women by men, and delivering over a large body of women intentionally, and many other women unintentionally, to insulting indignity at the pleasure of the police, has the genuine characteristics of tyranny. You say that you think there is no weight in the objection that the law applies to one sex only, inasmuch as enlistment does the same. To this I think you will see that my replies are unanswerable. In the first place, the laws that represent enlistment are not made by women only, themselves not liable to it, and then applied to men only who have no voice in making them, as is the case in those penalties or discipline proposed to be applied to prostitutes by a legislature which neither consists of, nor is elected by, any proportion of women. Moreover, so long as women who offer themselves as soldiers are not accepted, the being a soldier must be taken as a privilege, and not a penalty, of sex. If women were only not soldiers because they are incapable of the fatigue and labour, then those women who in men's clothes have proved themselves capable would not be ejected on their sex being discovered. So long as this is the case military service is as much a privilege of our aristocracy as it is in Mahomedan countries where Christians are not allowed to serve. And the discipline to which this aristocracy voluntarily submits itself through the voice of a legislature which itself elects, cannot be compared to the discipline inflicted by those who do not share it without the consent of those who alone are exposed to it. Secondly, if it was impossible for any man to expose himself to military discipline without a woman as his companion, and if he only was liable to the discipline or punishment, the case would be more nearly parallel. You must remember that no woman can render herself liable as a prostitute without a man for her accomplice; yet when it comes to the punishment, or, if you prefer so to consider it, to the discipline, we hear no more of him. Thus the man only is a soldier, and he subjects himself voluntarily to the discipline; a man and a woman must be associated in prostitution, the woman only is subjected to discipline, and that without her own consent.

3. There are important medical opinions against as well as in favour of the Acts. If the preponderance is in favour this carries no weight with me, for professional men look at questions from a professional point of view, it being a medical man's professional duty to ascertain disease as early as possible and put it under treatment at once. The professional association is quite sufficient to account for a medical bias. I suppose medical men would desire to place men also under the discipline, which would then be decidedly less odious and more effectual. We cannot take their authority for the half and then refuse it for the whole. Some of the warmest medical advocates for the Acts admit that their operation can never be satisfactory

till men also are submitted to them, which they say they know men will
never consent to.

4. With regard to those who object to the Contagious Diseases Acts as
encouraging vice, I do not undertake to defend all that they say, but I think
them so far in the right that even if there were the strongest reasons of other
kinds for the Act, it would to soldiers and ignorant persons always have this
for one of its drawbacks, and it cannot but seem that legal precautions taken
expressly to make that kind of indulgence safe are a license to it. There is no
parallel case of any indulgence or pursuit avowedly disgraceful and immoral
for which the Government provides safeguards. A parallel case would be the
supplying of stomach-pumps for drunkards, or arrangements for lending
money to gamblers who may otherwise be tempted into theft in moments of
desperation, and throwing out their wives and families. We have no such
parallels by which to prove to men of lax habits in this matter that we
disapprove of while taking care of them. It is tolerably plain, therefore, that
as a matter of fact the legislature does regard this with less disfavour than
any other practice generally considered immoral and injurious to society,
and the public evidence of its doing so much of necessity tend to remove
feelings of shame or disapprobation connected with it.

4.10   The Wolfenden Report and the law relating to prostitution (1957)

304. The present law seems to be based on the desire to protect the
prostitute from coercion and exploitation. When it was framed, the
prostitute may have been in some danger of coercion; but today, either
through the effectiveness of the law or through changes which have removed
some of the economic and social factors likely to result in a life of
prostitution, she is in less danger of coercion or exploitation against her will.

305. The popular impression of vast organisations in which women are
virtually enslaved is perhaps in part due to the indiscriminate use of words
which suggest an entirely passive role for the women concerned. We have,
for example, learned of an arrangement between several prostitutes and a
car-hire firm whereby the firm made large sums of money out of the use of
their cars by the prostitutes. The firm was said to 'run' a group of
prostitutes, with the implication that they organised the women's activities.
Another group of prostitutes lived in rooms, at various addresses, of which
one particular man was landlord. This man, who had several convictions for
brothel keeping and living on the earnings of prostitution, was said to be
'running several girls'. In both cases, however much unpleasant exploitation
there might appear to the outsider to be, and might indeed actually be, the
association between the prostitute and the 'exploiter' was entirely voluntary
and operated to mutual advantage.

306. It is in our view an over-simplification to think that those who live on
the earnings of prostitution are exploiting the prostitute as such. What they
are really exploiting is the whole complex of the relationship between
prostitute and customer; they are, in effect, exploiting the human
weaknesses which cause the customer to seek the prostitute and the

prostitute to meet the demand. The more direct methods with which we have dealt above are not the only means by which the trade is exploited; that it continues to thrive is due in no small measure to efforts deliberately made to excite the demand on which its prosperity depends. Abraham Flexner, in his work on 'Prostitution in Europe', to which the Street Offences Committee made reference, says (page 41) 'A very large constituent in what has been called the irresistible demand of natural instinct is nothing but suggestion and stimulation associated with alcohol, late hours and sensuous amusements'. At the present time, entertainments of a suggestive character, dubious advertisements, the sale of pornographic literature, contraceptives and 'aphrodisiac' drugs (sometimes all in one shop), and the sale of alcoholic liquor in premises frequented by prostitutes, all sustain the trade, and in turn themselves profit from it. With most of these evils the law attempts to deal so far as it can without unduly trespassing on the liberty of the individual; and, as in the case of prostitution itself, it is to educative measures rather than to amendment of the law that society must look for a remedy.

4.11   Sociological perspective on the Stephen Ward case

This extract is from an article by Louis Blom-Cooper, 'Prostitution: a socio-Legal Comment on the Case of Dr. Ward'.

The criminal proceedings against Dr Stephen Ward died with him on 3 August 1963; the issues, raised by prosecution brought against him for living on the earnings of prostitution, live on to haunt our memory of a man who fleetingly stood at the centre of a scandal that shook the British public's faith in its own morality, and at one time bore all the signs of a crisis that might even topple the government.

Dr Ward, a skilled and socially well-connected osteopath who displayed an untutored but not wholly unpleasing talent for painting, ran a curious ménage at his Marylebone Mews flat. But for the fact that one of his mistresses had experienced an adulterous association with a Minister of Defence, he might at least have escaped the clutches of the criminal law, if not the attentions of the police. But once the sorry tale of odd, and sometimes perverse, sexual practices was revealed to the public at large, the established order went into battle against this man, whose sole offence was a nonconformity in sexual matters that met with the same kind of relentless reaction from the prosecuting authorities that characterised the prosecution of *Lady Chatterley's Lover*.

Was Dr Ward's conduct so socially grave that it called for more than mere public censure, and if so did the full might of the legal system need to be invoked merely to record for posterity our society's disapprobation? Was Dr Ward's offence so clearly within that area of private behaviour which it is the law's business to curb by the agency of the criminal law?'

No one seriously questions the view that Ward's conduct was, by current standards of our society, immoral; indeed he put himself forward at the trial as an immoral man. And no doubt in less dramatically charged circumstances, where his liberty was not in direct jeopardy, he would similarly have been frank about his conduct (it might be that he would rather regard himself as amoral – a classic case of a creative psychopath). Nor were Miss Keeler and Miss Rice-Davies anything but adolescent drabs, for whom little public sympathy should be wasted – despite Lord Denning's jejune injunction to his readers not to judge them too harshly.

But immorality and criminality are far from co-extensive. It should not, and does not, follow that public condemnation of Ward's immoral behaviour should have been reflected in a judicial condemnation of him as a criminal. Yet the fact that he should have been prosecuted to conviction on two charges of living on the immoral earnings of prostitution while the girls on whom he partially lived (and, by all accounts, they upon him!) were not amenable to the criminal law, is a reflection of the law's inability to discriminate between immorality and criminality. Ward's conviction is a classic instance of the official and public attitude towards prostitution – which throughout this century has become increasingly tolerant – and the attitude towards the men with whom the prostitutes live – which remains relentlessly intolerant.

The English criminal law's activities against the *maquereau* date only from the Vagrancy Act 1898. It is significant that that Act provided that every male person who knowingly lives wholly or in part on the earnings of prostitution shall be deemed a rogue and a vagabond. Thus, the primary aim of the Victorians was to remove from public sight not only the prostitutes but also those who supposedly preyed or battened on these women. The Act added that the courts would presume a man was living on immoral earnings of a prostitute if he habitually lived with or controlled the prostitute; these provisions are substantially reproduced in the Sexual Offences Act 1956. The very fact that the offence should be related to other acts of vagrancy demonstrates markedly that our Victorian forbears were concerned with the public aspect of prostitution and those who engaged in what has always been a lawful trade.

The law – and the judges have lent ready support to it – has long visualised the *maquereau* as a lout or a bully who lives parasitically on the prostitute. If the present judiciary has tacitly abandoned the old notion that the offence of living on immoral earnings was designed to protect the prostitute from coercion or exploitation against her will, the view is still current that, but for the *maquereau*, the prostitute would be living a decent and honest life. The law in this respect is sadly out of touch with social realities.

The law has in fact never really made up its mind as to what it understands by the word 'prostitution'; instead it has dealt with the matter empirically, judging the matter largely on the amount of moralistic fulmination directed at the prostitute and her *maquereau*. Was Ward so wrong in limiting the definition of a prostitute to the woman who engages in sexual intercourse (or sexual perversions) 'without sentiment or feeling' for the male client who pays her? His definition was rejected, though no alternative was put forward. A satisfactory way of defining prostitution would be to stress the element of 'payment'. Prostitution can exist in its socially accepted sense only if there is a pre-existing contract of sale between the male client and the woman. If a woman regularly declines to have any sexual intercourse with men unless and until she is paid for the service, then she is no prostitute. Her discrimination in selecting the men she is prepared to go to bed with discloses a motive other than profit for indulging in sexual intercourse. Prostitution is the offering by a woman of her body simply for the return of financial gain to herself.

If the dividing line between promiscuity and prostitution has been blurred, so the offence of living on immoral earnings has become explicable only in terms of the law's attempt to counter what it regards as grave anti-social acts of prostitution, deserving to be labelled as criminal. The doubts about Dr Ward's trial thus reflect a much more fundamental ambivalence in the law's attitude towards promiscuous (and hence immoral) conduct. Society is constantly having to resolve the problem, how far sinful conduct should be punished by the criminal law. Prostitution, and the offences related to it, are a practical example of society's over-eagerness to translate immorality into criminality. About prostitution there is an assumption, both by the public and by the law that the activities of the *maquereau* are inherently criminal. The man who procures a woman for the purposes of prostitution – and but for whom the woman would not engage in this oldest profession – is certainly committing a grave anti-social act which the law is entitled to dub as criminal.

There is a further basic hypocrisy about the law's attitude to prostitution. Prostitution in this country is not in itself illegal. Yet the law does everything connected with the lawful trade to penalise those who engage in it. Prostitutes may not seek their customers in public places; landlords may not let flats to them at inflated rents, knowing that they are to be used for prostitution; publishers may not advertise the services of prostitutes in a directory; publicans, in London at least, may not knowingly permit prostitutes to meet their clients on public house premises; and, probably, newsagents may not display window notices advertising the whereabouts of prostitutes, even in thinly veiled language. The assumption that these restrictions upon the peripheral activities to prostitution will drastically, or even marginally, reduce the scale and temptations of prostitution has yet to be substantiated by solid social research. There is in fact the very gravest suspicion that the law does not care for social realities; it bases its action upon highly emotive opinion on what is best for the country's morals.

There might be sound reasons of social policy why any or all these activities should be condemned by the law. But if the sole reason for these offences is the moral revulsion they arouse, we should be more honest if we either removed them from the criminal statute book or made prostitution itself a crime, a step which we have always declined to take on the basis of a sound social policy that prostitution is certainly ineradicable and cannot even be severely curtailed by direct or indirect prohibition.

4.12   Instructions to the police on the Street Offences Act 1959

Home Office Circular 109/1959 deals with police procedure under s.2 of the Street Offences Act 1959. This section introduced the cautionary system which had to be operated before a prostitute could be held to have committed the offence of soliciting in public.

On the first occasion when a woman who has not previously been convicted of loitering or soliciting for the purpose of prostitution is seen loitering or soliciting in a street or public place for that purpose, the officer seeing her will obtain the assistance of a second officer as a witness, and when both officers, after having kept the woman under observation, are satisfied by her demeanour and conduct that she is in fact loitering or soliciting for the purpose of prostitution, they will tell her what they have seen and caution her. Details of the caution will subsequently be recorded at the police station and in a central register for the Metropolitan Police District. The two officers, after administering the caution, will ask the woman if she is willing to be put in touch with a moral welfare organisation or a probation officer, and invite her to call at the police station at a convenient time to see a woman police officer for these arrangements to be made, unless she prefers her name and address to be given to a welfare organisation or a probation officer without going to the station. If the woman continues to loiter or solicit for the purpose of prostitution, a second formal caution will be given in the street and recorded and a second offer will be made to put her in touch with a welfare officer or probation officer. She will not be arrested until she is seen loitering or soliciting on the third occasion.

4.13   Curbing the kerb-crawler

Lord Chorley *(b.1895) is a distinguished legal scholar, law reformer, and first editor of the* Modern Law Review. *The following extract is from his introductory speech on the Street Offences Bill, designed to plug a gap in the law which punishes prostitutes for soliciting in public but leaves unscathed the 'kerb-crawling' male who seeks to obtain a woman's sexual services. Although widely supported in principle, the Bill failed to obtain a second reading on the grounds that, as drafted, it bestowed alarmingly wide powers on the police which might have led to the arrest of innocent parties.*

Lord Chorley: My Lords, I beg to move that this Bill be read a second time. On May 27, 1965, in Preston, Lancashire, a man was observed by the police driving his car slowly about the streets and approaching various women to whom he spoke. The police had no doubt that his objective was to get one of these women to go away with him for purposes of sexual intercourse; and indeed most of the women, if not all, were known to be prostitutes. The police accordingly charged the man with soliciting for an immoral purpose under Section 32 of the Sexual Offences Act 1956, which makes it an offence for a man to solicit for immoral purposes. Before the justices, the point was taken that this section did not cover such a case as this, and the justices, who were satisfied that a *prima facie* case had been made out against the man, decided to state a case for the opinion of the High Court as to whether this point taken by the defence was correct or not. In the result the High Court, by a majority, held that the section was concerned with procuring and similar activities, and was not aimed at soliciting for ordinary sexual intercourse. The charge was accordingly dismissed.

Some people have read this case as meaning that a charge could not be brought in respect of what is commonly known as 'kerb crawling'; but its implications are very much wider than that and in effect have come to this: that a man cannot be dealt with under this section of the Sexual Offences Act for soliciting a woman for sexual or immoral purposes. The case of *Crook* v. *Edmondson*,[5] which was decided just two years ago in 1966, received a great deal of publicity at the time and indeed was received with a great deal of indignation in many quarters, an indignation which I must say I felt myself, because it underlined a fact which had been argued about a great deal during the passing of the Street Offences Act in 1959, that men and women were not placed on a par with each other in regard to this type of offence. There are really two causes why a great deal of indignation was felt about this and why this indignation still persists. The first, and I think the most important of the two, is that, as I say, it underlines the fact that in this part of the criminal law there is discrimination between men and women, and my main object in bringing this Bill before your Lordships' House to-day is to abolish this inequality.

My Lords, if I may say so, this is a particularly apposite time for us to take action of this kind. Your Lordships may have seen that in a little book which has recently been brought out to·celebrate this year, Human Rights Year, quite a point is made of the fact that there is still a great deal of inequality between men and women in respect of prostitution. Let us in 1968 secure this further human right. It is, of course, the right of women to secure their claim for equality with men in this sort of matter. And this year, as your Lordships will remember, is the 50th anniversary of the year in which women were first given some degree of political equality, when they won the vote. So, for both these reasons, it would be very appropriate for us to give this Bill a Second Reading.

It has been suggested that there are so few cases in which men are involved in soliciting that there is not much need to have further legislation. I think that this is quite wrong. 'Kerb crawling' which is very much in point in connection with this Bill, is good proof to the contrary; and already at the time of the Wolfenden Committee Report this practice of 'kerb crawling' had become a real nuisance which the Committee recognised, although they did not feel that they were called upon to make any recommendation about it.

Since that time, my Lords, this has undoubtedly become a much more

5. [1966] 2 Q.B. 81.

serious evil, especially in the larger cities. It was commented on, indeed, by Mr Justice Sachs in his judgment in the *Crook* v. *Edmondson* case. The Josephine Butler Society, too, which has been very much concerned, and is very much concerned to-day with this matter, and has taken a large part in the campaign for bringing this Bill before your Lordships' House, has a great deal of evidence that this is a very real nuisance in very many large towns up and down the country. I could take up quite a lot of your Lordships' time by quoting from material which has come to me over the last week since this Bill was published. I will content myself with two examples.

One was taken from an address given by a Liverpool magistrate, Miss White, J.P., a year or so ago. She said:

'In Liverpool this is now much more open and chiefly due to the use of cars. It is very persistent, particularly in certain areas of the city. Most unlikely women are molested, followed, and sometimes attacked. Victims have included a woman of 80 and women teachers on the staff of one of the schools, who have been given friendly protection by neighbouring housewives.'

There is a good deal more on the same sort of lines, which shows that this is just as rife in the Manchester area, and it is well known to be troublesome all over London.

I have a letter from a young woman who lives in the Notting Hill district, out of which I should like to quote a short passage:

'I am the eldest of a family of five daughters living in Notting Hill – a notorious area of London, but nevertheless one where many ordinary people live and work. In this area there is a constant stream of men in cars and on foot who spend their time accosting any female from the age of 12 to 60 at any time of the day or night. During my schooldays I used to dread the walk home … '

This is going on all over the country at the present time and it is high time it stopped. It is so well known that this is an evil that there is no need for me to spend longer in stressing it to your Lordships. I submit that it is clear enough that this 'kerb crawling' is a real nuisance, just as soliciting by women had become a real nuisance in London and other large towns before the Street Offences Act was passed.

4.14 A skirmish in the battle against adultery

Many who have argued for a strengthening of the moral fibre of the community through extension of the criminal law have taken adultery as their primary target, and this view was particularly prevalent during the period spanning the latter part of the eighteenth and the early part of the nineteenth centuries. In 1779 Shute Barrington, Bishop of Llandaff, brought in a Bill to prevent adulterers from remarrying within a specified period of time. Supported by, among others, the Duke of Richmond and Lord Chancellor Thurlow, the Bill passed the Lords but was thrown out in the Commons where the opposition was led by James Fox. (Much the same fate had befallen a similar Bill introduced by the Duke of Atholl in 1771.) The following is an extract from the debates in the Lords on the 1779 Bill (**Parliamentary History**, *11 and 30 March 1779.*).

Debates in the Lords on the Adultery Bill. March 11. The Bishop of *Llandaff* (Dr Shute Barrington) rose to propose a Bill 'for the more effectual Discouragement of the Crime of Adultery.' The learned prelate introduced this Bill with a feeling and eloquent exordium. He represented, with great pathos, the private miseries consequent on such offences, and the misfortunes to the state from a cause which became so much the more dangerous, from its being a domestic one. In the more ancient annals of our country, this offence has been much less frequent, because punished with greater severity; and it was remarkable that in the 17 years of his Majesty's reign, whom he might pronounce, without fearing the imputation of sacrilege, as exemplary a prince as any of his predecessors, there had been as many divorces as had happened during the whole history of the country put together, since its transactions had been submitted to written record. There were two reasons for this: the total extinction of the internal monitor of shame, in the present period, which had been felt by our forefathers with its due force, and kept them from the commission of an offence wherein that sensation was more particularly appealed to. The other reason was, an injudicious mitigation of the penal laws with regard to the commission of this crime. By the common law of England, no woman after a divorce was permitted to regain her dower, nor to marry again within a limited time. A method of evading this salutary statute had been discovered by making previous settlements, or by entering into private bonds; so that a woman might now enjoy as many conveniences of rank and situation after a compelled dismission from her husband, as after a separation from him by the hand of providence, and in a situation when she had merited every thing by her conjugal tenderness and fidelity. The learned bishop presented his Bill, which was read the first time.

March 30. The Bill was read a second time.

The Earl of *Effingham* objected to its commitment. He believed it to be totally inadequate to the purpose proposed, and that no possible reformation was likely to be the consequence of it. Instead of prohibiting the parties offending from marrying within a prescribed period, in his opinion, the most effectual punishment would be to compel them to an immediate marriage, within twelve hours after the decree of their lordships pronouncing the divorce.

The Bishop of *Llandaff* said, it was not by any means his expectation, to eradicate an evil of so confirmed a kind; but though the effort he had now made, might not prove adequate to the entire removal of the offence, yet if it contributed to stop the growing mischief, and to produce only a partial cure, it would not be without its advantages. He reminded the House of the shameful height to which the vice of adultery had risen amongst us, and especially in the higher ranks of life, to the great misfortune of some of the first families in the kingdom. He explained his intention to be that of fixing a brand of infamy on an adulteress, that might operate as a terror upon the mind, and prevent the so frequent commission of the crime.

The Earl of *Carlisle* thought that no penal statute could reach a mere immorality. The injunctions of a higher judicature were the laws by which such offenders were to be corrected; and if persons so far forget their duty as not to be intimidated by the precepts originating from that superior authority, he did not suppose they were capable of being affected by any other interposition. It was in his opinion unjust, that the weaker offender should be considered as the greater culprit. The man was to escape punishment by this Bill; all was to fall on the unfortunate woman, who generally possessed stronger inclinations, without an equal power of imposing that restraint of thought, and reasoning, concerning consequences, which the learned prelate had held out as the only protection against the offence.

The *Lord Chancellor* spoke with peculiar feeling, strength, and argument. He said the matter immediately before the House was, whether or no they would take into their consideration a method for the more effectually preventing the crime of adultery? That was the appellation ascribed to the Bill; and if they rejected it, they pronounced in form, that they were not disposed to put any restraint at all upon this abominable practice. Whether or no the means prescribed in the Bill were likely to prove adequate to the purpose, would be a subject for inquiry when the House should be in a committee upon it; at present, the plain question was, Do you, or do you not, think it worth your while to interpose by some method for the prevention of a crime that not only subverts domestic tranquility, but has a tendency, by contaminating the blood of illustrious families, to affect the welfare of the nation in its nearest interests? The Bill went generally to all mankind, to every husband and father in the kingdom; but it concerned their lordships more than any other order of people. A due regard for his posterity was to every man a near and dear object; to nobility, the most important to which they could possible advert. He begged the House to recollect, that the purity of the blood of their descendants, was, and must necessarily be, an essential consideration in the breast of all the peers of the kingdom. Every attempt to preserve the descent of peers unstained and perfectly pure, merited their immediate attention; for his part, he declared, he saw the importance of the Bill to the peerage so clearly, that if he had the blood of forty generations of nobility flowing in his veins, he could not be more anxious to procure it that assent and concurrence, which it deserved from their lordships. He did not agree with the noble lord who spoke last, who had said that adultery was a mere consideration of morality, and was not altogether a subject of human legislation. He observed, that when immorality went so far as openly to disturb the order of civil society, it was then necessary in every civilised state for the legislature to interfere.

4.15   *The futility of making adultery a crime*

Samuel Horsley *(1733-1806), Bishop of St Asaph (1802-06) and author of works on mathematics and theology, wrote as follows in a letter to John Bowlder in 1796.*

Against adultery laws will not be successful, because adultery is not reprobated by the public mind. I doubt whether a new statute upon the subject could be carried. Certainly not one that should make the punishment corporal. I think a law restraining the delinquent party from forming a new marriage before the death of the former consort, might have a good effect. But yet it would deserve serious consideration whether such a restraint might not be a temptation to private murthers. ...

4.16　Adultery: 'destructive of the best interests of society'

In 1800 the Duke of Auckland declared that 'Great Britain had preserved her existence amidst the paroxysms and convulsions and downfalls of nations, by the effect of our being a little less irreligious and a little less immoral than others', an assertion which met with a general cry of 'hear, hear' from his fellow peers (Sir L. Radzinowicz, A History of the English Criminal Law, *London, 1956, vol.3, p.201). Shortly after this, Lord Auckland brought in a Bill to prevent adulterers from remarrying and providing that every Bill of divorce should contain a clause to that effect. Despite wide support from peers (including several prelates) the Bill was defeated by 143 votes to 104 in the Commons (*Parliamentary History, *2 and 4 April and 10 June, 1800).*

Debate in the Lords on the Adultery Prevention Bill. April 2, Lord Auckland said, that he rose with reluctance to present a bill which might have come from others with more propriety and effect. But such of their lordships as had attended a late debate, respecting parliamentary proceedings in cases of divorce, would recollect, that he had happened to advert to a suggestion which received the concurrence of the whole House. From that moment he had thought it his duty to come forward; and he was now prepared to submit to their lordships the justice, propriety, and expediency of providing, that 'It shall not be lawful for the person, on account of whose adultery a marriage shall be dissolved, to intermarry with the person with whom the adultery shall have been committed.' Such a restriction was not new. It might be traced through different periods of history in the laws and practice of other nations. Indeed, in many of those nations, adultery had been punished as a capital crime; and even in this country, during the Commonwealth in 1650, it had been made felony without benefit of clergy. He was not desirous to imitate republics in the excesses of their puritanism or profligacy; but perhaps he ought to wish for the sake of the public morality, that the crime of adultery were subject to some chastisement beyond that of a civil action for pecuniary damages. And surely it was a strange system, which permitted the offending parties not only to go unpunished, but to form with each other that sacred contract which they had grossly violated, and in many cases to derive benefit from their offence. By the law of Scotland, in 1600, it was made unlawful for the adulterers to intermarry, and that law still continues in force. And even in this part of the united kingdom it is the law of the land, and recognized in the 107th canon of the church, that neither of the parties when divorced, even for cause of adultery, shall marry again in the lifetime of each other. Their lordships would recollect that with us, as in Roman Catholic countries, there exists no jurisdiction which can give divorce *a vinculo matrimonii*, except for causes which existed anterior to the marriage; a parliamentary bill of divorce is therefore a special interference, in a case for which the law has not provided; such bills in their origin were merely remedial and solely in favour of the injured party; but the offending party not having been excepted or restricted, had acquired, by inference and acquiescence, the supposed right of contracting a new marriage, even with the person with whom the adultery had been proved; and thus it was, that the interposition of the legislature was made beneficial to criminals, and that it gave hire and salary instead of punishment to an offence of heinous magnitude, both in its example and consequences. – The incongruity and evil tendency of such a result, had been strongly felt, as soon as parliamentary divorces became frequent. To the end of the seventeenth century, in a period of 150 years from the Reformation, the whole number of bills of divorce for adultery had not been more than three or four; the particulars might be found in the proceedings on the Duke of Norfolk's case, reported in the State Trials; and even during the first fifty years of the eighteenth century, the instances were rare. But the applications for these remedial bills having become scandulously frequent, towards the year 1771 the duke of Athol proposed a bill to prevent the intermarriage of the offending parties. That bill passed through the House of Lords without opposition, and was rejected in the House of Commons by a small majority. A similar bill was again brought forward in 1779, by the then bishop of Llandaff [supra], and it met with a similar fate. Was it, then reasonable to expect that the present moment would be more favourable to the same measure? He believed that it was. The promise of marriage in the event of detection and divorce, is a notorious ground of seduction, and the prohibition of eventual marriages, cannot fail to operate as a strong prevention of the crime in question. Under these impressions, he entertained the most sanguine hopes that the bill which he meant to propose would be adopted. He had, therefore, postponed for the present the intention of seeking the same object through the mode of a standing order. The bill would contain two provisions; the one to make it unlawful for the offending parties to intermarry; the other, to require that every bill of divorce shall contain a clause to prohibit such intermarriage. – The noble lord then presented a bill, 'for the more effectual Prevention of the Crime of Adultery.' The bill was read a first time, and ordered to be printed.

April 4. On the order of the day for the second reading of the bill,

The Duke of Clarence rose to oppose it. That the crime of adultery was a most pernicious crime, that it struck at the root of all domestic comfort, and was destructive of the best interests of society, was an idea not more strongly impressed on the minds of the right reverend prelates opposite than on his own. Happy should he be, therefore, to support any measure that had a tendency to give a check to the increase of adultery; but, highly as he thought of the talents of the noble lord who introduced the bill, and much as he admired the motives that had induced the noble lord to introduce it, he felt it his duty to oppose the bill, because it appeared to his mind as more likely to increase than to check the career of adultery. When he considered the consequences that would follow the operation of such a bill, he could not but consider it as a measure of the most fatal nature, to that description of persons who from the amiableness of their sex, were best entitled to compassion and liberality. His main objection to the bill was, that it contained no provision for the poor unfortunate female who should fall a victim to her own vanity, or weakness. It, on the contrary, took away from her almost the only means of remedy and satisfaction that the practice of the legislature in respect to divorce bills at present allowed her – the hopes of salving her reputation by a marriage with the man, whose arts had beguiled her of her virtue, deprived her of her husband's affections, and destroyed her domestic happiness.

Let their lordships recollect, that as divorce bills were only within the reach of persons of property and some rank in life, the wives of such persons, when fallen from their respectable situations, were in a manner expelled society, and deprived of the usual resorts for obtaining a livelihood. They could not work as menial servants; they were not instructed in any line of business: they could not beg. And what other line of providing the means of life was left open to them, but abandoning themselves to prostitution? It was a fact, to which he adverted with great pain, that among the divorce bills which had come to their bar in the course of a few years, several of them had been petitioned for by persons of high rank and title. Let their lordships therefore consider the case as their own. Let them ask themselves, whether they thought their own ladies, if by any misfortune it should be their fate to be parties complained of in divorce bills, ought to be turned over from their exalted situations, to all the misery and wretchedness to which, under the operation of the present bill, they would stand exposed! However deeply the prevalence of the crime of adultery was to be deplored, surely all consideration for the unfortunate of the most amiable sex was not to fall a sacrifice to their lordships' zeal to prevent a crime confessedly most pernicious to society! It had been said, that many of the recent divorces originated in a previous contract, between the offending parties, to intermarry when the first marriage should be dissolved. He greatly doubted that fact. He rather thought the virtue of the woman had in most cases been undermined by the artful persuasions of the man, to whose intrigues the consequent injury of the husband's honour and happiness was owing. There might possibly by a solitary instance of some collusion between the parties; but he must have the fact better established, that it had frequently been the case, before he could bring himself to give it credit. He could easily believe that divorces by the legislature increased the number of adulteries. When a divorce was obtained by an act of legislature, as the matter stood at present, it was open to the man who had been the instrument of the crime with the wife, to make the best amends in his power, by marrying her. But, looking at the case as a man of the world, he could not shut his eye to the pretty generally known fact, that the husband who, by suing for pecuniary damages, obtained a verdict, was considered not as a very honourable man, if when he received them, he put them in his own pocket, instead of returning them to the purse of the defendant. The royal duke compared the general effect of punishments with the crimes to which they were applied. He instanced the cases of treason, rebellion, mutiny, and desertion, in opposition to those of a baser nature, such as murder, robbery, burglary and other felonies, contending, that in each, in proportion as the punishment was rendered capital and severe, the crime rather increased than diminished. Mutiny, as a military offence, was parallel to rebellion, considered as a political and civil crime; but, increasing the severity of the punishment of desertion had not tended to check its frequency. To prove the inefficacy of capital punishments in cases of desertion, he need only instance when the duke de Choiseul was the French minister, in the war before the peace of 1763, an edict was issued, subjecting every deserter to be shot. Yet it was notorious that during this severe edict, there were more deserters than ever. He imputed many of the late divorces to the accidental effect of the war, which detained officers of the army and navy for a long time from their wives; but when peace should arrive, that effect would cease, and he had no doubt that applications for divorce bills would then diminish. His royal highness concluded with moving 'That the said bill be read a second time on this day four months'.

The Bishop of London addressed himself to the House, as guardians of the religion and morality of the country, and earnestly entreated them to pay due attention to a subject of the first importance to both. He complimented the illustrious duke on the honourable and eloquent manner in which he had stated his reasons for objecting to the bill, and rejoiced to hear from his royal highness, that he was a firm advocate for the religious principles of the Church of England, and for the morality of the people, as well as a detester of the foul crime of adultery. His lordship said, he had taken upon himself to come forward thus early in the debate, because he had a better opportunity of witnessing the increasing number of divorces than many other persons, since a great proportion of them originated in his own consistorial court. In a very short period the number had increased to 198; and unless some means were resorted to by the legislature to check their progress, the number in a few years would be so great, that it could not but undermine the best props and securities of society. That the present bill was all that was requisite to stop the fatal career of the crime of adultery, was more than could be expected; but it would do good to a certain extent; and until something more effectual should be proposed, it was worthy of cordial support.

The Earl of Guilford said, that every noble lord must deeply lament the prevalence of the crime of adultery; he could not, however, agree that the number of divorce bills was an infallible proof of the increase of adultery; on the contrary, it might be contended for as an argument the other way. Nor could he admit, that the morals of the people of this country were more vicious than those of antecedent periods. That divorce bills, by their number, established that fact, no man would agree, who looked back to what had been the case in France under the old government. It was well known that, during the monarchy no divorce was obtainable; and would any man deny that the crime of adultery was less frequent there, than it had been in Great Britain since the legislature had consented to grant divorce bills? He doubted, if the proposed bill were to pass, whether it would have any tendency to prevent the crime of adultery; though it was undeniable that it would operate as a merciless punishment upon the unfortunate female, who had sacrificed her honour. But surely the House would not adopt a remedy for a most crying evil, without some greater certainty of its being likely to be efficacious, than could be proved to be the case of the bill under consideration.

The Bishop of Durham said, that nothing could be more self evident, than that the rapidly increasing crime of adultery, threatened the most serious consequences to the morality and religion of the people of this country. That the proposed bill would not operate to the full extent of all that was desired, was a fact to be lamented; but would noble lords therefore refuse a measure calculated to operate as some check to its progress, because it did not promise to answer the whole of the wished-for purpose? Let but the present bill pass, and he would ask their lordships, whether they did not believe a woman would be more cautious than before in encouraging any man in his attempt upon her virtue? If, misled by an unhappy and unlawful passion, she once passed the rubicon, she would be taught that she could not repass it, that she could not patch up her reputation by marrying her paramour. In regard to what had fallen from the royal duke, that the woman would be driven to prostitution and vicious courses for a livelihood, it by no means followed as a necessary consequence. When she had manifested her contrition and repentance, she might marry again, and be restored to society; for though the bill interdicted her intermarrying with the adulterer, it left her at liberty to marry any other person. The ratio in which divorces had multiplied of late years would be seen from the fact, that from the reign of Henry the 8th down to the present king, not more than thirty or forty parliamentary divorces were obtained; whereas, during the present reign, no fewer than ninety-eight had taken place. Let the example afforded to the rising generation be considered, and the legislature must feel the imperious necessity of taking every possible step to avert the evil. With respect to the morals of the country, he must consider the evil complained of as a strong proof of their becoming worse; and among the chief cause of this was to be classed the promulgation of those principles by some of the most celebrated teachers of the school of infidelity, which inculcated that adultery was no crime, and which endeavour to bring the marriage contract into disrepute.

Lord Eldon observed, that the tenderness for the ecclesiastical courts, which some noble lords affected to think peculiar to the present bill, was what was uniformly inserted in every act of parliament, with the object of which those courts could have any concern. With regard to the propriety of allowing pecuniary damages for adultery, he would pause a long time before he could propose an alteration in that respect. As the law stood at present, it was competent to any man who was injured to bring his action for damages, and at the same time institute a prosecution in the ecclesiastical court; but whenever that happened, the judges in the courts below caused, of their own authority, one of the suits to be stopped; and he confessed that it would be better to regulate this by act of parliament than to leave it to the discretion of the judges. As to the noble lord who now presided in the court of King's-bench, if he was a legal recluse, he found means to obtain in the retirement of his study a great deal of learning, and in his practice a great deal of experience. That learned lord, as well as every other judge, was bound by his oath to state to the jury what he thought of the evidence, and of the case before him' and unless he was stript of his heart and his feelings, he could not be supposed to overlook any circumstances of collusion. The objection, that this bill would be productive of perjuries, was equally applicable to any bill under the authority of which oaths were to be administered. He declared, that he differed entirely from the sentiments just quoted, and was inclined to think, that whatever lord Thurlow might have said as an advocate when attorney-general, he would hold a different language as a legislator, and a member of that House. In this opinion he was the more confirmed, as that noble lord had recommended, that instead of confining the power of granting final divorces to the legislature, the ecclesiastical court should be empowered to grant a divorce *a vinculo matrimonii* – To come to the clause that prohibited the intermarriage of the adulterer and the adultress: if he had turned his attention to the bill for a century, he was persuaded that the result of the best attention he could bestow would be to prevent that intermarriage; and he was fortified in this opinion by the best writers, and by the experience which he had acquired even in his recluse walk of life. There were various kinds of seducers. There was what was called the honourable seducer, who laid his plan of seduction with a view of marrying the lady. Now, when this honourable seducer should find that there was a law to prevent that marriage, it would call him aside from the path he was pursing. As to the other seducer, which might be called the dishonourable one, when he reflected that he was to face a judge and a jury, and that he was to be punished, perhaps it would cool his appetite a little; and so far the punishment, not as a punishment, but as a prevention, would be found to have a good effect. It had been stated, that the woman was to be pitied, that she was sunk into the abyss of misery, and driven to a state of desperation; but should the clause in question teach her to reflect a little, would she not say to herself, 'this man cannot be an honourable seducer, for he knows that, by the law of the land, he cannot marry me after I have violated my conjugal vow'. Noble lords might talk of humanity to the unhappy lady; but was there no humanity owing to the public? What must be the feelings of relatives and friends on such an occasion? It was the first policy of any state to see that children should be virtuously educated; and where was the example to be sought but in parental affection and conjugal delicacy? As the law stood at present, by permitting the offending parties to intermarry, instead of a punishment, it would operate rather as an inducement to the commission of the crime. The number of divorces called for prevention, by punishment that would operate as such; and under that impression he should give the bill his support.

[During debate in the Commons] Mr Wilberforce said, that the question for the consideration of the House was, whether the crime of adultery had arisen to such a height as to require legislative provision? It could not be denied, that it was a crime which attacked the first germ of civil society. The Author of our holy religion had denounced it, and had dwelt upon it more particularly than upon any other. Marriage was by no means merely a civil contract: the state had a right to prescribe the ceremonies by which it should be contracted; but it was sanctified by religion, and was on that account more holy, and ought to be more indissoluble. No institution had been devised so well calculated to promote the happiness of man, and it ought to be regarded with the greatest reverence. In this light it could not long be viewed, if the present system were continued. Could it be a question, whether that should be made a crime in the code of English laws, which was already a moral offence of so deep a hue? — If he understood the lawyers right, there was not at present any penalty annexed to this crime. But it had been stated, that although there was no direct penalty, yet there was one practically, because the adulterer paid in damages to the husband what amounted to a heavy penalty. This circumstance was with him one great argument in favour of the bill, because he considered it improper that a penalty for a public offence should be paid in the shape of damages to an individual. A case might exist where the crime was consummated, yet where no penalty in damages could be inflicted. Suppose the case of a negligent and indifferent husband, ill-treating an amiable wife, while she was endeavouring, by the most persuasive of all eloquence, or continued love and kindness, to reclaim him: suppose, then, that an artful seducer should step in between her and the accomplishment of this desired object, and, by aggravating every fault of her husband, should induce her to deviate from the paths of virtue. Would any one say, that this was not the most guilty of mortals? Yet, should the husband bring an action against him, it would be said with justice, that the plaintiff was a careless, debauched, and profligate scoundrel, and that he ought to be non-suited. He could with ease state many other cases, where there was a loud call for punishment, yet where to give damages would be improper. We were now exactly in that state when a bill of this nature was necessary, and if we delayed much longer, it would be altogether ineffectual to stem the torrent of corruption. The principles of the people aere still good, though their practices were beginning to be very immoral; and it was well known, that bad habits would ruin the best principles. Our wealth had greatly increased, and had occasioned a corresponding increase of luxury, directly tending to introduce licentiousness of manners, and some regulations were indispensably necessary to counteract this tendency. The science of morals was better understood than in any former age, and propriety of character was more accurately marked; but by no means followed, that our actions were correspondingly laudable. Morals were formerly founded on religion; but the morality of the present day seemed to consist in a decorum of deportment, founded rather on the consideration of character than of religion. He would not deny but that in the reign of Charles 2nd there existed a most licentious court; and he could not omit this occasion of paying a just tribute of applause to the bright example which was exhibited by the court of the present day, and which, he was convinced, tended more than any circumstance to produce that moral decency so characteristic of these times. He therefore thought the present the proper time to pass the bill before the House. He thought the proposed punishment by no means too severe. Hitherto, the adulteress had been rewarded for her breach of the marriage vow, and there were many reasons why the intermarriage of the parties should be prohibited. It was the duty of legislatures to enact laws the best calculated to promote the present happiness of mankind. Even in this point of view it was very shortsighed to allow an opiate to be administered to the woman who had been guilty of such a crime, and to allow her to return to society to indulge in luxury and licentiousness, and to corrupt those around her by precept and example. He was greatly alarmed when he heard honour spoken of as contra-distinguished from honesty. This was false honour, the most dangerous of all principles. Against such principles he entered his strongest protest. It had been stated, that if the bill should pass, the number of adulteries would be increased, as the debauchee would then be more ready to prey upon the spoils of innocence, when there was no possibility of his being obliged to marry the woman he had seduced. He himself did not believe that the human heart could be so hardened, nor the moral principle so debased. But would not the removal of this restraint he more than counterbalanced by the ignominy which would attach upon the seducer, and the punishment he must expect to undergo? He would gladly give his vote for going into a committee. He considered this subject of much more importance than any question about peace or war, or any constitutional question; for, although the latter might have some remote influence on the comforts of families, yet the question then before the House went to the inmost recesses of domestic happiness; to the very foundations of civil society; and if the crime was suffered to go on unchecked, nothing could have a greater tendency to destroy the whole fabric of society.

4.17 Adultery and social morality: the view of Archbishop Fisher

Geoffrey Fisher *(1887-1972), Bishop of London 1939-45 and Archbishop of Canterbury 1945-61; the following speech on the subject of adultery was reported in* The Times, 23 December 1959.

'I think there ought always to be in the public mind the question "has adultery become such a public menace that the time has come when it ought to be made a criminal offence?".' *In reply to press comment on this, he then wrote that he had raised that question* 'to make people think. What forces in the community (apart from the Church) are actively trying to limit the tide of adultery? Public opinion, which once ostracised adulterers, does it no longer. Can nothing be done to show that if a third party breaks into a marriage and thereby inflicts an injury of the gravest and most anti-social kind on the institution of marriage, he is doing a serious public harm to society? ...'

4.18 The ambiguity of 'consent' in allegations of rape

François Petrus van den Heever *(1894-1956) was a South African judge and distinguished Roman-Dutch legal scholar. The judgment that follows is from a case decided in the Appellate Division of the South African Supreme Court concerning an allegation of rape.*

Another ground for accepting complainant's story in preference to that of appellant is the fact that she is alleged subsequently to have reproached him with having penetrated her and that she was distressed. One knows from the cases that even spouses may reproach each other with sexual acts, fully acquiesced in, which might lead to pregnancy. It is to be supposed that in illicit intercourse such reproaches are more frequent. Tears after the event are not necessarily indicative of absence of consent. They may be tears of remorse or apprehension. Gretchen's famous lament is no pointer to her having been ravished by Faust.

However, the main ground upon which I feel bound to differ from the judgment of the Court *a quo* is this. It assumes that where a man and a woman make a pact to indulge in sexual acts with each other short of natural sexual intercourse and, overcome by the stimuli so experienced, the woman succumbs, permits full copulation and comes to her senses only when it is too late, the man is guilty of rape because of his breach of the condition: 'thus far and no further.' In our law rape is a sub-species of *vis* ... It is essential that the victim's resistance be overcome by fear, force or fraud. When it is overcome by the prompting of her own passions, to the stimulation of which she consented, there can be no question of rape. I do not wish to suggest that once the male is sexually roused by lascivious acts permitted by the woman he may resort to *vis* and rape her with impunity. But excitation acquiesced in by an adult does not amount to *vis*.

In my judgment the Court *a quo* erred in convicting the appellant and the conviction and sentence should be set aside.

4.19   'The case against rape'

The following is an article by Tony Clifton from the Sunday Times, *21 December 1969.*

It is one of the elements of the laws governing rape that boyfriends can almost never be charged with raping their girlfriends – and if they are, they are almost invariably acquitted. Obviously because of their relationship juries are always likely to find there was consent. The human problem is that neither accused nor accuser, however innocent, can hope to emerge with reputations unscathed.

Because of the aftermath of such cases (last week's was an example) a growing body of criminologists would like to see the laws on sexual offences generally abolished. They argue that all known sexual offences including rape could just as easily be dealt with under the much less emotive charges of common assault, wounding and grievous bodily harm.

As the criminologist Louis Blom-Cooper says, 'The problem with sex offences is that they are now being judged against a background of emotion and moralising never encountered in other cases and this emotional upheaval can only cloud the issues being judged. The sexuality isn't relevant in these cases – an assault is an assault however it is committed.'

The Criminal Law Revision Committee, which is a body appointed by Parliament to review the law has sexual offences on the list of legislation it will be asked to examine by the Home Secretary. But they have a full list already and they will probably not reach Offences Against the Person (which includes sex offences) for another two years. And even then prospects of change are dim.

As one legal expert said this week, 'they won't change the laws on rape because the last revision of sexual offences laws was in 1956. And in terms of English law that means yesterday. Anyhow there seems to be a general feeling that the laws are working perfectly well as they are.'[6]

Until 1956 there was a ragbag of laws on sex offences dating from the last century. These were consolidated into the Sexual Offences Act. Rape itself has been a crime in England from time immemorial and has always been regarded as a serious crime except for an odd interlude in the thirteenth century when it was downgraded from a felony to a misdemeanour between the years 1275 and 1285. Since then it has been severely punished, often by death and can still be punished by life imprisonment.

The basic element of proving any case of rape is to show that intercourse took place without consent. This can mean violent rape where the victim is physically overpowered, but rape is proved if it is shown that the woman was drugged or made drunk to make her submit.

But 'consent' can be given and rape proved. In one celebrated case in the twenties a singing teacher was convicted of rape after he had had intercourse with a pupil who consented because the teacher had convinced her that the act would improve her singing.

A husband, however, cannot be charged with raping his wife – by her acceptance of the marriage vows she is taken to have given her consent to intercourse. This exception is bound to be tested in years ahead as more and more people live permanently together without marrying. Courts have not yet been called upon to decide whether a man has the same rights to intercourse with his common law wife as a married man has but such a case must come one day to try the wits of judge and jury.

The country which has far and away the most cases of rape brought to court each year is the U.S.A. Last year there were 27,100 cases of rape and attempted rape in that country, an increase on the year before of 1,770.

In Britain last year 330 men and one woman were charged with rape. (A woman can be charged if she assists a man to commit the offence.) Of this group, 218 or 65 per cent. were found guilty. Their punishments ranged from conditional discharge to life imprisonment.

The conviction rate of 65 per cent. is low. The rate for murder is 74 per cent., unlawful sexual intercourse with a girl under 16 is 89 per cent., malicious wounding 79 per cent., and indecent assault 77 per cent. The low figure for rape suggests that juries are extremely cautious in rape cases and also shows that rape is hard to prove.

'Rape is impossible without consent,' one of Britain's most famous pathologists said last week. 'The consent may be through fear or may be fatalistic after a struggle, but the fact is that a normal man cannot rape a normal woman who struggles unless he has assistance or knocks her out. And the minute you have consent of any kind you give defence lawyers room to manoeuvre.'

One senior police officer in an outlying borough estimated this week that half the rape complaints he saw never got to court. 'Most of these are cases

---

6. But see subsequent report by the Heilbron Advisory Group on the Law of Rape, Cmnd. 6352 of 1975.

of girls who have been found to be having intercourse with boy-friends and to protect themselves have claimed they were forced into the act. In these cases we can discover the truth easily enough.'

The last survey of sex offenders show that most of them are unmarried and most had left school at 14. Only 11 per cent. were known to have had any form of higher education. The largest single group were labourers and three per cent. were mental defectives. Many had been drinking when they committed offences and there was a higher percentage of men with deformities or disfigurements in the group than would be encountered in a normal population sample.

In a sense these were the classical rapists, the men who were prone to attack lone women on quiet roads or in parks or by bursting into their homes. Without being facetious they could be said to have been the men who by their violence gave rape a bad name. At the present time the man who is reported by a frustrated or angry girl-friend for rape is charged with the same crime as these men.

If the offence was changed to assault, all these men could be dealt with, but at the same time the stigma which now attaches even to men found innocent of rape would be removed.

4.20 Male chauvinism and the crime of rape

The following is an abridgment of an article on rape by Jill Tweedie, a journalist, which appeared in the Guardian, *3 January 1972.*

A little rough stuff ...

I was brought up in the diffuse but all-embracing belief that inside every male was a seething volcano of sex, a churning stream of lava kept under control only by dint of iron discipline on the man's part and extreme caution on mine. No one actually said so but all their attitudes screamed it. It was adjured to be 'careful' when I was with a man, I must never be guilty of 'leading him on,' I mustn't even flirt or I might get 'more than I bargained for.' As the Victorians prepared their daughters for marriage as lambs for the slaughter, so I was conditioned into accepting that my body was not my natural possession, a cosy kind of blanket that wrapped me round, but an indecent sexual object whose indiscreet use might, quite rightly, inflame men to dreadful deeds.

Breasts, they hinted, were not for the feeding of infants but dynamite directed against the sorely-tried male and to show them in any quantity was to risk driving decent men mad. Legs, uncovered beyond a certain point (and the certain point, in Victorian times, was the ankle), stopped being convenient walking aids and became twin red rags to the neighbourhood bulls. Shoulders, neck, hair, eyes, nose, lips: all had no normal functions that did not also carry the added weight of being designed to flare men's nostrils and start that inner volcano on its way to eruption.

The implication was always that men could not help themselves, that sexually they were at all times very nearly out of control and so it was my duty, as a woman, to cover myself and lower my eyes if I wanted to stay out of trouble, though exactly what trouble they never bothered to explain. The boys I grew up with absorbed this social propaganda eagerly and, as a result, were often brainwashed into total sexual irresponsibility, drunken engine drivers in charge of runaway trains with every one colluding to blame the drink.

Understandably, they matured with few restraints, leaping upon women in cars, thrusting themselves from all manner of dark corners and, when the protest came, switching quickly over to the drunken engine driver: 'What can I do, it's bigger than both of us, you are too beautiful, I can't help myself, you drive me wild.' The wretched girl, half flattered, half frightened, accepts the man's morality, knowing that society will take his side, not hers. After all, isn't she wearing false eyelashes, swooping neckline, soaring skirt? If unbridled passions are aroused, isn't it her fault? Isn't she, in fact, asking for it?

The next step back there in the dark corner – pant pant, grope grope – is rationalisation: Man's apparently inalienable right to believe that women who push them back and say no are actually, fundamentally, pulling them forward and saying yes. And here is revealed a dreadful tangle of emotions, an inextricable Gordian knot, a circle so vicious that it roots may well have vanished for good. Women, we are frequently told, are generally masochistic – it would be surprising, given their generations of submissive conditioning, if they were not, fantasies and all. And women, we are also frequently told, do not know their own minds until they are coerced.

And this belief allied to the myth of uncontrollable male sexuality and the convention that a woman's body is there not for herself but for men, leads straight along the primrose path of rape.

'Straw Dogs,' Sam Peckinpah's latest and bloodiest filmed contribution to sadism, illustrates all these points to sickening perfection. A young wife is raped by two village louts and Mr Peckinpah obviously believes she deserves everything she gets. After all, the shameless hussy has a) slept with one of the men before her marriage, b) wears no bra, c) pulls up her skirt to examine a ladder in her tights and, worst of all, d) appears to be keener, if anything, on sex than her husband. Heavens to Betsy, the girl's begging for it. On cue, in come the village rapists, she struggles, she gets belted, threatened with a gun and down she goes in the familiar foggy foggy dew. Ah, but wait now for the coup de grace, ladies and gentlemen. All is not lost. Our heroine is a woman like other women, despite her aching jaw and dislodged teeth. Soon, sweetly soon, her little arms steal round her rapist's neck and boom ta-ra boom, she's loving every minute of it.

At this point in the film a long sigh escapes the men in the audience and they lean back, triumphant. Didn't they always say? Didn't they always know in their bones? The ladies, God bless 'em, like nothing so much as a clout across the earholes and a couple of cauliflower ears to add spice to the act of love. Mild-mannered men (till now) curse their own gentleness and vow to be different in the future. Later in the film a teenage girl walks the village idiot out on a moonlit night, seduces him into kissing her and, by her accidental death, triggers off the last twenty minutes of mayhem and bloody murder. The message comes over crystal clear: flaunt yourself, however unconsciously, and you'll get your come-uppance, if you'll excuse the language, because rape is always the woman's fault. As the middle-aged manager of the cinema commented to me afterwards: 'If a gentleman makes a personal approach of this sort to a woman, most of the time she likes it.'

And, of course, women think so too – none more than the respectable middle-aged housewife. 'Straw Dogs' and, in particular, that rape scene, was discussed last week on a Granada television programme by a panel of Gallup Poll-picked men and women and all of them blamed the rape unanimously on the girl. One apple-cheeked lady, smiling brightly, pointed out that, after all, the girl had slept with one of the men before her marriage so what else but rape could she expect?

Unsurprisingly, given these feelings, the incidence of rape goes up in this country every year. In Washington, capital of rape (one woman every 15 minutes) official advice to females is to submit, advice echoed by a male friend of mine last week who pointed out with some asperity that there would be no violence in rape if women didn't struggle.

Unfortunately for such optimists violence, in many cases, appears to be the sine qua non of the act; many women are beaten up, mutilated, and killed *after* being raped. And, in direct contradiction to the paternal advice not to struggle, is the widely-held opinion that a woman really determined to resist rape will always succeed. 'Rape,' says one of Britain's best-known pathologists, 'is impossible without consent. The consent may be through fear or may be fatalistic after a struggle, but the fact is that a normal man cannot rape a normal woman who struggles unless he has assistance or knocks her out.' This, I regret to say, is one of the most scarlet of red herrings, another careful nail in the old coffin 'it's all woman's fault.'

Apart from the fact that fear *is* coercion, it has escaped this expert's attention that many men, particularly in American prisons, are raped by their fellow men for all their superior strength. But then, rape being a uniquely male crime it is obviously up to men to defend it, justify it and otherwise wash it out of existence. Certainly the idea of a man being raped by other men is rather more shocking, an event higher on the list of traumas.

If T.E. Lawrence had been a lady would experts have spent quite so much obsessive time tracing his subsequent behaviour back to a possible Turkish rape?

As far as I am concerned, rape is quite simply definable as any coercion, particularly the use or threatened use of physical strength, that makes a woman submit to intercourse against her will. That woman may be a vestal virgin or Salome of the Seven Veils – raped she is if she didn't want it.

But, of course, it is deeply ingrained in us that only a virgin can truly be raped: as the old saw puts it so endearingly, a slice from a cut cake is never missed … Any girl who would sink so low as to practise what society in general considers a sexual perversion has no right to that society's help when she is forced to do the same thing to a total stranger. It follows, therefore, that if you can prove a woman promiscuous, give evidence that she has intercourse with the men she chooses, she has stepped outside the pale and is fair game for any man.

In fact, the way British law and British prejudice stands at the moment, a woman's only redress in the law courts is her rape by a perfect stranger. A survey of sex offenders in England shows that most are unmarried and most had left school at 14. Only 11 per cent were known to have had any form of higher education, the largest single group were labourers, many had been drinking when they committed offences and there was a higher percentage of men with deformities or disfigurements in the group. From these figures one writer recently and predictably concluded that 'without being facetious they could be said to have been the men who by their violence gave rape a bad name'.[7] In other words, rape between acquaintances cannot happen, just as rape in marriage has no legal existence.

We know, of course, that it does. Incest, for example, is often a synonym for rape and a high percentage of all our grandmothers, at least, were raped on their wedding night and from then on through endless nights of marital struggle, apparently because few men ever thought it possible (because of the masculine moral edict imposed on women) that their wives could actually accept sex willingly. There must be thousands of households across the country where rape will be committed tonight, carefully camouflaged in the sacraments of marriage. Men drunk; men obstinate; men indignant will have intercourse with reluctant wives because they want to, because it is their right, because they have such overriding needs, because they are stronger.

A girl (how many girls?) was raped last month by more than eighty Pakistani soldiers and went out of her mind. How many men can truly say they see no connection, however small, between this extreme event and their own occasional behaviour?

4.21 Background to the reform of the law on incest

This Home Office memorandum concerns the Incest (Punishment) Bill 1903. The Bill, one of a long series of the subject, failed to react the Statute Book.

Incest (Punishment) Bill
(introduced by Col. Dalbriac, Lord Newark, and five other members)

Object of the Bill
At present incest (i.e. sexual intercourse between persons within the forbidden degrees of relationship) is not as such an offence of which the civil law of England take cognisance, though it is a crime in Scotland and in most civilised countries. The object of the Bill is to make incest between certain near relations punishable as a misdemeanour.

General Remarks
English law in excluding incest from the list of crimes in understood to proceed on the theory that it is so horrible and unnatural an offence as to be rarely, if ever, committed. Unfortunately the facts do not support this theory. Incestuous intercourse is undoubtedly very common. Exact statistics are not available, but out of 193 cases of rape and carnal knowledge of girls under 16 noted in the H.O. no less than 51 are incestuous

7. See 4.19.

– a proportion of more than 1 in 4.* In 49 cases the offence was committed by a father on his daughter, in one by an uncle on a niece, and in one by a nephew on an aunt.

These were of course cases in which either (1) the girl was under 16 or (2) there was no consent, i.e. they would have been equally punishable if the connexion had not been incestuous. But in view of them it can hardly be doubted that there must be many cases of incestuous intercourse with girls over 16 with their consent, which is at present not punishable.†

The desirability of a change in the law is well illustrated by the fact that more than one case is known to H.O. in which the Court appears to have strained the law in order that an act which was really incest might be treated as rape (and therefore punishable) ...

Effect of the Bill
The Bill will make it an offence

(1) for a male to have intercourse with his grandaughter, daughter, or sister if of the age of 13 or upwards (?intercourse with a girl under 13 is already an offence in *any circumstances*).

(2) for a female aged 16 or upwards to consent to her grandfather, father or brother having intercourse with her. But it is a sufficient defence for a female to prove that she acted under 'duress'. In either case relationship with or through illegitimates is reckoned.

The maximum penalty for either party to the offence is 7 years penal servitude. A man may in addition be deprived of his guardianship (if any). The enforcement of the Bill would probably be a matter of some difficulty. From the nature of the offence the evidence of the girl would usually be necessary in order to secure a conviction, and as she would be liable to punishment equally with the man unless she could prove 'duress', it would often be given unwillingly, if at all.

This difficulty is however not insuperable. Convictions appear to be obtained to some extent in Scotland ...

Amendment
If it is considered desirable to amend the Bill in committee the case of uncle and niece is the most important practical omission. The case of mother and son is also omitted, but its inclusion is hardly necessary.

---

* These figures relate to cases which have come before the H.O. on petition for remission of sentence or for other special reasons. They are only a small part of the total.

† Where there is so much incest punishable as rape it is practically certain that there is much unpunished and at present unpunishable.

Editors' Note:
These footnotes appeared as marginal annotations in the original: they were presumably written by one of the superiors of the anonymous civil servant author of the document.

Course to be taken in regard to the Bill
It is suggested that the second reading should be allowed subject to amendments in Committee if considered necessary.

4.22   Outrage against incest

This letter to the Home Secretary (Akers-Douglas) is from the 'Maidstone Social Purity Association', January 1905, calling for legislation to curb incest. No reply appears on the Home Office file.

The Vicarage, Maidstone
Dear Mr Akers-Douglas,

Though you will not remember me personally, I have a pleasant recollection of a cricket match, a good many years ago when I played for Mr Willie Hoare at Chilston Park. I am venturing, however to write to you, not as a private individual, but as President of the 'Maidstone Social Purity Association' on a subject of grave public importance, in the hope that, as Home Secretary, you may see your way to give it your practical, as well as, I do not doubt, your sympathetic attention. This 'Maidstone Social Purity Association' have knowledge of a very serious case of incest; a man having three children by a sister, and two more by the eldest girl, his own daughter, who was actually under 16 when this first child was born. There is no doubt about the facts. The case as regards the young girl might have been dealt with under the law for the Prevention of Cruelty to Children, but the law is not retrospective and, as the girl is now over 16, the law cannot be applied. We are informed that there is no law against incest, and that nothing can be done in such cases.

It is for this reason that we feel justified in appealing to the Home Secretary in the hope that, if possible, the legislature may introduce a Bill in the coming session of Parliament dealing with this terrible moral evil.

The case I have mentioned is as bad as any we can imagine possible, but the evil is said to be widespread and it is difficult to understand why the power of the law, which is brought to bear in so many ways on moral questions cannot be applied in the case of incest which is repugnant to the moral sense of the community. We feel sure of your sympathy with the object we have in view and we feel also that, if it is in your power to do anything, your desire to do so will be strengthened by having such a concrete case as I have quoted, brought to your notice.

If there is anything further that we can do in the way of helping this matter forward, or if you are in a position to give us any advice as to the way of dealing with particular cases, the Association I represent would be deeply grateful for information on the subject.

Trusting that I am not in any way out of order in bringing this matter before your notice.

Believe me to remain
Yours very faithfully,

Edward H. Hardcastle.

4.23   Incest, an unmentionable subject

Lord Halsbury *(1823-1921) was Lord Chancellor during the periods 1885-6, 1886-92, 1895-1905. A formidable figure, he was renowned for his conservatism which was reflected both in his judgments and in his political speeches in the House of Lords. This speech preceded the defeat of the Incest Bill 1903.*

The Lord Chancellor (The Earl of Halsbury); My Lords, I regret very much that the nature of this Bill is one which renders it repulsive to everybody to discuss it. I confess that I think that if the law which has prevailed for some centuries on the subject is to be altered some greater case ought to have been presented to your Lordships for so doing. The noble Earl says, I have no doubt quite accurately, that he has made private inquiry. But surely that is not the mode by which a complete alteration of the criminal law is to be justified. I believe that legislation of this character is calculated to do an infinite amount of mischief. The noble Earl says he is confident that certain newspapers will not make capital out of these cases. I do not know where his confidence comes from. It strikes me that anything of this sort would be eagerly grasped by some portion of the Press, who make these things more public than they otherwise would be. I wish to do every credit to the noble Earl and those who are acting with him, but I cannot help thinking that it is zeal without knowledge. Everyone who is familiar with the administration of the criminal law is well aware that the publicity given to an offence at one Assize Court produces a crop of similar offences at other Assizes; and these are cases which it is inadvisable to drag into the light of day. I do think that it is a reflection on the beginning of the twentieth century that it should be thought necessary to deal with this matter at all. I cannot help thinking that it has not been sufficiently discussed, or the other House would not have rashly passed such a Bill without some evidence as to the necessity for it. I confess that I am very much impressed by the wisdom of the view on these subjects which Tacitus ascribed to the Germans – *Diversitas supplicii illuc respicit, tanquam scelera ostendi oporteat, dum puniuntur, flagitia abscondi*. That is, I believe, the truèr view of what ought to be done in this matter, and it is with reluctance, because I believe I shall be running counter to the opinions of some whose views are worthy of consideration, but with a strong sense of duty, that I move that the Bill be read a second time this day six months.

4.24   Incest in Scotland

Report in The Guardian, *April 6, 1971.*

A man, aged 49, and his son's wife, aged 18, who ran away together, appeared with her in the High Court, Edinburgh, yesterday, charged with incest under an Act of 1567. T.S., a waterman, and M.C., both of Bo'ness, West Lothian, admitted having incestuous intercourse on three occasions. The couple had been in custody since March 15. Lord Avonside said he had looked into the background of 'this wretched affair' and took a lenient view. They would both be admonished. It is not an offence outside Scotland for a man to have intercourse with his daughter-in-law.

5

Family and Fecundity

Darwin observes that the history of man's moral development has been a continual extension in the objects of his 'social instincts and sympathies'. Originally man was an island, having regard only for himself and perhaps for those of a very narrow circle about him. Later he came to regard more and more 'not only the welfare, but the happiness of all his fellow men'; then 'his sympathies became more tender and widely diffused, extending to men of all races, to the imbecile, maimed and other useless members of society, and finally to the lower animals'.[1]

The history of the law resembles Darwin's account. There was probably never a pure Hobbesian state of nature in which no rights existed, except the individual's right of self-help. But in the earlier days it is fair to say that 'families' (including extended kinship groups and clans) were the exclusive concern of the law. Everyone outside that charmed circle was alien and rightless though even within the family, persons (especially women and minors) were often devoid of legal rights.

Maine pointed out how even under the *patria potestas* of the Romans the father had *jus vitae necisque* – the power of life and death – over his children. He had power of uncontrolled corporal chastisement; he could modify their personal condition at pleasure; give a wife to his son; give his daughter in marriage; divorce his children of either sex; transfer them to another family by adoption; he could even sell them.[2] The child was less than a person – merely an object, a thing.

The period of the late nineteenth and early twentieth century witnessed dramatic changes in the law protecting the interests of children. The era of child welfare, which has gathered pace throughout this century, has not yet culminated in the child being accorded legal rights *per se* – the principal reason being that the basic feature of the legal definition of the family (the father as titular head) will remain for some time. Even the later concept of the fatherless family is unlikely to encompass child rights. The Children Act 1975 only goes part of the way towards establishing the rights of children.

What has changed is that the father's right as master of his household has diminished to a position which, while no less masterful, is overlaid with more extensive duties and obligations. The duties of each member of the family are measured, at least in theory and in legal conception, according to the role each takes in the family, and role is perceived socially in terms of financial provider and economic dependency. Thus a complex matrix of

---

1. Charles Darwin, *Descent of Man*, 2nd ed. 1874, pp. 119, 120-1.
2. H.S. Maine, *Ancient Law*, 1930, p. 153.

corresponding rights and duties among the various members of the family marks out the relationships between those members. Although such a relationship does not eliminate or destroy the rights of any member, it can enhance or diminish the social meaningfulness of those rights.

Such rights as exist within the family are derived from the legal concept of 'status', a somewhat vacuous word although significant in describing the legal relationships between persons in society. Status is a concept of peculiar significance in legal theory – if only because of Henry Maine's famous dictum that 'the movement of progressive societies has hitherto been a movement from status to contract', meaning thereby that individuals create legal rights and obligations by agreement, and do not have those rights and obligations imposed on them by law.

Status is both a philosophical concept and a legal fiction, and once it is found to exist in a particular form certain practical legal consequences follow as a matter of course. Such principles as the obligation of a man to maintain a woman or a child raise questions which, to a greater or less extent, rest on, or are contingent upon, the existence of an acknowledged status.

Status is one of the lawyer's tools for legal reasoning – sometimes even, at its most rigid, a substitute for logic. Judges tend to ask themselves whether a particular status exists (for example, are these two people husband and wife?) and then to reify it – that is, mentally convert the concept into a thing. This approach means that the existence of a particular status – the rights and duties of those impressed with the attributes of that status – represents the starting point for a process of *a priori* reasoning. The lawyers proceed from abstract notions to their physical consequences – from assumed axioms and not from experience. Yet, if ever there was an area of social conduct where the law should proceed inductively – constructing legal rules from observable fact – it is in those cases of direct personal relationships which have induced the erection of such a concept as status. The lawyers' inability to view relationships outside the concept of status hampered changes in the law limiting the prohibited degrees of marriage (5.10, 5.11, and 5.12) and influenced decisions about polygamy (5.13) and artificial insemination (5.14, 5.15, and 5.16).

The clearest example in British society of the consequences of rigid adherence to status can be seen in the law's treatment of married women. Institutional writers, such as Bacon, Blackstone (5.2) and Mill (5.3) since the Middle Ages have testified to the inferior status of married women, that husbands had power and dominion over not only their wives' property but also their persons. Shakespeare did not overstate the law as spoken by Petrucchio in the *Taming of the Shrew*, that 'she is my goods, my chattels; she is my house, my household stuff, my field, my barn, my horse, my ox, my ass, my anything'. The shadows of dominion, ownership and servility still stalk about as if they were living realities, for married women's partial emancipation in this century has not yet led finally to female liberation.

Women are, as we have seen elsewhere, still handicapped in a variety of ways, largely as a result of their economic dependency on their husbands. These are the legacies of a society which for so long subordinated the interests of wives to those of their husbands. Their financial dependency finds a ready acknowledgment in recent divorce and ancillary matrimonial property legislation (followed by the Law Commission's tentative proposals on matrimonial property generally[3]) but sex discrimination even in these areas of property rights has not yet been eradicated.

Discrimination against women was statutorily forbidden at the end of the First World War in respect of all public functions, from appointments to civil or judicial office, and in entry into the civil, professional or vocational occupations. Fifty years later, the legislative move towards sexual equality can be seen to have materially but incompletely taken place. At the time of writing, anti-discrimination legislation has just been enacted.

Discriminatory practices still abound. The recent Conservative Party document, *Fair Shares for the Fair Sex* – an otherwise far-sighted report – smacked of the patronising male chauvinism so rightly resented by women. Occupationally, women still have many male preserves to breach, and even in those citadels of masculinity which have fallen to female invasion, the breach has been altogether on a miniscule scale. However, it must be conceded that a chink in the male armoury has been effected by the Anti-Discrimination Act 1975, which may, in the fulness of time, prove to be the beginning of the end of male superiority in many areas of life.

In one area of legal status, the twentieth century has witnessed a total swing of the pendulum. Until the end of the last century, children were, subject to some notable statutory exceptions, still regarded as the property of their fathers – their earning power was after all a significant element in a small family budget, a factor which has weighed in more recent debates about raising the school-leaving age. By 1925, paternal stranglehold had given way to equal parental rights and duties over children. The principle of the paramountcy of the child's welfare (echoed in the Guardianship of Minors Act 1971, re-enacting the 1925 Act) led in most cases to mothers gaining the upper hand in forensic tussles with the fathers of their children. For very young children it is almost axiomatic that the mother should be awarded custody (or at the very least, daily care and control) and, until the last few years, even older children were frequently left by the courts in the control of their mothers – a reflection of the general pattern of familial behaviour whereby men are generally content to leave the rearing of their children to their womenfolk.

However, if there are perceptible signs of a paternal revolution – a demand for joint custody of legitimate children and the statutory right of putative fathers since 1959 to apply for custody of their illegitimate offspring (to both of which rights the judiciary has afforded recognition) – it has also been accompanied by a new move to establish an independent status for children. The claim that children have rights that need to be specifically protected, detached from their parental link, is indicative of the breaking of the traditional concept of the family.

Given this conceptual framework of rights within the family, statutory provisions and judicial empiricism have together established a right, enforceable at law, in children. The child has the right to be maintained by the head of the family; he has the right to be educated; and he has the right

3. Law Com. 52, 1973.

to protection. But the rights of the child are imperfect, in the sense that they are enforceable not at his personal instance but by either one or other of his parents or a local authority exercising child welfare functions. There is as yet no person, independent of the child's family or of a child welfare agency, responsible for enforcing directly any rights a child may have. How can a child enforce its own rights against a parent when the latter is permitted to represent the child in court?

One example will suffice. In all adoption proceedings Parliament requires that the court shall appoint for the child a guardian *ad litem*, whose duty is to report confidentially to the court generally on the suitability of the prospective adopters. In the ensuing proceedings the guardian *ad litem* is a neutral expert, there to protect the interests of the child. However, he is not an independent advocate on behalf of the child. The adoption proceedings, if contested, will be between the natural parent and the prospective adopters in which the guardian, as the court officer, endeavours to maintain a degree of neutrality so as not to appear to influence the judicial decision. If the child were recognised as having legal rights independent of his parents or of any surrogate parent, he would be a party to any issue so crucially affecting his future welfare; since he cannot exercise independent judgment, he must have someone appointed as his advocate and not have foisted on him an agent of the social services.[3]

The imperfect legal rights of children are matched to a less marked degree by the position of married women (5.4, 5.5, 5.6, 5.7, and 5.8).

What is significant about the imperfection of rights within the family circle is the tentativeness with which the law has reflected social and moral attitudes towards the family. As each conflicting situation arises so the courts have reacted instinctively according to assumed moral standards.

What does the law regard as 'the family'? The problem came up in acute form in a recent case (5.1) involving the maintenance by landlords of housing according to local authority health standards. The tenant and his wife lived on one floor. The tenant's son, his wife and child occupied the second floor. The landlord contended, successfully, that the premises were not 'occupied by members of more than one family' within Sections 15 and 16 of the Housing Act 1961, so that he was not caught by the requirement to rectify lighting and washing facilities. The Court of Appeal blandly held that 'one family' meant 'one family and not one household' and the relations were all one family.

The 1961 Act and all preceding legislation on this subject, however, was essentially concerned with the nuclear family – a man and a woman joined in a socially recognised union together with the biological offspring of the spouses (but not necessarily biologically related, e.g., adopted children). The nuclear family is the basic social unit of our society, although it may not be the normal household unit. It may be embedded in an extended family unit – the sociological family. The Court of Appeal gave 'family' the meaning of an extended family unit as a result, not of a sociological approach, but of adherence to the moral concept of the blood tie.

Given the law's concept of the family, how have the courts wrestled with

3. Since this was written, major changes have been effected by the Children Act 1975.

the myriad of domestic problems which those affected have increasingly thrust upon the judges? Throughout the century the courts have struggled with the broken pieces of human earthenware within the context of a divorce law which stoutly maintained the concept of the matrimonial offence (5.8 and 5.9). Victorian morality permitted the discarding of a spouse – more frequently the man of his wife – only if the discarded spouse behaved with sexual or moral impropriety. Even the passing of the Divorce Reform Act 1969 did not produce the *volte-face* intended by its proponents. Although there is only one ground for divorce – the irretrievable breakdown of the marriage – the old grounds of adultery, desertion and cruelty (slightly disguised in modern parlance) are presumptive bases for asserting irretrievable breakdown. The experience of judges had led them to acknowledge that a reduction of the sum total of human misery can be achieved only by abandoning moral judgments of spouses' conduct. As a result the courts are gradually jettisoning blameworthiness and substituting the need to repair the lives of former marriage partners. Judges still, however, occasionally resort to the matrimonial offence concept for deciding issues of costs, maintenance and custody of children. For the lawyer, the aphorism *plus ça change* etc. has a particularly enduring application.

The hesitancy with which the courts are willing to abandon outmoded Victorian moral attitudes is exemplified in the area of man's increasing ability (and indeed, need) to control his own fertility. Parliament has now made provision for voluntary vasectomy on the National Health Service, a practice which some traditionalist lawyers might regard as mayhem (5.20) particularly if the operation were irreversible. Even if the courts would acknowledge that Parliamentary approval would remove such a stigma from this mode of sterilisation, it is clear that the operation would suffice as a continuing act of cruelty if not done with both spouses' consent. One recalls Lord Denning's classic remark in *Bravery* v. *Bravery* (5.21) that contraception is one thing; sterilisation is altogether beyond the legal pale.

Contraception may be widely accepted within the context of the domestic hearth but the use of contraceptives is regarded by some as iniquitous encouragment of extramarital sexual immorality. The sale of contraceptives by means of slot machines in public places has been declared an evil, and the proper object of legislation against the practice. Advocacy of automatic dispensers for contraceptives in schools was considered in the *Little Red Schoolbook* case as doing damage 'to the sort of helpful supportive relationship between children and teachers' needed to determine 'acceptable conduct'. If the law has acknowledged that husband and wife are not accountable (except to each other) for activity within marital privacy, intimacies outside the marriage bond can still claim no complete immunity from legal interference based upon moral censure.

5.1 *Judicial definition of the family unit*

Home v. **Royal Borough of Kensington and Chelsea**: *under the housing legislation a local authority has power to require landlords of premises 'occupied by members of more than one family' to carry out repairs. The question which the Court of Appeal had to consider was what constituted 'one family'. In the particular case the* *residential premises consisted of two floors above a shop. A man and his wife occupied the first floor; his son, with wife and child, occupied the second floor.*

[Lord Justice Sellers:] It has been submitted for the council that the judge has wrongly construed the statutory words and misdirected himself in not inquiring whether two families are occupying the house. The stress, it was submitted, was on multiple occupation, and here it was said there are two families and not one. The argument recognised that there was the blood relationship, the father and mother on the first floor and the son and his wife and children on the second, but it is said that they constituted two separate 'households.'

If 'household' had been the word used, the argument might have been convincing, but the word 'household' is used within the same section and can hardly have been used to replace 'family'. In so far as there is ambiguity there is a penalty of up to £100 for failure to comply with a notice (Housing Act, 1964, s. 65), and I agree with the judge that the legislation should have made it clear if the provisions were to apply to such circumstances as exist here. There is no separate letting. It is a family arrangement. Families can share things in common with less objection and inconvenience than can strangers. Where strangers have rights and require facilities it is more justified for local authorities to intervene than perhaps it is for them to intrude when only members of a family are concerned, although this is an argument which hardly lies with the landlord who has let premises so ill-equipped for use by anyone.

The expression 'a house which is occupied by members of more than one family' is to be found as far back as the Public Health Act, 1875, and apparently this is the first occasion when it has been sought to be relied on in circumstances such as these. Counsel for the council contended that Mr Allen, junior, was occupying a separate unit in the premises. The son had no agreement which prescribed the unit, and the family may well have moved freely between one floor's accommodation and the other, but assuming a separate unit the occupiers were not strangers but were members of a family.

The judge replied on *Brock* v. *Woolams* and *Standingford* v. *Probert*, and the appellant council submit that they have no application since they are decisions under the Rent Restrictions Acts and refer to tenants' rights and protection. They are perhaps not very helpful, but no other authority cited to us provided any guide. The relationship is clear. They are all members of one family living within the one house and there were no persons living in the house who were strangers or outside that family. I find it difficult to see that there was a defined unit or area of occupation. There is no finding to that effect in the judgment.

5.2   Blackstone on the unliberated woman

The status of eighteenth-century married women can be seen through the views of a contemporary lawyer who would have found it difficult to digest today's ideas about women's liberation.

By marriage, the husband and wife are one person in law: that is, the very being or legal existence of the woman is suspended during the marriage, or at least is incorporated and consolidated into that of the husband: under whose wing, protection, and *cover*, she performs every thing; and is therefore called in our law-french a *femme-covert, foemina viro co-operta*; is said to be *covert-baron*, or under the protection and influence of her husband, her *baron*, or lord; and her condition during her marriage is called her *coverture*. Upon this principle, of an union of person in husband and wife, depend almost all the legal rights, duties, and disabilities, that either of them acquire by the marriage. I speak not as present of the rights of property, but of such as are merely *personal*. For this reason, a man cannot grant any thing to his wife, or enter into covenant with her; for the grant would be to suppose her separate existence; and to covenant with her, would be only to covenant with himself: and therefore it is also generally true, that all compacts made between husband and wife, when single, are voided by the intermarriage. A woman indeed may be attorney for her husband; for that implies no separation from, but is rather a representation of, her lord. And a husband may also bequeath any thing to his wife by will; for that cannot take effect till the coverture is determined by his death. The husband is bound to provide his wife with necessaries by law, as much as himself: and if she contracts debts for them, he is obliged to pay them; but, for any thing besides necessaries, he is not chargeable. Also if a wife elopes, and lives with another man, the husband is not chargeable even for necessaries; at least if the person, who furnishes them, is sufficiently apprized of her elopement. If the wife be indebted before marriage, the husband is bound afterwards to pay the debt; for he has adopted her and her circumstances together. If the wife be injured in her person or her property, she can bring no action for redress without her husband's concurrence, and in his name, as well as her own: neither can she be sued, without making the husband a defendant. There is indeed one case where the wife shall sue and be sued as a feme sole, *viz.* where the husband has abjured the realm, or is banished; for then he is dead in law; and, the husband being thus disabled to sue for or defend the wife, it would be most unreasonable if she had no remedy, or could make no defence at all. ...

In the civil law the husband and the wife are considered as two distinct persons and may have separate estates, contracts, debts, and injuries; and therefore, in our ecclesiastical courts, a woman may sue and be sued without her husband.

But, though our law in general considers man and wife as one person, yet there are some instances in which she is separately considered; as inferior to him, and acting by his compulsion. And therefore all deeds executed, and acts done, by her, during her coverture, are void; except it be a fine, or the like matter of record, in which case she must be solely and secretly examined, to learn if her act be voluntary. She cannot by will devise lands to her husband, unless under special circumstances, for at the time of making it she is supposed to be under his coercion. And in some felonies, and other inferior crimes, committed by her, through constraint of her husband, the law excuses her: but this extends not to treason or murder.

The husband also (by the old law) might give his wife moderate correction. For, as he is to answer for her misbehaviour, the law thought it reasonable to intrust him with this power of restraining her, by domestic chastisement, in the same moderation that a man is allowed to correct his apprentices or children; for whom the master or parent is also liable in some cases to answer. But this power of correction was confined within reasonable bounds, and the husband was prohibited from using any violence to his wife, *aliter quam ad virum, ex causa regiminis et castigationis uxoris suae, licite et rationabiliter pertinet*. The civil law gave the husband the same, or a larger, authority over his wife: allowing him, for some misdemenors, *flagellis et fustibus acriter verberare uxorem*; for others, only *modicam casigationem adhibere*. But, with us, in the politer reign of Charles the second, this power of correction began to be doubted: and a wife may now have security of the peace against her husband; or, in return, a husband against his wife. Yet the lower rank of people, who were always fond of the old common law, still claim and exert their ancient privilege: and the courts of law will still permit a husband to restrain a wife of her liberty, in case of any gross misbehaviour.

These are the chief legal effects of marriage during the coverture; upon which we may observe, that even the disabilities, which the wife lies under, are for the most part intended for her protection and benefit. So great a favourite is the female sex of the laws of England.

5.3   Mill on the subjection of women

John Stuart Mill *(see 1.3) published this famous essay 'On the Subjection of Women' in 1869. It accords with the writer's libertarian beliefs, already discussed.*

It is not true that in all voluntary association between two people, one of them must be absolute master: still less that the law must determine which of them it shall be. The most frequent case of voluntary association, next to marriage, is partnership in business: and it is not found or thought necessary to enact that in every partnership, one partner shall have entire control over the concern, and the others shall be bound to obey his orders. No one would enter into partnership on terms which would subject him to the responsibilities of a principal, with only the powers and privileges of a clerk or agent. If the law dealt with other contracts as it does with marriage, it would ordain that one partner should administer the common business as if it was his private concern; that the others should have only delegated powers; and that this one should be designated by some general presumption of law, for example as being the eldest. The law never does this: nor does experience show it to be necessary that any theoretical inequality of power should exist between the partners, or that the partnership should have any other conditions than what they may themselves appoint by their articles of agreement. Yet it might seem that the exclusive power might be conceded with less danger to the rights and interests of the inferior, in the case of partnership than in that of marriage, since he is free to cancel the power by withdrawing from the connexion. The wife has no such power, and even if she had, it is almost always desirable that she should try all measures before resorting to it.

It is quite true that things which have to be decided every day, and cannot adjust themselves gradually, or wait for a compromise, ought to depend on one will: one person must have their sole control. But it does not follow that this should always be the same person. The natural arrangement is a division of powers between the two; each being absolute in the executive branch of their own department, and any change of system and principle requiring the consent of both. The division neither can nor should be pre-established by the law, since it must depend on individual capacities and suitabilities. If the two persons chose, they might pre-appoint it by the marriage contract, as pecuniary arrangements are now often pre-appointed. There would seldom be any difficulty in deciding such things by mutual consent, unless the marriage was one of those unhappy ones in which all other things, as well as this, become subjects of bickering and dispute. The division of rights would naturally follow the division of duties and functions; and that is already made by consent, or at all events not by law, but by general custom, modified and modifiable at the pleasure of the persons concerned.

A pertinacious adversary, pushed to extremities, may say, that husbands indeed are willing to be reasonable, and to make fair concessions to their partners without being compelled to it, but that wives are not: that if allowed any rights of their own, they will acknowledge no rights at all in any one else, and never will yield in anything, unless they can be compelled, by the man's mere authority, to yield in everything. This would have been said by many persons some generations ago, when satires on women were in vogue, and men thought it a clever thing to insult women for being what men made them. But it will be said by no one now who is worth replying to. It is not the doctrine of the present day that women are less susceptible of good feeling, and consideration for those with whom they are united by the strongest ties, than men are. On the contrary, we are perpetually told that women are better than men, by those who are totally opposed to treating them as if they were as good; so that the saying has passed into a piece of tiresome cant, intended to put a complimentary face upon an injury, and resembling those celebrations of royal clemency which, according to Gulliver, the king of Lilliput always prefixed to his most sanguinary decrees. If women are better than men in anything, it surely is in individual self-sacrifice for those of their own family. But I lay little stress on this, so long as they are universally taught that they are born and created for self-sacrifice. I believe that equality of rights would abate the exaggerated self-abnegation which is the present artificial ideal of feminine character, and that a good woman would not be more self-sacrificing than the best man: but on the other hand, men would be much more unselfish and self-sacrificing than at present, because they would no longer be taught to worship their own will as such a grand thing that it is actually the law for another rational being. There is nothing which men so easily learn as this self-worship: all privileged persons, and all privileged classes, have had it. The more we descend in the scale of humanity, the intenser it is; and most of all in those who are not, and can never expect to be, raised above any one except an unfortunate wife and children. The honourable exceptions are proportionally fewer than in the case of almost any other human infirmity.

Philosophy and religion, instead of keeping it in check, are generally suborned to defend it; and nothing controls it but that practical feeling of the equality of human beings, which is the theory of Christianity, but which Christianity will never practically teach, while it sanctions institutions grounded on an arbitrary preference of one human being over another.

There are, no doubt, women, as there are men, whom equality of consideration will not satisfy; with whom there is no peace while any will or wish is regarded but their own. Such persons are a proper subject for the law of divorce. They are only fit to live alone, and no human beings ought to be compelled to associate their lives with them. But the legal subordination tends to make such characters among women more, rather than less, frequent. If the man exerts his whole power, the woman is of course crushed: but if she is treated with indulgence, and permitted to assume power, there is no rule to set limits to her encroachments. The law, not determining her rights, but theoretically allowing her none at all, practically declares that the measure of what she has a right to, is what she can contrive to get.

5.4   Blackstone on divorce

Sir William Blackstone *(see 1.1) writes on divorce* a mensa et thoro *in the* Commentaries.

Divorce *a mensa et thoro* is when the marriage is just and lawful *ab initio*, and therefore the law is tender of dissolving it; but, for some supervenient cause, it becomes improper or impossible for the parties to live together: as in the case of intolerable ill temper, or adultery, in either of the parties. For the canon law, which the common law follows in this case, deems so highly and with such mysterious reverence of the nuptial tie, that it will not allow it to be unloosed for any cause whatsoever, that arises after the union is made. And this is said to be built on the divine revealed law; though that expressly assigns incontinence as a cause, and indeed the only cause, why a man may put away his wife and marry another. The civil law, which is partly of pagan original, allows many causes of absolute divorce; and some of them pretty severe ones: (as if a wife goes to the theatre or the public games, without the knowlege and consent of the husband) but among them adultery is the principal, and with reason named the first. But with us in England adultery is only a cause of separation from bed and board: for which the best reason that can be given, is, that if divorces were allowed to depend upon a matter within the power of either the parties, they would probably be extremely frequent; as was the case when divorces were allowed for canonical disabilities, on the mere confession of the parties, which is now prohibited by the canons. However, divorces *a vinculo matrimonii*, for adultery, have of late years been frequently granted by act of parliament.

5.5   Cruelty and the marriage union

Lord Stowell *(1745-1836) eventually became a judge of the High Court of Admiralty, which office he held for thirty years. He was the elder brother of Lord Chancellor Eldon. This extract is from his judgment in* Evans v. Evans *(1790) on cruelty and the nature of the marriage union.*

To vindicate the policy of the law is no necessary part of the office of a judge: but if it were, it would not be difficult to shew that the law in this respect has acted with its usual wisdom and humanity, with that true wisdom, and that real humanity, that regards the general interests of mankind. For though in particular cases, the repugnance of the law to dissolve the obligations of matrimonial cohabitation, may operate with great severity upon individuals; yet it must be carefully remembered, that the general happiness of the married life is secured by its indissolubility. When people understand that they *must* live together, except for a very few reasons known to the law, they learn to soften by mutual accommodation that yoke which they know they cannot shake off; they become good husbands, and good wives, from the necessity of remaining husbands and wives; for necessity is a powerful master in teaching the duties which it imposes. If it were once understood, that upon mutual disgust married persons might be legally separated, many couples, who now pass through the world with mutual comfort, with attention to their common offspring and to the moral order of civil society, might have been at this moment living in a state of mutual unkindness – in a state of estrangement from their common offspring – and in a state of the most licentious and unreserved immorality. In this case, as in many others, the happiness of some individuals must be sacrificed to the greater and more general good.

That the duty of cohabitation is released by the cruelty of one of the parties is admitted, but the question occurs, *What is cruelty?* In the present case it is hardly necessary for me to define it; because the facts here complained of are such as fall within the most restricted definition of cruelty; they affect not only the comfort, but they affect the health, and even the life of the party. I shall therefore decline the task of laying down a direct definition. This, however, must be understood, that it is the duty of courts, and consequently the inclination of courts, to keep the rule extremely strict. The causes must be grave and weighty, and such as shew an absolute impossibility that the duties of the married life can be discharged. In a state of personal danger no duties can be discharged; for the duty of self-preservation must take place before the duties of marriage, which are secondary both in commencement and in obligation; but what falls short of this is with great caution to be admitted. The rule of *per quod consortium amittitur* is but an inadequate test; for it still remains to be enquired, what conduct ought to produce that effect? whether the consortium is reasonably lost? and whether the party quitting has not too hastily abandoned the consortium?

What merely wounds the mental feelings is in few cases to be admitted, where they are not accompanied with bodily injury, either actual or menaced. Mere austerity of temper, petulance of manners, rudeness of language, a want of civil attention and accommodation, even occasional sallies of passion, if they do not threaten bodily harm, do not amount to legal cruelty; they are high moral offences in the marriage-state undoubtedly, not innocent surely in any state of life, but still they are not that cruelty against which the law can relieve. Under such conduct of either of the parties, for it may exist on one side as well as on the other, the suffering party must bear in some degree the consequences of an injudicious connection; must subdue by decent resistance or by prudent conciliation; and if this cannot be done, both must suffer in silence. And if it be complained that by this inactivity of the courts much injustice may be suffered, and much misery produced, the answer is, that courts of justice do not pretend to furnish cures for all the miseries of human life. They redress or punish gross violations of duty, but they go no farther; they cannot make men virtuous: and, as the happiness of the world depends upon its virtue, there may be such unhappiness in it which human laws cannot undertake to remove.

Still less is it cruelty, where it wounds not the natural feelings, but the acquired feelings arising from particular rank and situation; for the court has no scale of sensibilities, by which it can judge the quantum of injury done and felt; and therefore, though the court will not absolutely exclude considerations of that sort, where they are stated merely as a matter of aggravation, yet they cannot constitute cruelty where it would otherwise not have existed: of course, the denial of little indulgences and particular accommodations, which the delicacy of the world is apt to number among its necessaries, is not cruelty. It may, to be sure, be a harsh thing to refuse the use of a carriage, or the use of a servant; it may in many cases be extremely unhandsome, extremely disgraceful to the character of the husband; but the Ecclesiastical Court does not look to such matters: the great ends of marriage may very well be carried on without them; and if people will quarrel about such matters, and which they certainly may do in many cases with a great deal of acrimony, and sometimes with much reason, yet they must decide such matters as well as they can in their own domestic *forum.*

These are negative descriptions of cruelty; they shew only what is *not* cruelty, and are yet perhaps the safest definitions which can be given under the infinite variety of possible causes. ... In the older cases of this sort, which I have had the opportunity of looking into, I have observed that the danger of life, limb, or health, is usually inserted as a ground upon which the court has proceeded to a separation. This doctrine has been repeatedly applied by the court in the cases that have been cited. The court has never been driven off this ground. It has been always jealous of the inconvenience of departing from it, and I have heard of no one case cited, in which the court has granted a divorce without proof given of a *reasonable apprehension* of bodily hurt. I say an *apprehension*, because assuredly the court is not to wait till the hurt is actually done; but the apprehension must be *reasonable*: it must not be an apprehension arising merely from an exquisite and diseased sensibility of mind. Petty vexations applied to such a constitution of mind may certainly in time wear out the animal machine, but still they are not cases of legal relief; people must relieve themselves as well as they can by prudent resistance – by calling in the succours of religion and the consolation of friends; but the aid of courts is not to be resorted to in such cases with any effect.

The truth of the case, according to the impression which the whole of it makes upon my mind, is this: two persons marry together; both of good moral characters, but with something of warmth, and sensibility, in each of their tempers; the husband is occasionally inattentive; the wife has a vivacity that sometimes offends and sometimes is offended; something like unkindness is produced, and is then easily inflamed; the lady broods over petty resentments, which are anxiously fed by the busy whispers of humble confidantes; her complaints, aggravated by their reports, are carried to her relations, and meet perhaps with a facility of reception, from their honest, but well-intentioned, minds. A state of mutual irritation increases; something like incivility is continually practised; and, where it is not practised, it is continually suspected; every word, every act, every look, has a meaning attached to it; it becomes a contest of spirit, in form, between two persons eager to take, and not absolutely backward to give, mutual offence; at last the husband breaks up the family connection, and breaks it up with circumstances sufficiently expressive of disgust: treaties are attempted, and they miscarry, as they might be expected to do, in the hands of persons strongly disaffected towards each other; and then, for the very first time, as Dr Arnold has observed, a suit of cruelty is thought of; a libel is given in, black with criminating matter; recrimination comes from the other side; accusations rain heavy and thick on all sides, till all is involved in gloom, and the parties lose total sight of each other's real character, and of the truth of every one fact which is involved in the cause.

Out of this state of darkness and error it will not be easy for them to find their way. It were much to be wished that they could find it back again to domestic peace and happiness. Mr Evans has received a complete vindication of his character. Standing upon that ground, I trust he will act prudently and generously; for generosity is prudence in such circumstances. He will do well to remember, that the person he contends with is one over whom victory is painful; that she is one to whom he is bound by every tie that can fasten the heart of one human being to another; she is the partner of his bed! – the mother of his offspring! And, if mistakes have been committed, and grievous mistakes have been committed, most certainly, in this suit, she is still that person whose mistakes he is bound to cover, not only from his own notice, but, as far as he can, from that of every other person in the world.

Mrs Evans has likewise something to forget; mistakes have been made to her disadvantage too in this business: she, I say, has something to forget. And I hope she has not to learn, that the dignity of a wife cannot be violated by submission to a husband.

It would be happy indeed, if, by a mutual sacrifice of resentments, peace could possibly be re-established. It requires, indeed, great efforts of generosity, great exertions of prudence, on their own part, and on the part of those who are connected with them. If this cannot be done; if the breach is too far widened ever to be closed, Mrs Evans must find her way to relief; for, she must not continue upon her present footing, no, not for a moment: she must call in the intervention of prudent and respectable friends; and, if that is ineffectual, she must apply to the court, under the guidance of her counsel, or other persons by whom the matrimonial law of this kingdom is understood.

But, in taking this review, I rather digress from my province in giving advice: my province is merely to give judgment; to pronounce upon what I take to be the result of the facts laid before me. Considering, then, all those facts, with the most conscientious care, and with the most conscientious application of my understanding to their result, I am of opinion, that Mr Evans is exculpated from the charge of unmanly and unlawful cruelty. I therefore pronounce, *that Mrs Evans has failed in the proof of her libel, and dismiss Mr Evans from all further observance of justice in this behalf.*

5.6 Gladstone's views of the religious implications of divorce

William Gladstone *(1809-98), the famous Victorian statesman and Liberal Prime Minister in the latter part of the nineteenth century, was well known as a devout high churchman, and his religious views strongly coloured his speeches and writings on social issues such as divorce. His objections to the Divorce Bill of 1857 which secularised the law of divorce stemmed largely from the fact that, as originally drafted, it required clergymen to remarry divorcees in their churches. The following extract is from his article 'The Bill for Divorce',* Quarterly Review, *July 1857.*

The legislation now threatened will be, we do not hesitate to say, an intolerable burden upon conscience; and it will in our opinion strike a blow at the time-honoured union between Church and State heavier than any which it has yet received. Nor is it less an insult to our religion – supposing for a moment that it were worked not by men but by steam, or by water-power like the prayer-mill in Thibet – that we should pretend to efface, by a merely civil process, a rite which that religion consecrates as 'a great mystery of the Gospel'.

A time may come, when society cannot bear the strictness of the Christian law, and will reject the drill, that is necessary to make the soldier. It will then doubtless largely fall back upon that lower conception of marriage, which treats it as a purely civil contract between individuals. It may be said that that time has already come, in a country like England: where, according to the last returns, out of one hundred and sixty thousand marriages, seven thousand six hundred, a number relatively small but absolutely considerable, were celebrated by the Registrar, and therefore with no special religious authority. We are far from saying that the law offends by permitting such marriages as these to persons whose consciences do not enable them to enter into marriage by the way properly Christian. So, then, if there must be re-marriage, let that too be the Registrar's privilege. The day, when marriage is made dissoluble by law in England, will at best be noted in our Calendar with charcoal, not with chalk. But if we are not strong enough to hold the lower portion of society up to Christianity down to the lowered and lowering level of society. Let the salt of the earth still keep its savour, and the darkness of the body be illumined, as far as it may, by the eye that still wakes within it.

5.7 Reform of divorce laws in 1920: the views of a prelate and a judge

The Matrimonial Causes Act 1920 ended the gross anomaly whereby a husband could divorce his wife for adultery alone, but a wife had to prove in addition to adultery either cruelty or desertion in order to divorce her husband. The first extract is from a speech on the Bill by Randall Davidson (1848-1930), an extremely active and politically astute Archbishop of Canterbury. It is followed by part of a speech by Lord Coleridge (1857-1927) judge of the Queen's Bench Division 1907-23 and son of Lord Chief Justice Coleridge. It shows clearly the impact that personal experience can have upon the professional philosophy of a judge.

The Archbishop of Canterbury: Not only are you taking an irrevocable step, but you are dealing in all this with a very sacred thing touching the home life of England. You are – I do not scruple to say it – on holy ground. It is very easy for the zealous reformer to point in scorn or pity or indignation at the case of domestic strife and misery, which are known to all men, and to ask, 'Is that what you call a sacred thing? Is that what you uphold as the glory of matrimony? Is that what you want to safeguard and preserve?' There are, I think, some 9,000,000 married couples in this country. The cases we are talking about to-night are in comparison the veriest handful. We do want to consider them and we do want to help them if we may; but beware lest in your mode of helping these you bring unrest, apprehension, and distress into homes, not ten times but a thousand times as numerous, and beware also lest you open a door which will be used by ten people whom you do not want to use it for every one for whose benefit you made the opening. That, I believe, is the fundamental fact which underlies our action in this matter. I would say that to my mind the moment at which we are asked to do this is the very worst one for dealing quietly and soberly with these particular things. The whole of our life in Europe is seething. In parts of Europe the wildest proposals, social and otherwise, are in the air. I noted a moment ago the abnormal character of our present Divorce Court figures and how little it bears on our ordinary life; but when we look afield every sort of outrageous scheme is finding supporters.

Lord Coleridge: My Lords, my sole reason for wishing to intervene in this debate is that I think it may be useful if I speak from personal experience in the working of the Divorce Court. For six months last year I sat as Judge in that Court, and during that period I disposed of some 1,500 cases. I think that is ground for my expressing my own opinion based upon experience.

I approached my work with the general settled opinion that the restriction on divorce should not be relaxed. I had not thought deeply on the subject, I admit; I accepted the views of general opinion, and I thought that they were sound in the interests of morality, in the interests of the matrimonial home, believing that the more people were forced to live together the more likelihood there was of their differences being composed. I am not ashamed to confess that experience entirely changed my views. I was perplexed; I was depressed; indeed, I may almost say that I was appalled at the amount of human unhappiness with which I was confronted.

And there were some curious loopholes in the law. For instance, it is the policy of the law that collusion between the parties should be a bar to any matrimonial relief, and I found myself bound to decide upon this issue and to discover what both parties were desirous of concealing from me. Imagine my astonishment when I found that I was precluded by Act of Parliament from asking the very questions which were necessary to bring those facts to light. That defect is cured by this Bill. Collusion may be a desirable or an undesirable bar to divorce, but if it exists it is asking the Judge to play but a sorry part where he is obliged to pronounce decrees which he often thinks, even almost knows, are collusively obtained, and at the same time to deprive him of the opportunity of all investigation. I have said that this defect is remedied by the Bill.

Now, again, there is a general opinion which exists – which has been emphasised by the most rev. Prelate, and which I think is the subject of almost general acceptance – that the same grounds should exist in regard to both sexes for obtaining a decree of divorce. As is well known the husband has only to prove adultery on the part of the wife to succeed, whereas the wife has to prove, in addition to adultery, either cruelty or desertion. The Courts have, from time to time, in the interest of wives, enlarged, and are continually enlarging, the definition of cruelty, but still its existence must be proved. As to desertion *prima facie* it is established no doubt if one party, without excuse, makes the other party live apart for two years. That is desertion, but that form of desertion is seldom proved. It is usually proved by the wife suing for restitution of conjugal right to be obeyed within fourteen days. The husband disobeys. Desertion is then proved, and the wife is entitled to a decree of divorce after proving adultery. How is it done? The wife writes a fondling letter to the husband whom she loathes, and asks her husband to return to her. The husband refuses, and the decree is duly pronounced. It may be said to be almost universally the case that no suit for the restitution of conjugal rights is brought without a wife having the proof of adultery as well. The wife, indeed, would be horrified if the husband obeyed the decree, and daily Judges are called upon to take part in this which is nothing but a sorry farce. All these evils that I have dwelt upon are removed by placing the sexes on the same footing.

I want to remove the idea that the vast increase in the applications for divorce necessarily indicates a growing moral degeneration. Statistics may be most misleading. For instance, a marked increase in crime may merely indicate an efficient police, and a marked decrease in crime may merely indicate an insufficient detective force. No, my Lords, there are reasons for this increase. First of all, the doors of the Divorce Court are not now open exlusively to the rich. Before 1914 no one but the well-to-do had access to the Divorce Court. Since 1914 a poorer class has been admitted. But even now, if a party can prove that he or she is not worth £50, it is a mistake (into which the most rev. Prelate has fallen) to say that their costs are all paid. That party who has not £50 need not pay the Court fees, but that party must pay all the out-of-pockets of the solicitor if a solicitor is employed, and must pay all the costs of, and incidental to, the party, or his or her witnesses, appearing in the Divorce Court; and I need hardly ask, how can a person who is not worth £50 be expected to bring witnesses from North Berwick and Penzance to the Divorce Court in London? But the effect of these Poor Persons Rules has been, no doubt, to bring the Court more within the access of the poor.

It may seem to be a paradox, but it is no paradox, to say that the increase in the applications for divorce is due to a raised moral standard. So long as the poor were excluded from the Divorce Court people living in irregular unions were morally pardoned by their neighbours. Now that the doors of the Divorce Court are enlarged the neighbours no longer overlook these irregularities; people find that the moral feeling of the street is against them and hurry to do homage to the higher standard of the street. Secondly, the fact that the custody of the children implies that the spouse getting their custody is free from moral blame is another reason for the struggle of the poor to obtain the custody of their children however burdensome such custody may be upon them. All these things seem to me to be fine and praise-worthy symptoms indicating a sound moral atmosphere and inconsistent with the mournful prospect of general moral decadence. These few observations from one having experience I thought possibly may not be unacceptable to the consideration of your Lordships' House.

5.8 *Modern divorce law reform: the Archbishop's working party*

One of the first major documents to come out of the newly formed Law Commission was a reflection upon changes in the divorce law which had been promoted in a startlingly progressive report by the Archbishop of Canterbury's Working Party on Divorce, Putting Asunder *(London, 1966) in which theological doctrine emerged happily married to sociological perspective. Here, an extract from* Putting Asunder *is followed by some key paragraphs (5.9) from the Law Commission's own paper,* Reform of the Grounds of Divorce: The Field of Choice.

13 ... To the people of a modern secular society ... talk of divorce and remarriage being contrary to reason and the law of nature is apt not to sound very meaningful. Even if they go as far as to admit the reality of such a law, they will want to know whose reason, and whose conception of the law, are being appealed to, since their own reason does not in fact tell them that divorce and remarriage are wrong. So it becomes clear that 'hardness of heart', or 'incredulity', is a very real factor to be reckoned with. Christians are driven to distinguish between those dictates of the law of nature which are apparent to all men of good will and those which seem clear to themselves but not to others, and to admit that apprehension of the latter owes more to faith and less to bare reason than the theologians once maintained. The lifelong obligation of the marriage covenant seems to fall into the second class.

14   In such circumstances it is right that Parliament should make provision for divorce and remarriage. Indeed it conforms with natural justice by so doing, since natural justice requires that human law should not be the tyrannical imposition upon the community of an alien code, but an expression of the community's own mind. If *per impossibile* the Christian minority to-day had power to impose on the nation a matrimonial law satisfactory to itself, to use the power would surely be unjust as well as socially disruptive.

15   It has also to be recognized that in a modern plural society the concept of human law is very different from that which obtained when the traditional theology of law was being formulated. Since theology lost its dominance legislators have been sceptical of metaphysics, regarding law as concerned only with the empirical – with what can be agreed independently of men's diverse religions and philosophies. So such intangibilities as a union of man and wife alleged to subsist after all common life has ceased are nowadays thought to be not the law's business. When therefore a modern court 'dissolves' a marriage, it is not making a pronouncement about the *vinculum matrimonii* in the traditional Christian sense of that term; for it does not take cognizance of any such thing. What it dissolves is the complex of legal rights and duties that make up the legal status of marriage.

17   There is ... nothing to forbid the Church's recognizing fully the validity of a secular divorce law within the secular sphere. It follows that it is right and proper for the Church to co-operate with the State, and for Christians to co-operate with secular humanists and others who are not Christians, in trying to make the divorce law as equitable and as little harmful to society as it can be made. Since *ex hypothesi* the State's matrimonial law is not meant to be a translation of the teaching of Jesus into legal terms, but allow properly for that 'hardness of heart' of which Jesus himself took account, the standard by which it is to be judged is certainly not the Church's own canon law and pastoral discipline. Any advice that the Church tenders to the State must rest, not upon doctrines that only Christians accept, but upon premises that enjoy wide acknowledgement in the nation as a whole. No one should think, therefore, that advice from the Church in this matter is bound to represent an ecclesiastical attempt to obtain legal enforcement of specifically Christian tenets.

5.9   *The Law Commission and reform of the grounds of divorce: the field of choice*

71   The basic weakness, as we see it, of the proposals of the Archbishop's Group is that they call for an elaborate, time-consuming and expensive investigation to satisfy the court that the marriage has irretrievably broken down. The realities of the situation are that unless the marriage had broken down the parties would not be before the court. Conceivably, it may not have broken down irretrievably, but if cohabitation has ended and both parties are convinced that reconciliation is impossible the chances of saving it are remote. The parties are likely to be better judges of the viability of their own marriage than a court can hope to be, even with the most elaborate and searching inquest.

72 As we see it, a divorce case based on breakdown should involve the determination of four questions: –

(a) Has the marriage broken down?

(b) If so, is there any reasonable prospect of a reconciliation?

(c) If not, is there any reason of public policy, including in particular justice to the parties and the children, why the marriage should not be dissolved?

(d) If not, what are the appropriate consequential arrangements to be made regarding the parties and the children?

The Archbishop's Group wish the answers to all these questions to be proved positively to the satisfaction of the court by means of an inquest into the whole of the married life. Under the alternative proposal that we are now considering, the court, *on proof of a period of separation*, would be prepared to assume a positive answer to (a) and, in the absence of evidence to the contrary, negative answers to (b) and (c). The ending of cohabitation and a sustained failure to resume it are the most cogent, objective, and justiciable indications of breakdown, and the objectives of a sound divorce law, as summarised in paragraph 15, might be better achieved by relying on these indications rather than on an attempted inquest, in all cases, into the whole marital history.

72 Question (a), as we have already said, is answered by the fact that the parties have separated and that divorce proceedings have been brought. Normally neither it, nor question (b) – the possibility of a reconciliation – requires investigation. If both parties, who are the best judges, have decided that their differences are irreconcilable, and if this is confirmed by the fact that they have parted for some time, the court does not need further proof on these points. If something in the pleadings or evidence led the court to think that there was a possibility of reconciliation, then, as we have already suggested, the court should be empowered to adjourn the hearing for a limited period so that the possibility could be explored. But the court would not attempt an inquest into the marriage to satisfy itself that the marriage had irretrievably broken down unless this was seriously disputed between the parties. Even if it was disputed, an adjournment for attempts at reconciliation would normally be more constructive than an inquest into the past.

5.10 A seventeenth-century case of marital consanguinity

Hains v. **Jessel**

Court of King's Bench

A day was appointed to hear counsel, why a prohibition should not be granted to the Spiritual Court of Worcester, to say a suit against Hains for marrying with the bastard daughter of his sister. And Sir Bartholomew Shower for the prohibition argued, that it was not prohibited by any law, for there was neither affinity nor consanguinity, for a bastard is *nullius filius* ...

It is no consideration to raise a use ... Dobbins *e contra*, that the original is, *ad proxinam sanguinis non accedat*; that the Jews made no difference, as to marriage, between bastards and others ... It seems to the Court that no prohibition should be granted, for though bastards are deprived of privileges by particular laws, the same reason prohibits them from marrying, as others. And it has been always held accordingly, especially where it is the child of a woman relation. And by Sir Bartholomew Shower's rule Hains might marry his own bastard, which doubtless could not be allowed.

Adjournatur.

5.11   Marriage to a deceased wife's sister

The Seventh Duke of Marlborough (*1822-83*) *made the following speech on the Marriage With A Deceased Wife's Sister Bill only a few days before his death and it was widely regarded by his contemporaries as one of his most effective contributions to debate. In the result, his opposition to the Bill was rewarded by its defeat at third reading by 145 votes to 140. It is interesting to note that two members of the Royal Family, the Prince of Wales and the Duke of Albany, voted in favour of the Bill, the former's espousal of this cause giving rise to some popular ribaldry at the time. Marriage with a deceased wife's sister was not legalised until 1907 (the former Prince of Wales now being called upon to give Royal Assent to the Bill); marriage to a brother's widow had to wait until 1921.*

The Duke of Marlborough, in rising to move, as an Amendment, that the Bill be read a third time that day six months, said, he would not have been justified in taking up the time of their Lordships, in asking their attention to the subject once more, with a view to the reconsideration of the decision arrived at on a recent occasion, were it not for the narrowness of the division on the second reading, and the nearly equally divided opinion in their Lordships' House. When the question came before them on the second reading, the arguments that were used by his noble Friend behind him (Earl Beauchamp), in opposition to the measure, were of such a forcible, exhaustive character, that he felt he would be unduly trespassing upon their Lordships' attention if he were to endeavour to recapitulate any of the arguments that had been used in opposition to the measure, or go at any great length into the subject. But it was only fair to consider what had taken place since the second reading of the Bill. The Bill had been in Committee of the Whole House, and had there been subjected to a furbishing process at the hands of the noble Earl opposite (the Earl of Dalhousie), and altered in a variety of ways, especially in regard to its retrospective application. While, to some extent, it had assumed a new appearance, he could not say that it was improved in its character. In fact, he considered the Bill to be in its present form a monstrosity, and he was reminded by it of the words '*Ut turpiter atrum Desinat in piscem mulier formosa superne*'. Perhaps, before he went into the one or two objections that he might take with reference to the Bill as it stood, he might be allowed to say a few words, as he had not yet addressed their Lordships upon the subject – he wished to say a few words on what appeared to him to be the religious aspect of the question. He must admit,

to a great extent, the force of the remarks which had fallen from Noble
Lords opposite, to the effect that it was difficult to discover, in exact terms,
any definite and express prohibition in the Scriptures against these
marriages which the Bill was intended to legalize; and, although the subject
had been treated in a very light and airy, and, indeed, jocose manner by the
noble and learned Lord opposite (Lord Bramwell), who always attracted
the House by the pungency of his remarks, yet, at the same time, he thought
it was almost a pity that they, who were opposed to the Bill, should
endeavour to rest the objections to it upon grounds that, to his mind, could
not be clearly proved, and to which exception might be taken. It had always
appeared to him that, if a marriage of this kind was expressly prohibited by
Holy Scripture, the prohibition would have been in so direct and
unmistakable terms that 'he who runs may read.' He must admit he could
not convince himself that any prohibition could be found in any such
unmistakable terms. But, it appeared to him that there was an argument of
a far higher and more weighty character that could be used, and that was
this – that they knew the words that fell from the Saviour in regard to
bigamy and the putting away of wives.

There were those who supported [the Bill] from pure and consciencious
motives, such as he had no doubt induced the noble Earl opposite and most
of their Lordships who voted with him, and who believed there was a
grievance, and that it ought to be removed. But there was another class of
persons who supported this Bill, and they were the avowed enemies of the
Established Church. The great body of Dissenters throughout the country
supported the Bill, and Her Majesty's Government also supported the Bill.
He had no doubt they did because the Dissenters were their friends, and
they would not offend them. Now, let their Lordships see what the effect of
this Bill would be if passed. In the first place, it would bring in a conflict
between the law of the Church and the law of the land. Now, they knew
what would be the consequence of that. There was another point. It was
said – 'If you pass this Bill, see what safeguards you have attached to it.' He
had seen a great deal of safeguards in his day. He had seen, from their own
side of the House, a Reform Bill brought forward which was full of
safeguards, and these safeguards had disappeared, very rapidly, one by one.
This Bill had also safeguards, and one of these was that these marriages
were not to be performed in churches. How did any rational man think that
it would be possible to maintain that provision? There was a very strong
feeling in the country about being married in church. A great many people
thought being married in church sanctified the operation, and that a
marriage in church was more a marriage than a marriage anywhere else.
And that was a very proper and legitimate feeling. But now their Lordships
put a stigma on the marriages dealt with by the Bill. They said they were
lawful, that there was nothing in them contrary to the laws of God or man,
yet they were not to be performed in church. The very first agitation that
took place after the passing of the Act would be for the performance of these
marriages in church. In that case, what would happen but this – that the
clergy would not solemnize these marriages, and the duty would be left to
Dissenting ministers? The beautiful Marriage Service of the Church would

not be used for this purpose, but would be superseded by some other form, till ultimately they would have brought about a state of things which would imperil the relation between Church and State, and bring about the common use of churches, the great object for which every Dissenter in the Kingdom had long been striving, and which every Radical in the Kingdom desired should become an accomplished fact. He had no doubt a great many noble Lords on that (the Conservative) side of the House supported the Bill for very different reasons – because they did not look beyond the present moment, and thought merely that an injustice had to be redressed and a long-standing dispute to be settled, and that if they passed this measure they would get rid of the difficulties and disputes that were connected with the question. But he appealed to noble Lords on that side of the House, and asked them, in view of the circumstances which he had explained, to pause before they gave a vote to assist in passing the Bill. They had seen the opinions that had been expressed by a Minister of the Crown. They had seen the way in which these opinions had been treated by his Colleagues. They had seen the state of feeling out-of-doors. They knew that the passing of a measure of this sort could not stop there, but that it would involve the obliteration of all the degrees of the Church with regard to affinity; that it would put a nail into the coffin of the Church; that it would seriously weaken, if not annihilate, the connection between Church and State. He appealed to noble Lords to take a wider and a more general view of this question; and, even if they did but delay it for another year, let them give the country another year's breathing-time to consider this measure. Let them see whether new thoughts and lights might not arise, and a new and better sentiment. He would implore noble Lords not to precipitate the passing of this measure by their votes or by their voices on the present occasion, as by so doing they would run the risk of destroying the Church they revered and endangering the Throne they loved. He moved that the Bill be read a third time that day six months.

5.12 *Marriage to a divorced wife's sister*

The controversy lingered on over the issue of marriage to a divorced wife's sister. The following extract is from a speech made by the Bishop of London (William Wand) who joined with his Primate in denouncing the Marriage (Enabling) Bill on the subject, introduced by Lord Mancroft in 1949. The Bill failed, but Lord Mancroft eventually succeeded with a similar measure in 1960.

The Lord Bishop of London: My Lords, I think we must all tremendously admire the courage of the noble Lord, Lord Mancroft in introducing this Bill. I am not sure whether I admired most his courage in introducing the Bill, the assaults that he made upon the members of the Government, or the sly 'digs' that he gave to the occupants of this particular Bench. In any case, he made an admirable speech. But as the debate has gone on this afternoon I have wondered whether, after all, his courage was quite so great as at first I thought it was, because he has been backed by a gallant phalanx of speakers who have all taken the same view and, so far, the only opposed view that we have had is that which has been uttered by the most reverend

Primate, my own revered leader. Your Lordships have spoken of the concerted ring on this particular Bench. I can count only three of us; I have not counted up the number of people who have spoken on the other side, but it comes to a considerable number.

I myself wish to take a line opposed to Lord Mancroft and those who have been supporting this Bill, and I do so for quite simple and clear reasons. I endorse the very careful and what seemed to me cogent arguments put forward by the most reverend Primate. I take a straight and definite opposition. I wish to oppose the Bill because I am quite definitely opposed to divorce in any shape or form; in other words, I take precisely the opposite view from that which was clearly stated by the noble Lord, Lord Schuster. He said he did not like divorce but thought the door to it ought to be opened as widely as possible. I also say that I do not like divorce, but I say that the door ought to be kept closed against it. On the whole I think my attitude is the more logical.

I recognise that both Lord Mancroft and, in this particular respect, my own leader, think it possible to discuss the logic of this Bill by separating it altogether from the subject of divorce – in other words, that this is a logical step to take; that as we have already opened the door to divorce, so it is logical to open it so much further for divorce in this particular instance. That is surely the argument: that one step has been taken, and therefore it is logical to take the next. But that is an argument pursued without reference to the whole of the surrounding circumstances. There used to be an old Latin tag in my schooldays, *facilis descensus averni* – if you take one step to the slope it is logical to take the other. But surely, if you have regard to the matter as a whole, it is entirely illogical to go down a slippery slope at all.

5.13 *A cultural conflict (1969)*

Alhaji Mohamed v. **Knott:** *this case arose out of a marriage in Nigeria between a Nigerian girl aged thirteen and a fellow Moslem, the marriage being valid under Moslem law and therefore potentially polygamous. The question decided by the juvenile justices was that the marriage was not recognised as valid in England and that since she had no parent or guardian a girl of her age was 'exposed to moral danger'. Accordingly, the justices made a fit person order committing her to the care of a local authority. On appeal to the High Court it was held that the marriage should be recognised as valid and that although a fit person order might be made in respect of a wife validly married to her husband, it was relevant to that issue to consider the mode of life of the young bride. What follows is an extract from the judgment of Lord Chief Justice Parker.*

Lord Parker: ... What did the justices find? ...

'Here is a girl, aged thirteen or possibly less, unable to speak English, living in London with a man twice her age to whom she has been married by Moslem law. He admits having had sexual intercourse with her at a time when according to the medical evidence the development of puberty had almost certainly not begun. He intends to resume intercourse as soon as he is satisfied that she is adequately protected by contraceptives from the risk of pregnancy. He admits that before the marriage he had intercourse with a woman by whom he has three illegitimate children. He further admits that since the marriage, which took place as recently as January of this year, he has had sexual relations with a prostitute in Nigeria from whom he contracted venereal disease. In our opinion a continuance of such an association notwithstanding the marriage, would be repugnant to any decent minded English man or woman. Our decision reflects that repugnance.'

I would never dream of suggesting that a decision by this bench of magistrates with this very experienced chairman, could ever be termed perverse; but having read that, I am convinced that they have misdirected themselves. When they say that 'a continuance of such an association notwithstanding the marriage, would be repugnant to any decent minded English man or woman', they are, I think, and can only be, considering the view of an Englishman or woman in relation to an English girl and our western way of life. I cannot myself think that decent minded English men or women, realising the way of life in which Rabi was brought up, and the appellant for that matter, would inevitably say that this is repugnant. It is certainly natural for a girl to marry at that age. They develop sooner, and there is nothing abhorrent in their way of life for a girl of thirteen to marry a man of twenty-five. Incidentally it was not until 1929 that, in this country, an age limit was put on marriage. Granted that the appellant may be said to be a bad lot, that he has done things in the past which perhaps nobody would approve of, it does not follow from that that the wife, happily married to the appellant, is under any moral danger by associating and living with him. For my part, as it seems to me, it could only be said that she was in moral danger if one was considering somebody brought up in, and living in, our way of life, and to hold that she is in moral danger in the circumstances of this case can only be arrived at, as it seems to me, by ignoring the way of life in which she was brought up, and the appellant was brought up.

5.14 *Artificial insemination as adultery?*

Maclennan v. **Maclennan**, *1958 S.L.T. 12. Is artificial insemination of a married woman by a donor other than her husband adultery in law? Traditionally it has been thought not to amount to adultery since that matrimonial offence has always required penetration by the male organ. In the judgment that follows, the Scottish trial judge, Lord Wheatley (a Roman Catholic) adhered to the traditional view. The legislature has never provided a specific solution to this difficult jurisprudential problem, but no doubt artificial insemination carried out without the husband's consent would be subsumed under the 'irretrievable breakdown' provisions of the Divorce Reform Act 1969 (which has not yet been extended to Scotland).*

[Lord Wheatley:] In the uncomplicated days before science began to innovate on the natural process of procreation, the lapse of time between the last act of marital intercourse and the birth of the child would have led to the inevitable inference that the defender had been guilty of an adulterous act with another man by means of the normal and natural physiological mechanism as a result of which the child was conceived. The defender, however, has tendered an explanation by way of defence, which is unique in the annals of our law, and which seeks to establish that she conceived the child not as a result of sexual intercourse with another man, as that phrase is commonly understood, but as a result of artificial insemination from a donor. She does not aver, however, that the pursuer was a consenting party to such an artificial process of conception, and the pursuer maintains that he never agreed to the defender adopting it, if in fact it ever took place. The defender submits that artificial insemination by a donor even without the consent of the husband is not adultery as the law understands and has interpreted that term, and that proof of conception by such means would rebut the inference which would otherwise be raised from the 14 months' period of non-access followed by the birth of a child. ... The term 'artificial insemination by a donor' is glibly used without any explanation of the process in the pleadings, it being apparently assumed that such unusual practices and interference with the natural processes of procreation fall within that omniscience on all wordly matters which is described, sometimes euphemistically and sometimes with a complimentary but quite unjustified faith, as 'judicial knowledge'. My own particular knowledge of this subject is culled from the articles thereon in some of the journals to which I was referred in the course of the debate. ...

Artificial insemination is the process whereby the seed of the male is extracted from the male body, enclosed in a receptacle, and subsequently inserted into the female sexual organ, presumably by means of a syringe, thereby reproducing in the end the same result as follows from the natural and unrestricted act of sexual intercourse. This scientific innovation on the natural processes substitutes a syringe containing male seed for the male sexual and reproductive organs, and the act of conception, if the seed eventually fertilizes, is achieved without the presence of the male body. Technically, although I have no particular knowledge of this, I presume that the woman could acquire the seed and operate the syringe herself, thereby excluding the presence of any other person during the actual insertion.

There are manifestly grave moral, ethical, social and personal considerations involved in the practice of artificial insemination in its various forms which will no doubt be fully deployed elsewhere. It is almost trite to say that a married woman who, without the consent of her husband, has the seed of a male donor injected into her person by mechanical means in order to procreate a child who would not be a child of the marriage has committed a grave and heinous breach of the contract of marriage. The question for my determination, however, is not the moral culpability of such an act but is whether such an act constitutes adultery in its legal meaning. A wife or a husband could commit an act of gross indecency with a member of the opposite sex which would be a complete violation of the marital relationship, but which could not be classified as adultery. It would indeed be easy, according to one's personal viewpoint, to allow oneself to be influenced by the moral, ethical, social and personal considerations to which I have referred and to reach a conclusion based on these considerations, but this problem which I am called upon to solve must be decided by the objective standard of legal principles as these have been developed and must be confined to the narrow issue of whether this form of insemination constitutes adultery in the eyes of the law. If it is not adultery, although a grave breach of the marriage contract, that is a matter for the legislature if it be thought that a separate legal remedy should be provided.

In determining whether the marital offence (which I opine it to be whatever view one takes of its nature) of being impregnated by the seed of another man without the husband's consent constitutes adultery in its legal sense, one naturally seeks a solution from the definitions of 'adultery' in the works of our leading legal writers or in reported decisions. Some of our great legal writers however do not even seek to define it, while others, in referring to it, use terms which are more descriptive than definitive. This may be due to the fact that in earlier days when life was regulated by the natural rather than the scientific order of things, people knew what was meant by adultery and what its concomitants were. Where, however, attempts were made to describe adultery if not to provide an exhaustive definition of it, the idea of *conjunctio corporum* seems to be an inherent concomitant – a conception of the process which incidentally can likewise be found in the book of Deuteronomy, the writings of St. Paul and the works of the Canonists. The idea that adultery might be committed by a woman alone in the privacy of her bedroom aided and abetted only by a syringe containing semen was one with which the earlier jurists had no occasion to wrestle.

... I ... derive ... the following propositions, according at least to the law of England.

1. For adultery to be committed there must be the two parties physically present and engaging in the sexual act at the same time.

2. To constitute the sexual act there must be an act of union involving some degree of penetration of the female organ by the male organ.

3. It is not a necessary concomitant of adultery that male seed should be deposited in the female's ovum.

4. The placing of the male seed in the female ovum need not necessarily result from the sexual act, and if it does not, but is placed there by some other means, there is no sexual intercourse.

Just as artificial insemination extracts procreation entirely from the nexus of human relationships in or outside the marriage, so does the extraction of the nexus of human relationship from the act of procreation remove artificial insemination from the classification of sexual intercourse. If my views be correct, then it follows logically that artificial insemination by a donor without the consent of the husband is not adultery as the law interprets that term.

5.15 A Church of England reaction to the judgment in Maclennan

Lord Wheatley's judgment prompted a reaction from the then Archbishop of Canterbury, Dr Fisher, urging legislation on the topic 'to preserve the integrity of marriage and of the family'.

If many people get confused over the difference between crime and sin, I doubt not that some will get confused by this judgment.

They know that the Church says that adultery is a sin: they read that A.I.D. is not adultery: and some of them will get a quite illogical impression that if A.I.D. is not adultery, then it cannot be a sin either.

The Judge, of course, pointed out with great care and emphasis that, whether it was legally adultery or not, A.I.D. raises 'grave moral, ethical, social and personal considerations'; and he said further that a married woman who by this means had a child 'who would not be the child of her marriage had committed a grave and heinous offence' against the contract of marriage. Whether A.I.D. should be regarded by law as adultery for legal purposes is a matter for lawyers. Whether it is against the interests of social or personal morality, whether or no it is a sin, is a matter of great Christian concern.

I am told that recently in a discussion of A.I.D. on television a clergyman of the Church of England said that the Church had given no guidance on this matter. He was very wrong; and it is a serious thing for a clergyman thus to mislead a nationwide audience. In 1948 S.P.C.K. published a report of 70 pages entitled *Artificial Human Insemination*, being the report of a commission appointed by me as Archbishop of Canterbury in December, 1945. The chairman of the commission was the then Bishop of London, Dr Wand. Though it has not been formally adopted as an official document of the Church of England, it records for the guidance of the Church the considered judgment of eminent Church doctors, lawyers, and theologians, and so far as I know has commanded the general approval of the Church ever since.

Two of its findings relate to A.I.D. and I should like to recall them at this time. The one is as follows:–

> A.I.D. involves a breach of the marriage. It violates the exclusive union set up between husband and wife. It defrauds the child begotten, and deceives both his putative kinsmen and society at large. For both donor and recipient the sexual act loses its personal character and becomes a mere transaction. For the child there must always be the risk of disclosure, deliberate or unintended, of the circumstances of his conception. We, therefore, judge A.I.D. to be wrong in principle and contrary to Christian standards.

That was the finding, deliberate and definite, with one dissentient, of this weighty and responsible commission. That brings me to the second finding of the commission that 'the evils necessarily involved in A.I.D. are so grave that early consideration should be given to the framing of legislation to make the practice a criminal offence'.

5.16 Artificial insemination and legal conspiracy: Lord Denning's view

The issue was subsequently debated in the House of Lords on a motion by Lord Blackford that artificial insemination of a married woman by a donor other than her husband is tantamount to adultery and that all children so conceived are illegitimate. This is an extract from a speech by Lord Denning.

Secrecy and deception are the badge of conspiracy. If the wife and the doctor agree together to keep secret the fact that a child is illegitimate and falsely to pretend that it is legitimate, they are guilty of a wicked conspiracy. If they do it without the knowledge or consent of the husband it is a gross fraud on the husband. He is made to maintain a child which is not his and which he is not liable by law to maintain. For centuries, in the old books you will find that when a woman, the mother of a bastard, agrees with others by fraud or concealment to saddle an innocent person with the maintenance of that child, it has been held to be an indictable conspiracy. Lord Holt so ruled in 1705, Mr Justice Buller, a very learned Judge, in 1788, and Lord Denman in 1834. It is, I believe, if done without the knowledge or consent of the husband a fraud and an unlawful, indictable conspiracy.

What is the effect of this contingent fraud, this potential fraud? Again if you look into the old books you will find that the fraudulent foisting off of a child as legitimate when it is not, has been held to be a conspiracy, because, as Lord Hardwicke, the Lord Chancellor, said, it impedes the due course of descent; and Lord Chief Justice Willes at the same time so ruled. So I say that this action, when done in fraud or potential fraud, is an unlawful conspiracy by both the wife and the doctor with her. And I have not mentioned the Register of Births. The conspiracy goes back long before that. The conspiracy is when the plot is hatched. But when it comes to a false statement in the Register of Births, there is not only the overt act of the conspiracy; there is an additional crime, the crime of perjury, making a false statement in a Register of Births, when it is said that the husband is the father when he is not.

So much for the conspiracy between the doctor and the wife. What about the agreement between the doctor and the donor? What have they agreed? The whole essence of it is that it should be secret, not told to anyone, not told to the mother or the child, told to no one. And for what purpose? So that the donor should evade the responsibilities which by law attach to him. The natural and probable consequence of this is that he gets exemption from maintenance or responsibility for his own child. If he could be detected and found he could be made liable to maintain this child, not by the wife herself, because she is a married woman, but through the National Assistance Board. So I say that there is a double unlawful conspiracy, by the doctor with the wife and by the doctor with the donor. And not only is that so in the criminal law; it also gives rise to damages by any person injured by it.

5.17   *The trial of Besant and Bradlaugh*

In 1877 **Annie Besant** (*1847-1933*) *and* **Charles Bradlaugh** (*1833-91*) *were tried before Lord Chief Justice Cockburn with 'Unlawfully, and wickedly devising and contriving and intending, as much in them lay, to vitiate and corrupt the morals as well of youth as of divers other liege subjects of our said Lady the Queen and to incite and encourage the said liege subjects to indecent, obscene, unnatural and immoral practices, and to bring them to a state of wickedness, lewdness and debauchery'. The subject of this extraordinary indictment was Charles Knowlton's* Fruits of Philosophy, *originally* *published in America in 1832 and concerned with the desirability of family limitation. Incensed by the conviction of a Bristol bookseller and of a publisher for circulating and publishing* Fruits of Philosophy, *Bradlaugh and Besant formed the Freethought Publishing Company to republish the book and force a confrontation with the prosecuting authorities. The two redoubtable defendants conducted their own case amid a blaze of publicity. Although they were convicted (but explicitly exonerated from imputations of corrupt motive) the conviction was reversed on a technicality when the case went to appeal.*

The trial generated a considerable momentum for birth control ideas and in its wake Besant published a widely distributed pamphlet, The Law of Population, *while Bradlaugh reconstituted the influential Malthusian League.*

The extract that follows is from the Lord Chief Justice's summing up to the jury.

The Lord Chief Justice, in summing up, said: Gentlemen of the jury: There is one point on which I think every one who has attended to this trial will cordially concur with the Solicitor-General, who has just addressed you – that is as to the mischievous character and effect of this prosecution. A more ill-advised and more injudicious proceeding in the way of a prosecution was probably never brought into a court of justice. Here is a book which has been published now for more than forty years, which appears never to have got into general circulation to any practical extent, and which by this injudicious proceeding has been resuscitated and sent into general circulation to the extent of thousands of copies ... Therefore, we have the case here, and however much we may deplore the rashness which set this prosecution going, we must deal with it as though it had had the sanction of the Crown, which I do not think it has, although the Solicitor-General appears to conduct it. It is not a Government prosecution, nor have we any evidence that it is a prosecution set on foot by any authority which we should be disposed to treat with any great amount of consideration, but it is a case certainly deserving of your most serious attention. There is one thing in which I cordially agree with the Solicitor-General, and that is that no better tribunal can be found in the world to judge of such a question as this than the average sound sense and enlightened judgment which is to be found in English society, and I quite agree with what has been said on both sides that the decision in this case, when I have told you what the indictment is, and what the law is, rests solely and entirely and exclusively with you ... Now, gentlemen, as I have already said, you are the judges in this matter, and you have had this book before you, and you have had it in all its details and in its general effects commented on by both sides, and by this time you must be pretty familiar with it. I am bound to tell you what the law says about it. Although it is a law of modern times, and unknown, I believe, to the old common law of England, and forming a portion of that part of our law which is called 'judge-made law', there it is – it is the law of the land, and we must all abide by it. It is not for the defendants to say that the law is a bad law, and inconsistent with that perfect freedom of discussion which is essential to the welfare of mankind. We are a law-abiding people, and no man has a right to set himself above the law and to defy the law. If the law is a bad law, an immoral law, or an impolitic law, and you have it in your power in any way to change it, to abrogate or reverse it, your duty, as a good citizen, would be to do so. But while the law exists it is your first and bounden duty as citizens to obey it; therefore, we must not listen to arguments upon moral obligations arising out of any motive or out of any desire to benefit humanity, or to do good to your species. You must not say, I will set the law at defiance, or, I will do what the law forbids. ... Now, gentlemen, the law is this – that whatever outrages public decency and actually tends to corrupt the public morals is an offence. It is not necessary to load it with all the opprobrious epithets which have been applied to this work. It is enough to say that the work is a corrupt publication, that it tends to corrupt the morals of the population, and that it is, therefore, an offence against morality. But we must be careful in applying this general principle of law when we come to its practical application, so as not to abridge the full and free right of public discussion, and the expression of public and private opinion on matters which are interesting to all, and materially affect the welfare of society. There is a difficulty in a case of this kind in determining whether that which is put forward in the shape of a publication is matter tending to vitiate and corrupt public morals, or whether it is matter which it is of interest to mankind to have discussed, and which calls for an expression of opinion upon it. Now, the Solicitor-General, in opening this case – as he did also in replying to the case for the defence – has asserted not only that this publication is filthy and obscene, but also that the purpose of it – and all the details are intended to lead up to that purpose – is inconsistent with public morality, so that we have to divide the consideration of the subject into two parts. In the first place, are there in this publication details inconsistent with decency – details calculated to enkindle the passions and desires of lust, and excite libidinous thoughts in the minds of the readers? Even if that should not be the case, the second point is whether the purpose advocated in the work and the purpose and effect of the details so elaborately given, is a purpose inconsistent with the morals of society?

5.18   *The Marie Stopes libel action*

Marie Stopes *(1880-1956), a notable biologist, was probably prompted to enter into a campaign for enlightened education in matters of sex and birth control by the sexual failure of her own marriage (annulled for non-consummation in 1916). She published two highly popular works on these subjects,* Married Love *(1918) and* Wise Parenthood *(1918), and in 1921 established a pioneering birth control clinic in North London.*

In 1922 a Roman Catholic Physician, Dr Halliday Sutherland, published Birth Control: A Statement of Christian Doctrine against the Neo-Malthusians *which alleged that Marie Stopes (described as 'a doctor of German philosophy (Munich)') had exposed the poor to experiment and that the methods used in her clinic had been described by a medical authority as 'the most harmful of which I have had experience'. Marie Stopes sued for libel; the defendants pleaded justification and fair comment. Represented by the redoubtable Patrick Hastings K.C., the action was lost at first instance, won on appeal and lost again in the House of Lords. The real significance of the case lies in the publicity it achieved.*

The following is an extract from the opening address of Mr Patrick Hastings.

Now I am going to tell you quite shortly what the work is, and I am going to try and express her beliefs. It is very difficult, but you must allow me to do it for this reason; she has written many books on this subject. One of them, and the one which I suppose is the best known, is a book which received an enormous amount of comment, some praise and some dispraise. It is a book which is known as *Married Love*. It is a book she wrote for the furtherance of the propaganda of birth control, and she is now President of the Society. This book will be put before you. I am not going to do it at this moment, although it may be necessary for you to see it. I just want to say this about it: there is scarcely a book in the world with regard to which it would not be possible to take sentences and paragraphs out of it and describe them as either coarse, licentious, stupid or evil. We are only concerned here, as far as I know, with the licentious side of it. But if one might even be permitted to draw a parallel from perhaps the oldest and greatest book in the world,we all know that you can take sentences or verses out of that and call attention to it. You have to look at these works as a whole. Now the purpose underlying every one of Dr Marie Stopes's books is this – and this is which differentiates her work from the work of any other of these people who have tried to do it during past years, whether it be Bradlaugh or any Malthusian or any other person who had similar ideas – her belief is this; not that birth control is intended to limit the population, as so many other people believe, and say that limitation of population is the only thing which can enable civilisation to endure, that is no part of Dr Stopes's view. What she believes in, and what she is seeking to teach is this; that the only possible chance of happiness for married people is to realise that marriage, and all that it conveys, is intended to be a joy to both, and not a curse to either. She, in the course of her researches, has heard not one, not hundreds, probably not thousands, more like tens of thousands of cases, which must be known to everyone of us, of women whose life is made a misery by the fear of being forced to have children when their health is bad – poor people with 8 or 10 children and no income, whose lives are made a curse to them. The result of that may be, and in her view often is, that the husband and wife become estranged, that the feelings of one another become changed from those of affection to hatred, ad sometimes contempt. I do not suppose it would be too much to say that her view is, that the Divorce Court is peopled with those who really began their misery because, for some reason or another, the natural affection, and the means of expression of affection between married people, is necessarily curtailed or injuriously prevented. Her teaching lies in this, that people should have children, but that they should have healthy children. They should have them at a time when they can be well brought up and properly cared for. Further than that, that women's lives should be made happy by their associations with their husbands – not miserable, and that husbands' lives should be made happy by the feeling that they have not got to treat their wives in a way which is going to cause misery or unhappiness to them. The whole principle of her teaching is composed in all these books. I hope I have faithfully reproduced it in a few words. She will tell you herself that it is, as I understand it, based upon those two ideas. Now if that is right, that that is the real view underlying this lady's motives, could any living person say that a woman whose ideals are as high as that should be subject to a writing such as that of Dr Sutherland? He may believe it; he may be a member of a Roman Catholic Church whose tenets I do not profess to express or understand. But he may be one who may say: When a woman and a man are married, the woman's duty is to go on having children as long as her husband so desires it. He may be one of those who say it is better that the wife should suffer miserably rather than that anything should be done to permit those two to live happily together. He may be right in saying it. He is quite entitled to say that Dr Marie Stopes is wrong in expressing her views, but what he is not entitled to do is to say that she is a criminal for expressing her views, that she is experimenting on poor people who are too poor and ignorant to defend themselves, to say nothing of the fact that he might perhaps take a little trouble with his own ideas of courtesy, and not describe her contemptuously as a Doctor of German Philosophy.

5.19 State intrusion upon personal relationships: an American view

Mr Justice Harlan *was Associate Justice of the US Supreme Court, mainly during the era of Chief Justice Warren, and retired shortly before his death in 1972. The dissenting judgment that follows is from* Poe *v.* Ullman *(1961) where the majority upheld the right of the Connecticut legislature to enforce anti-birth control laws by making the use of contraceptives by married persons and the giving of contraceptive advice to such persons a crime.*

Appellants contend that the Connecticut statute deprives them, as it unquestionably does, of a substantial measure of liberty in carrying on the most intimate of all personal relationships, and that it does so arbitrarily and without any rational, justifying purpose. The State, on the other hand, asserts that it is acting to protect the moral welfare of its citizenry, both directly, in that it considers the practice of contraception immoral in itself, and instrumentally, in that the availability of contraceptive material tends to minimize 'the disastrous consequence of dissolute action,' that is fornication and adultery.

The very inclusion of the category of morality among state concerns indicates that society is not limited in its objects only to the physical well-being of the community, but has traditionally concerned itself with the moral soundness of its people as well. Indeed to attempt a line between public behaviour and that which is purely consensual or solitary would be to withdraw from community concern a range of subjects with which every society in civilized times has found it necessary to deal. The laws regarding marriage which provide both when the sexual powers may be used and the legal and societal context in which children are born and brought up, as well as laws forbidding adultery, fornication and homosexual practices which express the negative of the proposition, confining sexuality to lawful marriage, form a pattern so deeply pressed into the substance of our social life that any Constitutional doctrine in this area must build upon that basis.

It is in this area of sexual morality, which contains many proscriptions of consensual behaviour having little or no direct impact on others, that the State of Connecticut has expressed its moral judgment that all use of contraceptives is improper. Appellants cite an impressive list of authorities who, from a great variety of points of view, commend the considered use of contraceptives by married couples. What they do not emphasize is that not too long ago the current of opinion was very probably quite the opposite, and that even today the issue is not free of controversy. Certainly, Connecticut's judgment is no more demonstrably correct or incorrect than are the varieties of judgment, expressed in law, on marriage and divorce, on adult consensual homosexuality, abortion, and sterilization, or euthanasia and suicide. If we had a case before us which required us to decide simply, and in abstraction, whether the moral judgment implicit in the application of the present statute to married couples was a sound one, the very controversial nature of these questions would, I think, require us to hesitate long before concluding that the Constitution precluded Connecticut from choosing as it has among these various views. ...

But, as might be expected, we are not presented simply with this moral judgment to be passed on as an abstract proposition. The secular state is not an examiner of consciences: it must operate in the realm of behaviour, of overt actions, and where it does so operate, not only the underlying, moral purpose of its operations, but also the *choice of means* becomes relevant to any Constitutional judgment on what is done. The moral presupposition on which appellants ask us to pass judgment could form the basis of a variety of legal rules and administrative choices, each presenting a different issue for adjudication. For example, one practical expression of the moral view propounded here might be the rule that a marriage in which only contraceptive relations had taken place had never been consummated and could be annulled. ... Again, the use of contraceptives might be made a ground for divorce, or perhaps tax benefits and subsidies could be provided for large families. Other examples also readily suggest themselves.

Precisely what is involved here is this: the State is asserting the right to enforce its moral judgment by intruding upon the most intimate details of the marital relation with the full power of the criminal law. Potentially, this could allow the deployment of all the incidental machinery of the criminal law, arrests, searches and seizures; inevitably, it must mean at the very least the lodging of criminal charges, a public trial, and testimony as to the *corpus delicti*. Nor could any imaginable elaboration of presumptions, testimonial privileges, or other safeguards, alleviate the necessity for testimony as to the mode and manner of the married couples' sexual relations, or at least the opportunity for the accused to make denial of the charges. In sum, the statute allows the State to enquire into, prove and punish married people for the private use of their marital intimacy.

Adultery, homosexuality and the like are sexual intimacies which the State forbids altogether, but the intimacy of husband and wife is necessarily an essential and accepted feature of the institution of marriage, an institution which the State not only must allow, but which always and in every age it has fostered and protected. It is one thing when the State exerts its power either to forbid extra-marital sexuality altogether, or to say who may marry, but it is quite another when, having acknowledged a marriage and the intimacies inherent in it, it undertakes to regulate by means of the criminal law the details of that intimacy.

In sum, even though the State has determined that the use of contraceptives is as iniquitous as any act of extra-marital sexual immorality, the intrusion of the whole machinery of the criminal law into the very heart of marital privacy, requiring husband and wife to render account before a criminal tribunal of their uses of that intimacy, is surely a very different thing indeed from punishing those who establish intimacies which the law has always forbidden and which can have no claim to social protection.

5.20 Vasectomy and mayhem

Glanville Williams, *in* Sanctity of Life and the Criminal Law, *wrote on sterilisation and the legal doctrine of mayhem. This is of some contemporary interest in view of the enactment of the National Health Service (Family Planning) Amendment Act 1972 which empowers local authorities to set up clinics providing vasectomy operations under the National Health Service.*

The legality of sterilization at common law is problematical where there are no clinical indications and the operation is performed merely for eugenic reasons or as a form of birth control. Even in states possessing measures for eugenic sterilization, the legality of (other) contraceptive sterilization is generally left to be determined by the common law, though, in two, such voluntary sterilization is expressly disallowed by statute. One state that formerly prohibited sterilization except for therapeutic or eugenic reasons has since abandoned the prohibition, thus restoring the question to the common law.

The issue at common law is whether the patient can validly consent to the operation for non-therapeutic reasons. If he cannot, the operation is a criminal battery upon him by the surgeon, perhaps an aggravated form of battery such as a battery with intent to do grievous bodily harm; the patient himself may also be held guilty of a misdemenour. Whether consent can validly be given to a surgical operation is generally said to rest upon public policy. The only decided case of anything approaching relevancy in any common-law jurisdiction is a case of the first year of James I, mentioned by Chief Justice Coke, where 'a young strong and lustie rogue, to make himself impotent, thereby to have the more colour to begge or to be relieved without putting himself to any labour, caused his companion to strike off his left hand; and both of them were indicted, fined and ransomed therefor'. There is obviously a good deal of difference between the amputation of a member like a hand, when the individual becomes less able to work and may be a charge on the public funds, and an operation that is of interest only from the point of view of the production of another generation.

It is sometimes said that a person cannot effectively consent to the commission of a maim (mayhem) upon himself, and the question then resolves itself into whether sterilization is a maim. In principle, a maim was some injury that lessened a person's ability to fight and defend himself, such as cutting off a hand or even knocking out a tooth (which would impair his power to bite an adversary), and castration was also held to be a maim, because it was thought to diminish bodily vigour or courage. Sterilization has no effect upon mental or muscular vigour and so should not be held to be a maim. Also, vasectomy is not a maim because the legal meaning of a maim (as contrasted with a wound) is that it is permanent; the possibility of a reversal operation means that the prosecution cannot prove that vasectomy is permanent. Again, the law of maim seems historically to have no application to women. Even if all these difficulties are surmounted, it may be questioned whether the antiquated law of maim affords a satisfactory basis for a conclusion as to the defence of consent. It seems unlikely that a person would today commit a criminal offence by having his teeth extracted without adequate reason.

It may be taken as reasonably certain that the courts would uphold a voluntary sterilization submitted to on eugenic grounds. The single difficulty here is in respect of the reality of consent when a feeble-minded person is sterilized ...

The troublesome area is the 'sterilization of convenience'. The only possible evil that can be discerned even in these sterilizations (there is no evil, but only good, in eugenic sterilizations) is that this is against public policy because it imperils the future of the race. This appears to be an unrealistic attitude, neglecting the strength of the reproductive instinct. Moreover, since the mere decision of an individual not to procreate cannot be regarded as against public policy, it should follow that the undergoing of an operation to give effect to this decision is legal. It may be said that this decision that consent cannot be given to a sadistic act is unsupported by previous authority and of doubtful wisdom and policy. The question whether sadistic and masochistic practices should be penalized is a legislative one on which the opinion of medical experts, among others, would be important; it is not proper to be settled by pretended deduction from the theory of things *mala in se*.

These arguments are advanced in full consciousness that they are quite likely to be rejected by some judges, who may decide, when the question arises, that 'sterilization for convenience', at least if the medical evidence is that it is irremediable, is a criminal offence. It may be of some importance, in this connection, that judges belong to the male sex, since, as has been shown, males have a stronger instinctive reaction against sterilization than females. (The tendency to accumulate irrational arguments against sterilization is observable even in purported scientific literature.) A psychologist might predict that a male judge would tend to look with a kindlier eye upon female sterilization than upon male vasectomy; he does not feel the former as such an immediate threat to his own security. Legally, however, it seems impossible to differentiate between the sexes, except possibly confining the theory of maim to the fighting sex. Another governing factor may be the religious affiliation of the judge, who may be influenced by the traditional view that any divergence from sexual custom is sinful. This is more likely to happen in England than in the United States, where experience has been obtained of the working of legal sterilization.

In an English divorce case [*Bravery* v. *Bravery*, 5.21] Lord Justice Denning (now Lord Denning) took occasion to say, though it was in no way necessary for the decision, that sterilization was an offence when done to enable a man to have the pleasure of sexual intercourse without shouldering the responsibilities attached to it. However, this old-fashioned view, which overlooked the change of opinion that had occurred with respect to contraception, was not concurred in by the other two judges, who expressly left the question open. Lord Justice Denning himself agreed that sterilization was lawful when done with consent for just cause, and he gave the example of preventing the transmission of hereditary disease. It may be pointed out that even in this case, where the operation is admitted to be lawful, vasectomy allows a man to have the pleasure of sexual intercourse without its responsibilities. Any attempt to assign 'just causes' for sterilization would involve the courts in a somewhat intricate inquiry into the health of each marital partner, their eugenic endowment and economic circumstances, their capacity to make use of contraceptives, and the prospect of unfavourable psychological reactions to sterilization. These matters seem to be unsuitable for decision as incident to an inquiry whether a common-law crime has been committed. On an issue of this character, where there are strong religious and other differences of opinion, it seems only right that the legal question should be decided in favour of liberty, unless the legislature intervenes to answer it otherwise.

5.21   Sterilisation and 'cruelty' in marriage

Lord Justice Denning *(as he then was) dissented in* Bravery *v.* Bravery *(1954) on the lawfulness of sterilisation.*

Denning L.J. The parties married on October 25, 1934, when the husband was 25 and the wife 21. They lived very happily together for two years until a son was born to them on December 19, 1936. About 18 months later, in 1938, a shocking thing took place. The husband underwent an operation to have himself sterilised. He was the porter at a London hospital. One of the surgeons operated upon him, and he was attended by the sister and staff nurse.

This operation provokes several questions. The first is: Why did the husband have this done? Let me give his answer in his own words. Counsel asked him: 'What was the immediate cause of the operation? (A.) It was because of my wife's attitude towards the boy. He was not a baby to be caressed and loved. He was a show-piece.' Again: 'Why did you agree to have an operation for sterilisation? (A.) Because my wife was so installed. She was so installed with the home, and with this baby she had. (Q.) You said the baby was a show-piece? (A.) Yes. (Q.) In what way? (A.) She wanted to have him perfectly dressed, and when he was tiny, if there was the least thing missing, she would be absolutely beside herself.'

Those answers throw a flood of light on the husband's mentality. Why did he object to the wife treating the baby as a show-piece? Although he did not realize it, he must in some strange way have been jealous of the place which the child had in the wife's affections; and his jealousy found expression in a determination not to give her any more children, seeing that was the way she treated this baby. But it may well be asked why go to the length of sterilisation? Why not use contraceptives? Both agreed that ever since the birth of the child, they had been having intercourse using contraceptives. He was the one who used them, not she. And yet he went and had himself sterilised. It is, as the commissioner said, 'an amazing story'; and it was done simply because he was jealous of the baby. He did it so as to 'pay her out' for making so much of it. That seems to me to be cruelty in itself.

An ordinary surgical operation, which is done for the sake of a man's health, with his consent, is, of course, perfectly lawful because there is just cause for it. But when there is no just cause or excuse for an operation, it is unlawful, even though the man consents to it. The classic instance is a case reported by Lord Coke, tried at Leicester in 1604, when a 'young strong and lustie rogue, to make him impotent,' got his companion to cut off his left hand so that he might avoid work and be able the better to beg. Both were found guilty on indictment of a criminal offence. A later instance can be given from early Victorian days when soldiers, as part of their drill, had to bite cartridges. A soldier got a dentist to pull out his front teeth so as to avoid the drill. In the opinion of Stephen J. both were guilty of a criminal offence. (See Stephen's Digest of Criminal Law, 3rd ed., p. 142.) Another instance is an operation for abortion, which is 'unlawful' within the statute unless it is necessary to prevent serious injury to health. Likewise with a sterilisation operation. When it is done with the man's consent for a just cause, it is quite lawful; as, for instance, when it is done to prevent the transmission of an hereditary disease. But when it is done without just cause or excuse, it is unlawful, even though the man consents to it. Take a case where a sterilisation operation is done so as to enable a man to have the pleasure of sexual intercourse, without shouldering the responsibilities attaching to it. The operation then is plainly injurious to the public interest. It is degrading to the man himself. It is injurious to his wife and to any woman whom he may marry, to say nothing of the way it opens to licentiousness; and, unlike contraceptives, it allows no room for a change of mind on either side. It is illegal, even though the man consents to it; for it comes within the principle stated by Stephen J. (who was a great authority on criminal law) in *Regina* v. *Coney*: 'The Principle as to consent seems to me to be this: When one person is indicted for inflicting personal injury upon another, the consent of the person who sustains the injury is no defence to the person who inflicts the injury, if the injury is of such a nature or is inflicted under such circumstances, that its infliction is injurious to the public as well as to the person injured.' That principle is well illustrated by *Rex* v. *Donovan* and clearly covers cases of sterilisation.

Those cases under the criminal law have a bearing on the problem now before the court; because the divorce law, like the criminal law, has to have regard to the public interest, and consent should not be an absolute bar in all cases. If a husband undergoes an operation for sterilisation without just cause or excuse, he strikes at the very root of the marriage relationship. The divorce courts should not countenance such an operation any more than the criminal courts. It is severe cruelty. Even assuming that the wife, when young and inexperienced, consented to it, she ought not to be bound by it when in later years she suffers in health on account of it, especially when she was not warned that it might affect her health.

I would therefore, for myself, have allowed this appeal.

Appeal dismissed. Leave to appeal to
the House of Lords refused

5.22 Sterilisation and the Constitution of the United States of America: 'Three generations of imbeciles are enough'

Mr Justice Holmes *(1841-1935) was a great American judge and jurist. The following is an extract from a characteristically robust judgment on sterilisation by consent in* Buck *v.* Bell *(1925) a case which related to the constitutionality of the Virginia Statute permitting sterilisation. In a subsequent decision involving an Oklahoma statute in 1942, the Supreme Court reversed its earlier policy favouring sterilisation legislation. In* Skinner *v.* Oklahoma *it declared unconstitutional a statute which authorised the compulsory sterilisation of habitual criminals convicted of 'felonies involving moral turpitude'.*

We have seen ... more than once that the public welfare may call upon its best citizens for their lives. It would be strange if it could not call upon those who already sap the strength of the State for these lesser sacrifices, often not felt to be such by those concerned, in order to prevent our being swamped with incompetents. It is better for all the world, if instead of waiting to execute degenerate offspring for crime, or to let them starve for their imbecility, society can prevent those who are manifestly unfit from continuing their kind. The principle that sustains compulsory vaccination is broad enough to cover cutting the Fallopian tubes. Three generations of imbeciles are enough.

5.23 The Catholic view of sterilisation

Norman St. John Stevas *is Conservative MP for Colchester, lawyer, journalist, author, and editor of the works of Walter Bagehot. A prominent Roman Catholic propagandist, he published* Law and Morals *(London, 1964) which sets out the Catholic viewpoint on various aspects of the debate about law and morality: the following extract deals with sterilisation.*

The Catholic Church condemns all forms of direct sterilisation, whether compulsory or voluntary. Her condemnation is based on traditional Christian ethics which lay great emphasis on the essential creatureliness of man. Man is not the absolute master of his own body, but holds it on trust for God's purposes. His procreative faculty is one of man's most important endowments and save in cases of grave necessity he is not free to do away with it at will. Sterilization involves not only a mutilation of the body but the deprivation of a major faculty. In the early Church some persons, misunderstanding the meaning of Matthew 19.12 ('there be eunuchs who have made themselves eunuchs for the kingdom of heaven's sake'), castrated themselves. Such practices were condemned both by canon law and the Fathers of the Church. Castration, they taught, for the spiritual end of preserving chastity is ineffectual, and in any case is wrong because it is a kind of suicide, and implies that the body which God has created is in itself evil. Implicitly it denies free will and the providence of God.

In the Middle Ages St Thomas developed Catholic teaching holding that a man who mutilates his body commits a threefold offence: against the natural law of self-preservation and proper self-love: against the community of which he is a part; and also against God. To mutilate the body in order to preserve chastity is disproportionate. St Thomas allowed one exception to his rule, the removal of a diseased part of the body for the good of the whole. 'If, however,' he writes in the *Summa Theologica*, 'the member be decayed and therefore a source of corruption to the whole body, then it is lawful with the consent of the owner of the member, to cut away the member for the welfare of the whole body, since each one is entrusted with the care of his own welfare. The same applies if it be done with the consent of the person whose business it is to care for the welfare of the person who has a decayed member; otherwise it is altogether unlawful to maim anyone.' In his Encyclical *Casti Connubii*, Pius XI confirmed the teaching of St Thomas. 'Christian teaching established,' he wrote, 'and the light of human reason makes it most clear, that private individuals have no other power over the members of their bodies than that which pertains to their natural ends; and they are not free to destroy or mutilate their members, or in any other way render themselves unfit for their natural functions, except when no other provision can be made for the good of the whole body.'

6

The Sanctity of Human Life

In 1956 Professor Glanville Williams delivered the Carpenter Lectures in the United States on the subject 'The Sanctity of Life and the Criminal Law'. In his introduction to the published edition of the lectures he succinctly states the theme of the work and some of the questions he hopes to answer:

> Much of the law of murder rests upon pragmatic considerations of the most obvious kind. Law has been called the cement of society, and certainly society would fall to pieces if men could murder with impunity. Yet there are forms of murder or near-murder the prohibition of which is rather the expression of a philosophical attitude than the outcome of social necessity. These are infanticide, abortion and suicide. Each extends the disapprobation of murder to particular situations which raise special legal, moral, religious and social problems. The prohibition of killing imposed by these three crimes does not rest upon considerations of public security. If it can be justified at all, this must be ethico-religious or on racial grounds. There are related problems, all of them highly prickly in the present state of opinion. To what extent should the procreation of children be controlled by law? What should be the legal attitude to sterilization and artificial insemination? To what extent can the law effectively, and to what extent should it properly, penalize one who, perhaps from motives of humanity, kills another with his consent?[1]

This admirable statement could hardly be improved upon for our present purpose. Though some of the matters included by Glanville Williams are treated by us in other chapters, it is to him that the reader should turn for a much fuller discussion of these issues than is possible here.

Sanctity of life is a value which in one shape or form can be identified in most developed systems of law although the legal guise in which such a value appears may vary widely. It is at its most emphatic in those systems founded upon a Judaeo-Christian, or Mohammedan, or Hindu ethic.

In some societies and at some points in time human life has been held cheap. The Biblical commandment forbidding homicide has not restrained the Christian church itself from bloodshed or from countenancing a death penalty administered by the State. The extensive provision of capital punishment in the nineteenth-century criminal code reflected an ordering of priorities in which the taking of property was valued at the same cost as the

---

1. Glanville Williams, *The Sanctity of Life and the Criminal Law*, London, 1958, pp. 11-12.

taking or endangering of life (see Chapter 2) undermining the principle that a hierarchy of punishment should bear at least some tenuous relationship to society's attitudes to crime.

The Christian churches have always opposed the taking of life (subject to qualifications already mentioned). This opposition has been complicated in one respect, highly relevant to the arguments that follow, by the belief that death before absolution jeopardises the immortal soul of the victim. Hamlet declined to kill Claudius while the latter was at prayer on the understandable, if uncharitable grounds that his soul would thereby find an undeserved refuge in Heaven. This doctrine would seemingly encounter an insurmountable hurdle if applied to unborn, part-born, or newborn children whose souls have not yet been contaminated by wordly wickedness. However, this hurdle was temporarily overcome by a doctrine of original sin devised by St Augustine – but then modified by St Thomas Aquinas, and finally buried by Darwinism. Evolutionary theory is hardly compatible with a doctrine which founds an important area of contemporary *mores* upon a literal interpretation of the Book of Genesis.

The compartments into which the law places various violations of the principle of sanctity of life can be arranged along a continuum. At one end is the act of procreation with which current English law is little concerned, apart from providing criminal sanctions against deviant sexual activity of various kinds and imposing a minimum age of consent. In English law no penal sanctions are imposed for 'sins' like adultery (but see Chapter 4), masturbation, and fornication, though the criminal law does concern itself to various degrees with bestiality, buggery, and exhibitionism (the incongruities abounding in this field are discussed elsewhere). At the point of fertilisation the law begins to take a closer interest, and some societies make it illegal to disseminate information about contraception (see Chapter 7). Advertisements for contraceptive advice centres, contraceptives themselves, or for clinics specialising in treatment of venereal diseases may still fall foul of such legislation as the Indecent Advertisements Acts (or of informal 'rules of good taste' laid down by such bodies as London Transport – in respect of advertisements – or the B.B.C.).

The Roman Catholic Church still holds contraception other than by use of the safe period to be a mortal sin; but modern English law does not lend its support to this view. The real confluence of modern jurisprudence and views about the sanctity of life (based partly upon religious doctrine but supported by a variety of secular arguments) begins at the next point along the continuum – at the point beyond the aid of contraception as such,[2] where a child is conceived. Here, one embarks upon that singularly tortuous road leading from abortion (before or after a foetus has 'quickened') to child destruction, to infanticide, to child-murder – and one encounters a plethora of arbitrary definitions and dividing lines which do little to enhance the law's reputation for consistency and rationality.

The subject of abortion raises one issue with theological as well as medical implications; when does 'life' begin? (Contrast this with

2. There is a further blurring of the boundaries, particularly as regards the development of the 'morning after' contraceptive pill.

euthanasia, discussed below, where one must ask instead when life is finally extinguished). Sir William Blackstone[3] argued that life enters the body at 'quickening' (when the child begins to move in the uterus) and the Act of 1803 which first made abortion a criminal offence imposed harsher penalties after quickening. (Certainly there are good *medical* grounds for terminating a pregnancy in its early stages, but that was not the reason for this legal distinction.)

In 1846 the Criminal Law Commission suggested that abortion should cease to be an offence 'when such act is done in good faith with the intention of saving the life of the mother', although the suggestion was not taken up when the law was re-enacted in the Offences Against the Person Act 1861. However, the proviso was included, when (after a long struggle dating back to 1867) the new offence of child destruction (the killing of an infant before it becomes separated from its mother[4]) was created by the Infant Life Preservation Act 1929.

Abortions have always taken place illegally and no doubt *de facto* abortions have often occurred in the guise of other forms of surgery. Pressure for reform of the law had been growing in the early part of this century and a Committee of Inquiry on the subject was set up in 1937 under Norman Birkett Q.C. (which received evidence critical of the uncertain legal position in which doctors found themselves, from, *inter alia*, the B.M.A). Meanwhile a prominent gynaecologist, Alex Bourne, took the law into his own hands by performing an abortion upon the young victim of a brutal rape and ensuring that the issue was finally fought out in open court. In his celebrated summing-up of the case (6.2) Mr Justice Macnaghten told the jury that the proviso in the 1929 Act could be read into the Act of 1861, a decision nonsensical in strictly legal terms but one which breathed life into a brutally inflexible area of law.

The rule in *R. v. Bourne* was regarded as the definitive statement of the law up to the mid-1960s and had further been extended by *R. v. Bergmann and Ferguson*[5] which held that good faith was sufficient ground in the absence of firm evidence that the woman's health was in fact endangered. It was clear, however, that the law was still ambiguous and throughout the 1950s there developed a strong body of opinion that the grounds for legal abortion should be both consolidated and extended to cover eugenic and social grounds. The Magistrates' Association urged reform in 1955, and the Abortion Law Reform Association (founded as early as 1936) became increasingly active. The latter provoked the formation in 1967 of a counter-group, the Society for the Protection of the Unborn Child, which expressly dissociated itself from an exclusively Roman Catholic basis. There followed an unpalatable campaign sometimes couched in extravagantly emotive language. Formidable opposition came from the medical bodies but, after several false starts, David Steel's Abortion Bill was steered through Parliament in 1966 with the Government's blessing (6.3). The aftermath of

3. *op.cit.*, Book I.
4. Not to be confused with infanticide, the mother killing her child within one year of its birth (Infanticide Act 1922, as amended).
5. May 1948; cited in Williams, *op.cit.*, p.154.

the legislation has been the subject of a major inquiry.[6] At the time of writing (1975) a Bill to curb some of the unsavoury profiteering of referral agencies is being debated by Parliament.

The problem of euthanasia follows logically from that of abortion, though its implications are somewhat more complicated, and both involve difficult problems of medical ethics. 'Mercy killing', more self-evidently than an abortion carried out in the darkly anonymous uterine cavity, involves the killing (in both Christian doctrinal and legal terms, murder) of a living and breathing human being. Sometimes the 'victim' is indeed a newly-born. infant; sometimes it is questionable whether that infant, a grotesquely distorted 'monster', can strictly be called human at all. How will a doctor react to a situation where an overriding commitment to saving life results in the preservation of a creature so deformed that his life can only be perpetual misery to himself and to those around him? What of the more adult person, in full possession of his faculties, lying in incurably dreadful pain and wanting to die? – many doctors would barely hesitate before administering a dose of morphine, the ostensible purpose of which is analgesic but the inevitable secondary effect fatal. But what if the medical issue is not as clear-cut or the person administering the fatal dose is a close friend or relative, rather than a doctor?

Sir Thomas More's Utopian mercy (6.4) is not reflected in English law: the crime is murder, or at best manslaughter. In practice, however, the severity of the law has usually been mitigated by less severe sentences (6.7). Successive attempts have been made since the 1920s to permit voluntary euthanasia and a vigorous pressure group, the Voluntary Euthanasia Legalisation Society, was formed in 1932 to promote the cause. Nevertheless, this is one area of conscience where reform has stuck in Parliament's gullet. Doctors have revealed their own personal dilemmas (6.5 and 6.6) but in the end a succession of Bills on the subject has foundered, largely on the difficult issue of 'consent'; the most recent was in 1969.

Both the Church of England and the Catholic Church have always taken a very strong line against euthanasia. But in May 1971 Archbishop Ramsay was reported as saying 'that he did not think that doctors were duty bound to prolong the lives of patients whose cases were hopeless. He would not take any hard or fast line on euthanasia, but it did need more Christian exploration'.[7] In March 1975 the Church Information Office published a sensitive review of this subject in a report aptly entitled *On Dying Well*.

Like euthanasia, suicide is a matter of personal choice. However, the suicide is an instrument of his own destruction and does not, except in a suicide pact, involve another person. Suicide is in some respects the ultimate reflection of human freedom: Seneca argued plausibly that 'slavery loses its bitterness when by a step I can pass to liberty. Against all the injuries of life, I have the refuge in death'.[8] Cicero argued that a free man, if captured into

6. See the Report of the Committee on the Working of the Abortions Act (chaired by Mrs Justice Lane), Cmnd. 5579 of 1974.

7. The *Guardian*, 3 May 1971; quoted by Williams, *op.cit.*, p.228.

8. Quoted by Williams, *op.cit.*, p.228.

slavery with no hope of escape, actually should kill himself. But while some societies have accepted suicide as a private issue or as a more or less acceptable social mechanism (e.g., Japan) Christian doctrine has frowned heavily upon self destruction.

The traditional attitude of English law towards suicide and attempted suicide (6.8 and 6.9) is founded on feudal tradition requiring the forfeiture of a suicide's goods to the Crown, as in all felonies.[9] It was this practice, as well as the non-entitlement of the suicide to Christian burial, that lay behind the time-hallowed words used by coroners, 'suicide while the balance of his mind was disturbed'.

Doody's case (6.10) firmly established in 1854 the criminality of attempted suicide. The cruelty of a law which added punishment to the burdens of profoundly unhappy people was often mitigated in practice by nominal sentences or by police forbearance to prosecute,[10] though sadly this was not always the case (6.11). The enactment of the Suicide Act 1961 (6.12) did something to humanise the law in accordance with the *mores* of a mid-twentieth-century society possessing sociological insights denied to its forbears.

6.1   Punishment of abortion

Charles Mercier *in* Crime and Criminals *(1918) provides a view of the medical-legal rules concerning abortion (cited in Glanville Williams,* op.cit., *pp.197-8).*

The procuring of abortion with the consent of the woman wrongs no one. It prevents the foetus from attaining complete development, but the life of the foetus is scarcely begun, and it is yet far from being conscious, and has not even an independent existence. It would strain the meaning of words intolerably to look upon the action as a wrong done to the foetus, nor can it be considered a wrong to the mother, who freely and eagerly consents to it. It does, indeed, endanger the life of the mother, but I know of no instance in which an act, otherwise innocent, is regarded as a crime because it endangers the life of the actor, or in which an operation, freely consented to by the subject for the benefit to be obtained by it, is considered on the same ground a crime. No. The only ground upon which the procuring of abortion can be held to be a crime is that it infringes the racial principle. It deprives the community of a potential citizen. As the potential citizen is farther from the stage of actuality than the infant, it should seem that the crime is of less gravity than infanticide; but it is in fact reprobated more severely and punished with greater severity,* and the reasons seem to be two: first, it

9. Finally abolished by the Forfeiture Act 1870, though by then forfeiture had fallen into desuetude.

10. In 1916 the Metropolitan Police introduced a policy towards these attempted suicides, who had relatives willing to care for them, of placing them in the care of such relatives without initiating prosecutions. The practice was adopted by other forces.

* That is to say, in practice. In 1918, when Mercier wrote, infanticide was in English law a kind of murder, as it still is if the jury are not satisfied of mental unbalance. Convictions for murder by way of neonaticide have always, however, been hard to obtain; and the capital sentence (in the days when it applied) was regularly commuted. [Footnote by Glanville Williams.]

attracts to itself none of the sympathy that is felt for the mother who kills her illegitimate child, and who is usually assumed to be an innocent, confiding creature who has been led away by the arts of the seducer; and second, that around the practice of abortion clings some of the odium that attaches to the arts of the pander. Both reasons seem destitute of foundation. The mother of an illegitimate child is as often as not the seducer rather than the seduced, and the women who apply to have abortion procured are in many cases married and chaste. I can discover no sound reason in ethics for the great severity with which the procuring of abortion is punished by law.

6.2　Abortion: the case of Dr Alex Bourne

R. v. Bourne *(1939). This is an extract from the celebrated direction to the jury of Mr Justice Macnaghten in a case where a distinguished surgeon, Alex Bourne, performed an abortion on a young girl who had become pregnant as a result of being raped by four soldiers. Wishing to see the law clarified, Bourne made sure that he was prosecuted. Macnaghten's summing-up was the guideline for those who favoured therapeutic abortion, but its authority remained somewhat uncertain. The Abortion Act 1967 has consigned it to the legal history books. (Bourne was acquitted.)*

The charge against Mr Bourne is made under s. 58 of the Offences Against the Person Act, 1861, that he unlawfully procured the miscarriage of the girl who was the first witness in the case. It is a very grave crime, and judging by the cases that come before the Court it is a crime by no means uncommon. This is the second case at the present session of this Court where a charge has been preferred of an offence against this section, and I only mention the other case to show you how different the case now before you is from the type of case which usually comes before a criminal court. In that other case a woman without any medical skill or medical qualifications did what is alleged against Mr Bourne here; she unlawfully used an instrument for the purpose of procuring the miscarriage of a pregnant girl; she did it for money; £2-5s. was her fee; a pound was paid on making the appointment, and she came from a distance to a place in London to perform the operation. She used her instrument, and, within an interval of time measured not by minutes but by seconds, the victim of her malpractice was dead on the floor. That is the class of case which usually comes before the Court.

The case here is very different. A man of the highest skill, openly, in one of our great hospitals, performs the operation. Whether it was legal or illegal you will have to determine, but he performs the operation as an act of charity, without fee or reward, and unquestionably believing that he was doing the right thing, and that he ought, in the performance of his duty as a member of a profession devoted to the alleviation of human suffering, to do it. That is the case you have to try today.

In this case, therefore, my direction to you in law is this – that the burden rests on the Crown to satisfy you beyond reasonable doubt that the defendant did not procure the miscarriage of the girl in good faith for the purpose only of preserving her life. If the Crown fails to satisfy you of that, the defendant is entitled by the law of this land to a verdict of acquittal. If, on the other hand, you are satisfied that what the defendant did was not done by him in good faith for the purpose only of preserving the life of the girl, it is your duty to find him guilty. It is said, and I think said rightly, that this is a case of great importance to the public and, more especially, to the medical profession; but you will observe that it has nothing to do with the ordinary case of procuring abortion to which I have already referred. In those cases the operation is performed by a person of no skill, with no medical qualifications, and there is no pretence that it is done for the preservation of the mother's life. Cases of that sort are in no way affected by the consideration of the question which is put before you today.

Here let me diverge for one moment to touch upon a matter that has been mentioned to you, the various views which are held with regard to this operation. Apparently there is a great difference of opinion even in the medical profession itself. Some there may be, for all I know, who hold the view that the fact that a woman desires the operation to be performed is a sufficient justification for it. Well, that is not the law: the desire of a woman to be relieved of her pregnancy is no justification at all for performing the operation. On the other hand there are people who, from what are said to be religious reasons, object to the operation being performed under any circumstances. That is not the law either. On the contrary, a person who holds such an opinion ought not to be an obstetrical surgeon, for if a case arose where the life of the woman could be saved by performing the operation and the doctor refused to perform it because of his religious opinions and the woman died, he would be in grave peril of being brought before this Court on a charge of manslaughter by negligence. He would have no better defence than a person who, again for some religious reason, refused to call in a doctor to attend his sick child, where a doctor could have been called in and the life of the child could have been saved. If the father, for a so-called religious reason, refused to call in a doctor, he also is answerable to the criminal law for the death of his child. I mention these two extreme views merely to show that the law lies between them. It permits the termination of pregnancy for the purpose of preserving the life of the mother.

These general considerations have to be applied to the particular facts of this case; the verdict of the jury must depend on the facts of the case proved before them. The girl in this case was under the age of fifteen, for she has attained that age within the last ten days. It is no doubt very undesirable that a young girl should be delivered of a child. Parliament has recently raised the age of marriage for a girl from twelve to sixteen, presumably on the view that a girl under the age of sixteen ought not to marry and have a child. The medical evidence given here confirms that view; the pelvic bones are not set until a girl is eighteen, and it is an observation that appeals to one's common sense that it must be injurious to a girl that she should go through the state of pregnancy and finally of labour when she is of tender years. Then, too, you must consider the evidence about the effect of rape, especially on a child, as this girl was. Here you have the evidence of Dr

Rees, a gentleman of eminence in the profession, that from his experience the mental effect produced by pregnancy brought about by the terrible rape which Dr Gorsky described to you, must be most prejudicial. You are the judges of the facts and it is for you to say what weight should be given to the testimony of the witnesses; but no doubt you will think it is only common sense that a girl who for nine months has to carry in her body the reminder of the dreadful scene and then go through the pangs of childbirth must suffer great mental anguish, unless indeed she be feeble-minded or belongs to the class described as 'the prostitute class', a Dolores 'marked cross from the womb and perverse'. You will remember that the defendant said that if he had found that this girl was feeble-minded or had what he called a 'prostitute mind' he would not have performed the operation, because in such a case the pregnancy would not have affected her mind. But in the case of a normal, decent girl brought up in a normal, decent way you may well think that Dr Rees was not overstating the effect of the continuance of the pregnancy when he said that it would be likely to make her a mental wreck, with all the disastrous consequences that would follow from that.

6.3   Reforming the law on abortion, 1966

Leo Abse and **Norman St.John Stevas** *speaking on David Steel's Abortion Bill;*
the Bill was read a second time by 223 votes to 29.

[Mr Leo Abse:] Hon. Members on this side of the House, and many on the other side, too, must believe that, ideally, a society should be such that every child, whether born fatherless, whether born handicapped, whether born in a palace or in a manger, should be received with warmth and be endowed with care. This is our starting point. Let no one suppose that a Bill of this kind can be a triumph for the community. There are societies which are impatient of doctrines which place the same ultimate worth on each personality. These societies are ready to rid themselves of all the weak, whom they regard as encumbrances. The Nazi society, the great life deniers, killed off the aged and the mentally backward. The primitive African tribes, which some of us may have known from our military experience during the war, still commit infanticide against a child lacking a limb, and not long ago the Chinese were leaving the new-born female child to die of exposure and succouring only the male child.

Respect for life is the cornerstone of our society today. Every failure that we make to plan so that every life can live out its full potentiality within its puny transient span is a defeat, just as every hanging of a murderer or traitor is a defeat for the community, and a sign that the community does not know how to gain loyalty and is admitting its failure to deal with its failures.

Other hon. Members have said that they wanted to declare their prejudices or philosophies, and I think that I should make mine. Speaking as a humanist concerned with life, not with after-life, I find myself with a deep sense of unease about the approach to a Bill of this kind. The lack of frankness in the Amendment [i.e., to reject the Bill] is not made any the more attractive by this sickly reference to the humanitarianism of its sponsors.

I prefer the more robust attitude which the Royal College has adopted on this question. It said quite bluntly that those without specialised knowledge, and this includes members of the medical profession, are influenced in taking what they regard as a humanitarian attitude to the induction of abortion by a failure to appreciate what is involved. The Royal College of Obstetricians do not regard abortion as a trivial operation free from risks, and they say that there are serious risks. It would be unfortunate if, as a result of this debate, when clearly a more permissive atmosphere is part of the ambience of this Parliament, it were thought that we were treating abortion lightly, that it was a case of something like taking out a tooth. It should be emphasised that it is a serious act, and figures show that the maternal mortality rate of legal abortions in Denmark is three times our own, including the legalised abortions that take place here.

[Mr Norman St.John Stevas:] The Bill is fundamentally flawed because it rests upon denial of the sacred character and value of human life. The principle was recently reaffirmed by the House when it voted for the abolition of the death penalty. This principle is not one dependent on the recondite speculations of scholastic theologians as to when the soul does or does not enter the body, because nobody can know that. It rests upon the moral principle, all but universally accepted, that human life has an intrinsic value in itself, and that innocent human life should never be taken.

The acceptance of this principle has had a profound effect on the character of our society, on it is based not only the concept of liberty, but those of equality and fraternity as well.

Of course, there is scope for argument about when the right to life begins, but it is of profound significance that modern microbiology has confirmed the assertions of theologians that human life is fully present from the moment of conception and there is no qualitative difference between the embryo and the born child. There is only a difference of development. The embryo has a life of its own and has the full potentiality of becoming a human being. Therefore, it cannot be treated as mere animal matter to be excised from the womb and thrown aside and discarded in a dustbin or incinerator.

6.4   Euthanasia in Utopia

Sir Thomas More *(1478-1535) became Wolsey's successor as Lord Chancellor in 1529 but resigned in 1532, having vexed the King by opposing any relaxation in the laws of heresy. He was beheaded for treason in 1535. His* Utopia *(1516) is a far-seeing commentary upon man's social condition: this extract deals with euthanasia.*

The sick (as I said) [the Utopians] see to with great affection, and let nothing at all pass, concerning either physic or good diet, whereby they may be restored again to their health. Them that be sick of incurable diseases they comfort with sitting by them, with talking with them, and, to be short, with all manner of helps that may be. But if the disease be not only incurable, but also full of continual pain and anguish, then the priests and the magistrates exhort the man, seeing he is not able to do any duty of life, and by overliving his own death is noisome and irksome to other, and grievous to himself; that he will determine with himself no longer to cherish that pestilent and painful disease: and seeing his life is to him but a torment, that he will not be unwilling to die, but rather take a good hope to him, and either despatch himself out of that painful life, as out of a prison or a rack of torment, or else suffer himself willingly to be rid out of it by other. And in so doing they tell him he shall do wisely, seeing by his death he shall lose no commodity, but end his pain. And because in that act he shall follow the counsel of the priests, that is to say, of the interpreters of God's will and pleasure, they show him that he shall do like a godly and virtuous man. They that be thus persuaded finish their lives willingly, either with hunger, or else die in their sleep without any feeling of death. But they cause none such to die against his will; nor they use no less diligence and attendance about him; believing this to be an honourable death. Else he that killeth himself before that the priest and the council have allowed the cause of his death, him, as unworthy both of the earth and of fire, they cast unburied into some stinking marsh.

6.5   *A professional view of mercy killing*

Lord Dawson of Penn, *the distinguished royal physician, is speaking here upon the Voluntary Euthanasia (Legalisation) Bill in 1936; the Bill was refused a second reading by 35 votes to 14.*

[Lord Dawson of Penn:] It was an accepted tradition of the medical profession that it was the duty of the medical man to continue the struggle for life right up to the end. With time that has changed. There has gradually crept into medical opinion, as there has crept into lay opinion, the feeling that one should make the act of dying more gentle and more peaceful even if it does involve curtailment of the length of life. That has become increasingly the custom. This may be taken as something accepted. If once you admit that you are going to curtail life by a single day, you are granting the principle that you must look at life from the point of view of its quality rather than its quantity under these special circumstances. We do not lay down edicts for these things. It is a gradual growth of thought and feeling that entwines itself into the texture of our thoughts, and it is fair to say that it is equally entwining itself into the texture of the thoughts of laymen. There is no disharmony in this matter, in the main, between the thoughts of the laity and the thoughts of the doctors.

When you pass from what I may call the act of dying, to lives which are burdened by incurable disease, and where the gap between that stage of illness and death becomes wider, it may be fully admitted that the difficulty is greater, yet I would give as my deliberate opinion that there is a quiet and cautious but irresistible move to look at life and suffering from the more humane attitude, and in face of a disease which is undoubtedly incurable, and when the patient is carrying a great load of suffering, our first thoughts should be the assuagement of pain even if it does involve the shortening of life. This steady and silent change of opinion, common to doctors and laity alike, is, I suggest, due firstly, to a growing regard for quality of life as distinct from mere quality; and, secondly, to the greater importance and attention attached generally to the soothing and suppression of suffering in general, both of body and mind. Take, for instance, the multiplication of means – anaesthetics in midwifery and dentistry, the inducement of sleep prior to anaesthesia – and as for drugs to assuage pain and bring sleep and forgetfulness to the troubled mind, their name is legion.

6.6 The doctor's dilemma

*Another distinguished doctor, **Lord Segal**, spoke three decades later, in 1969, on the same subject. He concluded that to legislate for euthanasia was both premature and unlikely to assist the individual doctor called upon to decide whether to respond to his patient's wish to die.*

[Lord Segal]: My Lords, anyone who is at all conscious of the fallibility of human judgment, especially in matters affecting life and death, must feel how difficult it is to vote in favour of this Bill. Especially in this House, where we are used to legislating largely on the basis of known facts, how difficult must it be for us to embark upon legislation into the realms of the unknown. Parliament has already passed an Act abolishing capital punishment, and here we are asked to pass a Bill legalising the capital sentence upon those who are ill or stricken or in pain.

The other curious feature of this debate is that there has been no insistent demand for euthanasia coming from doctors, although this Bill sets out ostensibly to protect their interests. The demand for euthanasia is almost entirely from the one side, on behalf on the patients. Of course doctors must, at some time or other in the course of their experience, have to decide whether or not they are in favour of mercy killing; but they are, so far as I am aware, content to continue to tend their patients under the existing sanctions.

I well remember, as a young assistant some forty years ago, having to decide on my first case of mercy killing. For three days a young mother had been going through her first labour and was desperately longing for her child. The baby's head was impacted in her pelvis and it was far too late to perform a caesarean operation. It was a choice between her life and that of the child. The chief obstetrician of a large London hospital was called, and he decided to sacrifice the child. When the operation was over, I was left in charge of a straightforward labour, to deliver what he had made sure would be a dead child. But after a mass of broken cranial and cerebral tissue emerged, the head was born, and to everyone's horror the macerated foetus began to cry. There were six or seven student nurses all round, and each and every one of us was equally horrified. The mother would soon come out of her anaesthetic and demand to see her baby. All I could do was to ask the labour ward sister to supervise the third stage and to undertake to bath the baby myself. I asked the nurse to keep on adding a few more extra jugfuls of warm water to the bath, and immersed the baby head first. I suppose they could have laid an accusation against me of wilful murder, or at least of infanticide, but luckily the nurses all understood and, after their initial dismay, they acquiesced in what was done. That was over forty years ago, and in the same circumstances I would do the same again today.

At the other end of the scale, I remember the case of an old man of 82 with a massive cerebral haemorrhage. He lay in a deep coma for two weeks, and consultants had agreed there was no hope of his recovery. I remember deliberating to myself whether or not to hasten the end, and finally decided to inject twice the lethal dose of a certain drug. It had no effect at all. Then I gave four times, then eight times the lethal dose, but still he went on persisting in a deep coma. I felt as if there was some higher force deciding his fate beyond the power of the drug, and decided there and then to allow him to die without further medical intervention.

So often the greatest of specialists are fallible in their judgments. Even Clause 8 of this Bill, which seeks to lay down an entitlement to drugs, can often be at variance with medical experience. I remember a patient in her early forties in the terminal stages of cancer – a brilliant artist, the beauty of whose features were masked by the lines of her suffering. She knew she was shortly to die, and needed twice-daily injections of a pain-killing drug. One morning, as she lay on her death-bed in her studio, she began to talk of her paintings on the walls, and to my surprise after a while she said, 'The pain seems much easier now; I do not think I shall need my injection after all'. So there is also a limit to the patient's entitlement to lethal drugs, which the doctor, if he is wise, will always administer with caution.

As one closely connected with the work of the National Society for Mentally Handicapped Children, I have heard of no insistent demand for euthanasia or mercy killing on the part of any of the parents, who often have to carry the heavy burden of caring for these children for the greater part of their lives. Sometimes, on the contrary, these parents speak of the depths of love and affection which they receive from the children in return. I have often been dubious about those lines of Robert Louis Stevenson:

> Glad did I live and gladly die,
> And I laid me down with a will.

He was dying of tuberculosis on an island in the Pacific, in his early forties. Had he been alive today his tuberculosis would certainly have been cured. He would have been able to complete his unfinished novel, *Weir of Hermiston*, perhaps the greatest of all his novels, and would have enriched the world's literature with many more great masterpieces.

So many patients say they welcome death, but next morning the sun comes shining in through the window; they feel that God is still in His Heaven; and there is once more the will to live. No doctor can shirk the duty of sitting at the patient's bedside as he faces death. At times the Angel of Death is hovering so close he can almost hear the beating of his wings. But every doctor, in his mission of mercy, will have to hearken to the patient's plea and then decide the issue for himself. Permissive legislation is not likely to lighten his burden. He must struggle with his own conscience, and will invariably prefer to continue under the existing sanctions.

6.7   Varieties of mercy killing

An assortment of recent instances of mercy killings follows, showing a variety of judicial response to situations of this kind.

The *Guardian*, 22 April 1966:
After hearing evidence at an inquest in Pontypool (Monmouthshire) yesterday on a man convicted last year of killing his 12-year-old son by sleeping tablets and gas poisoning, the Monmouthshire coroner, Mr Kenneth Treasure, said:

'I am quite certain in my own mind that the deceased was morally perfectly correct in taking the course he did take in connection with his incurable little son. Legally, of course, he was wrong.' Although the father was convicted and punished, the punishment was obviously because of the moral issues of a minimal nature.

'One often wonders if one would react in the same way if this dreadful calamity happened to one. All I can say is that if I found myself in circumstances like the deceased, I hope I would have the moral courage to do what he did.'

The coroner recorded a verdict that Mr G.(45), of Pontypool, took his own life at a time when he was mentally upset – 'suicide in a period of depression.' Mr Treasure said that death was due to carbon monoxide and aspirin poisoning.

Police Sergeant Douglas Moon said that he found eight photographs of Mr G.'s son on the table near the bed.

The *Guardian*, 17 February 1970:
A man who killed his wife after devotedly nursing her for 11 years was given a conditional discharge at Staffordshire Assizes, at Stafford yesterday.

Mr E. (53), of Dudley, had pleaded not guilty to murdering his wife M. aged 48, but guilty of manslaughter. His pleas were accepted by the court.

Mr Frank Blennerhassett, Q.C. prosecuting, said that Mr E., a greengrocer, had nursed his wife night and day while she slowly died from disseminated sclerosis. She went blind at Christmas and prayed for death so he placed a pillow over her face and killed her. 'The anguish and despair became more than both of them could bear,' he said.

Psychiatrists had agreed that at the time, E.'s responsibility was diminished because of a mental trauma.

Passing sentence, Mr Justice Cooke said:

'However much one may sympathise, a mercy killing is something which the law will not tolerate, does not allow and must punish. But I am entitled to take into account the fact that you were not fully responsible for your actions at the time.'

The *Guardian*, 3 March 1970:
A woman 'called upon to endure more than her ordinary share of unhappiness and misery' suffocated three of her children with a pillow.

This was stated at Hampshire Assizes, Winchester, yesterday. The woman is P.B. (26). She was put on probation for three years. Mr Justice Hinchcliffe told her: 'I am satisfied this is a case where warm sympathy and support will be the best for you, rather than any form of retribution or punishment.'

B., of Hampshire, admitted the manslaughter of the children on the grounds of diminished responsibility. She pleaded not guilty to murdering them and this plea was accepted.

Mr Lewis McCreery, Q.C., prosecuting, said that when she was 15 she became pregnant by a schoolboy of the same age. The child was adopted. When she was 19 she became pregnant again by the same young man and they got married. The marriage lasted for about four years and two more children were born.

While she was pregnant with the third child her husband left her for another woman. B. then met Mr J., a married man with two children, and lived with him.

In 1968 Mr J. left her to return to his wife, but he came back to B. and she became pregnant by him. J. started associating with another woman, a married woman, and B. took an overdose of sleeping tablets for which she was treated in hospital. Before their child was born J. left her again but returned at intervals.

Finally Mr J. told her he intended to marry the other woman. On November 3, B. telephoned Hampshire Ambulance Service and said: 'Come quickly. I have killed my children and have done something to myself.'

She had suffocated N., aged 6, S., aged 5, and D., nearly 3, and tried to take her own life by gassing herself. When this seemed too slow she had drunk fluid containing creosote.

The *Guardian*, 6 October 1971:
After a particularly difficult night with her spastic son, it was stated at Shropshire Assizes at Shrewsbury yesterday, a 57-year-old woman knelt and prayed at his bedside, and then shot him with a humane killer.

Mrs F., of Shropshire, denied murdering her son H., aged 31, on June 28, but admitted manslaughter and was put on probation for three years. The pleas, which Mr Kenneth Jones, Q.C., said were entered on the ground of diminished responsibility, were accepted.

After putting Mrs F. on probation, Mr Justice Ashworth gave a warning against people assuming that courts condoned mercy killings.

'Every court in the world,' he said, 'has sympathy with people who are driven to make an end to a tragic human being such as H. was, but the law does not allow it, and no court would be doing its duty if it just as a matter of course treats persons in the tragic position of Mrs F. by placing them on probation.

'We must leave it to courts at the right time and the right place to show mercy, but it must not be assumed.'

Mr Stephen Tumin, prosecuting, said Mrs F. was devoted to H. She was a woman of excellent character, of high reputation, and there was no slur or attack on her integrity or her courage.

He was exceptionally difficult on the last night, and at 5.30 a.m. she called her doctor saying she had shot H. Mrs F. told police later: 'I had reached the limit. I had to do it. I was afraid I would die before he did.'

L.J. Blom-Cooper and T.P. Morris, *A Calendar of Murder*, (London, 1964, p.63):
M. (47), a prison officer, was described as 'quite passionately devoted' to his daughter (12) who had been an imbecile since birth, could neither walk nor talk, and was subject to terrible epileptic seizures. M. was alleged to have killed her with an overdose of drugs at their home.

Defence pleaded diminished responsibility, and the senior Medical Officer of Durham Prison (where M. worked) said that accused was suffering from acute nervous depression. The prosecution offered no rebutting medical evidence and M. was found guilty of manslaughter under section 2, the jury adding a strong recommendation for mercy, Durham Assizes, 27.10.1958. M.'s sentence of 3 years' imprisonment was reduced on appeal to 12 months' imprisonment on the grounds that the judge had not given full weight to the jury's recommendation.

[Authors' note: The first prison officer in this century to be indicted for murder. His colleagues in the prison service rallied round him and collected a large sum of money to ensure his financial security after he came out of prison.]

ibid., p.150:
Mrs M. (28), a widow, who was in part-time employment, became very depressed and worried about her financial prospects and about the prospects for the children, so she turned on the gas tap in the room in which they were all sleeping. Mrs M. was found unconscious but survived.

Defence pleaded diminished responsibility on account of acute melancholia and Mrs M. was convicted of manslaughter under Section 2 at York Assizes, 12.2.1960. Sentencing her to 2 years' imprisonment, Mr Justice Salmon said: 'This is one of the most terribly sad cases which I have ever had to deal with.'

6.8   The crime of suicide

Hales v. **Petit** (*1562*). *This is part of an early judgment by the Court of Common Pleas on the nature of the offence of suicide.*

And afterwards this same term the Justices argued, viz. Weston, Anthony Brown, and the Lord Dyer. But I only heard the Lord Dyer, and therefore what I say concerning the other two, I deliver only upon credible report. And all the justices argued that the forfeiture of the goods and chattels real and personal shall have relation to the act done by Sir James Hales in his life-time, which was the cause of his death, viz. the throwing himself into the water. And upon this the Lord Dyer said, that five things are to be considered in this case. First, the quality of the offence of Sir James Hales; secondly, to whom the offence is committed; thirdly, what shall he forfeit;

fourthly, from what time the forfeiture shall commence; and fifthly, if the term here shall be taken from the wife. And as to the quality of the offence which Sir James has here committed, he said, it is in a degree of murder, and not of homicide or manslaughter, for homicide is the killing a man feloniously without malice prepense, but murder is the killing a man with malice prepense. And here the killing of himself was prepensed and resolved in his mind before the act was done. And also it agrees in another point with the ancient definition of murder, viz. that *murdrum est occulta hominum occisio, nullo praesente, nullo sciente*; so that always he who determines to kill himself, determines by the instigation of the devil to do it secretly, *nullo praesente, nullo sciente*, lest he should else be prevented from doing it. Wherefore the quality of the offence is murder.

As to the second point, it is an offence against nature, against God, and against the King. Against nature, because it is contrary to the rules of self-preservation, which is the principle of nature, for every thing living does by instinct of nature defend itself from destruction, and then to destroy one's self is contrary to nature, and a thing most horrible. Against God, in that it is a breach of His commandment, *thou shalt not kill*; and to kill himself, by which act he kills in presumption his own soul, is a greater offence than to kill another. Against the King in that hereby he has lost a subject, and (as Brown termed it) he being the head has lost one of his mystical members. Also he has offended the King, in giving such an example to his subjects, and it belongs to the King, who has the government of the people, to take care that no evil example be given them, and an evil example is an offence against him.

6.9   Blackstone's view of suicide

William Blackstone *(see 1.1)* Commentaries, *op.cit., Book IV, p.189.*

Self-murder, the pretended heroism, but real cowardice, of the Stoic philosophers, who destroyed themselves to avoid those ills which they had not the fortitude to endure, though the attempting it seems to be countenanced by the civil law, yet was punished by the Athenian law with cutting off the hand, which committed the desperate deed. And also the law of England wisely and religiously considers, that no man hath a power to destroy life, but by commission from God, the author of it: and, as the suicide is guilty of a double offence; one spiritual, in invading the prerogative of the Almighty, and rushing into his immediate presence uncalled for; the other temporal, against the king, who hath an interest in the preservation of all his subjects; the law has therefore ranked this among the highest crimes, making it a peculiar species of felony, a felony committed on one's self. And this admits of accessories before the fact, as well as other felonies; for if one persuades another to kill himself, and he does so, the adviser is guilty of murder. A *felo de se* therefore is he that deliberately puts an end to his own existence, or commits any unlawful malicious act, the consequence of which is his own death: as if attempting to kill another, he runs upon his antagonist's sword; or, shooting at another, the gun bursts and kills himself. The party must be of years of discretion, and in his senses, else it is no crime. But this excuse ought not to be restrained to that length, to which our coroner's juries are apt to carry it, *viz.* that the very act of suicide is an evidence of insanity; as if every man, who acts contrary to reason, had no reason at all: for the same argument would prove every other criminal *non compos*, as well as the self-murderer.

6.10   Imprisonment for attempted suicide

R. v. **Doody** (*1854*), *the direction to the jury on attempted suicide as a misdemeanour. Until the Suicide Act 1961,* felo de se *and attempted suicide remained crimes; since the Act, any aiding, abetting, counselling or procuring of another to commit suicide remains an offence; a survivor of a suicide pact may be guilty of manslaughter for the death of the other party to the pact (see 6.12).*

The prisoner was indicted for unlawfully attempting to commit suicide at Wolverhampton, on the 5th of March, 1854.

It appeared that the prisoner was at the George Inn, Wolverhampton, on the night of the 5th March, and about ten o'clock went to the water-closet. He was soon afterwards found there, suspended to a beam by a scarf tied round his neck. He was cut down and animation restored. On being taken into custody and charged with the offence, he stated that he had led a bad course of life and had no money or friends. He now said in his defence that he had been drinking for nine days before, and did not know what he was doing. There was some evidence to show that, although he was partially intoxicated, he was quite capable of taking care of himself.

Wightman, J., told the jury that the offence charged constituted, beyond all doubt, a misdemeanor at Common Law. The question for them to consider was whether the prisoner had a mind capable of contemplating the act charged, and whether he did, in fact intend to take away his life. The prisoner alleged in his defence that he was drunk at the time, which must be taken to mean that he had no deliberate intention to destroy his life; for the mere fact of drunkenness in this, as in other cases, is not of itself an excuse for the crime, but it is a material fact in order to arrive at the conclusion whether or no the prisoner really intended to destroy his life.

Verdict guilty. Sentence three months' imprisonment.

6.11   The rationale of imprisonment for attempted suicide

Glanville Williams *cites instances of severe prison sentences for attempted suicide.*

It would be interesting to know on what principle of selection a small minority (43 out of 5,220 [in 1955]) were selected for incarceration in prison. Can it be that there was no other principle than the idiosyncrasy of the judge or magistrate?

Three illustrations may be given of actual cases, of various dates, where a sentence of imprisonment was imposed.

In 1938 a woman attempted to commit suicide by swallowing spoons, and from that date until 1940, when she was prosecuted, she was in hospital.

The magistrates' court sentenced her to six months' imprisonment, but fortunately this sentence was reversed on appeal, the Recorder saying:

'When this woman left hospital she had rid herself of her mental instability and was recovered. I cannot imagine a more certain way of bringing about a return of her mental condition than sentencing her to prison for six months.'[11]

In 1950 the Rochester Bench sent a woman to Holloway for six months for a second attempt at suicide. Her mother had died in a mental home, and she herself had shown other symptoms of being unbalanced. In announcing the sentence the Chairman said: 'You have been here before and we gave you every opportunity to go straight.' No appeal was taken.[12]

In 1955 a man, after arrest on a charge of larceny, attempted to commit suicide in his cell (or, at least, gave the appearance of such an attempt, by cutting his neck with glass, though as he then proceeded to call the gaoler the seriousness of his intention was open to doubt). The Recorder sentenced him to two years' imprisonment for the larceny and two years for the attempted suicide, the two sentences to run consecutively. On appeal the sentence for attempted suicide was reduced to what was called the 'nominal' one of one month. The Lord Chief Justice expressly disagreed with the opinion expressed by the Recorder that 'self-murder is one of the most serious crimes on our calendar'.[13]

These illustrations show how the law of attempted suicide creates a standing danger of maladministration of justice, especially when individual judges and magistrates may base their decisions upon religious opinions that are no longer held by what may be called enlightened opinion. They disprove the theory, advanced by some apologists for the present law,[14] that people are never sent to prison for attempted suicide except in the fulness of Christian love.

6.12   *The Suicide Bill, 1961*

The following are extracts from the second reading speeches in the House of Lords by the Bishop of Carlisle (Dr Bloomer) and Lord Denning.

[The Lord Bishop of Carlisle:] The problem which this Bill seeks to solve is to frame a law which aims at doing three things: ministering compassion, protecting society and upholding the sanctity of human life. Those three objects need to be kept clearly in mind. In my judgment, the Bill secures the first object – that is, compassion – by taking suicide out of the criminal list, and I shall be very glad indeed to support that clause. It is right, and I believe that it should be so dealt with. In Clause 2, the Bill attempts to secure what I referred to as the second and third objects – the protection of society and the upholding of the sanctity of life. Clause 2 makes it a crime to

11. 5 *Howard Journal* 228 (1940).
12. *Chatham Observer*, September 16, 1949; January 20, 27, 1950.
13. *Regina* v. *French*, *The Times* (London), December 13, 1955.
14. Sir W. Norwood East: *Medical Aspects of Crime* (London, 1936), p.142; Cecil Binney: *Crime and Abnormality* (London, 1949), pp. 132-3.

encourage or assist or tempt anyone to take his own life. It is concerned with the protection of life in society.

Now while Clause 2 helps to protect society, I am not satisfied that it is sufficiently strong to uphold the sanctity of life, and it is on this point that I want to concentrate. I want to be assured that in this Bill there is something of law that secures and makes very clear to everyone the sanctity of human life. To abrogate the rule of law whereby suicide is a crime is right; but in doing so there must, in my judgment, be enough left in the law to convey to everyone that to take life, one's own life, is literally a dreadful thing, contrary to natural instinct and contrary to natural law. I am satisfied, as I say, that Clause 2 is strong enough to show how dreadful it is to assist in helping another to take his life – it does that; it prescribes the penalty – but I submit that it is not strong enough to show how dreadful and how contrary to nature it is to take one's own life.

In proceeding with this Bill, we have to think of how it will be interpreted, not by those who are experts in the law or by those whose minds are trained to think in very exact terms; we have to think of how a change in the law will be interpreted in the setting of society as it is, of society in general. It may be a surprise to many of your Lordships to hear me say this, but I believe it is true, that a large proportion of people regard what is lawful as permissible and therefore right, and what is unlawful as forbidden and therefore wrong. We may lament that they should make legal distinctions coincide with moral distinctions, but it is understandable that many people just take that as the normal way of looking at things. If I were persuaded that this Bill contained a strong enough witness to the sanctity of life, I would wholeheartedly support it, and I want to support it. At the moment I am not so persuaded. I hope it will not be regarded as an impertinence – it is not meant to be – if I say that I am not even satisfied with this report produced by a Committee of my own Church, because I feel that there is not strong enough witness borne in it to what I call the sacredness of every human life. I want the Bill amended to make it crystal clear that suicide, even when legally permissible, is still a dreadful offence against nature.

I know it is a difficult subject, and I have only an amateurish knowledge of natural law, but I cannot help but think that natural law would determine the taking of one's life as unlawful. I want this law carried out in such a way that the person who attempts suicide unsuccessfully is not punished for the attempt. I do not want punishment brought in at all; it is not appropriate. I want to see some notice taken of the unfortunate person who attempts suicide and fails, and that he or she is given medical treatment. If that provision were in the Bill, the law would be administering not punishment but compassion, through medical treatment. At the same time, it would be seen that the law took cognisance of an attempt to commit suicide, and thus would be a dissuasion against suicide which all can understand. As the Bill stands at present, it seems to me that, if enacted, this law would take no notice at all of an unsuccessful attempt at suicide unless such attempt had been prompted or assisted by another person.

[Lord Denning]: My Lords, if your Lordships approve this Bill, it will end a most interesting chapter of our English law, because for nearly a thousand years suicide has been regarded as the most heinous of felonies – the felony of self-murder. In consequence, attempted suicide was a crime, a suicide pact was murder, and helping another to commit suicide was also murder. I say 'for nearly a thousand years', because it was King Edgar, nearly one thousand years ago, who decreed that it was a crime for a man to take his own life, denied him burial rights and laid down that all his goods were to be forfeited.

The reason for that law was stated by Blackstone to be founded, as it was, on our religion. The law of England, he said, wisely and religiously decreed that no man had power to destroy life except by commission by God, the author of it. He said that it was twofold; that one was spiritual. He said that to commit suicide was invading the prerogative of the Almighty, by rushing into His presence uncalled for. The other was temporal, against the King, because the King had an interest in the preservation of all his subjects. Those being the reasons for the law, the punishment which we inflicted for hundreds of years was twofold. First, on the corpse was inflicted ignominious burial. The suicide was buried at a cross-roads with a stake through his body and a stone on his face. Indeed, that continued until 1824, and the last suicide who was buried at the cross-roads was at Grosvenor Place. Even after that, until 1882, a suicide had to be buried by night; and ever since 1882 up to this day, according to the law of the Church of England, a suicide is not entitled to Christian burial. You will remember the gravediggers' scene in *Hamlet* and how Shakespeare puts into the mouth of the gravedigger these words: 'Is she to be buried in Christian burial that wilfully seeks her own salvation?'

It never has been so. I expect that now that suicide is to be no longer a crime – and I am glad to say it – a suicide will be permitted by Ecclesiastical Law a Christian burial, maybe with an alternative form of service recommended. That would be a final end to the law of dishonour in the courts. That was one angle of the punishment.

The other angle was to forfeit the goods, lands or leases of a suicide to the King. The great case, on which Shakespeare founded the scene of Ophelia, was the case in which Sir James Hale threw himself into the river at Canterbury, and the question was whether his widow would be entitled to his lease of the Graveney Marshes on his death [see 6.8]. The Judges held that the widow was not entitled, and it went to the Crown. That forfeiture existed until 1870, when we abolished it. But there is one form of forfeiture which exists to this day and which I hope this Bill, when passed, will do away with – monies on insurance policies.

I should like to give your Lordships a concrete case in which I was concerned some 20 years ago, the case of a Major Rowlandson. He owed some £40,000 to his creditors but he had £80,000 on life assurance policies, which said that they were payable even if he died by his own hands, sane or insane, after the first year. They were due to expire at three o'clock on a summer afternoon and he had not got the money to renew the premiums. At quarter past two, he went to his solicitor in Chancery Lane and saw him, came out at quarter to three, hailed a taxicab and said to the driver: 'Drive me to my flat in Albemarle Street and as you pass St. James's Palace clock, look at the time and note it.' The taxi driver did so. It was three minutes to three. The cab was going up St James's Street when the driver heard a shot and got out of his cab. There was Major Rowlandson, dead, at one minute to three, just in time, you might think, for the insurance policy monies to be payable. But the insurance company refused to pay. I happened to be led in the case by Sir William Jowitt, who tried to persuade the jury that Major Rowlandson was of unsound mind, but the Judge directed the jury that he was doing the act of a gallant English gentleman, killing himself for the sake of his creditors. The jury found him of sound mind, and although we appealed on the law right up to this House, it was held in your Lordships' House, sitting judicially, that no man could take a benefit from a crime, and suicide was the most heinous crime known to the law. So the policy monies were not recoverable, and the premiums were not recoverable, because suicide is a crime by English law.

It is different in Scotland, next door, where it has never been a crime; it is different in South Africa, where it is not a crime. But in most other parts of the Commonwealth it still is a crime and still will be, by law, if this Bill passes. The consequence is that policies are not payable and insurance companies can repudiate their liabilities contracted to pay on death. One of the benefits of this Bill when it passes is that suicide will no longer be a crime and insurance companies will have to honour their liabilities on their policies; all forfeitures will be gone; all dishonouring of the corpse will be gone.

7

Obscenity

No branch of the law more directly or more nearly attempts to mirror and define the morality of society than the law controlling the written word and the pictorial publication. Throughout history men have been moved, largely by fear, to suppress books. Mostly, suppression has been induced by the fact that the literature has been politically objectionable or religiously heretical. With the growing freedom accorded to men to think and say what they like, books were banned only because they were 'obscene', although from time to time they offended more against the political than against the personal morality of society.

Gulliver's Travels has been banned in Ireland as being both obscene and detrimental to both government and morals; Hans Andersen's *Fairy Tales* were banned by Nicholas I of Russia, who also suppressed *Uncle Tom's Cabin* and *The Scarlet Letter*; Jack London's *The Call of the Wild* was banned as too radical in Italy and Yugoslavia in 1929. If it be objected that these were the aberrations of erstwhile undemocratic societies, there are recent examples of political censorship *via* the agency of the obscenity laws. Some people would acknowledge the contention of Richard Neville at the conclusion of the *Oz* trial (7.13) that the prosecution of the 'Schoolkids Issue' No.28 was political in the broadest sense of that term; and those who think that the publication was more than just a pandering to the baser instincts of its potential readership, could hardly fail to see in the conviction, in 1971, of the publisher of *The Little Red Schoolbook*, a naked attempt to stifle anarchic views propounded to schoolchildren – again by the device of the law proscribing obscenity.

Public tastes and standards change; with these changes, fashions in prosecution change. To trace the trends of criminal prosecutions against books is to throw light on the social and political history of a country and England is no exception. Until the Victorian era mere bawdiness was never suppressed: the mediaeval church set its face exclusively against heresy and Boccaccio, with his *Decameron* (in 1958 Swindon magistrates made Britain look silly by ordering copies of the book to be burned) Chaucer, and Rabelais were admired for their literary art, while their bawdiness went unscathed. It was only with the advent of Swiftian smut that obscenity fell foul of public opinion and ultimately the law.

During the fifteenth and sixteenth centuries the English monarchy controlled printing, and at the same time quietly assumed prerogative rights through the Star Chamber, which largely exercised powers to suppress seditious and heretical works. The abolition of the Star Chamber in 1640 left Parliament with the power of controlling the printing presses. The eighteenth century saw the period of fullest freedom for English literature.

Sporadic prosecutions for obscenity were rebuffed by the ordinary courts as being matters for the ecclesiastical Courts until, in 1727, in *R. v. Curl*,[1] the Common Law courts for the first time assumed jurisdiction. The book involved was pornographic, entitled *Venus in the Cloister, or The Nun in her Smock*. The court adopted the Attorney-General's argument that an obscene publication constituted an offence at common law as tending to corrupt the morals of the King's subjects. There the matter rested – inexplicably – for 150 years until the Hicklin judgment (7.1) of 1868, the *fons et origo* of the present law.

Eleven years earlier, the legislature had intervened with Lord Campbell's Obscene Publications Act. That Act was aimed at restricting the output of pornography by conferring powers on lay magistrates to order the destruction of offensive and offending literature. As Lord Brougham prophetically observed in attacking the legislation, it constituted an indirect threat to serious literature. The threat remained dormant for a decade or more, for censorship was effectively exercised by a prudish public opinion, to which the literary giants of the period meekly submitted.

Then the Act was invoked in the Hicklin case, which concerned the publication *The Confessional Unmasked*, designed to expose 'the iniquity of the confessional and the questions put to females in confession'. In his famous judgment, Chief Justice Cockburn laid down the test which has become both hallowed in the law and the bane of legal advisers: the test is 'whether the tendency of the matter charged as obscene is to deprave and corrupt those whose minds are open to such immoral influences and into whose hands a publication of this sort may fall'. These words were echoed by the same judge in 1877 at the trial of Annie Besant and Charles Bradlaugh (5.17) for publishing a book on birth control, *The Fruits of Philosophy* (advertisements on matters of family planning generally have not escaped the law's attention [7.2]).

The legal net was cast far and wide. The test of a tendency to deprave and corrupt, moreover, found expression in the Obscene Publications Act 1959 – it has not been productive of easy interpretation or consistent application by the courts.

The breadth of the law's proscription is fictionally exemplified in Sir Alan Herbert's *Uncommon Law*. He envisaged a public schoolmaster having to answer an application for a destruction order of the Greek and Latin classics. The presiding magistrate's remarks, if he deigned to give reasons for the destruction order, might be as follows: 'We have read with particular repugnance the record of the alleged god Zeus, whose habit it is to assume the shape of swans, bulls and other animals, and, thus disguised, to force his unwelcome attentions upon defenceless females of good character'. And on the item-by-item approach, which the Court of Appeal (in the *Oz* appeal) has said is the right approach to judging the obscenity of a magazine or book comprising a number of unconnected items, the whole of such a work would be legally damned.

The shifting sands of moral attitudes in various countries towards obscene publications is seen in the legal career of D.H. Lawrence's *Lady*

1. (1727) 2 Stra.788.

Chatterley's Lover, which was first published in Florence in 1928 with a first edition of 1000 copies sold to subscribers at two guineas a copy. Since then it has had sporadic brushes with the law. After initial harangues from unanimous, strident critics – 'most evil outpourings: sewers of French pornography: literary cesspool; book snapped up by degenerate booksellers and British decadents' – few copies of the unexpurgated version circulated until the last twenty years. Publishers, emboldened by the change in literary *mores*, began to chance their arms, some achieving their ambitions unscathed (Lawrence's own views can be found at 7.7).

In the United States a Federal Court declared the book free from the smirch of obscenity with which the Postmaster-General had labelled it. In 1930 the book had achieved extra-judicial prominence in the famed 'decency debates' in the Senate between Senator Bronson Cutting from New Mexico, who was in favour of modifying the censorship laws, and Senator Reed Smoot of Utah. Cutting enraged and taunted Smoot by witty insinuations that 'Lady Chatterley was a favourite with the Mormon senator'. American readers' freedom to indulge their sensual traits stemmed from the classic judgment of Judge Woolsey, upheld by the Federal Court of Appeal (7.5), when he released James Joyce's *Ulysses* to the public in 1933. The same approach characterised the American Judge, Van Pelt Bryan, in his judgment in the Lady Chatterley case. He held that the court's decision was not to depend on the book's effect upon 'the irresponsible, the immature or the sensually minded'. To be obscene it must offend 'the average man of normal sensual impulses' and 'exceed the limits of tolerance imposed by the current standards of the community'.

Expurgated copies of *Lady Chatterley's Lover* found their way on to the market and occasionally fell foul of the law. In 1953 the book was removed from the shelves of two bookshops in England. When a destruction order was sought, the magistrate declared the book 'absolute rubbish', and said that, had he read the unexpurgated version, he'd have chucked it on the fire.

Perhaps the quaintest handling by any judiciary came from the Japanese Supreme Court, in a country whose law has only recently become imbued with any part of the Judaeo-Christian legal ethic of the West. That court held that it was a work of art, but that it was nevertheless obscene because it inculcated in the mind of the reader a sense of shame. Such a sense could be envisaged in the embarrassment which ordinary people find in reciting obscenity 'within the family circle or at a public gathering'. When *Lady Chatterley* was prosecuted in England under the new legislation of 1959, it had a narrow escape, although we shall never know whether the jury found it not obscene, or having thought it was obscene excused it on the grounds that it was of such literary merit as to be for the public good and hence not outside the law. In the course of the trial of Penguin Books, publishers of a cheap paperback edition, the courts were bombarded by a bevy of experts, tallying twenty-four in all. Ten confidently said that the book was not obscene, eight declared positively it was obscene, and six were not certain whether it was or not. A galaxy of English-speaking literary critics and other experts had (as they were to do frequently in later cases) paraded in the witness-box at the Old Bailey. Subsequently, in the *Oz* case, the Court of Appeal clamped down on expert evidence, saying that experts may be called only on the defence of public good – that is, that the work is in the interest of science, literature, art or learning.

In the *Oz* case, the criticism by Judge Argyle amounted to an assertion that most of the defence witnesses could not qualify as experts, either as to obscenity or to the public good of the work being published. Legal historians may recall how disdainfully even literary critics were treated in pre-1959 days and even since then (7.9). In the prosecution of Radclyffe Hall's *The Well of Loneliness*, a book depicting Lesbianism, a leading critic of his day, Mr Desmond MacCarthy, was examined by Mr Norman (later Lord) Birkett. When he was asked the sixty-four dollar question of whether the book had literary merit, the magistrates correctly disallowed the question, declaring that 'a book may be a fine piece of literature and yet be obscene'. If morality were to find expression in legal decisions it was to be only from the tribunal (magistrate or jury) unaided by those versed in the literary arts.

The 1959 Obscene Publications Act was a riposte to a spate of prosecutions in the 1950s, involving five respectable publishers. The first (Werner Laurie, for publishing an innocuous novel *Julia*) pleaded guilty in order to save time and money. The second, Secker and Warburg, was resoundingly acquitted to the accompaniment of a memorable and inspired summing-up from Mr Justice Stable (7.6). The third, Hutchinson, was convicted over *September in Quinze*, which defamed a notorious ex-monarch living sybaritically on the Riviera. The fourth was acquitted after two juries disagreed (Heinemann: *The Image and the Search*) and the fifth (Arthur Barker: *The Man in Control*) was acquitted, seemingly because no one could understand what was supposed to be wrong with the book.

Against this background of unhappy and ill-chosen prosecutions, honest publishers sought refuge in protective legislation. Parliament gave it to them, by acknowledging that works of merit, even if obscene, should escape the law's clutches. But simultaneously, this Act declared its ceaseless vigil and fight against pornography, and the courts continued to be faced with impossible value-judgments (7.8). There the matter uneasily rests for the present,[2] although there are sporadic attempts to re-define obscenity or to limit severely the law's operation (7.10).

The moral sense of the public towards obscene publications is not easy to gauge. It can find its reflection only in the courts' interpretation of the law and in juries' verdicts on individual publications which come under forensic scrutiny. The latter provides an unreliable test, in that the individual prosecution may catch a passing mood or suffer a quirkish result. The former provides the more legally authoritative (but not necessarily more socially accepable) guide.

2. In the 1973/74 session, Parliament was called upon to discuss the Conservative Government's Cinematograph and Indecent Displays Bill, a measure designed to stamp out the offensive advertising and display of indecent material in public. Opponents of the Bill expressed deep concern about the potential breadth of the legislation, the lack of a legal definition of indecency, and the absence of any provision for a defence on grounds of literary merit or public interest. The Bill expired with the premature dissolution of Parliament in February 1974, and the new Home Secretary, Mr Roy Jenkins, announced his unwillingness to re-introduce the Bill.

7.1 *The legal test of obscenity: the Hicklin case*

R. v. **Hicklin** *(1868). In this extract Lord Chief Justice Cockburn lays down the classic test of obscenity. (The summons related to anti-Catholic tracts entitled 'The Confessional Unmasked'.)*

[Lord Cockburn:] ... I think the test of obscenity is this, whether the tendency of the matter charged as obscenity is to deprave and corrupt those whose minds are open to such immoral influences, and into whose hands a publication of this sort may fall. Now, with regard to this work, it is quite certain that it would suggest to the minds of the young of either sex, or even to persons of more advanced years, thoughts of a most impure and libidinous character. The very reason why this work is put forward to expose the practices of the Roman Catholic confessional is the tendency of questions, involving practices and propensities of a certain description, to do mischief to the minds of those to whom such questions are addressed, by suggesting thoughts and desires which otherwise would not have occurred to their minds. If that be the case as between the priest and the person confessing, it manifestly must equally be so when the whole is put into the shape of a series of paragraphs, one following upon another, each involving some impure practices, some of them of the most filthy and disgusting and unnatural description it is possible to imagine. I take it therefore, that, apart from the ulterior object which the publisher of this work had in view, the work itself is, in every sense of the term, an obscene publication, and that, consequently, as the law of England does not allow of any obscene publication, such publication is indictable ... It seems to me that the effect of this work is mischievous and against the law, and is not to be justified because the immediate object of the publication is not to deprave the public mind, but, it may be, to destroy and extirpate Roman Catholicism. I think the old sound and honest maxim, that you shall not do evil that good may come, is applicable in law as well as in morals; and here we have a certain and positive evil produced for the purpose of effecting an uncertain, remote, and very doubtful good.

7.2 *The case of the obscene sandwich board*

This letter was written by the Chief Constable of Birmingham to the Home Office, concerning police action to be taken against a man carrying sandwich boards advertising contraceptives.

10th January, 1908

Sir,
 I have the honour to direct your attention to a class of advertisement which appears in the newspapers, which is highly objectionable; but which the Indecent Advertisements Act[3] does not touch.

3. Indecent Advertisements Act 1889, 52 and 53 Vict. c.18. The Act restricts advertisements relating to venereal diseases and their treatment.

I ... enclose copy of [a report] from P.C. Abbots ... relative to a class of advertisement which has been exhibited in the streets here by sandwichmen.

I wish to direct your attention to the fact that the present law dealing with indecent advertisements is too narrow in its limits, and that it would be desirable in my opinion to obtain larger Parliamentary powers to put down indecent advertisements.

I think I have already written to you relative to the practice of persons, who sell 'French Letters' and other appliances, in watching newspapers and sending advertisements of check pessaries, soluble pessaries, and other means for preventing conception, and also of sending private letters, to young married women, when notification of the birth of a baby appears in the papers. I have had numerous letters concerning this from husbands of all classes in life, both from noblemen and labouring men complaining of this sort of literature being sent addressed to their wives.

[The enclosed report was as follows:]

Central November 19th, 1906.

Re Complaint by Chief Constable of man carrying Sandwich boards in Bull Street.
P.C.A.44. Joseph Abbots reports for the information of Sup. McManus D.C.C. that at 4.30 p.m. Monday Nov. the 19th 06, he was on duty in Corporation Street, near to Bull Street when the Chief Constable came to P.C. and called his attention to a man named George Edwards residing at the Model Lodging House, Summer Lane who was carrying Sandwich boards which were about 3 feet by 2 feet 3 inches in size in Bull Street, with the following advertisement printed thereon:-

> For the best and cheapest Medical Surgical and Rubber Appliances call or write Newton and Co 188 Summer Lane
> (on one side, and, on the other side:)
> For Urinary troubles Gravel Stones Etc try Urethene, a Uric Acid Solvent.
> Newton, Specialist, 188 Summer Lane.

The man Edwards stated that he had been carrying these boards about the City for the past three weeks and had not been spoken to by the Police before. P.C. advised the man to take the boards in for the time being which he did.

7.3   Obscenity and indecency judicially defined

M'Gowan v. **Langmuir** *(1931). In the following extract Lord Sands, judge of the Scottish Court of Session and procurator of the Church of Scotland, delivers a judgment drawing a distinction between obscenity and indecency,*

This case concerns the keeping for sale of indecent or obscene prints. I do not think that the two words 'indecent' and 'obscene' are synonymous. The one may shade into the other, but there is a difference of meaning. It is easier to illustrate than define, and I illustrate thus. For a male bather to enter the water nude in the presence of ladies would be indecent, but it would not necessarily be obscene. But if he directed the attention of a lady to a certain member of his body his conduct would certainly be obscene. The matter might perhaps be roughtly expressed thus in the ascending scale: Positive–Immodest; Comparative–Indecent; Superlative–Obscene. These, however, are not rigid categories. The same conduct which in certain circumstances may merit only the milder description may in other circumstances deserve a harder one. 'Indecent' is a milder term than 'obscene' and as it satisfies the purposes of this case if the prints in question are indecent, I shall apply that test.

In using the expression indecency in relation to this case, I am, of course, referring to decency and indecency in relation to sex, and to nudity, and to physiological functions; for the words 'decent' or 'indecent' are often used in relation to matters of conduct which have no such significance. 'Indecent' in the sense which I am considering, I take to mean contrary to decency in relation to exposure, gesture, or language in accordance with the standards which prevail in the country at the time. These standards have varied in different ages, and they vary today in different countries. If I recollect aright this observation is as old as Herodotus. There is nothing indecent in the human frame. Such a suggestion would be a libel upon nature. But the most venerable record in history recognises that, whilst nakedness is innocent, shame comes with the consciousness of nakedness – 'They were both naked the man and his wife and were not ashamed ... and the eyes of them both were opened and they knew that they were naked and they sewed fig leaves together, and made themselves aprons'. Except among some of the lowest savages the public exposure of certain parts of the human body to the gaze of members of the opposite sex has been regarded as indecent so far back as historical records extend. Even the wave-tossed and half-drowned Ulysses,

> With his strong hand broke from a goodly tree
> A leafy bough that he might hide his shame

before he ventured to approach fair Nausicaa and her maidens. The story of the sons of Noah shows that in certain circumstances this veto was not limited to exposure as between members of the opposite sex.

Under a convention however, which extends far back in the history of civilisation, an exception has been recognised to the general rule that, what it is deemed indecent publicly to expose, it is indecent to depict for public exhibition. That convention concerns works of art. There have been differences of opinion as to how far that convention should extend, but into that one need not enter. The concession, if such it be regarded, to art is hedged in certain ways. The nude must be impersonal. A picture of the nude which a householder might display in his drawing room as a work of art would, however perfect in that regard, be regarded as grossly indecent if the person depicted were his wife or daughter. This, as it appears to me, illustrates the relativity of indecency, and how impossible it may often be to pronounce upon it apart from circumstances. A picture of Mrs Brown, to which only the very strait-laced might take exception if displayed as a work of art in a remote city, might be grossly indecent if displayed in Brown's drawing room in Edinburgh.

7.4 The Supreme Court of the United States of America and the Ginzburg Case

Alistair Cooke, *distinguished Anglo-American commentator, writes in* The Guardian *(March 24 1966) on the U.S. Supreme Court's handling of the Ginzburg obscenity prosecution.*

The Supreme court of the United States has decided that there is such a thing as an obscene book. There was nothing slapdash about this shattering judgment. It only just squeaked through a loudly divided court, with Justices Warren, Brennan, Clark, White and Fortas carrying the day over the dissenting voices of Justices Harlan, Stewart, and, of course, Douglas and Black.

But it is an historic ruling, and while it has already saddened the civil libertarians who think and see no evil, it is expected to strike panic among the pornography pedlars who, since the court gates opened to admit the naïve Lady Chatterley, have ridden high, wide, and handsome on the subsequent flood of garbage.

Only a few years after four-letter words required dots between the first letter and the last, it was possible to publish almost anything in the United States, an excess of liberty that came to the ears of the most notorious pornographic printing press in France, which, finding the current puritanism of Paris too binding, emigrated to the land of the free and has been minting fortunes ever since.

The Court had before it three cases, and it had better be said at once, lest it be thought that Washington has gone square, that it began by restoring Fanny Hill to the waiting arms of the college boys, from which she was rudely snatched in Boston, and suppressed as an obscenity.

The Court decided by six to three that Massachusetts was in the wrong; that John Cleland's 'Memoirs of a Woman of Pleasure' failed to meet the modern test of obscenity which the Court defined in *Roth* v. *the United States* in 1957. This asked 'Whether to the average person, applying contemporary community standards, the dominant theme of the material taken as a whole, appeals to prurient interest.'

Until yesterday, the Court had applied this test to all the obscenity cases that came before it; not surprisingly, it set all of them free, since the definition is as full of escape hatches as a knitted sweater. Some books might only inflame the un-average person.

What is a 'contemporary' standard? In Las Vegas? In Concord, Massachusetts? How about a contemporary 'non-community' standard? And how, if most of the material is foul but not the 'dominant' theme? Who, anyway, wants to 'take the material as a whole'? The most nimble pornographers ave always, like the censor in 'Gentlemen Prefer Blondes,' snipped out the erotic parts and run them over and over.

Anyway, Fanny Hill is okay, according to Mr Justice Brennan, who delivered the verdict, because it is 'not utterly without redeeming social value.' Justice Tom Clark couldn't have agreed less. In his dissent, he digested every pornographic incident in the book and then declared that he could not 'stomach' it.

The second case upheld the conviction of one Edward Mishin, of Yonkers, N.Y., on a charge of publishing 'spankers' and 'bondage' books, the cognoscenti's terms for books devoted to sexual sadism and masochism.

Mr Mishkin's lawyers did their best for him by quoting the Roth test and saying that the books did not appeal to 'the prurient interest' of 'average people' but were designed to appeal only to perverts! Mr Justice Brennan had them there. He said, in that case, the books were designed to appeal to 'the prurient interest of perverts,' not presumably to their Boy Scout interludes.

The most important case, and the one that is expected to cause a large broom to whisk through the land in pursuit of slick-paper sex, bosomy paperbacks, theatre marquees, and sex advertising in general, was that of Ralph Ginzburg, a dedicated and today thoroughly disgusted student of erotica.

He had been fined £10,000 and sentenced to five years in gaol for sending, through the mails, his magazine 'Eros,' also a newsletter 'Liaison' and a short book, 'The Housewife's Handbook on Selective Promiscuity.' Mr Ginzburg's main aim was to 'keep sex an art and prevent it from becoming a science.'

The Court went beyond the present fashion of arguing whether or not a book has literary value. Even Mr Ginzburg's lawyers admitted that 'Eros' had none.

The Court moved on to new and hazardous ground by considering, and deploring, the style of the advertising and promotion, the circulars boosting the three publications (even the fact that the publishers had sought mailing privileges from the postmaster of Intercourse and Blue Ball, two towns in Pennsylvania) and finding that all this was 'permeated with the leer of the sensualist.'

In other words, the new, extended test of obscenity takes in the motives of the publisher and the character of his advertising.

Justice Brennan, for the majority, found that 'Eros' was 'created, represented, and sold solely as a claimed instrument of the sexual stimulation it would bring' and like the other two publications was out to 'render it available to exploitation by those who would make a business of pandering to the widespread weakness for titillation by pornography.'

It had, therefore, 'no claim to the shelter of the First Amendment,' the clause of the Bill of Rights which guarantees freedom of speech and expression.

Mr Ginzburg, to the amazement of the legal world, and his own, will go to serve his stiff sentence, leaving behind only the assurance that 'future generations of Americans will look back at today's decision with shame and remorse.' Meanwhile, get out the warrants, men; Times Square, the revived burlesque houses, and the newspaper advertising pages are waiting for you.

7.5   A defence of Ulysses

U.S. *v.* **Ulysses**, *(1934). James Joyce's brilliant novel* Ulysses *(first published in 1922 and banned in Britain until 1936) was seized by the immigration authorities of the United States in 1933. Judge Woolsey's celebrated decision declaring the book not obscene was upheld by the Federal Court of Appeal. Here follows part of the judgment from Judge Augustus Hand (concurred in by his famous cousin Judge Learned Hand) and part of a dissent by Judge Manton (who, five years later, was convicted of taking bribes for premature disclosure of his judgments).*

[Judge Hand:] James Joyce, the author of *Ulysses*, may be regarded as a pioneer among those writers who have adopted the 'stream of consciousness' method of presenting fiction, which has attracted considerable attention in academic and literary circles. In this field *Ulysses* is rated as a book of considerable power by persons whose opinions are entitled to weight. Indeed it has become a sort of contemporary classic, dealing with a new subject-matter. It attempts to depict the thoughts and lay bare the souls of a number of people, some of them intellectuals and some social outcasts and nothing more, with a literalism that leaves nothing unsaid. Certain of its passages are of beauty and undoubted distinction, while others are of a vulgarity that is extreme and the book as a whole has a realism characteristic of the present age. It is supposed to portray the thoughts of the principal characters during a period of about eighteen hours.

We may discount the laudation of *Ulysses* by some of its admirers and reject the view that it will permanently stand among the great works of literature, but it is fair to say that it is a sincere portrayal with skilful artistry of the 'streams of consciousness' of its characters. Though the depiction happily is not of the 'stream of consciousness' of all men and perhaps of only those of a morbid type, it seems to be sincere, truthful, relevant to the subject, and executed with real art. Joyce, in the words of *Paradise Lost*, had dealt with 'things unattempted yet in prose or rime' – with things that very likely might better have remained 'unattempted', but his book shows originality and is a work of symmetry and excellent craftsmanship of a sort. The question before us is whether such a book of artistic merit and scientific insight should be regarded as 'obscene' within section 305 (a) of the Tariff Act.

That numerous long passages in *Ulysses* contain matter that is obscene under any fair definition of the word cannot be gainsaid; yet they are relevant to the purpose of depicting the thoughts of the characters and are introduced to give meaning to the whole, rather than to promote lust or portray filth for its own sake. The net effect even of portions most open to attack, such as the closing monologue of the wife of Leopold Bloom, is pitiful and tragic, rather than lustful. The book depicts the souls of men and women that are by turns bewildered and keenly apprehensive, sordid and aspiring, ugly and beautiful, hateful and loving. In the end one feels, more than anything else, pity and sorrow for the confusion, misery, and degradation of humanity. Page after page of the book is, or seems to be, incomprehensible. But many passages show the trained hand of an artist, who can at one moment adapt to perfection the style of an ancient chronicler, and at another become a veritable personifaction of Thomas Carlyle. In numerous places there are found originality, beauty, and distinction. The book as a whole is not pornographic, and, while in not a few spots it is coarse, blasphemous, and obscene, it does not, in our opinion, tend to promote lust. The erotic passages are submerged in the book as a whole and have little resultant effect. If these are to make the book subject to confiscation, by the same test *Venus and Adonis, Hamlet, Romeo and Juliet,* and the story told in the Eighth Book of the *Odyssey* by the bard Demodocus of how Ares and Aphrodite were entrapped in a net spread by the outraged Hephaestus amid the laughter of the immortal gods, as well as many other classics, would have to be suppressed. Indeed, it may be questioned whether the obscene passages in *Romeo and Juliet* were as necessary to the development of the play as those in the monologue of Mrs Bloom are to the depiction of the latter's tortured soul.

It is unnecessary to add illustrations to show that, in the administration of statutes aimed at the suppression of immoral books, standard works of literature have not been barred merely because they contained *some* obscene passages, and that confiscation for such a reason would destroy much that is precious in order to benefit a few.

It is settled, at least so far as this court is concerned, that works of physiology, medicine, science, and sex instruction are not within the statute, though to some extent and among some persons they may tend to promote lustful thoughts. We think the same immunity should apply to literature as to science, where the presentation, when viewed objectively, is sincere, and the erotic matter is not introduced to promote lust and does not furnish the dominant note of the publication. The question in each case is whether a publication taken as a whole has a libidinous effect. The book before us has such portentous length, is written with such evident truthfulness in its depiction of certain types of humanity, and is so little erotic in its result, that it does not fall within the forbidden class.

The main difference between many standard works and *Ulysses* is its far nore abundant use of coarse and colloquial words and presentation of dirty scenes, rather than in any excess of prurient suggestion. We do not think that *Ulysses,* taken as a whole, tends to promote lust, and its criticised passages do this no more than scores of standard books that are constantly bought and sold. Indeed a book of physiology in the hands of adolescents may be more objectionable on this ground than almost anything else.

It is true that the motive of an author to promote good morals is not the test of whether a book is obscene, and it may also be true that the applicability of the statute does not depend on the persons to whom a publication is likely to be distributed. The importation of obscene books is prohibited generally, and no provision is made permitting such importation because of the character of those to whom they are sold. While any construction of the statute that will fit all cases is difficult, we believe that the proper test of whether a given book is obscene is itss dominant effect. In applying this test, relevancy of the objectionable parts of the theme, the established reputation

of the work in the estimation of approved critics, if the book is modern, and
the verdict of the past, if it is ancient, are persuasive pieces of evidence; for
works of art are not likely to sustain a high position with no better warrant
for their existence than their obscene content.

It may be that *Ulysses* will not last as a substantial contribution to
literature, and it is certainly easy to believe that, in spite of the opinion of
Joyce's laudators, the immortals will still reign, but the same thing may be
said of current works of art and music and of many other serious efforts of
the mind. Art certainly cannot advance under compulsion to traditional
forms, and nothing in such a field is more stifling to progress than limitation
of the right to experiment with a new technique. The foolish judgments of
Lord Eldon about one hundred years ago, proscribing the works of Byron
and Southey, and the finding by the jury under a charge by Lord Denman
that the publication of Shelley's 'Queen Mab' was an indictable offence, are
a warning to all who have to determine the limits of the field within which
authors may exercise themselves.

[Judge Manton:] Congress passed this statute against obscenity for the
protection of the great mass of our people; the unusual literator can, or
thinks he can, protect himself. The people do not exist for the sake of
literature, to give the author fame, the publisher wealth, and the book a
market. On the contrary, literature exists for the sake of the people, to
refresh the weary, to console the sad, to hearten the dull and downcast, to
increase man's interest in the world, his joy of living, and his sympathy in
all sorts and conditions of men. Art for art's sake is heartless and soon grows
artless; art for the public market is not art at all, but commerce; art for the
people's service is a noble, vital, and permanent element of human life.

The public is content with the standard of saleability; the prigs with the
standard of preciosity. The people need and deserve a moral standard; it
should be a point of honour with men of letters to maintain it. Masterpieces
have never been produced by men given to obscenity or lustful thoughts –
men who have no Master. Reverence for good work is the foundation of
literary character. A refusal to imitate obscenity or to load a book with it is
an author's professional chastity.

Good work in literature has its permanent mark; it is like all good work,
noble and lasting. It requires a human aim – to cheer, console, purify, or
ennoble the life of people. Without this aim, literature has never sent an
arrow close to the mark. It is by good work only that men of letters can
justify their right to a place in the world.

7.6 *The Philanderer Case*

R. *v.* **Secker and Warburg** *(1954). This is the summing-up by Mr Justice Stable
in the* Philanderer *obscenity case; the defendants were acquitted.*

The test of obscenity to be applied today is extracted from a decision of 1868
[*R v. Hicklin*, see 7.1]; it is this: '... whether the tendency of the matter
charged as obscenity is to deprave and corrupt those whose minds are open
to such immoral influences, and into whose hands a publication of this sort
may fall.' Because this test was laid down in 1868, that does not mean that

you have to consider whether this book is an obscene book by the standards of nearly a century ago. Your task is to decide whether you think that the tendency of the book is to deprave those whose minds today are open to such immoral influences and into whose hands the book may fall in this year, or last year when it was published in this country. Considering the curious change of approach from one age to another, it is not uninteresting to observe that in the course of the argument of the case in 1868 the rhetorical question was asked: 'What can be more obscene than many pictures publicly exhibited, as the Venus in the Dulwich Gallery?' There are some who think with reverence that man is fashioned in the image of God, and you know that babies are not born in this world, be they of either sex, dressed up in a frock-coat or an equivalent feminine garment.

We are not sitting here as judges of taste. We are not here to say whether we like a book of this kind. We are not here to say whether we think it would be a good thing if books like this were never written. You are here trying a criminal charge and in a criminal court you cannot find a verdict of 'Guilty' against the accused, unless, on the evidence that you have heard, you and each one of you are fully satisfied that the charge against the accused person has been proved.

Remember the charge is a charge that the tendency of the book is to corrupt and deprave. The charge is not that the tendency of the book is either to shock or to disgust. That is not a criminal offence. Then you say 'Well, corrupt or deprave whom?' and again the test: those whose minds are open to such immoral influences and into whose hands a publication of this sort may fall. What, exactly, does that mean? Are we to take our literary standards as being the level of something that is suitable for a fourteen-year-old schoolgirl? Or do we go even further back than that, and are we to be reduced to the sort of books that one reads as a child in the nursery? The answer to that is: Of course not. A mass of literature, great literature, from many angles is wholly unsuitable for reading by the adolescent, but that does not mean that the publisher is guilty of a criminal offence for making those works available to the general public.

You have heard a good deal about the putting of ideas into young heads. But is it really books that put ideas into young heads, or is it nature? When a child, be it a boy or a girl, passing from a state of blissful ignorance, reaches the most perilous part of life's journey which we call 'adolescence', and finds itself traversing an unknown country without a map, without a compass, and sometimes, I am afraid, from a bad home, without a guide, it is this natural change from childhood to maturity that puts ideas into its young head. It is the business of parents and teachers and the environment of society, so far as is possible, to see that those ideas are wisely and naturally directed to the ultimate fulfilment of a balanced individual life.

This is a book which obviously and admittedly is absorbed with sex, the relationship between the male and the female of the human species. I, personally, approach that great mystery with profound interest and at the same time a very deep sense of reverence. It is not our fault that but for the love of men and women and the act of sex, the human race would have ceased to exist thousands of years ago. It is not our fault that the moment in, shall we say, an over-civilized world – if 'civilized' is an appropriate word –

sex ceases to be one of the great motive forces in human life, the human race will cease to exist. It is the essential condition of the survival and development of the human race, for whatever ultimate purpose it has been brought into this world. Speaking, as I am sure I do, to a representative group of people, nine men and three women, each one of you I am sure is of good will and anxious that in the solution of this great mystery today we should achieve some conception which will lead to great personal happiness between individuals of the opposite sex in millions of homes throughout this island, which, after all, is the only possible foundation upon which one could build a vigorous, a strong and a useful nation.

Rome and Greece, it is not uninteresting to reflect, elevated human love to a cult, if not a religion, but when we reach the Middle Ages we find an entirely different approach. The priesthood was compelled to be sexless, and a particular qualitative holiness was attached to the monks and nuns who dedicated themselves to cloisters and sheltered lives. You may think that it is lucky that they were not all quite as holy as that because otherwise, if they had been, we should none of us have been here today.

When you approach this matter which – let us face it – throughout the ages has been one of absorbing interest to men and women, you get these two schools of thought which are poles apart, and in between those two extremes you have a wide variety of opinion. At one extreme you get the conception, I venture to think, of the mediaeval church, that sex is sin; that the whole thing is dirty; that it was a mistake from beginning to end (and, if it was, it was the great Creator of life who made the mistake and not you or I); that the less that is said about this wholly distasteful topic the better; let it be covered up and let us pretend that it does not exist. In referring to the arrival of a particular day, reference is made to 'the happy event on Monday' instead of saying 'a baby was born on Monday' – it means exactly the same thing – and in speech and behaviour the utmost degree of reticence is observed. I suppose the high tide was obtained in the Victorian era, possibly as a reaction against the coarseness of the Georges and the rather libertine attitude of the Regency, when I understand that in some houses legs of tables were actually draped and rather stricter females never referred as such to gentlemen's legs but called them their 'understandings'.

It is equally important that we should have an understanding of how life is lived and how the human mind is working in those parts of the world which, although not separated from us in point of time, are separated from us in point of space. At a time like today, when ideas and creeds and processes of thought seem, to some extent, to be in the melting pot, this is more than ever necessary, for people are bewildered and puzzled to know in what direction humanity is headed. If we are to understand how life, for example, is lived in the United States, France, Germany, or elsewhere, the contemporary novels of those nations may afford us some guide, and to those of us who have not the time or the opportunity or the money or the inclination to travel, it may even be the only guide. This is an American novel written by an American, published originally in New York and purporting to depict the lives of people living today in New York, to portray their speech and their attitude in general towards this particular aspect of life. If we are going to read novels about how things go on in New York, it would not be of much assistance, would it, if, contrary to the fact, we were led to suppose that in New York no unmarried woman of teenage had disabused her mind of the idea that babies are brought by storks or are sometimes found in cabbage plots or under gooseberry bushes?

You may think that this is a very crude work; but that it is not, perhaps, altogether an exaggerated picture of the approach that is being made in America towards the great problem of sex. You may think that if this does reflect the approach on the other side of the Atlantic towards this great question, it is just as well that we should know it and that we must not close our eyes or our minds to the truth because it might conceivably corrupt or deprave any somewhat puerile young mind.

You may agree that it is a good book, or a bad book, or a moderate book. It is at least a book. It is the creation of a human mind and it depicts the people created in their particular environment. If you look at the front page, you will see the text. It is taken from a Victorian poet, Browning: 'What of soul was left, I wonder, when the kissing had to stop?' and I suppose men and women of all ages have wondered that.

7.7 Lawrence hits back

D.H. Lawrence (*1885-1930*) *wrote this essay on 'Pornography and Obscenity' in 1929, a year after the publication of* Lady Chatterley's Lover. *The extract is taken from the Penguin anthology,* A Propos of Lady Chatterley's Lover and Other Essays (*Harmondsworth, 1961, pp. 60* ff).

Nobody knows what [the word obscene] means. Suppose it were derived from *obscena*; that which might not be represented on the stage; how much further are you? None! What is obscene to Tom is not obscene to Lucy or Joe, and really, the meaning of a word has to wait for majorities to decide it. If a play shocks ten people in an audience, and doesn't shock the remaining five hundred, then it is obscene to ten and innocuous to five hundred; hence the play is not obscene, by majority. But Hamlet shocked all the Cromwellian Puritans, and shocks nobody today, and some of Aristophanes shocks everybody today, and didn't galvanize the later Greeks at all, apparently. Man is a changeable beast, and words change their meanings with him, and things are not what they seemed and what's what becomes what isn't, and if we think we know where we are it's only because we are so rapidly being translated to the majority, everything to the mob, the mob, the mob. They know what is obscene and what isn't, they do. If the lower ten million doesn't know better than the upper ten men, then there's something wrong with mathematics. Take a vote on it! Show hands, and prove it by count! *Vox populi, vox Dei. Odi profanum vulgus! Profanum vulgus.*

So it comes down to this; if you are talking to the mob, the meaning of your words is the mob-meaning, decided by majority. As somebody wrote to me: the American law on obscenity is very plain, and America is going to enforce the law. Quite, my dear, quite, quite, quite! The mob knows all about obscenity. Mild little words that rhyme with spit or farce are the height of obscenity. Supposing a printer put 'h' in the place of 'p', by mistake, in that mere word spit? Then the great American public knows that this man has committed an obscenity, an indecency, that his act was lewd, and as a compositor he was pornographical. You can't tamper with the great public, British or American. *Vox populi, vox Dei*, don't you know. If you don't we'll let you know it. At the same time, this *vox Dei* shouts with praise over moving-pictures and books and newspaper accounts that seem, to a sinful nature like mine, completely disgusting and obscene. Like a real prude and Puritan, I have to look the other way. When obscenity becomes mawkish, which is its palatable form for the public, and when the *Vox populi, vox Dei* is hoarse with sentimental indecency, then I have to steer away, like a Pharisee, afraid of being contaminated. There is a certain kind of sticky universal pitch that I refuse to touch.

So again, it comes down to this: you accept the majority, the mob, and its decisions, or you don't. You bow down before the *Vox populi, vox Dei*, or you plug your ears not to hear its obscene howl. You perform your antics to please the vast public, *Deus ex machina*, or you refuse to perform for the public at all, unless now and then to pull its elephantine and ignominious leg.

When it comes to the meaning of anything, even the simplest word, then you must pause. Because there are two great categories of meaning, for ever separate. There is mob-meaning, and there is individual meaning.

Business is discovering the individual, dynamic meaning of words, and poetry is losing it. Poetry more and more and more tends to far-fetch its word-meanings, and this results once again in mob-meanings, which arouse only a mob reaction in the individual. For every man has a mob self and an individual self, in varying proportions. Some men are almost all mob-self, incapable of imaginative individual responses. The worst specimens of mob-self are usually to be found in the professions, lawyers, professors, clergymen, and so on. The business man, much maligned, has a tough outside mob-self, and a scared, floundering, yet still alive individual self. The public, which is feeble-minded like an idiot, will never be able to preserve its individual reactions from the tricks of the exploiter. The public is always exploited and always will be exploited. The methods of exploitation merely vary. Today the public is tickled into laying the golden egg. With imaginative words and individual meanings it is tricked into giving the great goose-cackle of mob-acquiescence. *Vox populi, vox Dei*. It has always been so, and will always be so. Why? Because the public has not enough wit to distinguish between mob-meanings and individual meanings. The mass is for ever vulgar, because it can't distinguish between its own original feelings and feelings which are diddled into existence by the exploiter. The public is always profane, because it is controlled from the outside, by the trickster, and never from the inside, by its own sincerity. The mob is always obscene, because it is always second-hand.

Which brings us back to our subject of pornography and obscenity. The reaction to any word may be, in any individual, either a mob-reaction or an individual reaction. It is up to the individual to ask himself: Is my reaction individual, or am I merely reacting from my mob-self?

When it comes to the so-called obscene words, I should say that hardly one person in a million escapes mob-reaction. The first reaction is almost sure to be mob-reaction, mob-indignation, condemnation. And the mob gets no further. But the real individual has second thoughts and says: am I really shocked? Do I *really* feel outraged and indignant? And the answer of any individual is bound to be: No, I am not shocked, not outraged, nor indignant. I know the word, and take it for what it is, and I am not going to be jockeyed into making a mountain out of a molehill, not for all the law in the world.

Now if the use of a few so-called obscene words will startle man or woman out of a mob-habit into an individual state, well and good. And word prudery is so universal a mob-habit that it is time we were startled out of it.

But still we have only tackled obscenity, and the problem of pornography goes even deeper. When a man is startled into his individual self, he still may not be able to know, inside himself, whether Rabelais is or is not pornographic: and over Aretino or even Boccaccio he may perhaps puzzle in vain, torn between different emotions.

One essay on pornography, I remember, comes to the conclusion that pornography in art is that which is calculated to arouse sexual desire, or sexual excitement. And stress is laid on the fact, whether the author or artist *intended* to arouse sexual feelings. It is the old vexed question of intention, become so dull today, when we know how strong and influential our unconscious intentions are. And why a man should be held guilty of his conscious intentions, and innocent of his unconscious intentions, I don't know, since every man is more made up of unconscious intentions than of conscious ones. I am what I am, not merely what I think I am.

However! We take it, I assume, that *pornography* is something base, something unpleasant. In short, we don't like it. And why don't we like it? Because it arouses sexual feelings?

I think not. No matter how hard we may pretend otherwise, most of us rather like a moderate rousing of our sex. It warms us, stimulates us like sunshine on a grey day. After a century or two of Puritanism, this is still true of most people. Only the mob-habit of condemning any form of sex is too strong to let us admit it naturally. And there are, of course, many people who are genuinely repelled by the simplest and most natural stirrings of sexual feeling. But these people are perverts who have fallen into hatred of their fellow men: thwarted, disappointed, unfulfilled people, of whom, alas, our civilization contains so many. And they nearly always enjoy some unsimple and unnatural form of sex excitement, secretly.

Even quite advanced art critics would try to make us believe that any picture or book which had 'sex appeal' was *ipso facto* a bad book or picture. This is just canting hypocrisy. Half the great poems, pictures, music, stories of the whole world are great by virtue of the beauty of their sex appeal. Titian or Renoir, the *Song of Solomon* or *Jane Eyre*; Mozart or *Annie Laurie*, the loveliness is all interwoven with sex appeal, sex stimulus, call it what you will. Even Michelangelo, who rather hated sex, can't help filling the Cornucopia with phallic acorns. Sex is a very powerful, beneficial, and necessary stimulus in human life, and we are all grateful when we feel its warm, natural flow through us, like a form of sunshine.

So we can dismiss the idea that sex appeal in art is pornography. It may be so to the grey Puritan, but the grey Puritan is a sick man, soul and body sick, so why should we bother about his hallucinations? Sex appeal, of course, varies enormously. There are endless different kinds, and endless degrees of each kind. Perhaps it may be argued that a mild degree of sex appeal is not pornographical, whereas a high degree is. But this is a fallacy. Boccaccio at his hottest seems to me less pornographical than *Pamela* or *Clarissa Harlowe* or even *Jane Eyre*, or a host of modern books or films which pass uncensored. At the same time Wagner's *Tristan and Isolde* seems to me very near to pornography, and so, even, do some quite popular Christian hymns.

7.8   *The* International Times *case*

'Diogenes' wrote about the International Times *prosecution in* New Society *29 January 1970; the case later went to the House of Lords as* Knuller *v.* D.P.P. *(1973) where the Law Lords spurned a golden opportunity to overrule their earlier decision in* Shaw *(see 1.9).*

The committal of the directors of the *International Times* for trial at the Old Bailey, on charges arising out of their alleged insertion in their magazine of advertisements through whose medium homosexuals made contact with one another, is an illustration of the maxim that small cases and large principles often go hand in hand.

The charges do not spring, as they so often do in the field of obscenity, from old statutes concerned with customs and excise or the Post Office, but from the common-law itself. The allegation is that the defendants by their actions conspired to corrupt public morals and to outrage public decency.

It will come as a surprise to many to learn that such a flexible and wide-ranging offence has survived the reforms of the 'permissive society.' In 1774, in the heyday of the common law, Lord Mansfield, the Chief Justice, proclaimed: 'Whatever is *contra bonos mores et decorum*, the principles of our law prohibit, and the King's Court, as the general censor and guardian of the public manner, is bound to restrain and punish.'

As the body of statutorily defined crimes grew, the pace of development of common law crimes diminished. But then in 1962, in *Shaw* v. *the Director of Public Prosecutions*, the House of Lords resurrected the ancient offence. In that case the defendant had published a magazine called *Ladies' Directory* which contained the names, addresses and other particulars of prostitutes, with the object of assisting them to ply their trade, and derive profit. Lord Simonds upholding the conviction intoned: 'In the sphere of the criminal law, I entertain no doubts that there remains in the courts of law a residual power to enforce the supreme and fundamental purpose of the law, to conserve not only the safety and order but also the moral welfare of the state, and that it is their duty to guard it against attacks which may be the more insidious because they are novel and unprepared for.'

It was indeed an *obiter dictum* of Lord Simonds that underlay the charge in the present case. 'Let is be supposed that at some future – perhaps early – date, homosexual practices were publicly advocated and encouraged by pamphlet and advertisement? Or must we wait until parliament finds time to deal with such conduct? I say that it is for Her Majesty's judges to play the part which Lord Mansfield pointed out to them.'

The danger in such reasoning is apparent. The courts do not, in reliance on it, so much anticipate as bypass parliament's decision. Since the Sexual Offences Act, 1967, it is no longer unlawful to indulge in homosexual acts in private. Public opinion expressed through its elected representatives has ruled on the matter. It is entirely wrong that a man's liberty should depend on the view of what twelve men take to be the public morality, but will in fact only be their own.

Further, and worse, the doctrine offends against the basic principle of legality: *nullum crimen sine lege*. The vague ambit of the offence threatens all; for who can know in advance whether he has transgressed or not? The ultimate effect is the same as that of retroactive legislation.

The issue then is not whether the defendants are guilty of the offence charged, but whether they or anyone should ever be charged with such an offence.

7.9　*The right to defend 'obscene' literature*

The Guardian, *August 30 1970: 'Academics' Defence of Filth Appeals J.P.'*

Uproar broke out in court at Brighton yesterday when a local bookseller was fined £230 and ordered to pay 180 guineas prosecution costs for selling obscene books.

The bookseller, William Huxford Butler (33), of Over Street, Brighton, had denied 10 summonses that he sold obscene books at the Unicorn Bookshop, Gloucester Road, Brighton, and opposed an application to forfeit the books.

Earlier the prosecution had withdrawn summons concerning one book with a four-letter word in its title. Mr Michael Worsley, prosecuting, accepted that this book was not in fact on sale at the shop.

The chairman of the magistrates, Mr Herbert Ripper, said: 'May I say how appalled my colleagues and I have been at the filth that has been produced at this court and the fact that responsible people, including members of the university faculty, have come here to defend it. It is something which is completely indefensible from our points of view. We hope these remarks will be conveyed to the university authorities.'

Shouts of 'rubbish' broke out in the court and a young man refused to sit down and protested: 'I will not accept the legality of this court.' He was ejected.

When the shouting stopped Mr Ripper added: 'That is all I have to say.' A man in the gallery replied: 'You said enough, man.'

The magistrates imposed fines of £25 each on eight of the summonses and £30 on a ninth summons over a book called 'Poems' by Giorno. Of this book the chairman said: 'This is the most filthy book I have had to read.'

Mr Leslie Joseph, defending said: 'There are many normal and decent people in this country who find it shocking and distasteful that this prosecution should take place.' He said that items, objected to in the nine summonses, were openly on sale in bookshops and were also in public libraries throughout the country.

Mr Joseph said that most of these magazines and books were intended for universities and scholars.

7.10   The Arts Council report

The following is an extract from the conclusions of the Report of the Working Party under the chairmanship of Mr John Montgomerie, set up by the Arts Council to review the laws of obscenity (1969). The report advocated repeal of the Obscene Publications Acts 1959 and 1964 for a trial period of five years. On 24 July 1969 in reply to a question by Mr Ben Whitaker M.P., the Labour Home Secretary, while acknowledging defects in the existing law, said he was unconvinced that repeal of the obscenity statues was the appropriate solution.

The foregoing analysis had led the Working Party firmly to the conclusion that the laws against obscenity, while constituting a danger to the innocent private individual, provide no serious benefit to the public. The basic problem of founding a law that can be accepted on so subjective a concept as obscenity appears to be insuperable. Any formula of definition must be doomed to beg the question, so there can be little hope of formulating alternative legislation with more than peripheral improvements.

The Working Party therefore recommends that the Obscene Publications Acts of 1959 and 1964 should be repealed and should not be replaced for a trial period of five years or even at the expiration of five years from that date unless Parliament should otherwise determine. The Theatres Act 1968 should be brought into line.

It also recommends that certain other relevant Acts should be amended or repealed. Many of these have been or could be used as a basis for indirect censorship and contain words such as 'indecent' and 'profane' which are no more capable of definition than 'obscene' but which may be used to circumvent any need to establish harmful consequences.

We recognise, however, that it is reasonable to protect individuals who may be affronted by offensive displays or behaviour in public places. There are various Acts dealing with this, for which we would substitute a single section so that there should be no overlapping.

We would not seek to interfere with the existing arrangements under which the British Board of Film Censors classifies films into various categories. Television is not in practice affected by the Obscenity Acts and we are content that the B.B.C. and I.T.A. should be left to conduct their programmes on their own responsibility, with such regard as they see fit to pay to ascertainable public opinion.

We would leave intact the Children and Young Persons (Harmful Publications) Act 1955.

7.11   Miller on censorship in the theatre

Jonathan Miller, *physician, playwright, humourist and critic wrote this article on theatre censorship for the* Guardian, *16 October 1967, before the liberalisation of the law by the Theatres Act 1968.*

There can be no serious argument about theatrical censorship. It's an awkward, silly thing and no one who thinks carefully about it could seriously want it to survive. But nevertheless it's very hard to imagine it vanishing altogether. Censorship is only partly administered by the officials who bear the title. It is the expression of the General Will and if people are outraged by the blasphemy, obscenity, or violence of a public spectacle they will use all the other machinery of the common law to see that the offence is wiped out.

But what is censorship anyway? It's not quite like the other prohibitions we lay upon ourselves for it only deals with representations of certain acts and not with the acts themselves. It forbids scenes as opposed to deeds. Often enough the deeds shown in a prohibited scene are not in themselves illegal. They become illicit, however, when acted out in front of an audience.

Censorship then is a taboo on certain sorts of public mimicry. It has something in common, therefore, with the ancient ban upon mimesis in general. Men have always been slightly uneasy about reproductions and replicas. Even language, which is only a replica of the world in a very complex and indirect way, is touched with the same sacred dread. Certain names of God must never be said aloud, and there are still people frightened to hear a mass spoken backwards.

In modern censorship, most of whose bans involve very sophisticated rationalisations, there are still remains of this fear of mimicry as a thing in itself. For example, it is still very difficult to mimic living Heads of State on the English stage. The pastiche may be quite innocent, but for the censor such imitations are *never* innocent. Statesmen and monarchs have to lie in their vaults for several generations befor anyone can safely revive them in living effigy.

This has changed in the past eight years. Peter Cook took a risk when he did Macmillan in 'Beyond the Fringe'. And he confined himself to some vocal mannerisms and a few vaguely characteristic gestures. Now, however, six years later, the telly satirists vanish behind such elaborate make-up that they actually become identified, or at least confused, with their subjects. Perhaps the censors have made a blunder by relaxing their rules here. Perhaps mimicry does have a certain destructive magic; though there is nothing occult about it. Imitation, like graphic caricature, undermines the power of its victim by showing up his essential nature. It suggests to an audience that the man they feared or admired is simple and predictable. Reduced to a few characteristic lines or gestures, he becomes as powerless and innocuous as a puppet.

The effect is very strong indeed and often goes beyond satire to generate a diffuse contempt for the victim simply for being so open to imitation. I sometimes think, therefore, that the free exercise of political mimicry has brought a dangerous note of generalised ridicule into the political scene. It suggests to a public, amused by such pastiches, that *all* politicians are imitable clowns and that democracy is a farce worked by goons. So there are grounds for regretting the original relaxation of the ban on political imitation. But they are not sufficient to merit a reverse.

Blasphemy – I do not really care about it one way or the other. It seems petty to censor it but antediluvian to care.

The main discussion about censorship, however, centres on sex, excretion and violently inflicted pain. It is all about the body and the primitive extremes of pain and pleasure. We are embarrassed to show these in public. And particularly to a public whose individual members are unknown to each other. The famous device of the club performance illustrates this last point nicely. It is nothing more than a legal wangle now, but it rests on a very substantial superstition – that people bound together by some formal affinity (and therefore theoretically, at least, known to each other) are somehow protected from the black magic of collectively experienced depravity.

This is one of the reasons why T.V. censorship is so much stricter when it comes to questions of sex and violence. Quite apart from the fact that telly creeps like a cat burglar into the sleeping household, there is the question of the vast, fragmented, mutual anonymity of the audience.

It is easy to see how this ban on carnal spectacle came into existence. One of the things that gives it away is the list of bodily functions, pains and pleasures the imitations of which are *not* banned on the stage. Gluttony never runs into any trouble. No one ever shuts down a pie-eating contest and the film censor never touched the disgusting scenes in 'Henry the Eighth' where Charles Laughton gobbled a chicken whole. Sloth is all right and so is anger. Even fear unto death is no problem; except for children, of course. The censor is only moved to act when it comes to the display and exercise of what we call the private parts.

Censorship here is nothing more than a legal corollary of public modesty. It is part and parcel of the whole delicate machinery of etiquette to whose changes its own development is tied. So long as we continue to lock ourselves in segregated lavatories, fasten our flies and sit with our knees together when travelling on buses, the abolition of formal censorship will change very little in the content of public performance.

In some ways the censor protects the performers and authors from public anger. His certificate deters independent prosecutions. And in recent years, the Lord Chamberlain, despite some absurd lapses of intelligence, has actually walked a few steps *ahead* of public modesty. Not far enough to outrage any audience into a protest against their moral guardian's laxity; and yet not so timidly in step that theatrical development stood still. I shall not be altogether delighted to see him go for I fear the grass-root movement which might fill his place.

I doubt if there will ever be a total relaxation of the informal censorship of sexual spectacle. As Desmond Morris has indicated, most of the devices of modesty and etiquette are ways of quenching, or at least controlling, the exceptional lust of the human ape. Our whole social structure is built on an elaborately cantilevered system of repressions and permissions. Man has been endowed with unprecedented sexual appetite. This has been developed in order to encourage certain advantageous patterns of breeding and child rearing. But radiant sexual energy has to be focused and screened, so that the community is not thrown into chaos. Out of this necessity come clothes and bedrooms, locked toilets, curtains and bathing machines. And sexual censorship. But man has moved a long way from his origins. The biological imperatives have possibly weakened.

Will man, in the future, be able to get along in society without the tissue of sexual restraints and manners of which censorship is only a small part? There are signs that we are changing a great deal in this respect. Faster than ever before. The whole pattern of pairing and marriage seems to be changing and it was for this that the edifice of modesty was once raised.

But modesty itself has been a fickle value. We have always given irregular and changeable emphasis to it, just as the customs of marriage and child rearing have changed and changed about. If censorship alters now, it is not in a mood of abstract permission, capriciously granting freedom to art, when everything else is strict. Censorship has changed because the whole *mood* and *aim* of society have altered too. I doubt if it is even useful to say that society as a whole has become permissive. The very idea of permission suggests that there is some final standard of decorum from which everything else is a more or less certified deviation.

The fact is, we have begun to alter some of our fundamental concepts on the nature of human appetite itself. The idea of permission makes it look as if we were irresponsibly letting condemned sins out on parole. It's a very penological view of human nature. I prefer to see it as a comprehensive change of mind which involves a new moral classification of our appetites and desires. Censorship simply follows the new categories.

One of the consequences of this new recognition we have given to sexual desire is that the satisfaction obtained from the experience of violence must also change its emphasis. Or that at least is the hope to be obtained from following the Freudian theory of the instincts and their repression. From this point of view sadism arises from the violence we do to our infantile energies and wishes. By being more intelligent (not simply permissive) in the way in which we train the young infant it is to be hoped that the pleasure got from pain and torment will diminish. Once that happens censorship of violent spectacle must become irrelevant.

But the millennium anticipated by such political Freudians as Norman O. Brown and Herbert Marcuse has not yet arrived. Violence and pain still provide an evil satisfaction which the remoralisation of sex has not yet exorcised. Here, perhaps, is the one place where censorship still has a rational use. There *do* seem to be grounds for believing that constant exposure to scenes of brutality and sadism coursens the mind of a mass audience and facilitates the acting out of their own violent lusts. But the case is not cut and dried. It is hard to know *which* scenes really do the damage. Artless brutality sickens all but the sick and these people are bent on mischief anyway.

The danger, if there is any, lies in performances which actually escape the censor's scrutiny. I am thinking here of films like 'Bonnie and Clyde' which *could* deprave, not through the blood and pain they show, but by the cool, attractive elegance with which violence is presented. By what the Earl of Shaftesbury condemned as 'this false relish which is governed rather by what immediately strikes the Sense than by what consequently and by reflection pleases the mind and satisfies the Thought and Reason.'

But even here I am doubtful about the use of censorship. The connection between an audience *sees* and what it *does* as a result, is obscure to say the least. And in principle I am unhappy about the use of the law as a prophylactic device. The law works upon deeds and not upon moods. Even if it *could* be shown that certain moods make criminal deeds more likely there is something reassuring about the act requirement of criminal law. Censoring scenes of violence has something in common with the preventive detention of psychopathic personalities whose dangerous state of mind has not yet actually resulted in a cime.

It's not exactly the same, of course. There is a great difference between the detention of a dangerous man and the banning of a dangerously suggestive movie. But there is a principle of jurisprudence which the two cases have in common.

Once this business of policing the *mood* of the public is admitted, other sorts of censorship and legal action are admitted too. It might be argued, for example, that films which advertise the pleasures of possessions and wealth produce a mood of dangerous acquisitiveness which could just tip the balance in people poised on the edge of theft or financial dishonesty. It is a reasonable psychological theory but it is also a dangerous precedent.

What is more, this approach to law inverts the priorities of constructive social actial. People who would increase the severity of censorship in the belief that it is 'immoral spectacle' which lies at the root of our current disorder, ignore the complex *institutional* basis of society's mood and behaviour. If we *are* more lawless, venal and depraved than before (which is by no means certain anyway) I doubt very much whether the quality of public spectacle has anything more than a marginal part to play. The great controversy about modern censorship is possibly more damaging than what is actually banned. There is more pressing business in hand.

7.12   Obscenity: where to draw the line

Dennis Barker *in the* Guardian *(13 March 1971) provides a journalist's view of a judge's pronouncements on obscenity and the permissive society.*

A judge yesterday spoke about 'a line of conduct below which behaviour is regarded as abnormal or perverse and abóve which it is regarded as normal'. [His Honour, Judge] King-Hamilton, was beginning his summing up at the Central Criminal Court in the case against the book 'The Mouth and Oral Sex'.

He told the jury that some people thought the pendulum had swung too far towards permissiveness and it was time it began to swing back. 'If you share that view, it would only be proper to take it into account if you are convinced that it coincides with the view of the public at large.'

It would not be right to do this, if the jury believed it to be a minority view. 'You must not shut your eyes to what is going on around you, if you believe that what is going on around you is widely accepted by the public at large.'

The jury might feel that the climate was not set by authors or playrights or film producers. 'They set the trend,' he said. 'The author may put four-letter words into his book, a play may have nude scenes, and a film may shown an act of sexual intercourse. The fact that many people, perhaps many people, buy such a book, or see such plays and go to such films, does not necessarily mean that the general standard is set by these people.'

The general standard, by which the jury had to judge, was set by the public as a whole. 'In a civilised society, such as we like to think ours is – although sometimes one begins to doubt it – there must be a line of conduct below which behaviour is regarded as abnormal or perverse and above which it is regarded as normal. There must be a line below which things are regarded as obscene and above which they are regarded as not being obscene. These two lines do not necessarily coincide. It is the public which fixes the position of these lines.'

Christopher Kypreos, of The Running Man Press, faces four charges of procuring to be sent through the post a packet containing an indecent circular promoting the book. He faces one charge of having for publication for gain obscene articles – copies of the book. He denies all the charges.

Remarks on Rome's decline and its relevance to present day 'decadence' in England, made earlier in the week by the judge, were attacked by Mr Jeremy Hutchinson, QC, defending, in his closing speech. The judge had asked a medical witness if he knew 'as an historical fact' that 'Rome fell because of many years of decadence and immorality.' Later he rephrased his question.

Mr Hutchinson asked: 'Was it permissive books that brought the Empire down, or was it something more important, something called Christianity? Was it an Empire we all want to preserve? People held in bondage without any rights, without any freedom?'

Mr Hutchinson said it was 'terribly easy' to think of the past as better than the present and that everything was going to the dogs. He referred to a quotation in the book, a passage quoted from Victorian times, and to which the prosecution took exception.

'In Victorian times, what was the position?' asked Mr Hutchinson. 'There were industrialists going to church, very proper and moral when in their factories children were working 14 to 16 hours a day at the age of 10. You have judges of the greatest possible rectitude who were in fact still hanging people for stealing and later were happily sentencing people to the cat o' nine tails and transportation. In Leicester Square – you talk now about prostitutes – there were hundreds of prostitutes outside the theatres when the gentlemen came out of their reputable and honorable clubs in the evening. Why were all those prostitutes there?'

'When it is said that now we are decadent therefore you, the jury should stand up and find this gentleman here guilty of publishing this book, not because of the book's obscenity but because it will be in some way a protest against the decadence of our society, I ask you first not to act on that basis, and secondly not to accept what is perhaps the inference as to whether this world we live in, in England, is in fact more decadent than it was a little while ago.'

7.13 Children's liberation

Part of **Richard Neville's** *speech to the jury in the Oz obsenity trial in July 1971, on the freedom of children. At the Old Bailey the defendants were convicted; but on appeal their convictions were, with the exception of one count, quashed.*

There are many groups today who are making demands for freedom. These demands of course frighten the established order and I think the charges against me result partly from such fear. This is not surprising. Many people were frightened by the call to abolish slavery and they put forward all sorts of arguments as to why such abolition would lead to the decline and fall of our civilisation.

Many people say similar things about the current demands for children's rights. Just as many people hotly opposed the idea of women ever having the vote.

During this case we shall hear more about the increasing agitation of children and the relevance and importance of their demands for all of us. If their demands strike you as impudence, remember that children do not even have the most basic freedoms. They do not have freedom of dress or appearance. They do not have freedom to participate significantly in deciding what they should learn. They do not have freedom of expression – this incident reported last week is typical. A schoolboy claimed in his school magazine that the meals were unhygienic. Instead of answering the allegations, the headmaster merely confiscated all the copies of the magazine and tore off the front page which contained the offending story. That example may seem rather trivial ... but how would you like to be treated like that? What if you published a letter in a local paper attacking the council and the mayor came along and ripped the offending pages out of every copy?

There was also the case of the young teacher in Stepney – evidently very popular – who had to borrow money in order to publish his pupils' poems. He then got sacked for his pains. Another boy, called Martin Woodhams, got sentenced to a caning when he expressed his frustrations and dreams in a school essay. Martin refused the cane and was punished by suspension.

Against this essay, the headmaster used the all-purpose excuse of every censor – that the essay was obscene.

One of the reasons we invited adolescents to edit a special issue of *Oz* was to combat this tendency for everyone to try and shut them up. We were interested in what they had to say. But we didn't want to be like the headmasters who censor everything they don't happen to agree with.

So we advertised in Issue 26 for any schoolchildren between the ages of 14 and 18 to come and edit *Oz*. We offered them freedom from editorial interference, and we kept our promise. As the prosecution witness, Vivian Berger, has shown, there was no coercion of any kind, and our assistance and advice was confined almost exclusively to technical matters. They would not be caned or sent to Coventry if we didn't like what they wrote or drew. *Oz* 28 is the result of this experiment. 'Schoolkids issue' it says on the cover – which means, of course, the issue *edited* by schoolchildren, not aimed at them.

The Prosecution's case assumes that the children wished only to implant lustful and perverted desires. But most of the articles have little to do with sex and are concerned to question authoritarian attitudes on many subjects. The article entitled Weekend Drop Out is a sensitive and coherent call to reform the school system. I draw your attention especially to the illustration under the heading 'School Atrocities', of a teacher molesting a boy, which seems to sum up all the suppressed violence and hypocrisy of institutions.

'Sadism in *Oz*' said the headlines two nights ago, after the prosecutor's speech. Is this sadistic? Is it not the behaviour it depicts which is sadistic? This illustration surely communicates disgust and abhorrence at such practices.

This magazine consists of 48 pages, including the front and back cover. Like most magazines, it is a mixture of the original and the derivative ... some bits boring, others fascinating, some bits solemn, others satirical ... corny in some places, crude in others ... all in all a gutsy and entertaining read for 20 pence. It contains varied attacks on accepted attitudes, which as far as I know is not yet against the law ... in fact it contains varied attacks on *Oz* Magazine itself, which I doubt can be the cause of this prosecution.

But remember, if you convict us at the end of this trial, you are in reality convicting schoolchildren. And if you convict schoolchildren, then you yourselves must accept some responsibility for their guilt.

7.14   *The Festival of Light*

Moral outrage against 'permissiveness' is nothing new (see 8.1 and 8.2). In the 1930s a body called the Public Morality Council actively campaigned against literary obscenity. More recently, in the early 1970s, something of a crusade against 'the permissive society' was promoted by a number of people, the most prominent of whom were Mary Whitehouse and Lord Longford. The campaign crystallised in a vociferous pressure group (Christian-based, but not exclusively religious in orientation) called the Festival of Light. The following news item give an impression of the character of their activities (Guardian, 18 April 1973).

A grand incitement to decency and the good life arrived in London yesterday. It came in the shape of Mrs Mary Whitehouse and a petition signed by 1,350,000 people demanding the reform of the Obscenity Laws and greater protection for children from the inroads of public indecency.

'We are fighting for freedom and against that tiny minority who are fouling the country,' said Mrs Whitehouse before the petition was handed in at 10 Downing Street. 'We do not look on our fight as being repressive.' On the contrary, she said, it was a struggle for freedom.

Judging from speeches by Mrs Whitehouse and the Rev. Eddie Stride of the Festival of Light at a conference yesterday the silent majority is marching now, hell-bent on freedom. They demand a freedom from television programmes which contain '*double entendres*'; from public display of indecent and salacious advertisements; and from obscene material posted through the letter box. Mrs Whitehouse said this was often opened by widows.

'We are tired with the infantile preoccupation with sex organs,' she added. The petition was out to reverse the kind of thinking which made such preoccupations possible and visible in some artistic form.

At least two speakers were at pains to point out that they were not puritans concerned to kill all joy in life – not even sexual joy, provided it was contained within a loving marriage.

'Sex is for loving not for having', said Mr Stride. That was the motto of the Festival.

The petition asks the Government to ensure:

(1)   That the present Obscenity Law be reformed in order to make it 'an effective instrument for the maintenance of public decency.'

(2)   That the Obscenity Law be amended to cover broadcasting.

(3)   That special legislation be introduced to safeguard school children from exposure to teaching material portraying behaviour which, when performed in public, would constitute an offence against public decency.

An accompanying letter to Mr Heath says that Vice Komissar Nielsen of the Danish State Police, who was present at the conference, had informed the organisers of the position that 'violent sex crimes have increased in Denmark since the abolition of the sex laws.'

They had risen from 2,461 to 2,702 in 1971. In 1965 there were 12 cases of rape and 28 cases of attempted rape while by 1971 these figures had risen to 32 and 64 respectively.

8

Religion

The prevalent *mores* of British society have their roots deeply embedded in the doctrines of Christianity. Increasing secularisation has to some extent been recognised by institutional reform and by changes in the law. There has, however, been a time lag and the metamorphosis is incomplete. Many of the subjects dealt with elsewhere in this book have strong religious overtones – one encounters a variety of religious views reflected in such matters as punishment and the law concerning sanctity of human life, while incest was exclusively an ecclesiastical offence until 1908. Sometimes, as with the law of abortion, the views of a church have had a direct influence upon legal development. The present chapter is concerned with areas of law which are most clearly ecclesiastical in character, in particular the laws covering blasphemy and Sunday observance.

Religious bodies have always been vigorous and effective pressure groups and, until free-thinking became respectable, their political opponents, as well as swimming against the tide of popular opinion, faced formidable legal sanctions imposed under laws of blasphemy and heresy. Contemporary movements, like the Festival of Light (7.14), directed against the permissive society have their eighteenth-century counterparts in, for example, a society founded at the turn of that century to enforce a royal petition against the plethora of immorality and vice that was said to exist at that time[1] (8.1 and 8.2). Religious groups have fought a series of rearguard actions against the secularisation of the law, and bishops of the Church of England in the nineteenth century were vocal and, for the most part, ultra-reactionary members of a reactionary House of Lords that voted down a succession of social reforms.[2] In the present anthology, pride of place has been accorded to groups (mainly secular) whose efforts have been directed at changing the law, rather than at maintaining it.

In Britain, the Church of England still retains its incongruous position as the established church conferring, *inter alia*, the right of bishops to twenty-six seats in the House of Lords. The monarch must be an Anglican, and is titular head of the Church. Until the passage of the Lord Chancellor (Tenure of Office and Discharge of Ecclesiastical Functions) Act, as recently as 1974, it was doubtful whether a Roman Catholic could become Lord Chancellor. Ordained clergy of the Church cannot sit in the Commons.[3]

1. See Sir Leon Radzinowicz, *A History of English Criminal Law*, London, 1956, Vol. 3, Chapter 6.

2. The illiberalism of the nineteenth-century House of Lords is documented, albeit in a rather tendentious fashion, in a Fabian Tract, *Lords and Commons*, by F. Hardie and R.S.W. Pollard (Tract 123, 1948).

3. See *Re McManaway* [1951] A.C. 161.

Yet Britain is not, and never has been, either ethnically or religiously homogeneous. Minority religious and racial groups have increasingly made their views felt and undermined the rationality of the case for maintaining an established church. Laws appropriate to an age which saw nonconformity as synonymous with heresy have required (but not always received) radical up-dating to accommodate the needs of a manifestly and self-consciously pluralist society. To what extent has this happened?

The fight for religious toleration has been both long and turbulent and there are various legislative landmarks strewn along the way – the Toleration Act 1689; the Catholic Emancipation Act 1829; the removal of constitutional discrimination against the Jews in 1846; and the Oaths Act 1888, passed after Charles Bradlaugh's spirited, and at times violent, fight against the bigotry that denied the electorate a right to be represented by its chosen M.P. simply because he was a professed atheist. The battles between church and secular courts were of a rather different nature. Certainly they had to do with toleration in the broadest sense, but they were more akin to the kinds of demarcation dispute which have occurred throughout the history of the courts. Jurisdiction was at one time an issue involving both power and hard cash, as well as reflecting more general pressures on the *status quo* brought about by changes in the structure of society and government.

Ecclesiastical courts still exist but their functions are limited to such matters as Church discipline. The last heretic to be burned by decree of an ecclesiastical tribunal was the unfortunate Legate (*sic*) who went to the stake in 1612. The growing ecclesiastical jurisdiction of secular courts began in 1618 when it was held that an analogy with sedition permitted blasphemous libel to be prosecuted outside the ecclesiastical courts for protection of State security. In 1676, in Taylor's case (8.7) it was held that Christianity was part of English law, a decision which had long-term repercussions and which survived (though more than somewhat battered) until the mid-nineteenth century.

The judgment of Lord Chief Justice Coleridge in *R.* v. *Ramsey and Foote*[4] divorced the civil law from its uneasy union with the doctrines of a church which no longer exercised a monopoly of spiritual power in British society. And in 1917 in *Bowman* v. *The Secular Society* (8.10) the House of Lords, considering the civil issue of the validity of a charitable trust, underlined the division by holding that the objects of a company were not criminal because of its denial of the validity of Christianity.

Bowman's case is the last recorded instance of the higher courts reviewing the crime of blasphemy and in that case it was stressed that the crime was still extant, even though dormant. Three years earlier, in 1914, the Attorney-General Sir John Simon had been asked by the Home Secretary for his opinion upon the state of the law. He arrived at the conclusion that the crime of blasphemy survived but that its repeal was neither practicable nor necessary (8.9).

Perhaps this is one branch of law which may still be sprung upon a hapless and unsuspecting defendant. There has, Professor Street says, 'been

4. (1883) 15 Cox C.C. 231.

only one subsequent prosecution for blasphemy of the slightest importance'. In *R*. v. *Gott*[5] the Court of Criminal Appeal held, in effect, that causing offence to someone of strong religious feeling was not to be the true test of what constitutes blasphemy – 'the real issue was whether they might provoke a breach of the peace by anyone sympathetic to Christian ideals even though not a practising Christian'.[6] The weapon can be unsheathed even today (8.12) though the sympathy of the courts for such prosecutions could hardly be taken for granted. The State's interest in retaining the crime of blasphemy lies in the realm of public order where it has far more potent weapons at its disposal, such as the Public Order Act and, more recently, the Race Relations Acts. In a pluralist society, with a plurality of faiths and a strong vein of agnosticism and atheism, the Church of England has much to lose in trying to reassert its earlier pre-eminence by trying to breathe new life into relics of canon law.

Perhaps the most obvious reminder of religious values imposed in a legal context is the law relating to Sunday observance. The notorious 'British Sunday' with its amorphous mixture of laws on the opening of shops and on the enjoyment of public entertainment and sports has been the subject of a fascinating and successful political battle to defend the seeming indefensible against apparently hopeless odds.[7] A battle led by the Lord's Day Observance Society (8.5) formed as long ago as 1831, and backed by a small but vocal group of peers and M.P.s, has kept a mass of seventeenth-century legislation on the statute books. Notwithstanding the worthy and sensible (if rather dull) Crathorne Report on various aspects of the law on Sunday observance published in 1964 (8.6) a determined minority has managed to defeat a succession of Sunday Entertainment Bills brought by backbenchers. No major political party has been willing to espouse a cause which has traditionally lain outside the sphere of party-political commitment, though the Labour Government in 1969-70 did offer timetabling facilities to assist the passage of a Bill on this subject. The Bill failed despite Government help, and it is paradoxical that the Sunday Theatre Act 1972, permitting theatrical performance on Sundays, was enacted under a Conservative administration. However, it did so by default since the usually vigilant opponents of reform were outflanked in the Commons where the Bill was allowed through all its stages without debate. The President of the Lord's Day Observance Society remarked that this was the 'blackest day in the history of the British Sunday'.[8]

It seems likely that the British Sunday will retain at least some of its distinctive character for a considerable time to come, though entry into the European Common Market may eventually have some impact upon it. The argument retains a flavour of outmoded religious fundamentalism into which politicians are fearful of straying, although there are more persuasive social arguments against reform, for example, the need to promote the cause of leisure, and the problems arising from extending the noise and bustle of

---

5. (1921) 17 Cr. App.R.87.
6. H. Street, *Freedom, The Individual and the Law*, 3rd ed., 1972, p.188.
7. See P.G. Richards, *Parliament and Conscience*, London, 1971, Chapter 8.
8. See Gavin Drewry, 'Sabbath Laws', *New Law Journal*, 122, pp. 501-2.

Saturday sport to Sundays. The advocates of reform have never shown the same determination as their opponents, and the latter have found it comparatively easy to exploit private members' procedures which, in the absence of Government support, are geared only to the enactment of wholly uncontroversial measures. Anomalies abound – only in 1951 did Parliament abolish the notorious common informer procedure which provided rich pickings for predatory individuals who were willing to sue their fellow citizens for statutory penalties, mostly for breaches of Sunday observance laws. And the anomalies have provoked ingenious attempts to circumvent the law: in 1972 for example, a furniture shop, forbidden to ply its trade on a Sunday resorted to 'giving away' suites of furniture with highly priced carrots, since vegetables can be sold on the sabbath.[9] This action was baulked by the courts, but there can be no doubt that much of the law in this field is in a mess.

There are no easy answers. In a pluralistic society undergoing continuing change there are pressures for law reform which can be met only by treading upon the susceptibilities of people, once in a majority, who still feel strongly about their beliefs. Perhaps the basic problem stems, as in so many areas discussed in this book, from the tendency to leave old laws to serve new purposes, with governments and politicians being too timid to give a firm lead in the direction of change.

8.1   *The Proclamation Society*

In 1787 **William Wilberforce** *(see 1.2) conceived the idea of prompting the setting up of voluntary associations for the promotion of public virtue. As an initial step he induced the Privy Council to issue the 'Proclamation for the Encouragement of Piety and Virtue', the text of which is set out below. The document following it is the prospectus of the Society for Giving Effect to His Majesty's Proclamation, established in the autumn of 1787 with the Duke of Montague as its first president and with a formidable array of patrons. The Society gave way in 1801 to a new 'Society for the Suppression of Vice and the Encouragement of Religion and Virtue, throughout the United Kingdom, to consist of Members of the Established Church', which also enjoyed wide support. Other bodies, smaller, but similar in their objectives, grew up at the same time both in London and in the provinces. (See Sir Leon Radzinowicz,* A History of the English Criminal Law, *vol. 3, pp. 141* ff.*)*

A PROCLAMATION for the encouragement of PIETY and VIRTUE; and for preventing and punishing of VICE, PROFANENESS, and IMMORALITY, issued by George the Third (June 1, 1787).

WHEREAS we cannot but observe, with inexpressible concern, the rapid progress of impiety and licentiousness, and that deluge of profaneness, immorality, and every kind of vice, which, to the scandal of our holy religion, and to the evil example of our loving subjects, hath broken in upon this nation: we therefore, esteeming it our indispensable duty to exert the

9.   *Waller* v. *Hardy* (1972) 70 L.G.R.331.

authority committed to us for the suppression of these spreading evils, fearing lest that they should provoke God's wrath and indignation against us, and humbly acknowledging that we cannot expect the blessing and goodness of Almighty God (by whom Kings reign, and on which we entirely rely) to make our reign happy and prosperous to ourself and our people, without a religious observance of God's holy laws; to the intent that religion, piety, and good manners, may (according to our most hearty desire) flourish and increase under our administration and government, have thought fit, by the advice of our privy council, to issue this our royal proclamation, and do hereby declare our royal purpose and resolution to discountenance and punish all manner of vice, profaneness, and immorality, in all persons of whatsoever degree or quality, within this our realm, and particularly in such as are employed near our royal person; and that, for the encouragement of religion and morality, we will, upon all occasions, distinguish persons of piety and virtue, by marks of our royal favour: and we do expect and require, that all persons of honour, or in place of authority, will give good example by their own piety and virtue, and to their utmost contribute to the discountenancing persons of dissolute and debauched lives, and they, being reduced by that means to shame and contempt for their loose and evil actions and behaviour, may be thereby also enforced the sooner to reform their ill habits and practices, and that the visible displeasure of good men towards them may (as far as it is possible) supply what the laws (probably) cannot altogether prevent: and we do hereby strictly enjoin and prohibit all our loving subjects, of what degree or quality soever, from playing, on the Lord's day, at dice, cards, or any other game whatsoever, either in publick or private houses, or other place or places whatsoever: and we do hereby require and command them, and every of them, decently and reverently to attend the worship of God on the Lord's day, on pain of our highest displeasure, and of being proceeded against with the utmost rigour that may be by law. And, for the more effectual reforming all such persons, who, by reason of their dissolute lives and conversation, are a scandal to our kingdom, our further pleasure is, and we do hereby strictly charge and command all our judges, mayors, sheriffs, justices of the peace, and all other our officers and ministers, both ecclesiastical and civil, and all other our subjects, to be very vigilant and strict in the discovery, and the effectual prosecution and punishment of all persons who shall be guilty of excessive drinking, blasphemy, profane swearing and cursing, lewdness, profanation of the Lord's day, or other dissolute, immoral, or disorderly practices; and that they take care also effectually to suppress all publick gaming houses, and other loose and disorderly houses, and all unlicensed public shews, interludes, and places of entertainment, using the utmost caution in licensing the same: also to suppress all loose and licentious prints, books, and publications, dispersing poison to the minds of the young and unwary, and to punish the publishers and venders thereof; and to put in execution the statute made in the twenty-ninth year of the reign of the late King Charles the Second, intitled, 'An Act for the better Observation of the Lord's Day, commonly called Sunday;' and also an act of parliament made in the ninth year of the reign of the late King William the Third, intitled, 'An Act for the more effectual suppressing of Blasphemy and Profaneness;' and also an act passed in the twenty-first year of our reign, intitled, 'An Act for preventing certain Abuses and Profanations on the Lord's Day, called Sunday;' and all other laws now in force for the punishing and suppressing any of the vices aforesaid; and also to suppress and prevent all gaming whatsoever, in publick or private houses, on the Lord's day; and likewise that they take effectual care to prevent all persons keeping taverns, chocolate houses, coffee houses, or other publick houses whatsoever, from selling wine, chocolate, coffee, ale, beer, or other liquors, or receiving or permitting guests to be or remain in such their houses in the time of divine service on the Lord's day, as they will answer it to Almighty God, and upon pain of our highest displeasure. And, for the more effectual proceeding herein, we do hereby direct and command all our judges of assize, and justices of the peace, to give strict charge at their respective assizes and sessions, for the due prosecution and punishment of all persons that shall presume to offend in any of the crimes aforesaid; and also of all persons that, contrary to their duty, shall be remiss or negligent in putting the said laws in execution; and that they do, at their respective assizes and quarter sessions of the peace, cause this our royal proclamation to be publickly read in open court immediately before the charge is given. And we do hereby further charge and command every minister in his respective parish church or chapel to read, or cause to be read, this our proclamation at least four times in every year, immediately after divine service, and to incite and stir up their respective auditors to the practice of piety and virtue, and the avoiding all immorality and profaneness. And, to the end that all vice and debauchery may be prevented, and religion and virtue practised by all officers, private soldiers, mariners, and others who are employed in our service by sea and land, we do hereby strictly charge and command all our commanders and officers whatsoever, that they do take care to avoid all profaneness, debauchery, and other immoralities, and that by their own good and virtuous lives and conversation they do set good examples to such as are under their care and authority; and likewise take care of and inspect the behaviour of all such as are under them, and punish all those who shall be guilty of any of the offences aforesaid, as they will be answerable for the ill consequences of their neglect herein.

Given at our court at St. James's, the first day of June, one thousand seven hundred and eighty-seven, in the twenty-seventh year of our reign.

God save the King.

8.2 *Prospectus of the society for enforcing the King's proclamation against vice and immorality (1787)*

We, the undersigned, truly sensible of His Majesty's tender and watchful concern for the happiness of his people, manifested in his late royal Proclamation, and being convinced of the necessity, in the present juncture, of our attending to His Majesty's call on all his faithful subjects to check the rapid progress of impiety and licentiousness, to promote a spirit of decency and good order, and enforce a stricter execution of the laws against vice and immorality, do agree to form ourselves into a Society, for the purpose of carrying His Majesty's gracious recommendation into effect.

2. With this view we will be ourselves, and will countenance and encourage others in being, vigilant in the effectual prosecution and punishment of such criminal and disorderly practices as are within reach of the law.

3. We will endeavour to afford the Magistracy such assistance in the discharge of their duty as the nature of the case may require.

*DUKE OF MONTAGU, PRESIDENT.

Duke of Buccleugh	Archbishop of York
Marlborough	Bishop of Hereford
Northumberland	Chichester
Grafton	St. Asaph
Chandos	*Salisbury
*Marquis of Buckingham	Peterborough
Lord Ailesbury	Ely
Hopetoun	Rochester
Dartmouth	Chester
Guilford	Oxford
North	Lincoln
Radnor	Bangor
Effingham	Lichfield
Brudenell	Gloucester
Harcourt	Norwich
*Muncaster	Llandaff
*Sir Lloyd Kenyon	St. David's
*William Dolben	Bristol
Henry Hoghton	*Mr Morton Pitt
James Long	*Samuel Thornton
*Charles Middleton	*Wilberforce
*Mr Mainwaring	*Edwards Freeman
*Brook Watson	Richard Milnes
Archbishop of Canterbury	*Rev. Dr. Glasse

8.3 Blackstone on profanation of the Lord's day

Profanation of the lord's day, vulgarly (but improperly) called *Sabbath-breaking*, is [an] offence against God and religion, punished by the municipal law of England. For, besides the notorious indecency and scandal, of permitting any secular business to be publicly transacted on that day, in a country professing christianity, and the corruption of morals which usually follows it's profanation, the keeping one day in seven holy, as a time of relaxation and refreshment as well as for public worship, is of admirable service to a state, considered merely as a civil institution. It

* The names to which asterisks are annexed are those of members of the Committee.

humanizes by the help of conversation and society the manners of the lower classes; which would otherwise degenerate into a sordid ferocity and savage selfishness of spirit: it enables the industrious workman to pursue his occupation in the ensuing week with health and chearfulness: it imprints on the minds of the people that sense of their duty to God, so necessary to make them good citizens; but which yet would be worn out and defaced by an unremitted continuance of labour, without any stated times of recalling them to the worship of their maker. And therefore the laws of king Athelstan forbad all merchandizing on the lord's day, under very severe penalties. And by the statute 27 Hen. VI. c. 5. no fair or market shall be held on the principal festivals, good friday, or any sunday (except the four sundays in harvest) on pain of forfeiting the goods exposed to sale. And, since by the statute 1 Car. I. c. 1. no person shall assemble, out of their own parishes, for any sport whatsoever upon this day; nor, in their parishes, shall use any bull or bear baiting, interludes, plays, or other *unlawful* exercises, or pastimes; on pain that every offender shall pay 3*s*. 4*d*. to the poor. This statute does not prohibit, but rather impliedly allows, any innocent recreation or amusement, within their respective parishes, even on the lord's day, after divine service is over. But by statute 29 Car. II. c. 7. no person is allowed to *work* on the lord's day, or use any boat or barge, or expose any goods to sale; except meat in public houses, milk at certain hours, and works of necessity or charity, on forfeiture of 5*s*. Nor shall any drover, carrier, or the like, travel upon that day, under pain of twenty shillings.

8.4   Mill attacks the Sabbatarians

John Stuart Mill, *in a letter to the secretary of the Sunday League, November 1856, denounced the League's aims.*

November 1856

Sir, – I beg to acknowledge your letter of the 3rd instant asking my objections to the address of the National Sunday League.

The passage to which I principally object, and which has hitherto made it impossible for me, consistently with my own convictions, to subscribe to the League, is the following: 'They themselves would be the first to oppose the opening of any frivolous and vicious places of amusement.'

That the committee should limit their own endeavours to the opening of institutions of a more or less scientific or literary character on Sundays may, possibly, be judicious; but it is not necessary for this purpose that they should join in stigmatising the broader principle, the recognition of which I think should be their ultimate aim. With regard to 'vicious places of amusement', if there be any such, I would not desire that they should be open on any day of the week. Any place unfit to be open on Sunday is unfit to be open at all. But with regard to 'frivolous' amusements I no more think myself justified in limiting the people to intellectual than to religious occupations on that day; and the committee cannot but feel that if their disclaimer does them any service with those whom it is intended to conciliate, it will be by being understood as a protest against permitting, for example, music, dancing, and the theatre, all of which I should wish to be as free on the seventh (or rather the first) as on any other day of the week.

I am also unable to give my adhesion to various expressions in the Declaration which partake of the nature of a compliance with cant; such as the 'desecration of the Sunday, and the preservation of its original purpose of a day of devotion.' The devotion which is not felt equally at all times does not deserve the name; and it is one thing to regard the observance of a holiday from ordinary work on one day in the week as a highly beneficial institution, and another to ascribe any sacredness to the day, a notion so forcibly repudiated in the quotations from great religious authorities on your fourth page, and which I hold to be as mere a superstition as any of the analogous prejudices which existed in times antecedent to Christianity.

8.5   The Lord's Day Observance Society

'Lord's Day Observance Act 1780' was part of a tract issued by the Lord's Day Observance Society in the 1920s. The L.D.O.S. was founded in 1831 and flourishes to this day as a pressure group opposed to the secularisation of the Christian sabbath. It has successfully opposed a number of Private Members' Bills on such matters as Sunday entertainments.

The Lord's Day Observance Act, 1780, is a statutory bulwark of our priceless heritage, the British Sunday. I ask those who think lightly of this heritage: Where would Britain have been without the hallowed and hallowing influences of the matchless British Sunday? Britain's Prime Minister, the Rt. Hon. Mr. J. Ramsay Macdonald, M.P., has paid a great tribute to the influences of the Christian Sunday on our Nation's life. Here are his words:

> The British Sunday is a great heritage, which has strengthened the National Character and sustained the life of the people. To reduce it to the Continental Pattern is to destroy an invaluable National Asset.

Why are the enemy clamouring to wipe the Lord's Day Observance Act, 1780, off the Statute Book? Because of the financial advantages which, they admit, would accrue to them. The Agitation, stripped of all its plausibleness, is the most sordid agitation which has ever been engineered for breaking down Britain's quiet, reverent Sundays. Let no one be under any illusion on that point. Sunday Opening would mean, it is estimated, £10,250,000 (ten million two hundred and fifty thousand pounds) extra revenue per annum for the Theatre and Cinema and Prize Fight Saloon Owners. Sunday Opening, on the other hand, would also mean that tens of thousands of Cinema and Theatre Employees would lose their Sunday Rest – Christian Churches would be hindered in their mission – God's hallowed Day would be Trampled Down on 52 Sunday afternoons and on 52 Sunday evenings every year. 4,000 Cinema Halls and 597 Theatres up and down the country are involved.

The Forces of Mammon are advancing! The Enemy is at the Gates! Shall any of us who are members of Christian Churches betray the Lord's Day by opening the gates to let the Sunday Destroyers in?

Christian men and women, it is evident, must prepare themselves for an intense fight to save the Lord's Day in our land. Let none of us hearken to the voices of compromise. The issues are too vital for compromise. *No secular Film can possibly take the place of Divine Worship. No Stage Play or Vaudeville Show or Prize Fight can possibly be right on the LORD'S Day.* If we believe in National Righteousness let us nail our colours to the mast, and stand for the Christian Sunday as the God-given Day of Rest and Worship. Do not, when pressed by apologists for Sunday Amusements, agree to any amendments which would whittle away the purpose of the Act – the safeguarding of the Nation's Day of Rest.

Let us, in short, resist any tampering with the Lord's Day Observance Act, 1780: the Act of Parliament which, in the last resort, is Britain's Protection against the Continental Sunday.

8.6   *The Crathorne Report*

This is part of the Report of the Crathorne Committee on the Law on Sunday Observance.

36. The current Sunday observance laws are still largely based on principles laid down in the 17th and 18th centuries, namely, that church attendance and religious conformity should be encouraged by prohibiting secular activities and restricting employment that might attract people away from their religious observance; also that entertainments and amusements profaned the Lord's Day and should be prohibited.

37. The laws no longer secure the purpose of encouraging church attendance and any attempt to do so by legislation would now be considered contrary to the freedom of the individual. The churches themselves no longer claim such a privilege in law; in their evidence to us we noted such remarks as 'the laws of the country are designed for the well-being of a pluralist society', 'Church attendance cannot be compelled by legislation' and 'Christians will not attempt to force others into Christian observance on Sunday or otherwise'.

38. Neither do the laws now 'prevent abuses and profanations' on Sunday because the entertainments and amusements to which the prohibition applies are not considered profane or improper in themselves (except by a small minority of the public). Most of our witnesses, including the representatives of the churches, who were opposed to Sunday entertainments on other grounds, agreed that there was no objection to these forms of entertainment in themselves, and that there was no theological or ethical reason why they should be prohibited. The modern view appears to be that if an entertainment is improper on Sunday it is just as undesirable on weekdays.

39. We came to the conclusion, therefore, that the statutes of the 17th and 18th centuries are no longer needed to secure their original purposes. The modifications to these statutes introduced in the 1930s ... were made to meet pressing needs of the 20th century but no modern principles or policies in relation to Sunday observance were formulated. When the Gowers Committee reviewed the Sunday trading law in 1947 they said that one of their difficulties was –

that the policy underlying Sunday closing depends in part on spiritual questions that evoke deep feeling and admit of no authoritative expression of opinion except after weighing a body of evidence that has not been necessary for the rest of our task.

Clearly our first object was to seek from our witnesses their views on whether there should be any Sunday observance legislation and, if so, on what principles it should be based.

40. The British Council of Churches and the Roman Catholic Body in England and Wales both considered that the traditional character of Sunday should be preserved for the Christian community and for the wellbeing of national and family life. They submitted that Sunday should provide an opportunity first, for corporate worship and, second, for rest and recreation and for family pursuits. They stressed that corporate worship on the first day of the week was fundamental to Christian doctrine and practice and that no other day would be an acceptable substitute. While Christians claim no privileged position, they hoped that any revision of the law would make it easier rather than more difficult for them to observe Sunday according to Christian practice.

41. The Council said that, even if employment did not interfere with worship, Sunday should not just be another working day. The Christian pattern of spending the day in relaxation and family pursuits had a special value to national and family life quite apart from its religious basis and they said that this view was supported in the wider community outside the churches. It might be true that regular churchgoers constituted only 12 per cent. to 15 per cent. of the population, but the Council thought that at least half the remainder were in sympathy and maintained some connection with the church. The Roman Catholic Body expressed similar views; their church required its members to 'rest from servile work' in order to devote themselves to the worship of God. Nowadays 'servile work' was commonly understood as the unnecessary pursuit on Sundays of a person's weekday work. Neither the Council nor the Roman Catholic Body condemned entertainments and recreations in themselves on Sunday provided that they did not interfere with worship and relaxation or make unreasonable demands on the labour of others. They stressed that, as both parents were often working during the week, Sunday provided a unique opportunity for family pursuits and for strengthening family ties. They considered that these objects could be achieved only by statutory restrictions on those activities that caused a disproportionate amount of employment or disturbance on Sunday.

42. The Council of Churches for Wales agreed in principle with the evidence submitted by the British Council of Churches but they felt that the character and tradition of Wales should receive special consideration. They claimed that, in Welsh-speaking Wales, nearly 70 per cent. were actively connected with a Christian community that upheld the sanctity of Sunday. They said that the strength of the views of Welsh-speaking people had been shown in the poll taken under the Licensing Act 1961 when eight counties had voted against the opening of licensed premises on Sundays. The witnesses could not define 'Welsh-speaking Wales' in terms of districts or as

a percentage of the population of Wales. They thought that the law should be modernised and that its object should be to promote the Christian observance of Sunday. If the existing restrictions were relaxed for England, they were not in favour of the relaxation applying to Wales without first testing local opinion by means of a poll in each borough or county district.

43. The Lord's Day Observance Society told us that they were founded in 1831:—

> for the dual purpose of preserving Sunday, as the national day of rest, from the encroachments of commercial and other activities which would imperil that institution and of promoting the observance of Sunday as the Lord's Day for worship and Christian service.

44. The Society had 35,000 individual subscribers and also received subscriptions from some 2,000 churches drawn from most Protestant denominations. Their evidence was based on the principle that Sunday should be preserved by law as a day for worship and for rest and quiet. In order that the maximum number of people should have an opportunity of spending Sunday in this way, the Society strongly opposed any relaxation of the existing statutory restrictions. They submitted that the law should be strengthened to prevent evasions and to improve its enforcement. In their view the law should be based on Christian principles even if the liberty of some individuals had to be curtailed for the benefit of the community.

45. Other Churches and religious organisations wrote to us in general terms in favour of maintaining the traditional English Sunday as a day of worship and rest. They argued that the pressure for relaxation of the law came from a profit-seeking minority and that most people did not wish for any change. They stressed the value of the traditional Sunday to national and family life and to the moral and religious training of young people.

46. We received evidence from a wide variety of organisations including local authority associations, trade unions, organisations of traders, representatives of employers and employees in the entertainment industry, controlling bodies of national sports and organisations concerned with the enforcement of the law. Among these witnesses there was a considerable measure of support for preserving the special character of the English Sunday. They said that apart from religious reasons, they regarded it as undesirable as a matter of social policy to make changes that would result in or encourage a substantial increase in the number of people who had to work on Sunday. We were given numerous examples of anomalies and uncertainties in the Sunday trading restrictions and of the anachronisms arising from the out-of-date laws governing Sunday entertainments and amusements. Those responsible for the administration and enforcement of the Sunday trading law told us that it had become virtually unenforceable in many respects. Similarly, the Association of Chief Police Officers told us that a large section of the general public regard the law on Sunday entertainments as obsolete and it was almost impossible to obtain any measure of support for its enforcement. They also said that it lent itself to circumvention by subterfuge which tended to bring the law into disrepute. We deal with this evidence in detail under the appropriate sections of our report. The evidence showed that the law no longer exercised an effective

control on Sunday trading and entertainments and that the gap between the law and modern practice was increasing. There appeared to be strong support from all these bodies for modernising the law on both entertainments and trading.

47. We did not receive enough evidence from individual members of the public to enable us to form any opinion ourselves of the views of the 'man in the street'. We considered whether we should seek to obtain this information through a social survey carried out on our behalf. We did not pursue this proposal because we were not all convinced that the considered views of members of the public on a complicated and controversial topic of this sort could be obtained by means of this type of investigation, and, at that stage, our enquiries indicated that it was unlikely that it could be carried out in the time available to us. We were, however, grateful to Social Surveys (Gallup Poll) Ltd. for supplying us with the results of a public opinion poll made in May, 1958 just before Mr Denis Howell's motion calling for a committee of enquiry was debated in the House of Commons. We judged that, of those who did express an opinion, a consistent and clear though small majority was in favour of reducing legal restrictions on Sunday activities.

48. There were some witnesses who, from religious convictions, looked upon Sunday recreation and work (apart from work of necessity) as contrary to Divine law. There were others who regarded all restrictions based on Sunday observance as an unjustifiable infringement of their freedom. Between these two extremes there was a considerable number of people who, for a variety of reasons, were in favour of keeping Sunday as a 'different' day. For practical purposes this 'difference' or special character of Sunday arises, apart from the tradition of worship, primarily from the conception of Sunday as a day of leisure in which a person is not required to pursue his weekday work (unless it is work of necessity) and is free to do as he chooses. Some witnesses also considered that entertainments and sports that caused an unreasonable amount of noise and disturbance should be prohibited on Sunday.

49. The freedom to choose how one spends Sunday poses a conflict of interest between those who wish to enjoy recreations and those who must work to provide those recreations and the necessary supporting services and so lose their own Sunday and their opportunity for worship, recreation and family pursuits. Most witnesses were in favour of some restriction on the number of people who had to work to provide recreation and services for others on Sunday, but there was no general agreement as to the extent of the restriction. A minority of witnesses were in favour of forbidding all public entertainments and sports, while the majority favoured a reasonable amount of work being allowed to provide recreation for others. Some thought that statutory restrictions were necessary to limit Sunday employment and others thought that it could be achieved by other means.

50. We could not consider these views in terms of the actual numbers involved because there are no offical statistics of the number of people employed on Sundays either in entertainments, sports and trading or in other trades and industries where no statutory restrictions exist. We were, however, able to obtain some general indication of the number of persons

likely to be affected by changes in the law from the following figures relating
to employment in England and Wales:–

		Number of persons employed	Per cent. of (d)
(a)	retail establishments (including working proprietors)	2,536,000*	12.22
(b)	cinemas, theatres, radio etc.	130,120†	.62
(c)	sports and other recreations	54,570†	.24
(d)	all industries	20,726,000†	—

51. We had to decide in relation to the various activities within our terms
of reference whether any statutory control was necessary and if so, to what
extent, in order to limit the number of persons required to work on Sunday
and to prevent undue noise and disturbance. We were guided by these
general considerations as far as possible; we appreciate that they leave
much scope for differences of opinion and we did not consider ourselves
bound by them where the evidence seemed to us to indicate a different
approach.

52. In framing our recommendations we have endeavoured to make
proposals which, if adopted, would produce a law that would be respected
and could be enforced. To achieve this, the law must be clear, certain, and
acceptable to a majority of the public.

8.7 A seventeenth-century case of blasphemy

Taylor's case (1676-77).

An information exhibited against him in the Crown Office, for uttering of
divers blasphemous expressions, horrible to hear, (viz.) that Jesus Christ
was a bastard and a whoremaster; religion was a cheat; and that he neither
feared God, the devil, or man.

Being upon his trial, he acknowledged the speaking of the words, except
the word bastard; and for the rest, he pretended to mean them in another
sense than they ordinarily bear, (viz.) whoremaster, i.e. that Christ was
master of the whore of Babylon, and such kind of evasions. But all the words
being proved by several witnesses, he was found guilty.

And Hale said, that such kind of wicked blasphemous words were not
only an offence to God and religion, but a crime against the laws, State and
Government, and therefore punishable in this Court. For to say, religion is a
cheat, is to dissolve all those obligations whereby the civil societies are
preserved, and that Christianity is parcel of the laws of England; and
therefore to reproach the Christian religion is to speak in subversion of the
law.

* Census of Retail Distribution for 1961 carried out by the Board of Trade
(paragraphs 140-141).

† Ministry of Labour Gazette, February 1964.

Wherefore they gave judgment upon him (viz.) to stand in the pillory in three several places, and to pay one thousand marks fine, and to find sureties for his good behaviour during life.

8.8   *Richard Carlile; an account of his 'mock-trial' for blasphemy*

Of those who fought in the nineteenth century for the rights of free speech and the right to publish, Richard Carlile (1790-1843) is a figure of immense importance whose deeds are now almost forgotten. In his publisher's shop at 55 Fleet Street he printed and published both Thomas Paine's theological works and Palmer's Principles of Nature.

In 1819 he faced his first trial – Carlile preferred to call this and all his other appearances in the criminal courts 'mock-trials' – for blasphemous libel before Lord Chief Justice Abbott and a special jury at the Guildhall, London. His first trial resulted in a fine of £1,500, imprisonment for three years and the providing of a surety for his good behaviour for the rest of his life. Undaunted, he and his wife continued to publish. Indeed Mary Carlile was herself convicted of publishing a correct account of the judicial proceedings in which Richard was convicted. Although he passionately believed in his right to publish matter which was clearly blasphemous Carlile appears not to have been an agnostic or atheist himself. In his later years, the only time when he was not intermittently in prison, he became a fervent religionist and denounced the works of Paine which he had fought so hard to publish.

The following piece is taken from the published transcript of the first day of his trial in October 1819.

Gentlemen, the book which I now hold in my hand, and which forms the subject of this prosecution, is entitled *The Theological Works of Thomas Paine*. I have already stated my motives for publishing it, which were of the best and purest description, namely to promote morality and free discussion on every subject. In a short preface to the work, I have stated my reasons for its publication, and I shall read it, in order that they may not be mistaken:

'In presenting to the public the Theological Works of Thomas Paine, against which so senseless a clamour has hitherto been raised, the Publisher is actuated by but one simple motive, namely, an inquiry after truth. The very numerous inquiries for the *Age of Reason* since the reappearance of the Political Works, have been to the publisher an irresistible inducement to bring forth the present edition. From the applications that have been made to him, he is completely convinced, that the minds of his fellow citizens are fully and adequately prepared to discuss the merits and demerits of the system of religion which forms so prominent a feature in the establishments of the country. He fully anticipates the senseless and unmeaning charges of "impiety" and "blasphemy" that will be exhibited against him by the ignorant and the interested; by the bigot and the hypocrite; to these, however, he is perfectly indifferent, satisfied as he is that this object is to arrive at the truth, and to promote the interests of fair and honest discussion.

'The publisher flatters himself that the present collection will be published from time to time, so as to defeat the hopes and wishes of those whose object it has been to suppress them. He confidently anticipates, that when free discussion on all subjects, whether political or theological, literary or scientific, shall be tolerated, that then, and then only, will the human mind, by progressive improvement, arrive at that state, which may be deservedly termed the Age of Reason.'

Gentlemen, my only reason for publishing the works of Mr Paine has been an anxious and sincere desire to promote the cause of truth and free discussion. I am convinced in my own mind, that they are calculated to improve morality by promoting inquiry; that they tend to exalt our notions of the Deity; and lead us to a belief of his excellence and love for man. These were my motives for republishing his works, and these are motives which produce a satisfaction within me, that no prosecution, that no persecution, will be able to destroy. I consider the publication as essential to the interest and welfare of the country, and having acted under that impression, I stand acquitted of all the malicious intention imputed to me by my persecutors. Gentlemen, I now proceed to call your attention to the work, which, is divided into Three Parts, and is called *The Age of Reason, Part the First being an Investigation of True and Fabulous Theology, by Thomas Paine*. It commences thus:

It has been my intention, for several years past to publish my thoughts upon religion; I am well aware of the difficulties that attend the subject, and from that consideration, had reserved it to a more advanced period of life. I intended it to be the last offering I should make to my fellow citizens of all nations, and that at a time when the purity of the motive that induced me to it, could not admit of a question, even by those who might disapprove the work.

Gentlemen, Mr Paine was nearly 60 years of age when he wrote the paragraph I have just read to you. He was then in France, it was at the period of the French revolution, when he could not be sure of his existence for a single day; and when, having written under such circumstances, he must certainly be entitled to the praise of sincerity, and of a thorough conviction of the rectitude of his intentions.

[*Carlile proceeded to quote at length from Paine's theological works*]

This, Gentlemen, finishes the first part of the *Age of Reason*, and I now ask you, or rather I leave you to judge for yourselves, whether there is to be found in it a single sentence hostile to the cause of justice, or morality, or tending to discourage the mind of man? No Gentlemen, it does not, but on the contrary it contains a finer system of ethics, and is more calculated to improve and exact the human faculties, than any thing which can be congregated, or formed from that Book which it so ably investigates. Two extracts only have been made from all that I have just read, and inserted in the Indictment which my persecutors have so zealously put together for the purpose of overwhelming me – and these two passages I have already noticed.

8.9   The Attorney-General's memorandum on the law of blasphemy

Sir John Simon *(1873-1954) when Attorney-General in 1914 was asked by the Home Office to give an opinion on the current state of the law of blasphemy. The following document was the result.*

Prosecutions for blasphemy in modern times are extremely rare, and when they take place they are not usually prosecutions under any Statute but under the common law.

The common law in reference to blasphemy has passed through three stages:–

(1) Originally common law prosecutions were based upon the allegation that what was complained of tended to sedition and commotion, and was likely to involve a disturbance of the peace. One reason for this view was that in so far as the offence did not tend to a breach of the peace, it was held to be a matter for the Ecclesiastical Courts alone. See, for example, *Trashe*'s case (1618) Hobart's Reports 236: *Atwood*'s case (1618) 2 Rolls Abridgement 78.

(2) In 1676 Sir Matthew Hale laid it down in *R. v. Taylor* (1676) 1.Ventr.293 [*see* 8.7] that 'Christianity is parcel of the laws of England and therefore to reproach the Christian religion is to speak in subversion of the law'. This view was applied in the eighteenth and early nineteenth centuries as a precedent for convicting persons of what was really heresy unaccompanied by any offensive or indecent expressions. For example, in *R. v. Woollston* (1729) Fitzy, an argument that the Gospel miracles were merely allegorical was held to amount to blasphemy; in 1763 in *R. v. Annet* 1.Wm. Bl.395 an attack on the Pentateuch was so regarded; in 1819 in *R. v. Carlile* 3 B & Ald.161 the publication and sale of Paine's 'Age of Reason' was held to be blasphemy; in 1841 in *R. v. Moxon* 2 Townsend's Mod. State Trials 356; Shelley's 'Queen Mab' was held to be a blasphemous libel and in 1842 Holyoake was convicted and sentenced to six months' imprisonment for asserting that he did not believe there was such a thing as God. The latest case which falls under this head is *Cowan* v. *Milbourne* (1867) L.R. 2.Ex.230 where a hiring out of rooms was held to be for an unlawful purpose because the tenant took the rooms for the purpose of giving lectures entitled 'The Character and Teachings of Christ; the former defective, the latter misleading' and 'The Bible shown to be no more inspired than any other book'.

(3) The view upon which Judges now act is that to constitute the offence of blasphemous libel there must be something indecent or offensive in the libel complained of. The origin of this view is to be found in the ruling of Coleridge J. in *R. v. Pooley*. (Bodmin Assizes July 1857) defining blasphemy as 'matter relating to God, Jesus Christ, the Bible or the Book of Common Prayer, *intended* to wound the feeling of mankind or to excite contempt and hatred against the Church by law established or to promote immorality.

Publications intended in good faith to propagate opinions on religious subjects, which the person who publishes them regards as true ... are not blasphemous merely because their publication is likely to wound the feeling of those who believe such opinions to be false, or because their general adoption might tend by lawful means to alterations in the constitution of the Church by law established'.

Coleridge L.C.J. followed this in his ruling in *R.* v. *Ramsey & Foote* (1883) 48 L.T. 733:– 'If the decencies of controversy are observed, even the fundamentals of religion may be attacked without a person being guilty of blasphemous libel', and he laid down that a publication is not blasphemous when 'what is aimed at is not insult to the opinions of the majority of Christians but a real, quiet, honest pursuit of truth'.

Sir James Stephen in his Digest of Criminal Law denies that this ruling is good law and thinks that a denial of the truth of Christianity in general, or of the existence of God is still blasphemy at common law. But there can be no doubt that the view of Coleridge L.C.J. has been since adopted. Thus, in *R.* v. *Boulter* 72 J.P. 188 Phillimore J. said:– 'A man is free to speak and teach what he pleases as to religious matters, though not as to morals. ... A man is not free in such places (i.e. public places) to use coarse ridicule on subjects which are sacred to most people in this country. He is free to use arguments'. He suggested a verdict for the accused, 'If he were writing in favour of his honest belief or unbelief, but not if he were making a scurrilous attack on the beliefs of most people in a public place'.

In the recent case of *Stewart*, which is the immediate occasion of the present Deputation, Lord Coleridge, who tried the case, appears to have followed the above statement of the law.

The main consequences which result from this review are as follows:–

(1) All Statute Law relating to blasphemy has long ago become a dead letter and such Statutes might well be repealed. (A possible exception might be made for a section in the Metropolitan Police Act, 1839, and the Town Police Clauses Act, 1847, which authorise summary proceedings for profanity in public places.)

(2) Modern judicial interpretation of the common law implies that no man can now be convicted for the bona fide expression of opinions honestly held and expressed for the purpose of converting others to those opinions.

(3) In the particular case of Stewart, there were strong circumstances to support the view that his attack upon orthodoxy was not bona fide; while he was speaking he was employing his wife to sell objectionable goods in a crowd of men, women and children which had collected.

(4) It seems certainly to be the fact that no offence is committed if the religious beliefs which are attacked are not those of the Church of England; this seems a gross anomaly.

(5) It seems to be well worth consideration whether it would not be proper to introduce a Bill to amend the Blasphemy Law which would

(*a*) repeal the old Blasphemy Statutes; and

(*b*) provide that publications, whether verbal or in writing, which are intended in good faith to propagate opinions on religious subjects shall not, in the absence of obscene or indecent matter, be deemed blasphemous or profane.

8.10 *Christianity not part of English law: Bowman's case*

Bowman v. **The Secular Society** (*1917*). *The following is part of an eloquent exposition by Lord Sumner (a Lord of Appeal) of the relationship between Christianity and English law. The question concerned the validity of a bequest to a society whose main object was the propagation of anti-Christian doctrines. Holding that Christianity is not part of the law of England he expressed the view that blasphemy, in the absence of scurrility or indecency inimical to public order, was not a criminal offence.*

If the respondents are an anti-Christian society, is the maxim that Christianity is part of the law of England true, and if so, in what sense? If Christianity is of the substance of our law, and if a Court of law must, nevertheless, adjudge possession of its property to a company whose every action seeks to subvert Christianity and bring that law to naught, then by such judgment it stultifies the law. So it was argued, and if the premise is right, I think the conclusion follows.

It is common ground that there is no instance recorded of a conviction for a blasphemous libel, from which the fact, or, at any rate, the supposition of the fact, of contumely and ribaldry has been absent, but this was suggested to be of no real significance for these reasons. Such prosecutions, it was said, often seem to be persecutions, and are therefore unpopular, and so only the gross cases have been proceeded against. This explains the immunity of the numerous agnostic or atheistic writings so much relied on by Secularists. All it really shows is that no one cares to prosecute such things till they become indecent, not that, decently put, they are not against the law. Personally I doubt all this. Orthodox zeal has never been lacking in this country. The Society for Carrying into Effect His Majesty's Proclamations against Vice and Immorality [see 8.2], which prosecuted Williams in 1797, has had many counterparts both before and since, and as anti-Christian writings are all the more insidious and effective for being couched in decorous terms, I think the fact that their authors are not prosecuted, while ribald blasphemers are, really shows that lawyers in general hold such writings to be lawful because decent, not that they are tolerable for their decency though unlawful in themselves. In fact, most men have thought that such writings are better punished with indifference than with imprisonment.

My Lords, with all respect for the great names of the lawyers who have used it, the phrase 'Christianity is part of the law of England' is really not law; it is rhetoric, as truly so as was Erskine's peroration when prosecuting Williams: 'No man can be expected to be faithful to the authority of man, who revolts against the Government of God.' One asks what part of our law may Christianity be, and what part of Christianity may it be that is part of our law? Best, C.J., once said in *Bird* v. *Holbrook* (a case of injury by setting a spring-gun): 'There is no act which Christianity forbids, that the law will not reach; if it were otherwise, Christianity would not be, as it has always been held to be, part of the law of England'; but this was rhetoric too. Spring-guns, indeed, were got rid of, not by Christianity, but by Act of Parliament. 'Thou shalt not steal' is part of our law. 'Thou shalt love thy neighbour as thyself' is not part of our law at all. Christianity has tolerated chattel slavery; not so the present law of England. Ours is, and always has been, a Christian State. The English family is built on Christian ideas, and if the national religion is not Christian there is none. English law may well be called a Christian law, but we apply many of its rules and most of its principles, with equal justice and equally good government, in heathen communities, and its sanctions, even in Courts of conscience, are material and not spiritual.

8.11 'Reasons for the Repeal of the Blasphemy Laws'

Part of a tract dated 1927, issued by the Society for the Abolition of the Blasphemy Laws in support of a Bill to repeal the ancient, but virtually unenforced, laws of blasphemy.

Blasphemy is an offence punishable by both Statute and Common Law.

So far as the statute 9 William III, c. 35, is concerned, there is no recorded instance of its having been taken as the basis of any direct prosecution for blasphemy. It, however, has been used to enforce the Common Law of blasphemy, and has also served as the ground upon which civil rights have been denied Freethinkers, such as the protection of copyright in published works, the care of children, etc.

(1) Under whatever form the law of blasphemy is applied, it must be regarded as an attack on opinion. So long as the test of 'decencies of controversy', when connected with religion, does not mean what the phrase means when applied to other controversial subjects, there is a discrimination which is determined by the opinion under discussion.

(2) There is no clear rule, and cannot well be one, as to what are the decencies of controversy. It must always be a matter of opinion whether, in view of all the circumstances, the language used is suitable or otherwise. The man charged with the offence cannot tell. He may be using language which to him is quite inoffensive. He cannot know whether the language he has used is 'blasphemous' or otherwise until a jury has settled the point. And, clearly, whether the language used by any one is likely to arouse strong feelings must be determined by education and environment. What would be suitable language in Whitechapel might be unsuitable in Mayfair. In these circumstances punishment for blasphemy becomes virtually a punishment for lack of education or of taste.

(3) A blasphemy law does not prevent blasphemy. It cannot prevent it being either spoken or written. The most deadly sarcasm, the most scathing ridicule, the fiercest invective, may safely be used by a man who is able to wield them with sufficent literary or oratorical skill. It is the poor man, the uneducated, who alone suffers.

(4) It is idle to suggest that a blasphemy law is necessary to protect the

religious feelings of people from coarse ridicule. First, the religious feelings of all people are not protected. If a man goes out into the highways and coarsely reviles the Roman Catholic doctrine of the mass, or some doctrine peculiar to the Jewish or Mohammedan religion, he may be charged under the ordinary law with inciting to a breach of the peace, or with using indecent language; but he cannot be charged with blasphemy. The religion protected by the Blasphemy Laws is practically that of the Church of England. Other Churches are protected only to the extent to which they hold doctrines in common with the Established Church. Second, the real, the only adequate guarantee of decency of controversy is the good taste and the education of the public. This is found adequate in the discussion of political and all other questions, and it should surely prove itself equally efficacious in the matter of religion.

(5) There is a growing dissatisfaction with this law of blasphemy. There has not been a single case of prosecution for blasphemy within recent years in which numbers of clergymen and others, in no way upholding the opinions of the person indicted, have not protested against the existence of such a law. They resent the imputation that their religion needs some special form of protection, and are anxious to divest it to the suspicion that it requires any other protection than that furnished by the common sense and good taste of the public. They claim that the manner in which the Blasphemy Laws are administered gives to many an obscure person a gigantic State advertisement, and so intensifies the evil it is intended to cure.

(6) The contention that if the present Bill becomes law there will be nothing to prevent people using coarse and indecent language in connection with religion is untrue. If the language used is genuinely indecent, and so offensive that it may lead to a breach of the peace, it can, under either heading, be dealt with by the ordinary law. The promoters of this Bill have no desire to encourage or to sanction offensive or indecent language. They merely desire that the law which operates shall function with all alike irrespective of their religious or non-religious beliefs. So long as the law applies to all alike, no one and no class has a special grievance. If the ordinary law is not strong enough to deal with abusive or coarse language in controversy, it should be strengthened. But a law passed and administered in the interest of one set of opinions, and existing for their protection, is alien to the liberal temper and destructive of the religious freedom which should exist in this country.

9.12   Private prosecution for blasphemy

The Times, *19 February 1971: report of the outcome of a private summons for blasphemy issued against two directors of a play.*

Summonses in a blasphemy case brought by the Dowager Lady Birdwood against two directors of the play *Council of Love* were withdrawn at Bow Steet Magistrates' Court yesterday.

The move by Mr Quentin Edwards, prosecuting for Lady Birdwood, followed evidence that Mr Jack Gold was not connected with the Criterion Theatre production after the first night and that Miss Eleanor Fazan took no part in the production after October 1.

Mr Edwards said Lady Birdwood had decided that it would not be right to press the prosecution.

Sir Frank Milton, Chief Metropolitan Magistrate, said there was not the least doubt that Lady Birdwood had been actuated by honourable motives. But on the evidence it was clear that, whether or not there was a prima facie case of an offence having been committed by someone, there was not a prima facie case of an offence having been committed by the two people named.

Mr John Mortimer, Q.C., for Miss Fazan, said she was not asking for costs, Mr David Jefferys, for Mr Gold, asked for costs, not against Lady Birdwood but from public funds. Sir Frank awarded him costs of £26.

Mr Edwards asked for summonses against the principal actors who had played the parts of Satan, God and Jesus Christ. Sir Frank refused to issue the summonses, which he said could have been applied for in the first place.

Mr Gold and Miss Fazan had faced a total of four summonses alleging that they blasphemed by directing a performance that vilified and ridiculed the Christian religion.

Lady Birdwood, of Philbeach Gardens, Earls Court, said she saw the play four times. In one scene God was portrayed as 'an old man, coughing and spluttering and wheezing – alternately, shouting and screaming, wearing a long, dirty robe and with matted hair'.

'It was a complete caricature. When I got home this caricature came between me and the God I worship – it intruded so badly.'

Christ, represented as anaemic, 'screamed and squealed'. The Virgin Mary in the play 'gave me the impression she was a voyeuse'.

Lady Birdwood said she did not sleep after the first night. Had she not been a fairly strong person 'it could have done me a lot of harm', she said.

8.13   The contemporary debate about blasphemy

Argument about the blasphemy laws continues to crop up in a variety of contexts. The outrage caused in Roman Catholic circles by a Danish film called The Love Life of Jesus Christ *prompted the following leading article in* The Times *(1 September 1973).*

Blasphemy in English Law

According to the reported view of the executive board of the Danish Film Institute the film provisionally entitled *The Love Life of Jesus Christ* is pornographic, obscene and blasphemous, and full of love, vibrancy, warmth, and humanity – a judgment that appears to provide for all eventualities except a flop. The enterprise has been denounced as blasphemous by the Pope, who is himself denounced (for allegedly heading a church which has for centuries stupefied and repressed the people) by the Danish Minister for Cultural Affairs, who is himself denounced for speaking out of turn by the Danish Minister for Religious Affairs, who is herself. ...

Leaving it to the Danes to sort out which portfolio the matter properly belongs to, one may speculate about what will happen if the film is completed, gets past Mr Stephen Murphy [then Chairman of the British

Board of Film Censors], and is shown here. We still have the offence of blasphemy. It is etiolated, but survives. The offence has a long and notable history, and has claimed victims as far apart as the son of Shelomith, Alcibiades the Athenian, and Charles Bradlaugh. It has had projected upon it different values at different periods of history. The Emperor Justinian cracked down on blasphemy in the sixth century since it imperilled the public safety by provoking the anger of God. Later Christian rulers proceeded against it on the different ground that an attack upon religion was in another aspect an attack upon the state. There was something of that behind the Williamite statute of 1697 and something too of an intention to keep unbelievers out of positions of public trust.

Nineteenth-century judges imported a distinction between denying fundamental truths of Christianity and so doing or so implying in a way that was contumelious, ribald, licentious, abusive, or provocative of disorder. The first you might do, the second you might not. In what was perhaps the latest major prosecution for blasphemy in England Mr Justice Avory, in 1922, described the offence as comprising 'indecent and offensive attacks on Christianity or the Scriptures or sacred persons or objects, calculated to outrage the feelings of the general body of the community'.

In 1930, a Bill was introduced to abolish the offence. It was argued, and many churchmen agreed, that the Christian religion neither needed, nor in the modern state deserved, this exceptional protection. The Government of the day was not quite ready for that. The Solicitor General put forward a saving amendment creating a new offence of doing anything calculated, 'by outraging the religious convictions of any other person', to provoke a breach of the peace. The abolitionists, taking the sensible view that, when it comes to legislation of a kind you dislike, better the old and toothless predator than a newly hatched gnat, dropped their Bill.

The official justification, if one were called for, of still having blasphemy an offence would probably rely on the breach-of-the peace argument. (And it appears that the Danish film, even before it has been made, has been provocative of commotion in Rome.) But that argument need not stand alone. One purpose served by laws against obscenity is to protect people against having their sense of decency outraged and to spare them the sight of the defilement of the public face of their society. Their religious feelings are deserving of as much consideration. But in both cases, before it is right to invoke the law, the sense of outrage must be shown to be deep, its extent across the community wide, and whatever it is that occasions it indubitably offensive.

[*This leader prompted a vigorous correspondence, two items of which appear below.*]

Sir, – The controversy over the Danish film *The Love Life of Jesus Christ* has, once again, brought into focus the need for some accepted norms for dealing with the lives of the prophets and of other spiritual and moral leaders of the human race. In this context your reflections on English law of blasphemy (*The Times*, September 1) are to the point and incisive. The legal aspect is definitely important and must be taken care of, but there is another dimension to the problem which also deserves some serious thought.

The limit of civilization among a people can hardly be measured by the yardstick of legal prohibitions. The moral sense of a society, its collective conscience, so to say, is more important. And the corruption of this collective conscience should be much more lamentable than the withering away of certain clauses of the criminal law.

Serious academic differences about tenets of religion are one thing; abusive, licentious and obscene allegations and their worldwide projection by printed words or through films is a different matter. Should a minority, irrespective of the fact that it is motivated by considerations of culture or commerce, be allowed to pollute the lives of men who had been the source of light and moral guidance for mankind throughout the ages and consequently injure the feelings of millions of people who hold them in esteem?

Although I belong to a religion other than Christianity, I feel equally aggrieved on what is purported to be the content of the alleged film. I firmly believe that all prophets of God and all founders of religions should be respected by all people.

The Muslims have protested on many occasions on the way the Prophet of Islam has been treated in European literature and by the communication media. Similar is our grief over outrages against Prophet Jesus and others. This kind of sacrilege should be brought to an end through a civilized consensus.

May I take this opportunity to suggest that a kind of an international convention may be developed about the way the lives and personalities of the prophets should be treated. This should be in the nature of a moral code, which may be framed at the initiative of the representatives of all major religions of the world. Once a consensus is developed on this Moral Convention, it may be adopted by the General Assembly of the United Nations and be ratified by its member states.

This convention should be woven into the moral fabric of society primarily through educational means. Legal provisions can be enacted in the light of this convention. The real need is to evolve a new moral realization resulting in a more civilized approach towards the religious leaders of the world. If it is a moral and legal crime to slander the honour of an individual or a family, it should be a greater crime to play with the honour of the moral leaders of the world whom people respect more than their parents or family dignitaries.

The time has come when something should be done to have a code of behaviour for this purpose. Those who have respect for great religious leaders as part of civilized behaviour should take initiative in this respect. This is an area of reform where people representing culture and religion both should cooperate and present a uniform approach towards an issue which is sensitive as well as delicate.

K. AHMAD,
Director General, The Islamic Foundation.

Sir, – On behalf of the National Secular Society, I am writing to protest against the call by Mr Ahmad, Director General of the Islamic Foundation, for an international blasphemy law ... In effect, he is demanding for 'all prophets of God and all founders of religion' a privileged immunity from any sort of comment deviating from the pious legends which the faithful believe.

Mr Ahmad sees as a major 'crime' the disparagement of 'the honour of the moral leaders of the world, whom people respect more than parents or family dignitaries'. Some people do, no doubt, revere their religious leaders to this fanatical degree, but in our opinion this is something to be deplored as inherently dangerous, not something to be applauded, let alone given international protection.

Moreover, many religions – including some whose revered founders are still alive – are very antisocial in their doctrines and practices, and if they were immune from outside criticism and counter-propaganda they would have it all their own way. Without controversy there can be no liberty, no progress.

This week's news from the Soviet Union shows, all too clearly, how laws restricting freedom of expression operate against intellectuals who may envisage something better than the status quo. National laws of this kind are bad enough, but at least there is the possibility of defection elsewhere. If religious censorship were backed by the United Nations it would be putting the clock back to the age of monolithic Christendom, when the Inquisition flourished.

The National Secular Society has always supported universal free speech and deplored all discrimination against minority religious groups; but some religionists (and these include some Christians as well as Muslims) deny the same freedoms to the non-believer. Even (to quote Mr Ahmad again) 'men who have been the source of light and moral guidance for mankind throughout the ages' (supposing, for the sake of argument, there were a consensus as to their identity) should surely be expected to hold their own in free competition with alternative theories of morality, either co-existing with them or being gradually superseded by them in the light of new knowledge and changing attitudes.

We uphold Mr Ahmad's right to assert 'There is one God, and Mahomet is His prophet', and the Christian's right to preach 'three persons in one God'; but we insist on the freethinker's equal right to say 'There are no gods, and human beings should turn away from such superstitions so as to concentrate their energies on the promotion of happiness on earth.'

Yours faithfully,
BARBARA SMOKER,
President, The National Secular Society

Documentary Sources

Chapter 1 The General Debate
1.1 William Blackstone, *Commentaries on the Laws of England*, London (eighth edition) 1778, Book IV, Chapter 4 ('Public Wrongs: Of Offences Against God and Religion'), pp. 41-2.
1.2 William Wilberforce, notes on 'The Importance of Legislative Measures for Promoting Public Morals', 1787 (published as an Appendix to *The Life of William Wilberforce*, by R.J. and S. Wilberforce, London, 1938).
1.3 John Stuart Mill, 'On Liberty', 1859.
1.4 John Stuart Mill, letter to E.W. Young (1867); reprinted in Hugh Elliot (ed.), *The Letters of John Stuart Mill*, London, 1910, Vol. 2, pp. 96-7.
1.5 Sir James Stephen, 'Liberty, Equality and Fraternity', *Cornhill Magazine*, 1873.
1.6 *Best* v. *Samuel Fox and Co. Ltd* [1952] A.C. 716, 727: Lord Porter.
1.7 Wolfenden Report on Homosexual Offences and Prostitution, Cmnd. 247 of 1957.
1.8 Lord Denning, reported in *The Times*, 27 September 1957.
1.9 *Shaw* v. *D.P.P.* [1962] A.C. 220, 266, 272: Viscount Simonds and Lord Reid.
1.10 Lord Devlin, 'Morals and the Criminal Law', Maccabaean Lecture 1957.
1.11 H.L.A. Hart, 'The Moderate and the Extreme Thesis', in *Law, Liberty and Morality*, London, 1963, pp. 48-52.
1.12 Speech by J. Enoch Powell on the Motor Cycle (Wearing of Helmets) Regulations, 1973; H.C. *Hansard*, 5 April 1973, cols. 757-61.
1.13 Judith N. Shklar, *Legalism*, Cambridge, Mass., 1964, pp. 30-1, 41-5, 88-90.
1.14 *Hayward* v. *Chaloner* [1968] 1Q.B. 120.

Chapter 2 Capital Punishment
2.1 William Paley, *Principles of Morals and Political Philosophy*, 1785.
2.2 Samuel Johnson, *The Rambler*, 20 April 1751.
2.3 Sir Samuel Romilly, entry in his *Journal*, 1810; from *Memoirs of Sir Samuel Romilly*, London, 1860, Vol. 2, pp. 325-8.
2.4 Petition from the Corporation of London opposing the death penalty for minor crimes against property, 1819; appendix to Vol. 1 of *A History of English Criminal Law*, by Sir Leon Radzinowicz, London, 1948.
2.5 Similar petition from the London jurors, 1831; *ibid*.

2.6 Editorial in the *Spectator*, 22 January 1831, on the non-efficacy of public hangings as a deterrent.

2.7 Charles Dickens, letter to the *Daily News*, 23 February 1846.

2.8 Sir James Stephen, 'Capital Punishments', *Fraser's Magazine*, June 1864.

2.9 Archbishop William Temple, 'The Death Penalty', *Spectator*, 1935.

2.10 Report of the Royal Commission on Capital Punishment, Cmd. 8932 of 1953.

2.11 Lord Goddard, speech on the Criminal Justice Bill, in H.L. *Hansard*, 28 April 1948, cols 489-93.

2.12 Lord Morris of Borth-y-Gest, speech on the motion to end capital punishment, 1969; H.L. *Hansard*, 17 December 1969, cols 1166-8.

2.13 John Sparrow and Louis Blom-Cooper, two letters on general deterrence. *The Times*, December 1969 and January 1970.

2.14 W.J.H. Sprott, 'Conflicts of Values', in *The Hanging Question*, ed. Louis Blom-Cooper, London, 1969.

Chapter 3 Non-Capital Punishment

3.1 Parliamentary return of public bodies calling for infliction of corporal punishment for offences against children, 1888.

3.2 High Court Judges' memorandum calling for the authorisation of flogging for certain offences, 1884.

3.3 Cadogan Report on Corporal Punishment, Cmd. 5684 of 1938, paras 59-61.

3.4 Report of the Advisory Council on the Treatment of Offenders, Cmnd. 1213 of 1960.

3.5 High Court Judges' memorandum on 'normal punishments', 1901; reprinted in R.M. Jackson, *Enforcing the Law*, London, 1967.

3.6 Samuel Johnson, essay on imprisonment for debt, *The Idler*, 16 September 1761.

3.7 Report of the Payne Committee on the Enforcement of Judgment Debts, Cmnd. 3909 of 1969.

3.8 Winston S. Churchill, speech on prisons, H.C. *Hansard*, 20 July 1910, vol. 19, col. 1354.

3.9 Hugh J. Klare, 'Striking a Balance in the Fight Against Crime', *The Times*, 31 March 1970.

3.10 Judith Shklar, *Legalism, op. cit.*, pp. 179-81, on war crimes trials.

Chapter 4 Human Sexuality

4.1 Alfred Kinsey *et al.*, *Sexual Behaviour in the Human Male*, 1948.

4.2 Bishop John Robinson, the Beckly Lecture to the Methodist Conference, 1972.

4.3 Peter Wildeblood, *Against the Law*, Harmondsworth, 1955, pp. 182-7. A homosexual's view of law and punishment.

4.4 Sir Henry Slesser, letter on homosexuality, *The Times*, 16 December 1957.

4.5 Leo Abse, speech introducing the Sexual Offences (No. 2) Bill, 1966 (H.C. *Hansard*, 19 December 1966, cols 1086-70).

4.6 Tom Harper, in the *Listener*, 27 September 1973.

5.10 *Hains* v. *Jessel* (1669) 1 Ld. Raym. 68, 91 E.R. 942: court refuses to allow a man to marry his sister's illegitimate daughter.

5.11 Duke of Marlborough, speech on Marriage with a Deceased Wife's Sister Bill, 1883 (H.L. *Hansard*, 28 June 1883, cols 1653-60).

5.12 Bishop Wand, speech on Bill legalising marriage to a divorced wife's sister, 1949 (H.L. *Hansard*, 21 March 1949, cols 718-19).

5.13 *Alhaji Mohamed* v. *Knott* [1969] 1 Q.B. 1.

5.14 *Maclennan* v. *Maclennan* (1958) S.L.T. 12: artificial insemination as adultery.

5.15 Archbishop Geoffrey Fisher, a reaction to *Maclennan*; *The Times*, 15 January 1958.

5.16 Lord Denning, speech in the House of Lords on artificial insemination, 1958 (H.L. *Hansard*, 26 February 1958, cols 944 *ff.*).

5.17 Lord Chief Justice Cockburn, summing up in trial of Charles Bradlaugh and Annie Besant, 1877.

5.18 Patrick Hastings, K.C., address to the jury in Marie Stopes' libel action, 1923.

5.19 Mr Justice Harlan, dissenting in *Poe* v. *Ullman*, 367 U.S. 497 (1961).

5.20 Glanville Williams, *Sanctity of Life and the Criminal Law* (London, 1957): on sterilisation and the doctrine of mayhem.

5.21 Lord Justice Denning, dissenting in *Bravery* v. *Bravery* [1954] 1 W.L.R. 1169, 1176: on sterilisation as cruelty.

5.22 Mr Justice Holmes, *Buck* v. *Bell*, 274 U.S. 200 (1925).

5.23 Norman St. John Stevas, *Law and Morals*, London, 1964, pp. 108-9.

Chapter 6 The Sanctity of Human Life

6.1 Charles Mercier, *Crime and Criminals* (1918), pp. 196-7; on abortion.

6.2 *R.* v. *Bourne* [1939] 1 K.B. 687: Mr Justice Macnaghten.

6.3 Leo Abse and Norman St. John Stevas, speeches on the Abortion Bill, 1966, H.C. *Hansard*, 22 July 1966, cols 1147-8 and 1155.

6.4 Sir Thomas More, *Utopia* (1516) on euthanasia.

6.5 Lord Dawson of Penn, speech on the Voluntary Euthanasia (Legalisation) Bill, 1936; H.L. *Hansard*, 1 December 1936, cols 480-1.

6.6 Lord Segal, speech on the Euthanasia Bill, 1969; H.L. *Hansard*, 25 March 1969, cols 1243-6.

6.7 Some recent instances of mercy killings.

6.8 *Hales* v. *Petit* (1562) 1 Plowden, at p. 261: the nature of suicide.

6.9 William Blackstone on suicide (*Commentaries*, Book IV, p. 189).

6.10 *R.* v. *Doody* (1854) 6 Cox C.C. 463: attempted suicide as a misdeameanour.

6.11 Glanville Williams, some examples of severe sentences for attempted suicide; *Sanctity of Life and the Criminal Law*, *op. cit.*, pp. 251-3.

6.12 Bishop Bloomer and Lord Denning, speeches on the Suicide Bill, 1961 (H.L. *Hansard*, 2 March 1961, cols 258-60 and 262-4).

Chapter 7 Obscenity

7.1 Lord Chief Justice Cockburn, test of obscenity in *Hicklin's Case* [1868] L.R. 3 Q.B. 360, 371.

7.2 Letter to the Home Office from the Chief Constable of Birmingham about a man carrying sandwich boards advertising contraceptives, 1908.

7.3 *M'Gowan* v. *Langmuir* (1931) S.C. 10: defining obscenity and indecency.

7.4 Alistair Cooke, article on the Ginzburg obscenity case, *The Guardian*, 24 March 1966.

7.5 *U.S.* v. *Ulysses*, 72 F. 2D. 705 (1934); judgments of Judges Hand and Manton.

7.6 *R.* v. *Secker and Warburg* [1954] 1 W.L.R. 1138; Mr Justice Stable's summing up.

7.7 D.H. Lawrence, essay 'Pornography and Obscenity', 1929: from *A Propos of Lady Chatterley's Lover and Other Essays* (1961).

7.8 'Diogenes', on the *International Times* case, *New Society*, 29 January 1970.

7.9 'Academics' Defence of Filth Appals J.P.', *Guardian*, 30 August 1970.

7.10 Arts Council Working Party, report 'The Obscenity Laws', 1969.

7.11 Jonathan Miller, article on theatre censorship, *Guardian*, 16 October 1971.

7.12 *Guardian* report on an obscenity prosecution and the 'permissive society', 13 March 1971.

7.13 Richard Neville, address to the jury in the *Oz* obscenity trial, 1971.

7.14 'The Festival of Light', *Guardian*, 18 April 1973.

Chapter 8 Religion

8.1 The King's 'Proclamation for the Encouragement of Piety and Virtue', 1787.

8.2 Prospectus of the Society for enforcing the King's Proclamation, 1787.

8.3 William Blackstone on sabbath observance; *Commentaries*, Book IV, pp. 63-4.

8.4 John Stuart Mill, letter to the secretary of the Sunday League, 1856; Elliot (ed.), *The Letters of John Stuart Mill*, Vol. 1, p. 189.

8.5 Tract published by the Lord's Day Observance Society.

8.6 Crathorne Report on the Laws on Sunday Observance, Cmnd. 2528 of 1964.

8.7 *Taylor's Case* (1676) 1 Ventris 293; 86 E.R. 189, on blasphemy.

8.8 Richard Carlile, an account of his 'mock-trial' for blasphemy, 1819.

8.9 Sir John Simon, Home Office memorandum on the law of blasphemy, 1914.

8.10 *Bowman* v. *The Secular Society* [1917] A.C. 452, on Christianity and English law.

8.11 Society for the Abolition of the Blasphemy Laws, tract dated 1927.

8.12 The Lady Birdwood blasphemy prosecution, *The Times*, 19 February 1971.

8.13 *The Times*, September 1973; leading article and correspondence on blasphemy today.